A GUIDE TO CRITICAL REVIEWS

Part I: *American Drama, 1900-1969.* 2d ed.
1973.

Part II: *The Musical, 1909-1974.* 2d ed. 1976.

Part III: *Foreign Drama, 1909-1977.* 2d ed. 1979.

Part IV: *The Screenplay, from "The Jazz Singer
to Dr. Strangelove."* 2 vols. 1971.

A Guide to Critical Reviews:

Part III:
Foreign Drama, 1909-1977

Second Edition

by

JAMES M. SALEM

The Scarecrow Press, Inc.
Metuchen, N.J., & London
1979

Library of Congress Cataloging in Publication Data (Revised)

Salem, James M
    A guide to critical reviews.

    CONTENTS: pt. 1. American drama, 1909-1969. --pt. 2.
The musical, 1909-1974. --pt. 3. Foreign drama, 1909-1977.
    1. Theater--New York (City)--Reviews--Indexes.
2. Drama--20th century--History and criticism--Addresses, es-
says, lectures--Indexes. I. Title.
Z5781. S16   1973   [PN2277. N5]   016. 809'2   73-3120
ISBN 0-8108-0608-8 (v. 1)
ISBN 0-8108-0959-1 (v. 2)
ISBN 0-8108-1226-6 (v. 3)

Copyright © 1979 by James M. Salem

Manufactured in the United States of America

FOREWORD

The purpose of Part III of A Guide to Critical Reviews (second edition) is to provide a bibliography of critical reviews of modern foreign plays produced on the New York stage from the 1909-1910 season to the season of 1976-1977. By rough count I have included over 2,300 productions of over 1,300 plays by 206 foreign dramatists (British, Continental, Canadian, South African, Puerto Rican). Broadway, Off Broadway, and Off Off Broadway productions are represented. In the case of foreign plays premiering abroad, or in American university or regional theaters (indicated by an asterisk in this bibliography), I have listed reviews without production information.

Playwrights included in this bibliography are presented alphabetically, with plays listed alphabetically under each dramatist. I have tried to cross-reference all the English translations of play titles I could find, and to include many of the foreign language titles as well.

My key source of production information is The Best Plays of the Year series (New York: Dodd, Mead and Co.), begun by Burns Mantle and currently directed by Otis L. Guernsey, Jr.

The reviews cited in this volume are those which appeared in American or Canadian periodicals and in the New York Times. With the exception of some now defunct dramatic periodicals like the Dramatic Mirror and the New York Clipper, most of the reviews should be available in college and public libraries. Reviews in other New York newspapers have not been indexed, but New York Theatre Critics' Reviews, which has reprinted reviews from the New York Journal-American, Daily News, Post, Mirror, World Telegram and Sun, Herald Tribune, and Times since 1940, has been cited for plays produced after that date.

As no attempt has been made to include critical articles from the scholarly journals, the student of modern drama should supplement this bibliography with the annual bibliographies in Modern Drama, PMLA, and Educational Theatre Journal. In addition, the "Continuing Checklist" published by The Shaw Review is valuable for items involving George Bernard Shaw, and Bulletin of Bibliography is important for bibliographies on many modern dramatists: Galsworthy, Jones, Pinero, Brieux, Schnitzler, Yeats, Chekhov, and Strindberg. Especially helpful is "A Selected Bibliography of

Bibliographies," compiled by Marvin Carlson, in <u>Modern Drama</u> VII (May 1965), 112-118.

In preparing this edition, I owe a debt of thanks to University of Alabama Reference Librarians Vi Ayer and Margene Biddle. I am also indebted to Donna, Tim, Betsy, and Jennifer Salem--who will do anything, I have learned, in order to recover the dining room table for the purpose for which it was intended.

James M. Salem

Tuscaloosa, Alabama
June 1978

CONTENTS

Ableman, Paul	1
Andreyev, Leonid Nikolayevitch	1
Anouilh, Jean	3
Ansky, S.	12
Archer, William	13
Auden, W. H.	14
Ayckbourn, Alan	15
Aymé, Marcel	16
Bagnold, Enid	16
Bahr, Hermann	17
Barrie, James M.	19
Baum, Vicki	26
Beckett, Samuel	26
Becque, Henry	32
Behan, Brendan	32
Benavente, Jacinto	34
Benelli, Sem	35
Bergstrom, Hjalmer	36
Bernard, Jean-Jacques	36
Besier, Rudolph	37
Betti, Ugo	39
Birabeau, André	40
Bjornson, Bjornstjerne	41
Bolitho, William	41
Bolt, Robert	42
Bolton, Guy	43
Borchert, Wolfgang	47
Bourdet, Edouard	47
Bowen, John	48
Brecht, Bertolt	49
Bridie, James	57
Brieux, Eugène	59
Bruckner, Ferdinand	61
Büchner, Georg	62
Camus, Albert	63
Capek, Karel	64
Carroll, Paul Vincent	66
Casella, Alberto	68
Chambers, C. Haddon	69
Chekhov, Anton	70
Chiarelli, Luigi	82
Christie, Agatha	82
Claudel, Paul	84
Cocteau, Jean	86
Colton, John	87
Copeau, Jacques	89
Coward, Noel	89
Dane, Clemence	99
D'Annunzio, Gabriele	101
de Ghelderode, Michel	101
de Hartog, Jan	103
Delaney, Shelagh	104
de Montherlant, Henri	104
de Musset, Alfred	105
de Porto-Riche, Georges	106
Deval, Jacques	106
Drinkwater, John	109
Duerrenmatt, Friedrich	111
Dumas, Alexandre fils	113
Dunsany, Lord	115
Dyer, Charles	116
Echegaray, Jose	117
Eliot, T. S.	117
England, Barry	121
Ervine, St. John	121
Fabbri, Diego	124
Feydeau, Georges	124
Frank, Bruno	127
Freeman, David E.	128
Friel, Brian	128
Frisch, Max	130
Fry, Christopher	131
Fugard, Athol	135
Galsworthy, John	137
García-Lorca, Federico	141
Genêt, Jean	143
Geraldy, Paul	145
Gide, André	146
Giraudoux, Jean	146
Gorki, Maxim	151
Granville-Barker, Harley	153
Gray, Simon	154
Greene, Graham	156

Gregory, Lady	157	Obey, Andre	235
Griffiths, Trevor	159	O'Casey, Sean	236
Guitry, Sacha	160	Orton, Joe	242
Hamilton, Patrick	162	Osborne, John	244
Hampton, Christopher	163	Pagnol, Marcel	248
Harwood, H. M.	164	Parker, Louis N.	249
Hauptmann, Gerhart	166	Phillips, Stephen	252
Hebbel, Friedrich	167	Pinero, Arthur Wing	252
Heijermans, Hermann	167	Pinero, Miguel	256
Hochhuth, Rolf	168	Pinter, Harold	256
Hochwälder, Fritz	170	Pirandello, Luigi	263
Hopkins, John	171	Priestley, J. B.	268
Houghton, Stanley	171	Quintero, Serafin and	
Housman, Laurence	172	Joaquin Alvarez	272
Hugo, Victor	173	Rattigan, Terence	273
Huxley, Aldous	174	Robertson, Thomas	279
Ibsen, Henrik	175	Robinson, Lennox	279
Ionesco, Eugene	187	Romains, Jules	281
Jerome, Helen	192	Rostand, Edmond	281
Job, Thomas	193	Ruskin, David	285
Johnston, Denis	194	Salacrou, Armand	286
Jones, Henry Arthur	195	Sardou, Victorien	286
Joyce, James	197	Sartre, Jean-Paul	288
Kaiser, Georg	197	Saunders, James	291
Katayev, Valentin	198	Savoir, Alfred	292
Kipphardt, Heinar	199	Schnitzler, Arthur	294
Knott, Frederick	199	Shaffer, Anthony	296
Kops, Bernard	201	Shaffer, Peter	296
Labiche, Eugene	201	Shairp, Mordaunt	299
Lawler, Ray	201	Shaw, George Bernard	300
Lenormand, Henri René	202	Shaw, Robert	326
Levy, Benn W.	202	Sherriff, R. C.	327
Lonsdale, Frederick	205	Shiels, George	328
Luke, Peter	208	Sigurjonsson, Johann	329
McCarthy, Justin		Simonov, Konstantin	329
Huntley	208	Simpson, N. F.	330
Maeterlinck, Maurice	208	Slade, Bernard	330
Marceau, Felicien	211	Smith, Dodie	331
Marcel, Gabriel	212	Sternheim, Carl	332
Marcus, Frank	212	Stoppard, Tom	333
Martinez-Sierra,		Storey, David	335
Gregorio	213	Strindberg, August	337
Masefield, John	214	Sudermann, Hermann	343
Maugham, W. Somerset	215	Synge, John Millington	344
Mauriac, Francois	221	Tabori, George	347
Milne, A. A.	221	Taylor, Tom	349
Molnar, Ferenc	225	Thomas, Brandon	349
Morley, Robert	231	Thomas, Dylan	350
Munro, C. K.	231	Toller, Ernst	351
Murray, T. C.	232	Tolstoy, Leo	352
Nestroy, Johann	233	Turgenev, Ivan	353
Nichols, Peter	233	Ustinov, Peter	354
Nichols, Robert	234	Vajda, Ernst	357

Vane, Sutton	358	Whiting, John	370
Verneuil, Louis	359	Wilde, Oscar	371
Vildrac, Charles	360	Williams, Emlyn	371
Von Hofmannsthal, Hugo	361	Wilson, John	377
Von Kleist, Heinrich	362	Winter, Keith	377
Wedekind, Frank	362	Wolf, Friedrich	378
Weiss, Peter	364	Wood, Mrs. Henry	378
Werfel, Franz	366	Yeats, William Butler	378
Wesker, Arnold	368	Zuckmayer, Carl	378
Wheeler, Hugh	369	Zweig, Stefan	381

About the Dramatists   383

Prolific Foreign Dramatists   388

Frequently Produced Foreign Dramatists   389

Successful Foreign Productions   390

New York Drama Critics' Circle Awards (Best Foreign Play)   397

Index of Co-Authors, Adaptors, and Translators   399

Index of Titles   404

FOREIGN DRAMA

ABLEMAN, PAUL

*Blue Comedy (Consists of Hank's Night and Madly in Love)
   Reviews:
     New York Times p. 26, Oct 23, 1968

Green Julia
   Productions:
     (Off Broadway) Opened November 16, 1972 for 147 performances.
     (Off Off Broadway) Opened February 10, 1977.
   Reviews:
     New York Times p. 42, Nov 17, 1972
     New Yorker 48:110, Dec 9, 1972
     Time 101:58, Feb 19, 1973

Hank's Night (see Blue Comedy)

Madly in Love (see Blue Comedy)

ALVAREZ QUINTERO, SERAFIN AND JOAQUIN see QUINTERO,
SERAFIN and JOAQUIN ALVAREZ

ANDREYEV, LEONID NIKOLAYEVITCH

Anathema
   Productions:
     Opened November 1910.
     Translated by Herman Bernstein. Opened April 10, 1923
       for 15 performances
   Reviews:
     Dramatic Mirror 64:7, Nov 30, 1910
     Independent 69:1327-8, Dec 15, 1910
     Nation 91:397-8, Oct 27, 1910
          116:500-1, Apr 25, 1923
     New York Clipper 71:14, Apr 18, 1923
     New York Times p. 16, Apr 11, 1923
              VII, p. 1, Apr 15, 1923

Beautiful Sabine Women (see The Sabine Women)

Devil in the Mind
Productions:
    Adapted by William L. Laurence. Opened May 1, 1931 for 11 performances.
Reviews:
    Commonweal 14:48-9, May 13, 1931
    New York Times p. 23, May 2, 1931

He Who Gets Slapped
Productions:
    Adapted by George Zilboorg. Opened January 9, 1922 for 182 performances.
    English version by Judith Guthrie. Opened March 20, 1946 for 46 performances
    (Off Broadway) Season of 1955-1956.
    (Off Off Broadway) Translated by Gregory Zilboorg. Opened November 17, 1967 for 9 performances.
    (Off Off Broadway) Season of 1974-75.
    (Off Off Broadway) Opened January 13, 1977.
Reviews:
    Bookman 55:61-2, Mar 1922
    Catholic World 163:168, May 1946
    Current Opinion 72:484-94, Apr 1922
    Dial 72:337-8, Mar 1922
    Dramatic Mirror 95:62, Mar 1922
    Everybody's Magazine 47:112-18, Dec 1922
    Hearst 41:85-7+, Jun 1922
    Independent 108:90-2, Jan 28, 1922
    Life (NY) 79:18, Jan 26, 1922
    Nation 114:103, Jan 25, 1922
         162:409, Apr 6, 1946
    New Republic 29:283-4, Feb 1, 1922
         114:479, Apr 8, 1946
    New York Clipper 69:20, Jan 18, 1922
    New York Theatre Critics' Reviews 1946:426
    New York Times p. 15, Jan 10, 1922
         II, p. 1, Mar 17, 1945
         p. 31, Mar 21, 1946
         II, p. 1, Mar 31, 1946
         p. 18, Feb 2, 1956
         VI, p. 28, Feb 12, 1956
    New Yorker 22:42, Mar 30, 1946
    Newsweek 27:84, Apr 1, 1946
    Saturday Review 29:34+, Apr 13, 1946
         39:30, Mar 24, 1956
    Theatre Arts 30:252+, May 1946
    Theatre Magazine 35:141+, Mar 1922
    Time 47:76, Apr 1, 1946

·na (Yekaterina Ivanovna)
Productions:
    Translated by Herman Bernstein. Opened February 25, 1929 for 19 performances.

Reviews:
Commonweal 9:571, Mar 20, 1929
Dial 86:440-2, May 1929
New York Times p. 30, Feb 26, 1929
Vogue 73:164+, Apr 13, 1929

The Life of Man
Productions:
Translated by Clarence L. Meader and Fred Newton Scott.
Opened January 14, 1917 for one performance.
Reviews:
New Republic 33:176-7, Jan 10, 1923
New York Times p. 7, Jan 15, 1917
Theatre Magazine 25:137+, Mar 1917

Love of One's Neighbor
Productions:
Translated by Thomas Seltzer. Opened February 19, 1915 in
repertory (Washington Square Players).
Reviews:
Green Book 13:1151-2, Jun 1915

The Sabine Women (Beautiful Sabine Women)
Productions:
Opened March 1920.
Reviews:
Independent 101:382, Mar 13, 1920
Weekly Review 2:441-2, Apr 24, 1920

The Waltz of the Dogs
Productions:
Translated by Herman Bernstein. Opened April 25, 1928 for
35 performances.
Reviews:
Dramatist 14:1170-71, Jul 1923
Nation 126:546, May 9, 1928
New York Times p. 31, Apr 26, 1928
Theatre Magazine 48:38-9, Jul 1928
Vogue 71:98, Jun 15, 1928

Yekaterina Ivanovna (see Katerina)

ANOUILH, JEAN

L'alouette (see The Lark)

Antigone
Productions:
English adaptation by Lewis Galantiere. Opened February
18, 1946 for 64 performances.
(Off Broadway) Season of 1955-1956.
(Off Broadway) Season of 1959-1960.

(Off Off Broadway) Season of 1974-1975.
(Off Broadway) Translated by Alex Szogyi.   Opened December
    9, 1975 for 40 performances.
Reviews:
    Catholic World 162:71-2, Apr 1946
    Commonweal 43:525-6, Mar 8, 1946
    Forum 105:752-3, Apr 1946
    Independent Woman 25:100, Apr 1946
    Life 20:73-5, Mar 18, 1946
    Nation 162:269, Mar 2, 1946
            182:347, Apr 21, 1956
    New Republic 114:317, Mar 4, 1946
    New York Theatre Critics' Reviews 1946:450
    New York Times p. 28, Jan 10, 1946
                    VI, p. 28, Jan 27, 1946
                    II, p. 1, Feb 17, 1946
                    p. 21, Feb 19, 1946
                    II, p. 1, Feb 24, 1946
                    p. 25, May 28, 1946
                    p. 32, Apr 3, 1956
                    p. 46, Sep 16, 1959
                    p. 16, Sep 16, 1959
                    p. 52, Dec 14, 1960
                    p. 43, Jun 19, 1967
    New Yorker 22:40-1, Mar 4, 1946
            35:964, Sep 26, 1959
    Newsweek 27:80, Mar 4, 1946
    Player's Magazine 24:32-4, Nov 1947
                    24:70, Dec 1947
    Saturday Review 29:24-6, Mar 9, 1946
    Time 47:54, Mar 4, 1946

Ardèle   (see also Cry of the Peacock)
    Productions:
        (Off Broadway) Adapted by Lucienne Hill.   Season of 1957-58.
    Reviews:
        New York Times p. 39, Apr 9, 1958
        Saturday Review 52:40, May 10, 1969

Augustus
    Productions:
        (Off Off Broadway) Opened October 1976.
    No Reviews.

Becket
    Productions:
        Translated by Lucienne Hill.   Opened October 5, 1960 for 193
            performances.
    Reviews:
        America 104:275-6, Nov 19, 1960
        Catholic World 192:191-2, Dec 1960
        Christian Century 77:1284-6, Nov 2, 1960
        Coronet 49:14, Jan 1961

Nation 191:336, Oct 29, 1960
    192:467-8, May 27, 1961
New Republic 143:22, Oct 17, 1960
New York Theatre Critics' Reviews 1960:222
New York Times II, p. 1, Oct 2, 1960
           p. 50, Oct 6, 1960
           II, p. 1, Oct 16, 1960
           p. 36, Oct 18, 1960
           p. 44, May 9, 1961
           p. 35, Jul 12, 1961
New Yorker 36:73-4, Oct 15, 1960
Newsweek 56:102, Oct 17, 1960
Reporter 23:45, Nov 24, 1960
Saturday Review 43:22, Oct 22, 1960
        44:26, May 27, 1961
Theatre Arts 44:9-11, Dec 1960
Time 76:54, Oct 17, 1960
    77:78, Apr 7, 1961

The Cavern
    Productions:
    Translated by Lucienne Hill.
    (Off Off Broadway) Season of 1967-68.
    (Off Off Broadway) Season of 1968-69.
    Reviews:
    Nation 205:125-6, Aug 14, 1967

Cher Antoine (see Dear Antoine)

Colombe (see Mademoiselle Colombe)

Cry of the Peacock (see also Ardèle)
    Productions:
    Adapted by Cecil Robson. Opened April 11, 1950 for two per-
    formances.
    Reviews:
    New York Theatre Critics' Reviews 1950:316
    New York Times p. 33, Apr 12, 1950
    New Yorker 26:60, Apr 22, 1950
    Newsweek 35:95, Apr 24, 1950
    Theatre Arts 34:16, Jun 1950

*Dear Antoine
    Reviews:
    New York Times p. 40, Oct 3, 1969
               p. 12, Jul 17, 1971
    New Yorker 45:196+, Nov 29, 1969
    Time 94:57, Nov 14, 1969

Dinner with the Family (see Le Rendevous de Senlis)

Eurydice (see Legend of Lovers)

The Fighting Cock
  Productions:
    Adapted by Lucienne Hill.   Opened December 8, 1959 for 87
      performances.
  Reviews:
    America 102:538, Jan 30, 1960
    Nation 189:495-6, Dec 26, 1959
    New Republic 142:20-1, Jan 4, 1960
    New York Theatre Critics' Reviews 1959:192
    New York Times p. 57, Dec 9, 1959
                    II, p. 3, Dec 20, 1959
    New Yorker 35:111-13, Feb 21, 1959
               35:79-81, Dec 19, 1959
    Newsweek 54:83, Dec 21, 1959
    Saturday Review 42:29-30, Jun 20, 1959
                    42:24, Dec 26, 1959
    Time 74:34, Dec 21, 1959

The Goldfish (see Les Poissons Rouges)

Humulus the Great
  Productions:
    (Off Off Broadway) Opened October 5, 1976.
  No Reviews.

*L'hurluberlu
  Reviews:
    New Yorker 35:111-13, Feb 21, 1959
    Saturday Review 42:29-30, Jun 20, 1959

L'Invitation au Chateau   (see Ring Round the Moon)

Jeannette   (see Romeo and Jeannette)

The Lark (L'alouette)
  Productions:
    Adapted by Lillian Hellman.   Opened Nov 17, 1955 for 229
      performances.
    (Off Off Broadway) Adapted by Lillian Hellman.   Opened Novem-
      ber 10, 1975.
  Reviews:
    America 90:420-1, Jan 23, 1954
            94:363, Dec 24, 1955
            95:109-10, Apr 28, 1956
    Catholic World 182:308-9, Jan 1952
    Commonweal 63:304, Dec 23, 1955
    Holiday 19:77+, Mar 1956
    Life 39:113-14+, Dec 12, 1955
    Nation 181:485-6, Dec 3, 1955
    New Republic 133:21, Dec 5, 1955
    New York Theatre Critics' Reviews 1955:206
    New York Times II, p. 3, Nov 29, 1953
                   p. 21, May 13, 1955

II, p. 1, Nov 13, 1955
    p. 20, Nov 18, 1955
II, p. 1, Nov 27, 1955
    VI, p. 28, Dec 4, 1955
New Yorker 31:112+, Dec 3, 1955
Newsweek 46:110, Nov 28, 1955
Reporter 13:31, Dec 29, 1955
Saturday Review 38:24, Feb 19, 1955
Theatre Arts 39:23, Apr 1955
         40:63-4+, Mar 1956
         40:8-10, May 1956
Time 66:76+, Nov 28, 1955

Legend of Lovers
Productions:
Adapted by Kitty Black from Anouilh's play Eurydice. Opened
    December 26, 1951 for 22 performances.
(Off Broadway) Opened Season of 1952-1953.
Reviews:
Commonweal 55:373-4, Jan 18, 1952
Nation 174:44, Jan 12, 1952
New York Theatre Critics' Reviews 1951:125
New York Times p. 67, Oct 17, 1948
         p. 17, Dec 27, 1951
         p. 40, Oct 28, 1959
New Yorker 27:46, Jan 5, 1952
         35:88+, Nov 7, 1959
Newsweek 39:36, Jan 7, 1952
Saturday Review 35:32, Jan 19, 1952
Theatre Arts 36:71, Mar 1952
Time 59:44, Jan 7, 1952

Mademoiselle Colombe (Colombe)
Productions:
Adapted by Louis Kronenberger. Opened January 6, 1954 for
    61 performances.
(Off Broadway) Adapted by Denis Cannan. Opened February
    23, 1965 for 13 performances.
Reviews:
America 90:426, Jan 23, 1954
Catholic World 178:467-8, Mar 1954
Commonweal 59:41-2, Feb 12, 1954
Life 36:59-60+, Feb 15, 1954
Nation 178:77-8, Jan 23, 1954
      178:98-9, Jan 30, 1954
New Republic 130:20-1, Jan 25, 1954
New York Theatre Critics' Reviews 1954:397
New York Times II, p. 3, Jan 3, 1954
         p. 26, Jan 7, 1954
         II, p. 1, Jan 17, 1954
         p. 33, Feb 24, 1965
New Yorker 29:52+, Jan 16, 1954

Newsweek 43:59, Jan 18, 1954
    65:93, Mar 15, 1965
Saturday Review 37:30-1, Jan 16, 1954
    37:59-60, Jan 23, 1954
Theatre Arts 38:14, Mar 1954
Time 63:54, Jan 18, 1954

Medea
    Productions:
        (Off Off Broadway) Season of 1971-72.
        (Off Off Broadway) Opened October 5, 1973.
    Reviews:
        New York Times p. 26, Jan 25, 1972

*Ne Reveillez pas Madame
    Reviews:
        Nation 213:90, Aug 2, 1971
        New York Times p. 29, Oct 24, 1970

Pauvre Bitos (see Poor Bitos)

Point of Departure
    Productions:
        (Off Off Broadway) Season of 1967-68.
    Reviews:
        New York Times II, p. 3, Feb 11, 1951

*Les Poissons Rouges (The Goldfish)
    Reviews:
        New York Times p. 39, Feb 3, 1970

Poor Bitos (Pauvre Bitos)
    Productions:
        Translated by Lucienne Hill. Opened November 14, 1964 for
            17 performances.
        (Off Off Broadway) Translated by Lucienne Hill. Opened Sea-
            son of 1969-1970.
    Reviews:
        Nation 184:554, Jun 22, 1957
            199:415-17, Nov 30, 1964
        New Republic 151:20-1, Dec 12, 1964
        New York Theatre Critics' Reviews 1964:147
        New York Times p. 40, Nov 16, 1964
        New Yorker 32:84+, Nov 3, 1956
        Newsweek 64:92, Nov 30, 1964
        Saturday Review 47:43, Dec 5, 1964
            49:55, Mar 5, 1966
        Time 84:104, Nov 27, 1964

The Rehearsal
    Productions:
        Opened November 27, 1952 for four performances.
        Adapted by Pamela Hansford Johnson and Kitty Black.

Opened September 23, 1963 for 110 performances.
(Off Off Broadway) Opened April 23, 1976.
(Off Broadway) Opened October 14, 1976 for 98 performances.
Reviews:
Commonweal 79:194, Nov 8, 1963
Nation 175:562-3, Dec 13, 1952
    197:245, Oct 19, 1963
National Review 15:406-7, Nov 5, 1963
New Republic 127:23, Dec 22, 1952
New York Theatre Critics' Reviews 1963:285
New York Times p. 22, Nov 28, 1952
              p. 23, Sep 3, 1957
              p. 45, Sep 24, 1963
              II, p. 1, Oct 20, 1963
              p. 37, Nov 15, 1976
New Yorker 39:133-4, Oct 5, 1963
Newsweek 62:96, Oct 7, 1963
Saturday Review 35:26, Dec 13, 1952
                46:30, Oct 12, 1963
Theatre Arts 47:10-11, Dec 1963
Time 82:63, Oct 4, 1963

Le Rendevous de Senlis (Dinner with the Family)
Productions:
(Off Broadway) Season of 1960-1961.
Reviews:
New York Times p. 39, Feb 28, 1961
New Yorker 37:114-15, Mar 11, 1961
Theatre Arts 45:56, May 1961
Time 77:45, Mar 17, 1961

*La Répétition
Reviews:
Christian Science Monitor Magazine p. 9, Nov 11, 1950

La Répétition Ou L'Amour Puni
Productions:
Opened November 27, 1952 for four performances.
Reviews:
Nation 175:652-3, Dec 13, 1952
New York Theatre Critics' Reviews 1952:175
New York Times p. 22, Nov 28, 1952
Saturday Review 35:26, Dec 13, 1952

*Restless Heart
Reviews:
New York Times p. 37, May 9, 1957

Ring Round the Moon (L'Invitation au Chateau)
Productions:
Translated by Christopher Fry. Opened November 23, 1950
for 68 performances.
(Off Broadway) Season of 1959-1960.

(Off Off Broadway) Opened December 1975.
Reviews:
Catholic World 172:307, Jan 1951
Christian Science Monitor Magazine p. 13, Dec 2, 1950
Commonweal 52:253, Dec 15, 1950
Nation 171:514, Dec 2, 1950
New Republic 122:21, Jun 5, 1950
     123:22, Dec 25, 1950
New York Theatre Critics' Reviews 1950:189
New York Times p. 29, Jan 27, 1950
     II, p. 4, Nov 19, 1950
     p. 30, Nov 24, 1950
     p. 28, Nov 2, 1968
     p. 57, Sep 28, 1975
New Yorker 26:78-9, Dec 2, 1950
Newsweek 36:74, Dec 4, 1950
Saturday Review 33:25-6, Dec 16, 1950
Theatre Arts 32:30, Feb 1948
     34:29+, Dec 1950
Time 56:64, Dec 4, 1950

Romeo and Jeannette (Jeannette)
 Productions:
  (Off Broadway) Translated by Miriam John. Opened March 24, 1960 for four performances.
  (Off Off Broadway) Translated by Miriam John. Opened December 11, 1969 for 12 performances.
 Reviews:
  New York Times p. 20, Mar 25, 1960
        p. 15, Mar 26, 1960
        p. 53, Dec 16, 1969
  Theatre Arts 31:44, May 1947
      33:40-1, Nov 1950
  Vogue 109:251, Mar 1, 1947

Thieves' Carnival
 Productions:
  (Off Broadway) Season of 1954-1955.
  (Off Off Broadway) Opened December 13, 1973.
 Reviews:
  Catholic World 181:148-9, May 1955
  Commonweal 62:183, May 20, 1955
  New Republic 132:28-9, Feb 21, 1955
  New York Times p. 21, Feb 2, 1955
        II, p. 1, Feb 13, 1955
        p. 52, Jun 5, 1967
        p. 57, Dec 26, 1973
        p. 12, Apr 24, 1975
  New Yorker 31:77-8, Feb 19, 1955
  Saturday Review 38:38, Dec 3, 1955
  Theatre Arts 40:18-19, Jan 1956

Time Remembered
  Productions:
      English version by Patricia Moyes.   Opened November 12,
          1957 for 248 performances.
      (Off Off Broadway) Opened January 1976.
  Reviews:
      America 98:355, Dec 14, 1957
      Catholic World 186:304, Jan 1958
      Christian Century 74:1448, Dec 4, 1957
      Dance Magazine 32:9, Feb 1958
      Life 43:73-4+, Dec 9, 1957
      Nation 185:415-16, Nov 30, 1957
      New York Theatre Critics' Reviews 1957:183
      New York Times p. 35, May 4, 1955
                    p. 41, Nov 13, 1957
                    II, p. 1, Nov 24, 1957
      New York Times Magazine p. 71, Oct 27, 1957
      New Yorker 33:77, Nov 23, 1957
      Newsweek 50:84, Nov 25, 1957
      Reporter 17:35, Dec 12, 1957
      Saturday Review 40:23, Nov 30, 1957
      Theatre Arts 41:71-2+, Oct 1957
                   22:19, Jan 1958
      Time 70:91, Nov 25, 1957

Traveller without Luggage
  Productions:
      Translated by Lucienne Hill.   Opened September 17, 1964 for
          44 performances.
  Reviews:
      Commonweal 81:73, Oct 9, 1964
      Nation 199:202, Oct 5, 1964
      New York Theatre Critics' Reviews 1964:226
      New York Times p. 26, Sep 18, 1964
      Newsweek 64:90-1, Sep 28, 1964
      Saturday Review 47:28, Oct 3, 1964
      Time 84:96, Sep 25, 1964
      Vogue 144:66, Nov 1, 1964

The Waltz of the Toreadors
  Productions:
      English version by Lucienne Hill.   Opened January 17,
          1957 for 132 performances.
      English version by Lucienne Hill.   Opened March 4,
          1958 for 31 performances.
      (Off Broadway) Season of 1958-1959.
      (Off Broadway) Season of 1959-1960.
      Translated by Lucienne Hill.   Opened September 13, 1973 for
          85 performances.
  Reviews:
      America 96:656, Mar 9, 1957
      Catholic World 184:469, Mar 1957
                     187:146, May 1958

Christian Century 74:201, Feb 13, 1957
Life 42:109-10, Feb 25, 1957
Nation 184:108, Feb 2, 1957
      186:261, Mar 22, 1958
      217:349, Oct 8, 1973
New Republic 126:21, Feb 11, 1957
New York Theatre Critics' Reviews 1957:390
                                  1958:334
                                  1973:232
New York Times p. 14, Dec 22, 1956
            VI, p. 58, Jan 6, 1957
            p. 17, Jan 18, 1957
            II, p. 1, Jan 27, 1957
            p. 37, May 5, 1958
            p. 36, May 1, 1959
            p. 63, Sep 13, 1973
            p. 31, Sep 14, 1973
            II, p. 1, Sep 23, 1973
            III, p. 5, Jan 7, 1977
New Yorker 32:68+, Jan 26, 1957
         49:59, Oct 1, 1973
Newsweek 49:84, Jan 28, 1957
        82:127, Sep 24, 1973
Review of Reviews 15:38, Nov 1, 1956
Saturday Review 39:30, Oct 13, 1956
              40:24, Feb 2, 1957
Theatre Arts 41:21+, Mar 1957
Time 69:50, Jan 28, 1957
     102:91, Sep 24, 1973

ANSKY, S. (Solomon Rappaport)

The Dybbuk
  Productions:
    English version by Henry G. Alsberg. Opened December 15,
      1925 for 120 performances.
    Opened December 13, 1926 for 111 performances in reper-
      tory.
    Opened December 16, 1926 for 41 performances.
    (Off Broadway) Opened October 1954.
    Translated by H. N. Bialik. Opened February 3, 1964 for 24
      performances.
    (Off Broadway) Opened September 19, 1972 for 8 performan-
      ces.
    (Off Broadway) Translated by Joseph Landis. Opened April 7,
      1975 for 8 performances.
    (Off Off Broadway) Opened October 30, 1976.
    (Off Off Broadway) Opened January 21, 1977.
  Reviews:
    Arts and Decoration 24:66, Feb 1926

Bookman 63:81, Mar 1926
Catholic World 122:665-7, Feb 1926
Dial 80:255-9, Mar 1926
Independent 116:332, Mar 20, 1926
Life (NY) 87:20, Jan 14, 1926
        89:21, Jan 27, 1927
Literary Digest 88:29, Jan 23, 1926
Nation 122:16, Jan 6, 1926
New Republic 45:187, Jun 6, 1926
        49:190-1, Jan 5, 1927
        118:28, May 24, 1948
        131:21-2, Nov 15, 1954
New York Theatre Critics' Reviews 1964:332
New York Times p. 22, Dec 16, 1925
        VII, p. 3, Dec 20, 1925
        p. 27, Dec 17, 1926
        p. 18, Feb 24, 1937
        p. 26, May 3, 1948
        p. 33, Oct 27, 1954
        II, p. 3, Oct 31, 1954
        p. 30, Feb 4, 1964
        p. 39, Sep 20, 1972
        p. 38, Sep 27, 1972
        II, p. 5, Feb 9, 1975
        p. 26, Apr 9, 1975
        p. 46, May 20, 1975
        XI, p. 33, Dec 19, 1976
New Yorker 53:47-8, Jan 2, 1978
Newsweek 63:90, Feb 17, 1964
        85:53, Mar 10, 1975
Saturday Review 143:559, Apr 9, 1927
Survey 55:572, Feb 1, 1926
Theatre Arts 10:72, 79, Feb 1926
        25:581, Aug 1941
        32:18, Jun 1948
Theatre Magazine 43:15+, May 1926
Vogue 67:74, Feb 15, 1926
Woman Citizen 10:16, Feb 1926

ANTHONY, C. L. see DODIE SMITH

ARCHER, WILLIAM

The Green Goddess
    Productions:
        Opened January 18, 1921 for 175 performances.
    Reviews:
        Bookman 53:276, May 1921
        Collier's 67:14, Feb 19, 1921

Current Opinion 71:319-31, Sep 1921
Dramatic Mirror 83:188, Jan 22, 1921
Dramatist 12:1067-9, Jul 1921
Everybody's 45:91-8, Sep 1921
Independent 105:129, Feb 5, 1921
Life (NY) 77:172, Feb 3, 1921
Nation 112:250, Feb 9, 1921
New York Clipper 68:19, Jan 26, 1921
New York Times p. 14, Jan 19, 1921
            VI, p. 1, Jan 23, 1921
            VI, p. 1, Jan 30, 1921
Outlook 127:330-1, Mar 2, 1921
Theatre Magazine 33:224, Mar 1921
            34:84+, Aug 1921
Weekly Review 4:112, Feb 2, 1921

AUDEN, W. H.

Ascent of F 6 (with Christopher Isherwood)
    Productions:
       (Off Broadway) Opened April 23, 1939 for one perfor-
         mance.
       (Off Broadway) Opened September 1949 in repertory.
    Reviews:
       Forum 97:355, Jun 1937
       New Republic 141:16-17, Nov 23, 1959
       New York Times p. 29, Aug 24, 1949
       Saturday Review 16:20, May 8, 1937
       Scholastic 31:23 E, Jan 15, 1938
       Scribner's Magazine 102:66+, Sep 1937
       Theatre Arts 21:355-6, May 1937

The Dance of Death
    Productions:
       Opened May 19, 1935 (Federal Theatre Project).
    Reviews:
       Theatre Arts 19:906-8, Dec 1935

Dog Beneath the Skin (with Christopher Isherwood)
    Productions:
       (Off Broadway) Opened July 21, 1947.
    Reviews:
       Commonweal 46:475-6, Aug 29, 1947
       Nation 141:626, Nov 27, 1935
       New Republic 85:79, Nov 27, 1935
            141:16-17, Nov 23, 1959
       Saturday Review 13:16, Nov 30, 1935
       Theatre Arts 19:906-8, Dec 1935

*For the Time Being
    Reviews:
       New York Times p. 42, Dec 18, 1957

AYCKBOURN, ALAN

Absurd Person Singular
    Productions:
        Opened October 8, 1974 for 592 performances.
    Reviews:
        America 131:234-5, Oct 26, 1974
        Nation 219:444, Nov 2, 1974
        New Republic 171:36+, Nov 9, 1974
        New York Theatre Critics' Reviews 1974:224
        New York Times p. 20, Aug 3, 1973
                      p. 40, Aug 18, 1974
                      p. 48, Oct 9, 1974
                      p. 30, Oct 11, 1974
                      II, p. 1, Oct 20, 1974
                      II, p. 7, Oct 20, 1974
        New Yorker 50:58+, Oct 21, 1974
        Newsweek 84:56, Oct 21, 1974
        Time 104:90, Oct 21, 1974

How the Other Half Loves
    Productions:
        Opened March 29, 1971 for 104 performances.
    Reviews:
        New York Times p. 23, Aug 7, 1970
                      p. 33, Sep 11, 1970
                      p. 23, Mar 30, 1971
                      II, p. 3, Apr 4, 1971
                      p. 40, Jun 16, 1971
        New Yorker 47:95, Apr 3, 1971
        Time 97:78, Apr 12, 1971

Living Together (see Norman Conquests)

The Norman Conquests (Table Manners, Living Together, and
    Round and Round the Garden)
    Productions:
        Opened December 7, 1975 for 228 performances.
    Reviews:
        America 134:inside back cover, Jan 17, 1976
        Nation 220:286, Mar 8, 1975
              221:700, Dec 27, 1975
        New York Theatre Critics' Reviews 1975:133
        New York Times p. 41, Sep 17, 1974
                      p. 42, Dec 8, 1975
                      II, p. 1, Dec 14, 1975
                      II, p. 6, Apr 30, 1976
        New Yorker 50:142+, Dec 2, 1974
                  51:60, Dec 22, 1975
        Newsweek 86:74, Dec 22, 1975
        Time 106:71, Dec 22, 1975

Round and Round the Garden (see The Norman Conquests)

Table Manners (see The Norman Conquests)

AYME, MARCEL

Clerambard
    Productions:
        (Off Broadway) Season of 1957-58.
        (Off Broadway) Opened March 14, 1964 for 8 performances.
    Reviews:
        Christian Century 74:1448, Dec 4, 1957
        Nation 185:441, Dec 7, 1957
        New York Times p. 22, Nov 8, 1957
                        II, p. 1, Nov 17, 1957
        Theatre Arts 42:26, Jan 1958

*Louisiana
    Reviews:
        New York Times p. 29, Sep 15, 1961

Moonbirds
    Productions:
        Adapted by John Pauker.
        Opened October 9, 1959 for 3 performances.
    Reviews:
        New York Theatre Critics' Reviews 1959:272
        New York Times p. 13, Oct 10, 1959
                        p. 15, Oct 12, 1959
        New Yorker 35:135-6, Oct 17, 1959
        Newsweek 54:80, Oct 19, 1959
        Theatre Arts 43:89, Dec 1959

BAGNOLD, ENID

The Chalk Garden
    Productions:
        Opened October 26, 1955 for 182 performances.
        (Off Off Broadway) Opened January 8, 1976.
    Reviews:
        America 94:195, Nov 12, 1955
        Catholic World 182:227, Dec 1955
        Commonweal 63:616, Mar 16, 1956
        Holiday 19:85+, May 1956
        Life 39:164-6, Dec 5, 1955
        Nation 181:426, Nov 12, 1955
                182:477-8, Jun 2, 1956
        New Republic 134:21, Mar 26, 1956
        New York Theatre Critics' Reviews 1955:227
        New York Times p. 29, Oct 27, 1955
                        II, p. 1, Nov 13, 1955
                        II, p. 3, Jan 1, 1956
        New Yorker 31:77, Nov 5, 1955

Reporter 13:31-2, Dec 29, 1955
Saturday Review 38:24, Nov 12, 1955
Theatre Arts 40:16, Jan 1956
    40:66-7, Feb 1956
    41:25, May 1957
Time 66:96, Nov 7, 1955

The Chinese Prime Minister
 Productions:
 Opened January 2, 1964 for 108 performances.
 Reviews:
 America 110:148, Jan 25, 1964
 Nation 198:80, Jan 20, 1964
 New Republic 150:28, Feb 1, 1964
 New York Theatre Critics' Reviews 1964:393
 New York Times II, p. 1, Dec 29, 1963
      X, p. 1, Dec 29, 1963
      p. 14, Jan 3, 1964
      II, p. 1, Jan 12, 1964
      p. 21, May 21, 1965
 New Yorker 39:69, Jan 11, 1964
 Newsweek 63:70, Jan 13, 1964
 Saturday Review 47:22, Jan 18, 1964
 Time 83:52, Jan 10, 1964

Gertie
 Productions:
 Opened January 30, 1952 for five performances.
 Reviews:
 Commonweal 55:470, Feb 15, 1952
 New York Theatre Critics' Reviews 1952:379
 New York Times p. 23, Jan 31, 1952
 New Yorker 27:56, Feb 9, 1952
 Newsweek 39:82, Feb 11, 1952
 Theatre Arts 36:71, Apr 1952
 Time 59:79, Feb 11, 1952

A Matter of Gravity
 Productions:
 Opened February 3, 1976 for 79 performances.
 Reviews:
 Nation 222:221-2, Feb 21, 1976
 New York Times p. 40, Feb 4, 1976
      II, p. 1, Feb 15, 1976
 New Yorker 51:52, Feb 16, 1976
 Newsweek 87:77, Feb 16, 1976
 Time 107:65, Feb 16, 1976

BAHR, HERMANN

The Concert
 Productions:

Adapted by Leo Ditrichstein. Opened October 4, 1910 for
264 performances.
Opened March 23, 1968 in repertory for 6 performances.
Reviews:
Blue Book 12:637-7, Jan 1911
Columbian 3:698+, Jan 1911
Dramatist 2:150-1, Apr 1911
Everybody's 24:120+, Jan 1911
Green Book 4:1221-2, Dec 1910
Hampton 25:824-6, Dec 1910
Harper's Weekly 54:18, Nov 12, 1910
Life (NY) 56:661, Oct 20, 1910
Metropolitan Magazine 33:524-5, Jan 1911
Munsey 44:409-11, Dec 1910
New York Times p. 52, Mar 25, 1968
Pearson 24:800-803, Dec 1910
Theatre Magazine 12:131-3, Nov 1910

Josephine
Productions:
Adapted by Dr. Washburn Freund. Opened January 28, 1918
for 24 performances.
Reviews:
Bookman 47:76, Mar 1918
Dramatic Mirror 78:5, Feb 19, 1918
Green Book 19:590-1+, Apr 1916
New York Dramatic News 65:7, Feb 2, 1916
New York Times p. 13, Jan 29, 1918

Das Konzert (see The Concert)

The Master
Productions:
Adapted by Benjamin F. Glazer. Opened December 5, 1916
for 47 performances.
Adapted by Benjamin F. Glazer. Opened February 19, 1918
for 15 perfomrances.
Reviews:
Dramatic Mirror 76:5+, Dec 16, 1916
International 11:29, Jan 1917
Life (NY) 68:1150, Dec 21, 1916
New York Dramatic News 63:22, Dec 9, 1916
New York Times p. 7, Dec 6, 1916
p. 10, Feb 20, 1918
North American Review 205:135-6, Jan 1917
Theatre Magazine 25:9+, Jan 1917

The Mongrel
Productions:
Adapted by Elmer Rice. Translated by Francis C. Fay.
Opened December 15, 1924 for 32 performances.

Reviews:
    Independent 114:51, Jan 10, 1925
    Living Age 324:70-6, Jan 3, 1925
    New York Times p. 28, Dec 16, 1924
    Theatre Magazine 40:62+, Feb 1925

The Poor Fool
    Productions:
        Translated by Mrs. F. E. Washburn Freund. Opened August
        30, 1916 in repertory (Washington Square Players).
    Reviews:
        Dramatic Mirror 77:7, Mar 31, 1917
        Theatre Magazine 25:278, May 1917

BARRIE, JAMES M.

The Admirable Crichton
    Productions:
        Opened March 9, 1931 for 56 performances.
        (Off Off Broadway) Opened December 2, 1976.
    Reviews:
        Catholic World 133:210, May 1931
        Commonweal 13:581, Mar 25, 1931
        Drama 21:10, Apr 1931
        Dramatist 7:623, Oct 1915
        Life (NY) 97:25, Mar 27, 1931
        Literary Digest 108:17, Mar 28, 1931
        Nation 132:336, Mar 25, 1931
               223:283-5, Sep 25, 1976
        New York Times p. 23, Mar 16, 1931
                    VIII, p. 1, Mar 29, 1931
        Theatre Arts 15:373-4, May 1931

The Adored One (see Legend of Lenora)

Alice-Sit-by-the-Fire
    Productions:
        Opened February 13, 1911 for 32 performances.
        Opened March 7, 1932 for 32 performances.
    Reviews:
        Bookman 33:136-7, Apr 1911
        Catholic World 135:77, Apr 1932
        Collier's 46:13, Mar 11, 1911
        Commonweal 15:579, Mar 23, 1932
        Dramatist 2:147, Apr 1911
        Green Book 5:900, May 1911
        Life (NY) 57:444, Mar 23, 1911
        New Republic 70:153-4, Mar 23, 1932
        New York Times p. 19, Mar 8, 1932
        Theatre Guild Magazine 9:25-6, Apr 1932
        Theatre Magazine 13:xi-xiii, Mar 1911

Barbara's Wedding
    Productions:
        Opened October 8, 1931 for 20 performances.
    Reviews:
        New Republic 68:300, Oct 28, 1931
        New York Times p. 21, Oct 9, 1931

The Boy David
    Productions:
        (Off Broadway) Opened April 20, 1941 in repertory.
    Reviews:
        Player's Magazine 15:11+, Jan-Feb 1939
        Theatre Arts 21:4, Jan 1937
                    21:193, Mar 1937

The Censor and the Dramatists
    Productions:
        Opened October 14, 1913 for 33 performances.
    Reviews:
        Harper's Weekly 58:24-5, Nov 15, 1913
        New York Dramatic Mirror 70:7, Oct 15, 1913
        New York Times p. 13, Oct 9, 1913
                    p. 11, Oct 15, 1913

Dear Brutus
    Productions:
        Opened December 23, 1918 for 184 performances.
        (Off Broadway) Opened July 1, 1946 in repertory.
    Reviews:
        Bellman 26:12-15, Jan 4, 1919
        Current Opinion 66:91-4, Feb 1919
        Dramatic Mirror 80:8, Jan 4, 1919
        Hearst 35:46+, Mar 1919
        Forum 61:243-4, Feb 1919
        Life 73:56, Jan 9, 1919
        Nation 105:601, Nov 29, 1917
                108:30, Jan 4, 1919
        New Republic 17:285, Jan 4, 1919
        New York Times p. 7, Dec 24, 1918
                    IV, p. 2, Dec 29, 1918
                    p. 9, Jan 8, 1919
        Theatre Magazine 29:77+, Feb 1919
                    29:156+, Mar 1919

*Dear Miss Phoebe
    Reviews:
        New York Times p. 13, Oct 14, 1950

Half an Hour
    Productions:
        Opened September 25, 1913 for 60 performances.

Reviews:
    Bookman 38:263-4, Nov 1913
    Dramatic Mirror 70:6, Oct 1, 1913
    Dramatist 5:392-4, Oct 1913
    Everybody's Magazine 29:807-8, Dec 1913
    Green Book 11:166-7, Jan 1914
    Harper's Weekly 58:25-6, Oct 18, 1913

A Kiss for Cinderella
    Productions:
        Opened December 25, 1916 for 152 performances.
        Opened March 10, 1942 for 48 performances.
    Reviews:
        Bellman 22:44-6, Jan 13, 1917
        Book News 35:244, Feb 1917
        Bookman 53:172-3, Apr 1921
        Catholic World 155:216, May 1942
        Commonweal 35:561, Mar 27, 1942
        Current Opinion 62:178-82, Mar 1917
        Dramatic Mirror 75:7, Apr 15, 1916
                        76:7, Dec 30, 1916
                        76:15, Dec 30, 1916
        Green Book 17:388+, Mar 1917
        Life (NY) 69:22, Jan 14, 1917
        Nation 102:522-3, May 11, 1916
               104:27, Jan 4, 1917
               154:348-9, Mar 21, 1942
        New Republic 9:269, Jan 6, 1917
                    106:398, Mar 23, 1942
        New York Dramatic News 63:40, Dec 30, 1916
        New York Theatre Critics' Reviews 1942:332
        New York Times p. 6, Mar 18, 1916
                      p. 9, Dec 26, 1916
                      II, p. 6, Jan 7, 1917
                      II, p. 6, Jan 14, 1917
                      p. 22, Mar 11, 1942
                      VIII, p. 15, Mar 15, 1942
        New Yorker 18:29, Mar 2, 1942
        Newsweek 19:59, Mar 23, 1942
        North American Review 205:296-7, Feb 1917
        Theatre Arts 25:86-7+, Feb 1917
                    26:289-90, May 1942
        Time 39:46, Mar 23, 1942

The Legend of Lenora (The Adored One)
    Productions:
        Opened January 5, 1914 for 136 performances.
        Opened March 24, 1927 for 16 performances.
    Reviews:
        Bookman 38:612-13, Feb 1914
        Current Opinion 56:194-5, Mar 1914
        International 8:68, Feb 1914
        Green Book 11:406-8+, Mar 1914

Harper's Weekly 58:5, Feb 14, 1914
Life (NY) 63:110-11, Jan 15, 1914
North American Review 199:192-3, Feb 1914
New York Times p. 6, Jan 6, 1914
      p. 22, Mar 30, 1927
      VII, p. 1, Apr 3, 1927
Outlook 106:580-1+, Mar 14, 1914
    106:668-9, Mar 28, 1914

The Little Minister
Productions:
 Opened January 11, 1916 for 79 performances.
 Opened March 23, 1925 for 16 performances.
Reviews:
 Dramatic Mirror 75:8, Jan 22, 1916
 Literary Digest 119:31, Jan 12, 1935
 Life (NY) 85:20 Apr 9, 1925
 Nation 102:85, Jan 20, 1916
 New York Times p. 13, Jan 12, 1916
      VI, p. 1, Jan 16, 1916
      p. 21, Mar 24, 1925
 Stage 14:92, Aug 1937
 Time 25:55, Jan 7, 1935
 Vanity Fair 43:42, Feb 1935

Mary Rose
Productions:
 Opened December 22, 1920 for 127 performances.
 Opened March 4, 1951 for 17 performances.
Reviews:
 Bookman 51:541, Jul 1920
     52:568, Feb 1921
 Current Opinion 69:63-5, Jul 1920
 Catholic World 173:148-9, May 1921
 Commonweal 53:589, Mar 23, 1951
 Dramatic Mirror 83:11, Jan 1, 1921
 Fortnightly Review 113:955-9, Jun 1920
 Independent 105:57, Jan 15, 1921
 Living Age 305:492-4, May 22, 1920
 Nation 112:48, Jan 12, 1921
 New York Clipper 68:18, Dec 29, 1920
 New York Theatre Critics' Reviews 1951:328
 New York Times p. 9, Dec 23, 1920
      VI, p. 3, Dec 26, 1920
      VII, p. 1, Apr 3, 1921
      p. 25, Mar 5, 1951
      II, p. 1, Mar 11, 1951
      p. 9, Jul 21, 1972
 New Yorker 27:54, Mar 17, 1951
 Outlook 127:11-12, Jan 5, 1921
 School and Society 73:185, Mar 24, 1951
 Touchstone 8:335, Feb 1921
 Theatre Arts 35:17, May 1951

Theatre Magazine 33:155+, Mar 1921
Weekly Review 4:18-19, Jan 5, 1921

The New Word
  Productions:
    Opened May 14, 1917 for 48 performances.
    Opened May 6, 1918 for 32 performances.
  Reviews:
    Nation 104:640, May 24, 1917
    New Republic 11:221, June 23, 1917
    New York Times p. 11, May 15, 1917
                 VIII, p. 5, May 20, 1917
                 p. 11, May 7, 1918
    Theatre Magazine 15:344+, Jun 1917

Old Friends
  Productions:
    Opened May 14, 1917 for 48 performances.
  Reviews:
    Theatre Magazine 25:374, Jun 1917

The Old Lady Shows Her Medals
  Productions:
    Opened May 14, 1917 for 48 performances.
    Opened March 7, 1932 for 32 performances
    (Off Broadway) Opened May 25, 1943 in repertory.
  Reviews:
    Commonweal 15:579, Mar 23, 1932
    Current Opinion 63:23-6, Jul 1917
    Dramatic Mirror 77:5+, May 26, 1917
    Life (NY) 69:910, May 24, 1917
    New Republic 11:221, Jun 23, 1917
    New York Dramatic News 64:2, May 26, 1917
    New York Times p. 11, May 15, 1917
                 VIII, p. 5, May 20, 1917
                 p. 19, Mar 8, 1932
    Theatre Magazine 25:374, Jun 1917

Peter Pan
  Productions:
    Opened December 23, 1912 for 24 performances.
    Opened December 21, 1915 for 23 performances.
    Opened November 6, 1924 for 96 performances.
    Opened November 26, 1928 for 48 performances.
    Opened April 24, 1950 for 321 performances.
  Reviews:
    Catholic World 171:226-7, Jun 1950
    Christian Science Monitor Magazine p. 4, Apr 29, 1950
    Commonweal 52:127-8, May 12, 1950
    Dramatic Mirror 69:4, Jan 1, 1913
                 75:9, Jan 1, 1916
    Harper's Weekly 56:9-10, Dec 28, 1912
    Life 28:89-90+, May 22, 1950

Life (NY) 84:18, Nov 27, 1924
Literary Digest 84:26-7, Jan 17, 1925
Musical America 70:4, May 1950
National Magazine 53:195, Dec 1924
New Republic 122:20, May 8, 1950
New York Times p. 11, Apr 14, 1913
            VIII, p. 6, Jan 2, 1916
            p. 16, Nov 7, 1924
            p. 36, Nov 27, 1928
            p. 27, Apr 25, 1950
            II, p. 1, Apr 30, 1950
New Yorker 26:50+, May 6, 1950
Outlook 139:51-2, Jan 14, 1925
Theatre Magazine 40:19, Jan 1925
Time 55:49, May 8, 1950

The Professor's Love Story
Productions:
Opened February 26, 1917 for 48 performances.
Reviews:
Dramatic Mirror 77:7, Mar 3, 1917
Green Book 17:773+, May 1917
Life (NY) 69:401, Mar 8, 1917
Nation 104:275, Mar 8, 1917
New York Dramatic News 64:2, Mar 3, 1917
New York Times p. 9, Feb 27, 1917
            III, p. 2, Mar 4, 1917
Theatre Magazine 25:212+, Apr 1917

Rosalind
Productions:
Opened September 6, 1915 for 48 performances.
Reviews:
Dramatic Mirror 74:8, Sep 8, 1915
Green Book 14:811-13, Nov 1915
Harper's Weekly 61:302, Sep 25, 1915
New Republic 4:185, Sep 18, 1915

Shall We Join the Ladies?
Productions:
Opened January 13, 1925 for 31 performances.
Reviews:
American Mercury 4:373-4, Mar 1925
Bookman 61:75-6, Mar 1925
New York Times p. 19, Jan 14, 1925

A Slice of Life
Productions:
Opened January 29, 1912 for 48 performances.
Reviews:
Bookman 35:171-2, Apr 1912
Dramatic Mirror 67:6, Feb 7, 1912
Everybody's Magazine 26:685-6, May 1912

Life (NY) 59:348-9, Feb 15, 1912
Theatre Magazine 15:75, Mar 1912

The Twelve Pound Look
Productions:
Opened February 13, 1911 for 32 performances.
Reviews:
Bookman 33:136-7, Apr 1911
Collier's 46:13, Mar 11, 1911
Dramatist 2:147, Apr 1911
Green Book 5:900, May 1911
Life (NY) 57:444, Mar 2, 1911
Pearson's Magazine 25:502-3, Apr 1911
Theatre Magazine 13:xi-xiii, Mar 1911

What Every Woman Knows
Productions:
Opened April 13, 1926 for 74 performances.
Opened November 8, 1946 for 21 performances.
Opened December 22, 1954 for 15 performances.
(Off Broadway) Opened May 28, 1975 for 71 performances.
Reviews:
Catholic World 164:260, Dec 1946
              180:389, Feb 1955
Commonweal 45:144, Nov 22, 1946
Nation 163:593, Nov 23, 1946
        180:37, Jan 8, 1955
New Republic 115:723+, Dec 2, 1946
New York Theatre Critics' Reviews 1946:268
                                  1954:208
New York Times VIII, p. 1, Apr 18, 1926
               II, p. 1, Nov 3, 1946
               p. 13, Nov 9, 1946
               p. 23, Sep 29, 1954
               p. 16, Dec 23, 1954
               p. 27, Jun 3, 1975
               II, p. 5, Jun 15, 1975
New Yorker 22:59, Nov 16, 1946
           30:44, Jan 1, 1955
           51:50+, Jun 16, 1975
Newsweek 28:97, Nov 18, 1946
         45:43, Jan 3, 1955
Saturday Review 29:28, Nov 30, 1946
               38:25, Jan 8, 1955
Theatre Arts 30:692, Dec 1946
            31:23, Jan 1947
Theatre Magazine 44:13, Jul 1926
Time 63:35, Jan 3, 1955

The Will
Productions:
Opened September 29, 1913 for 32 performances.

Reviews:
American Mercury 77:32, Mar 1914
Bookman 39:263-4, Nov 1913
Dramatist 5:395-6, Oct 1913
Everybody's Magazine 29:808-9, Dec 1913
Harper's Weekly 58:25-6, Oct 18, 1913
Theatre Magazine 18:143, Nov 1913

BAUM, VICKI

A Divine Drudge (with John Golden)
Productions:
Opened October 26, 1933 for 12 performances.
Reviews:
New York Times p. 22, Oct 7, 1933
Stage 10:28-9, Aug 1933

Grand Hotel
Productions:
Translated by W. A. Drake. Opened November 13, 1930 for
459 performances.
Reviews:
Bookman 72:515-16, Jan 1931
Catholic World 132:460-1, Jan 1931
Collier's 87:19+, Apr 11, 1931
Commonweal 13:497, Mar 4, 1931
Drama 21:11-12, Jan 1931
Life (NY) 96:34-5, Dec 5, 1930
Literary Digest 107:19-21, Dec 13, 1930
New Republic 65:72, Dec 3, 1930
New York Times p. 30, Nov 14, 1930
IX, p. 1, Nov 23, 1930
IX, p. 2, Nov 23, 1930
Outlook 156:554, Dec 3, 1930
Sketch Book 8:25, Jan 1931
Theatre Arts 15:896-8, Nov 1931
Theatre Guild Magazine 9:38-40, Oct 1931
Theatre Magazine 53:24+, Jan 1931
53:33-5+, Feb 1931

Summer Night (with Benjamin Glazer)
Productions:
Opened November 2, 1939 for 4 performances.
Reviews:
Commonweal 31:96, Nov 17, 1939
New York Times p. 17, Nov 3, 1939
Newsweek 14:32, Nov 13, 1939

BECKETT, SAMUEL

Act Without Words

Productions:
    (Off Broadway) Opened February 23, 1972 for 6 performances.
    (Off Broadway) Opened November 20, 1972 for 16 performan-
      ces in repertory.
    (Off Off Broadway) Opened December 4, 1975.
    (Off Off Broadway) Opened February 19, 1976.
Reviews:
    New York Theatre Critics' Reviews 1972:156+
    New York Times p. 24, Aug 29, 1972
                p. 53, Nov 21, 1972
                II, p. 1, Dec 3, 1972
    New Yorker 48:123, Dec 2, 1972
    Newsweek 80:70, Dec 4, 1972
    Time 100:22, Dec 11, 1972

En Attendant Godot (see Waiting for Godot)

The B- Beaver Animations
Productions:
    (Off Off Broadway) Season of 1974-75.
    (Off Off Broadway) Opened March 25, 1977.
Reviews:
    New York Times III, p. 4, Mar 25, 1977.

Cascando
Productions:
    (Off Off Broadway) Opened April 1, 1976.
    (Off Off Broadway) Opened November 5, 1976.
Reviews:
    New York Times p. 27, Apr 13, 1976
               III, p. 3, Nov 5, 1976

Come and Go
Productions:
    (Off Off Broadway) Season of 1974-75.
    (Off Off Broadway) Opened March 1975.
    (Off Off Broadway) Opened November 1976.
Reviews:
    New York Times p. 46, Oct 23, 1975
    Newsweek 85:80+, Apr 7, 1975

Embers
Productions:
    (Off Broadway) Season of 1960-61.
Reviews:
    New York Times p. 44, Oct 26, 1960

Endgame
Productions:
    (Off Broadway) Season of 1957-1958.
    (Off Broadway) Opened February 11, 1962 in repertory.
    (Off Off Broadway) Season of 1969-1970.
    (Off Broadway) Opened May 30, 1970 for 6 performances.

(Off Off Broadway) Opened February 2, 1973.
(Off Off Broadway) Opened April 11, 1974.
(Off Off Broadway) Opened March 1975.
(Off Broadway) Opened April 29, 1975 for 12 performances.
(Off Off Broadway) Opened January 17, 1976.
(Off Broadway) Opened March 15, 1977 for 80 performances.
Reviews:
America 128:144, Feb 17, 1973
Christian Century 75:282, Mar 5, 1958
Nation 186:145-6, Feb 15, 1958
     216:283, Feb 26, 1973
New York Times p. 32, Jan 29, 1958
           II, p. 1, Feb 16, 1958
           p. 27, Feb 12, 1962
           VI, p. 30, Feb 25, 1962
           p. 32, Feb 21, 1964
           p. 47, May 6, 1970
           p. 39, Feb 8, 1973
           II, p. 20, Feb 11, 1973
           p. 36, Mar 29, 1977
New Yorker 48:80, Feb 17, 1973
Newsweek 59:79, Feb 26, 1962
Saturday Review 41:28, Feb 15, 1958
Theatre Arts 42:26, Apr 1958
Time 101:80, Mar 5, 1973

Everyman
Productions:
(Off Off Broadway) Opened December 4, 1975.
No Reviews.

The Expelled
Productions:
(Off Off Broadway) Opened January 20, 1977.
No Reviews.

*Fin de Partie (Game Is Up)
Reviews:
Life 42:143, Apr 22, 1957

Game Is Up (see Fin de Partie)

Happy Days
Productions:
(Off Broadway) Opened September 17, 1961 for 28 performances.
(Off Broadway) Opened September 28, 1965 for 16 performances.
Opened October 12, 1968 in repertory for 3 performances.
(Off Broadway) Opened April 24, 1970 for 10 performances.
(Off Broadway) Opened November 20, 1972 for 16 performances.
(Off Off Broadway) Opened February 19, 1976.

Reviews:
  Christian Century 78:1208-9, Oct 11, 1961
  Commonweal 75:69-70, Oct 13, 1961
  Nation 193:234-5, Oct 7, 1961
      201:258-9, Oct 18, 1965
      215:597, Dec 11, 1972
  New Republic 145:45-6, Oct 2, 1961
  New York Theatre Critics' Reviews 1972:156+
  New York Times II, p. 1, Sep 17, 1961
              p. 36, Sep 18, 1961
              II, p. 1, Oct 1, 1961
              p. 27, Oct 31, 1963
              p. 45, Sep 14, 1965
              p. 54, Oct 14, 1968
              p. 32, Apr 25, 1970
              p. 24, Aug 29, 1972
              p. 53, Nov 21, 1972
              II, p. 1, Dec 3, 1972
              p. 34, Jul 1, 1975
  New Yorker 37:119, Sep 30, 1961
      40:102+, Feb 22, 1964
      48:123, Dec 2, 1972
  Newsweek 80:70, Dec 4, 1972
  Saturday Review 44:38, Oct 7, 1961
  Theatre Arts 45:57-8, Nov 1961
  Time 78:74, Sep 29, 1961
      109:122, Dec 11, 1972

Jack MacGowran in the Works of Samuel Beckett
  Productions:
  (Off Broadway) Opened November 19, 1970 for 67 performances.
  Reviews:
  Nation 211:605-6, Dec 7, 1970
  New Republic 163:20, Dec 12, 1970
  New York Times Critics' Reviews 1970:127
  New York Times p. 32, Apr 25, 1970
              p. 32, Nov 20, 1970
              p. 46, Nov 27, 1970
              II, p. 8, Nov 29, 1970
              II, p. 11, Dec 6, 1970
  New Yorker 46:142, Nov 28, 1970
  Time 96:48, Nov 30, 1970

Krapp's Last Tape
  Productions:
  (Off Broadway) Opened January 14, 1960 for 582 performances.
  (Off Broadway) Opened September 12, 1961 for 32 performan-
      ces.
  (Off Broadway) Opened October 31, 1965 for 168 performances.
  (Off Broadway) Opened November 22, 1972 in repertory for
      15 performances.
  (Off Off Broadway) Opened September 1975.
  (Off Off Broadway) Opened November 1976.

Reviews:
    Christian Century 77:256, Mar 2, 1960
    Nation 190:153, Feb 13, 1960
    New Republic 142:21, Feb 22, 1960
    New York Theatre Critics' Reviews 1972:156+
    New York Times p. 37, Jan 15, 1960
                   II, p. 1, Jan 31, 1960
                    p. 11, Feb 6, 1960
                    p. 47, Mar 29, 1960
                    p. 42, Jun 9, 1965
                    p. 41, Oct 11, 1968
                    p. 49, Nov 23, 1972
    New Yorker 35:75, Jan 23, 1960
               48:123, Dec 2, 1972
    Newsweek 80:70, Dec 4, 1972
    Saturday Review 43:28, Jan 30, 1960
    Time 100:122, Dec 11, 1972

The Lost Ones
    Productions:
        (Off Off Broadway) Opened March 1975.
        (Off Off Broadway) Opened October 16, 1975.
        (Off Off Broadway) Opened February 7, 1976.
    Reviews:
        New York Times p. 46, Oct 23, 1975
        Newsweek 85:80+, Apr 7, 1975

Not I
    Productions:
        (Off Broadway) Opened November 22, 1972 for 15 performan-
        ces in repertory.
    Reviews:
        America 127:525-6, Dec 16, 1972
        Nation 215:597, Dec 11, 1972
        New Republic 167:24, Dec 16, 1972
        New York Theatre Critics' Reviews 1972:156+
        New York Times p. 49, Nov 23, 1972
                    II, p. 1, Dec 3, 1972
        New Yorker 48:124, Dec 2, 1972
        Newsweek 80:70, Dec 4, 1972
        Time 100:122, Dec 11, 1972

Oh! Les Beaux Jours (see Happy Days)

Play
    Productions:
        (Off Broadway) Opened January 4, 1964 for 121 performances.
        (Off Off Broadway) Opened March 1975.
    Reviews:
        Commonweal 79:484-5, Jan 24, 1964
        Nation 198:106, Jan 27, 1964
        New Republic 150:30, Feb 1, 1964

New York Times p. 35, Jan 6, 1964
p. 46, Mar 25, 1964
p. 36, Apr 15, 1971
II, p. 1, Dec 3, 1972
p. 46, Oct 23, 1975
III, p. 8, Dec 10, 1976
Newsweek 85:80+, Apr 7, 1975
Saturday Review 47:25, Jan 25, 1964
Time 83:64, Jan 17, 1964
Vogue 143:22, Feb 15, 1964

Waiting for Godot
Productions:
Opened April 19, 1956 for 59 performances.
Opened January 21, 1957 for 6 performances.
(Off Broadway) Season of 1958-1959.
(Off Broadway) Opened April 22, 1968 in repertory for 11 performances.
(Off Broadway) Opened February 3, 1971 for 277 performances.
(Off Off Broadway) Season of 1973-1974.
(Off Off Broadway) Opened October 1, 1974.
(Off Off Broadway) Opened October 16, 1975.
(Off Broadway) Translated by Elmar Tophoven. Opened March 29, 1977 for 7 performances.
Reviews:
America 95:182+, May 12, 1956
95:265, Jun 9, 1956
Catholic World 183:227-8, Jun 1956
Christian Century 88:603-4, May 12, 1971
Commentary 51:78, Apr 1971
Commonweal 61:365-6, Dec 31, 1954
64:203, May 25, 1956
66:188+, May 17, 1957
Life 40:155-6+, May 7, 1956
Nation 182:387+, May 5, 1956
212:253-4, Feb 22, 1971
222:797-8, Jun 26, 1976
New Republic 134:20-1, May 14, 1956
176:20-1, Apr 23, 1977
New York Theatre Critics' Reviews 1957:385
1971:360
New York Times II, p. 3, Nov 13, 1955
II, p. 1, Apr 5, 1956
p. 21, Apr 20, 1956
II, p. 1, Apr 29, 1956
p. 25, Jan 22, 1957
p. 22, Aug 6, 1958
VI, p. 36, Sep 21, 1958
II, p. 3, Jan 31, 1965
p. 38, Apr 23, 1968
p. 48, Apr 6, 1970
p. 43, Jan 28, 1971

New York Times II, p. 1, Jan 31, 1971
p. 29, Feb 4, 1971
II, p. 1, Feb 14, 1971
p. 43, Jul 29, 1971
p. 62, Sep 20, 1973
II, p. 1, Jun 8, 1975
III, p. 19, Mar 31, 1977

New Yorker 32:89, May 5, 1956
32:25-6, May 19, 1956
46:78+, Feb 13, 1971
Newsweek 47:76, Apr 30, 1956
48:102, Sep 24, 1956
Reporter 13:43, Oct 20, 1955
Saturday Review 39:32, May 5, 1956
39:46, May 19, 1956
40:25, Feb 9, 1957
Theatre Arts 40:18, Jun 1956
40:33-5+, Aug 1956
41:16, Apr 1957
Time 67:55, Apr 30, 1956
69:108, Mar 18, 1957
97:61, Feb 15, 1971

BECQUE, HENRY

Parisienne
Productions:
Adapted by Ashley Dukes. Opened July 24, 1950 for 16 per-
formances.
Reviews:
Christian Science Monitor Magazine p. 9, Jul 29, 1950
New Republic 123:22, Aug 28, 1950
New York Times p. 24, Jul 25, 1950
Newsweek 36:74, Aug 7, 1950

BEHAN, BRENDAN

Borstal Boy
Productions:
Adapted for the stage by Frank McMahon. Opened March 31,
1970 for 143 performances.
Reviews:
America 122:483, May 2, 1970
Life 68:16, May 22, 1970
Nation 210:473, Apr 20, 1970
New York Theatre Critics' Reviews 1970:312
New York Times p. 39, Oct 11, 1967
p. 55, Oct 12, 1967
p. 38, Apr 1, 1970
II, p. 9, Apr 12, 1970

New York Times p. 13, Aug 1, 1970
New Yorker 46:81-2, Apr 11, 1970
Newsweek 75:83, Apr 13, 1970
Saturday Review 53:26, Apr 18, 1970
Time 95:97, Apr 13, 1970

The Hostage
  Productions:
    Opened September 20, 1960 for 127 performances.
    (Off Broadway) Opened December 12, 1961 for 545 performances.
    (Off Broadway) Season of 1966-1967 for 9 performances.
    (Off Broadway) Opened October 9, 1972 in repertory for 8 performances.
  Reviews:
    America 104:130, Oct 22, 1960
    Atlantic 203:65-7, Jun 1959
    Catholic World 192:126-7, Nov 1960
    Commonweal 75:389, Jan 5, 1962
    Horizon 3:113-14, Jan 1961
    Nation 191:236, Oct 8, 1960
            215:410-11, Oct 30, 1972
    New Republic 143:20-1, Oct 3, 1960
    New York Theatre Critics' Reviews 1960:239
    New York Times p. 28, Jul 10, 1959
                  p. 42, Sep 21, 1960
                  II, p. 1, Oct 2, 1960
                  II, p. 1, Oct 30, 1960
                  p. 55, Dec 13, 1961
                  p. 24, May 12, 1972
                  p. 50, Oct 11, 1972
    New Yorker 35:156, Apr 18, 1959
               36:128, Oct 1, 1960
               37:57-8, Dec 23, 1961
               48:76+, Oct 21, 1972
    Newsweek 56:57, Oct 3, 1960
    Reporter 23:45, Nov 24, 1960
    Saturday Review 43:32, Oct 8, 1960
                    45:30, May 19, 1962
    Theatre Arts 44:8-9, Nov 1960
    Time 76:59, Oct 3, 1960

*Posterity Be Damned
  Reviews:
    New York Times p. 47, Mar 29, 1960

Quare Fellow
  Productions:
    (Off Broadway) Season of 1958-1959.
  Reviews:
    Catholic World 188:420, Feb 1959
    Commonweal 69:438-9, Jan 23, 1959
    New York Times p. 24, Jul 25, 1956

New York Times p. 34, Nov 28, 1958
New Yorker 34:119-20, Dec 6, 1958
Newsweek 52:66-7, Dec 8, 1958
Saturday Review 41:27-8, Dec 13, 1958
Theatre Arts 43:66, Feb 1959
Time 70:82, Jul 29, 1958
    72:78+, Dec 8, 1958
Vogue 133:95+, Jan 1, 1959

BENAVENTE, JACINTO

The Bonds of Interest
Productions:
    Translated by John Garrett Underhill. Opened April 19, 1919
      for 32 performances.
    Translated by John Garrett Underhill. Opened October 14,
      1929 for 24 performances.
Reviews:
    Bellman 26:574-7, May 24, 1919
    New Republic 19:25, May 3, 1919
    New York Times p. 9, Apr 15, 1919
                IV, p. 2, Apr 20, 1919
                p. 34, Oct 15, 1929
                p. 7, Dec 1, 1951
                p. 43, May 7, 1958
    Poet Lore 32:244-50, Jun 1921
    Theatre Arts 13:878, Dec 1929
    Theatre Magazine 29:341+, May 31, 1919
                   50:66, Dec 1929
    Weekly Review 1:45, May 24, 1919

Field of Ermine
Productions:
    Adapted by John Garrett Underhill. Opened February 8, 1935
      for 11 performances.
Reviews:
    Drama 13:101, Dec 1922
    New Republic 82:78, Feb 27, 1935
    New York Times p. 10, Feb 9, 1935
    Theatre Arts 19:248, Apr 1935

His Widow's Husbands
Productions:
    Translated by John Garrett Underhill. Opened October 31,
      1917 in repertory (Washington Square Players).
Reviews:
    New York Times p. 13, Nov 1, 1917

The Passion Flower
Productions:
    Translated by John Garrett Underhill. Opened January 13,
      1920 for 144 performances.

Reviews:
  Arts and Decoration 12:344, Mar 1920
  Dramatic Mirror 82:131, Jan 29, 1920
  Independent 102:157, May 1, 1920
  Nation 110:152-3, Jan 21, 1920
  New York Clipper 67:25, Jan 21, 1920
  New York Times p. 12, Jan 14, 1920
  Theatre Magazine 31:183-4, Mar 1920
  Weekly Review 2:161, Feb 14, 1920

Saturday Night
  Productions:
  Opened October 25, 1926 for 13 performances.
  Reviews:
  New Republic 48:323, Nov 10, 1926
  New York Times p. 25, Oct 26, 1926
                VIII, p. 1, Nov 7, 1926
  Theatre Arts 11:11, Jan 1937

BENELLI, SEM

La Beffa (see The Jest)

The Jest (La Beffa)
  Productions:
  Adapted by Jean Richepin.   Opened December 5, 1910 in rep-
     ertory as La Beffa.
  Opened April 9, 1919 for 77 performances.
  Opened September 19, 1919 for 179 performances.
  Opened February 4, 1926 for 77 performances.
  Reviews:
  Arts and Decoration 12:396-7, Apr 1920
  Bellman 26:489-92, May 3, 1919
  Bookman 63:214, Apr 1926
  Current Opinion 66:364-7, Jun 1919
  Dial 66:534-7, May 31, 1919
  Drama 10:140-5, Jan 1920
  Forum 61:28-9, May 1919
  Hearst 36:46-7+, Jul 1919
  Literary Digest 61:28-9, May 10, 1919
  Nation 108:618-19, Apr 19, 1919
  New Republic 19:55, May 10, 1919
               19:397, Jul 23, 1919
  New York Times p. 9, Apr 10, 1919
             IV, p. 2, Apr 20, 1919
             IV, p. 2, May 4, 1919
             IV, p. 2, May 18, 1919
             IV, p. 2, Sep 28, 1919
                p. 22, Feb 5, 1926
            VIII, p. 1, Feb 14, 1926
  Theatre Magazine 29:324, May 1919
                   29:352-4, Jun 1919

Theatre Magazine 30:159, Sep 1919
43:11, Apr 1926
Vogue 67:126+, Apr 1, 1926
Weekly Review 1:131, Jun 21, 1919
2:626, Jun 16, 1920

BERGSTROM, HJALMER

Karen
  Productions:
    Translated by Edwin Bjorkman.   Opened January 7, 1918 for
      80 performances.
  Reviews:
    Dramatic Mirror 78:7, Jan 19, 1918
    Life (NY) 71:143, Jan 24, 1918
    Nation 106:273, Mar 7, 1918
    New York Times p. 13, Jan 1918
                    IV, p. 7, Jan 13, 1918

BERNARD, JEAN-JACQUES

Invitation to a Voyage
  Productions:
    Translated by Ernest Boyd.   Opened October 4, 1928 for 19
      performances.
  Reviews:
    American Mercury 15:504, Dec 1928
    New York Times p. 17, Oct 5, 1928
    Vogue 72:122+, Nov 24, 1928

Martine
  Productions:
    Translated by Helen Grayson.   Opened April 4, 1928 for 16
      performances.
  Reviews:
    New Republic 54:272-3, Apr 18, 1928
    New York Times p. 19, Apr 15, 1928
    Vogue 71:114, Jun 1, 1928

The Springtime of Others
  Productions:
    (Off Off Broadway) Translated by Thomas Luce.   Opened May
      1976.
  No Reviews.

*Unquiet Spirit
  Reviews:
    New York Times p. 25, May 31, 1950

BESIER, RUDOLPH

The Barretts of Wimpole Street
　　Productions:
　　　　Opened February 9, 1931 for 370 performances.
　　　　Opened February 25, 1935 for 24 performances.
　　　　Opened March 26, 1945 for 88 performances.
　　Reviews:
　　　　Arts and Decoration 34:46, Apr 1931
　　　　Bookman 73:182-3, Apr 1931
　　　　Canadian Forum 12:316, May 1932
　　　　Catholic World 133:79-80, Apr 1931
　　　　　　　　161:169, May 1945
　　　　Commonweal 13:469, Feb 25, 1931
　　　　　　　　41:648, Apr 13, 1945
　　　　Golden Book 13:64-6, May 1931
　　　　Harper's Bazaar 79:116-17+, Oct 1945
　　　　Life (NY) 97:18, Feb 27, 1931
　　　　Life 18:105-8, Apr 16, 1945
　　　　Literary Digest 108:18-19, Mar 7, 1931
　　　　Nation 132:224-5, Feb 25, 1931
　　　　　　　　139:419, Oct 10, 1934
　　　　New Republic 112:447, Apr 9, 1945
　　　　New York Times p. 25, Feb 10, 1931
　　　　　　　　VIII, p. 1, Feb 15, 1931
　　　　　　　　VIII, p. 1, Feb 22, 1931
　　　　　　　　VIII, p. 3, Feb 7, 1932
　　　　　　　　p. 16, Feb 26, 1935
　　　　　　　　p. 23, Mar 27, 1945
　　　　　　　　II, p. 1, Apr 1, 1945
　　　　　　　　p. 23, Mar 7, 1950
　　　　　　　　II, p. 2, Mar 12, 1950
　　　　Newsweek 25:87, Apr 9, 1945
　　　　Outlook 157:311, Feb 25, 1931
　　　　Saturday Review 7:726, Apr 11, 1931
　　　　　　　　28:20-2, Apr 7, 1945
　　　　Sketch Book 8:21, Jul 1931
　　　　Theatre Arts 15:273-7, Apr 1931
　　　　　　　　19:258, Apr 1935
　　　　Theatre Magazine 53:8+, Mar 1931
　　　　　　　　53:24, Apr 1931
　　　　Time 45:88, Apr 9, 1945
　　　　Vanity Fair 35:38+, Mar 1931
　　　　Vogue 77:77+, Apr 1, 1931
　　　　Woman's Journal ns16:12-13, Mar 1931
　　　　Yale Review 20:817-18, Summer 1931

Don
　　Productions:
　　　　Opened December 30, 1909 in repertory.
　　Reviews:
　　　　Bookman 31:139-41, Apr 1910
　　　　Current Literature 48:421-7, Apr 1910

Dramatic Mirror 63:5, Jan 8, 1910
Dramatist 2:155-6, Apr 1911
Forum 43:188-9, Feb 1910
Hampton 24:410, Mar 1910
Harper's Weekly 54:25, Jan 22, 1910
Life (NY) 55:92, Jan 3, 1910
Metropolitan Magazine 32:390-1, Jun 1910
Theatre Magazine 11:35-6+, Feb 1910

Her Country (with Sybil Spottiswood)
Productions:
Opened February 21, 1918 for 76 performances.
Reviews:
Dramatic Mirror 78:5, Mar 9, 1918
Green Book 19:773+, May 1918
New Republic 14:177, Mar 9, 1918
New York Dramatic News 65:3, Mar 2, 1918
New York Times p. 12, Feb 22, 1918
Theatre Magazine 27:207, Apr 1918
27:260-8, Apr 1918

Lady Patricia
Productions:
Opened February 26, 1912 for 32 performances.
Reviews:
American Playwright 1:75-6, Mar 1913
Bookman 35:172-3, Apr 1912
Collier's 48:34, Mar 16, 1912
Dramatic Mirror 67:6, Feb 28, 1912
Dramatist 3:244-5, Apr 1912
Everybody's Magazine 26:688, May 1912
Green Book 7:907-9+, May 1912
7:975-7, May 1912
Leslie's Weekly 114:193, Mar 14, 1912
Life (NY) 59:540, Mar 14, 1912
Munsey 47:282, May 1912
Nation 93:321, Oct 5, 1911
Red Book 19:177-82, May 1912
Theatre Magazine 15:108+, Apr 1912

A Lesson in Love (with May Edgington)
Productions:
Opened September 24, 1923 for 72 performances.
Reviews:
Bookman 58:306, Nov 1923
Nation 117:412, Oct 10, 1923
New York Times p. 10, Sep 25, 1923
II, p. 1, Sep 30 1923
Theatre Magazine 38:75, Nov 1923

Olive Latimer's Husband
Productions:
Opened January 7, 1910 for one performance.
No Reviews.

Secrets (with May Edgington)
    Productions:
        Opened December 25, 1922 for 168 performances.
    Reviews:
        Current Opinion 75:61-6+, Jul 1923
        Drama 14:57, Nov 1923
        Nation 116:128, Jan 31, 1923
        New York Clipper 70:20, Jan 10, 1923
        New York Times p. 11, Dec 26, 1922
                        VII, p. 1, Dec 31, 1922
        Theatre Magazine 37:15, Feb 1923
                        37:28+, Apr 1923

BETTI, UGO

The Burnt Flowerbed
    Productions:
        (Off Broadway) Translated by Henry Reed.   Opened July 2,
            1974 for 48 performances.
    Reviews:
        New York Times p. 29, Jul 25, 1974

Corruption in the Palace of Justice
    Productions:
        (Off Broadway) Translated by Henry Reed.   Opened October 8,
            1963 for 103 performances.
    Reviews:
        Catholic World 198:199-200, Dec 1963
        Nation 197:306, Nov 9, 1963
        New Republic 149:26+, Dec 21, 1963
        New York Times p. 49, Oct 9, 1963
        New Yorker 39:100+, Oct 19, 1963
        Newsweek 62:72, Nov 18, 1963
        Theatre Arts 48:68, Jan 1964
        Time 82:75, Oct 25, 1963

The Gambler
    Productions:
        Adapted by Alfred Drake and Edward Eager.   Opened October
            13, 1952 for 24 performances.
        (Off Off Broadway) Season of 1968-1969.
        (Off Off Broadway) Opened October 18, 1973.
    Reviews:
        Commonweal 56:119, Nov 7, 1952
        New Republic 127:23, Oct 27, 1952
        New York Theatre Critics' Reviews 1952:241
        New York Times p. 40, Oct 14, 1952
        New Yorker 28:78-80, Oct 25, 1952
        Saturday Review 35:26, Nov 1, 1952
        Theatre Arts 36:25-6, Dec 1952
        Time 60:76, Oct 27, 1952

Island of the Goats
Productions:
   English version by Henry Reed.   Opened October 4, 1955 for
      7 performances.
Reviews:
   New York Theatre Critics' Reviews 1955:260
   New York Times p. 40, Oct 5, 1955
   New Yorker 31:81, Oct 15, 1955
   Theatre Arts 39:23, Dec 1955

Landslide at North Station
Productions:
   (Off Off Broadway) Opened May 1977.
No Reviews.

The Queen and the Rebels
Productions:
   (Off Broadway) Opened February 25, 1965 for 22 performances.
Reviews:
   New York Times p. 16, Feb 26, 1965
   New Yorker 41:80, Mar 6, 1965

Summertime
Productions:
   (Off Off Broadway) Season of 1969-1970.
No Reviews.

Time of Vengeance
Productions:
   (Off Broadway) Season of 1959-1960.
Reviews:
   Nation 190:19, Jan 2, 1960
   New York Times p. 39, Dec 11, 1959
                  II, p. 1, Dec 27, 1959

Troubled Waters
Productions:
   (Off Broadway) Translated by Gino Rizzo and William Meri-
      wether.   Opened June 3, 1965 for 5 performances.
Reviews:
   Nation 200:681, Jun 21, 1965
   New York Times p. 40, Jun 4, 1965

BIRABEAU, ANDRE

Dame Nature
Productions:
   Adapted by Patricia Collinge.   Based on Wedekind's The
      Awakening of Spring.   Opened September 26, 1938 for 48
      performances.
Reviews:
   Commonweal 28:644, Oct 14, 1938

Nation 147:362, Oct 8, 1938
New Republic 96:271, Oct 12, 1938
New York Times p. 24, Sep 27, 1938
Newsweek 12:28, Oct 10, 1938
Theatre Arts 22:782-3, Nov 1938
Time 32:49, Oct 10, 1938

Little Dark Horse
  Productions:
    Adapted by Theresa Helburn. Opened November 16, 1941 for
      9 performances.
  Reviews:
    New York Theatre Critics' Reviews 1941:218
    New York Times p. 14, Nov 14, 1941

BJORNSON, BJORN-STJERNE

*Mary Stuart in Scotland
  Reviews:
    New York Times p. 31, Sep 1, 1960

When the Young Vine Blooms
  Productions:
    Translated by Arvid Paulson. Opened November 16, 1915 for
      23 performances.
  Reviews:
    Dramatic Mirror 74:8, Nov 27, 1915
    New York Times p. 11, Nov 17, 1915

BOLITHO, WILLIAM

Overture
  Productions:
    Opened December 5, 1930 for 41 performances.
  Reviews:
    Arts and Decoration 34:48, Feb 1931
    Bookman 73:72, Mar 1931
    Catholic World 132:593-4, Feb 1931
    Commonweal 13:217-18, Dec 24, 1930
    Drama 21:14, Jan 1931
    Nation 131:714+, Dec 24, 1930
    New Republic 65:165-6, Dec 24, 1930
    New York Times p. 31, Nov 25, 1930
                    p. 26, Dec 8, 1930
                    IX, p. 1, Dec 14, 1930
    Outlook 156:629, Dec 17, 1930
    Theatre Arts 15:96+, Feb 1931
    Theatre Magazine 53:24-5, Feb 1931
    Vanity Fair 35:82, Feb 1931
    Vogue 77:39+, Feb 1, 1931

BOLT, ROBERT

Flowering Cherry
  Productions:
    Opened October 21, 1959 for 5 performances.
  Reviews:
    New York Theatre Critics' Reviews 1959:247
    New York Times p. 46, Oct 22, 1959
    New Yorker 35:136, Oct 31, 1959
    Theatre Arts 43:88, Dec 1959
    Time 74:30, Nov 2, 1959

*Gentle Jack
  Reviews:
    New York Times p. 50, Nov 29, 1963

A Man for All Seasons
  Productions:
    Opened November 22, 1961 for 637 performances.
    Opened January 27, 1964 for 17 performances.
  Reviews:
    America 106:452, Jan 6, 1962
            107:184-7, Apr 28, 1962
    Catholic World 194:255-6, Jan 1962
    Christian Century 79:87-9, Jan 17, 1962
    Commonweal 75:317-18, Dec 18, 1961
    Life 52:55-7+, Jan 12, 1962
    Nation 193:480, Dec 9, 1961
    New Republic 145:28-30, Dec 11, 1961
    New York Theatre Critics' Reviews 1961:164
    New York Times II, p. 1, Nov 19, 1961
                    p. 51, Nov 23, 1961
                    II, p. 1, Dec 3, 1961
                    II, p. 1, Sep 23, 1962
                    p. 15, May 11, 1963
                    p. 24, Jan 28, 1964
    New Yorker 37:117, Dec 2, 1961
    Newsweek 58:78, Dec 4, 1961
    Reporter 26:38, Jan 4, 1962
    Saturday Review 44:27, Dec 16, 1961
                    45:27, Sep 15, 1962
    Theatre Arts 46:10-11, Feb 1962
    Time 78:64, Dec 1, 1961

*The Tiger and the Horse
  Reviews:
    New York Times p. 26, Aug 25, 1960

Vivat! Vivat Regina!
  Productions:
    Opened January 20, 1972 for 116 performances.
  Reviews:
    America 126:181-2, Feb 19, 1972

Catholic World 212:313-14, Mar 1971
Nation 214:189, Feb 7, 1972
New York Theatre Critics' Reviews 1972:385
New York Times p. 80, May 24, 1970
          p. 21, Jul 20, 1970
          p. 20, Jul 28, 1970
          p. 50, Jan 20, 1972
          p. 27, Jan 21, 1972
          II, p. 1, Jan 30, 1972
          II, p. 1, Feb 6, 1972
          p. 55, Apr 26, 1972
New Yorker 46:160-1, Nov 14, 1970
          47:72, Jan 29, 1972
Newsweek 79:83, Jan 31, 1972
Saturday Review 55:62, Feb 12, 1972
Time 99:71, Jan 31, 1972

BOLTON, GUY

Adam and Eva (with George Middleton)
   Productions:
      Opened September 13, 1919 for 312 performances.
   Reviews:
      Current Opinion 68:782-8, Jun 1920
      Dramatic Mirror 80:1503, Sep 25, 1919
      Dramatist 10:969-70, Oct 1919
      Hearst 38:41-3+, Jul 1920
      Life (NY) 74:548-9, Sep 25, 1919
      New York Times p. 15, Sep 16, 1919
               IV, p. 2, Sep 21, 1919

Anastasia
   Productions:
      Adapted from a play by Marcelle Maurette. Opened December
      29, 1954 for 272 performances.
   Reviews:
      America 92:461, Jan 29, 1955
      Catholic World 180:386, Feb 1955
      Commonweal 61:582-3, Mar 4, 1955
      Life 38:32-3, Feb 14, 1955
      Nation 180:24, Jan 22, 1955
      New Republic 132:22, Feb 7, 1955
      New York Theatre Critics' Reviews 1954:192
      New York Times II, p. 3, Dec 26, 1954
               p. 13, Dec 30, 1954
               II, p. 1, Jan 16, 1955
      New Yorker 30:66, Jan 8, 1955
      Newsweek 45:62, Jan 10, 1955
      Saturday Review 38:31, Jan 15, 1955
      Theatre Arts 39:19+, Mar 1955
               39:28+, Jun 1955
               40:34-61, May 1956
      Time 65:35, Jan 10, 1955

The Cave Girl (with George Middleton)
    Productions:
        Opened August 18, 1920 for 37 performances.
    Reviews:
        Dramatic Mirror p. 9, Jul 3, 1920
                          p. 371, Aug 28, 1920
        Independent 103:261, Sep 4, 1920
        New York Clipper 68:19, Aug 25, 1920
        New York Times p. 12, Aug 19, 1920
        Theatre 32:242, Oct 1920

Chicken Feed (Wages for Wives)
    Productions:
        Opened September 24, 1923 for 144 performances.
    Reviews:
        Nation 117:412, Oct 10, 1923
        New York Times p. 10, Sep 25, 1923
        Theatre Magazine 38:56+, Nov 1923

Child of Fortune
    Productions:
        Adapted from Wings of the Dove by Henry James.   Opened
            November 13, 1956 for 23 performances.
    Reviews:
        Commonweal 65:383, Jan 11, 1957
        New York Theatre Critics' Reviews 1956:209
        New York Times p. 41, Nov 14, 1956
        New Yorker 32:124, Nov 24, 1956
        Saturday Review 39:50, Dec 1, 1956
        Theatre Arts 41:27, Jan 1957
        Time 68:58, Nov 26, 1956

Children (with Tom Carlton)
    Productions:
        Opened October 4, 1915 in repertory (Washington Square
            Players).
    Reviews:
        Dramatic Mirror 75:8, Apr 1, 1916
        New York Times p. 9, Mar 21, 1916

The Fallen Idol
    Productions:
        Opened January 23, 1915 for nine performances.
    Reviews:
        Current Opinion 58:177-8, Mar 1915
        Dramatic Mirror 73:24, Jan 27, 1915
        Green Book 13:765-6, Apr 1915
        Life (NY) 65:196, Feb 4, 1915
        New York Dramatic News 60:17, Jan 30, 1915
        New York Times p. 9, Jan 25, 1915
        Theatre Magazine 21:149, Mar 1915

The Five Million (with Frank Mandel)
  Productions:
    Opened July 8, 1919 for 91 performances.
  Reviews:
    Current Opinion 67:160-4, Sep 1919
    Forum 62:243-4, Aug 1919
    Hearst 36:42-3+, Oct 1919
    New York Times p. 14, Jul 9, 1919
    Theatre Magazine 30:149, Sep 1919

Golden Wings (R.A.F.) (with William Jay)
  Productions:
    Opened December 8, 1941 for six performances.
  Reviews:
    New York Theatre Critics' Reviews 1941:178
    New York Times p. 33, Nov 25, 1941
                  p. 46, Dec 9, 1941
    Newsweek 18:61, Dec 22, 1941
    Theatre Arts 26:79, Feb 1942

Grounds for Divorce   (see entry under Vajda, Ernest)

*Leave It to Jeeves
  Reviews:
    New York Times p. 89, Aug 13, 1972

The Light of the World (with George Middleton)
  Productions:
    Opened January 6, 1920 for 31 performances.
  Reviews:
    Dramatic Mirror 82:51, Jan 15, 1920
    Life (NY) 75:148, Jan 22, 1920
    New York Clipper 67:25, Jan 14, 1920
    New York Times p. 17, Jan 7, 1920
    Theatre Magazine 31:142, Feb 1920

The Nightcap (with Max Marcin)
  Productions:
    Opened August 15, 1921 for 96 performances.
  Reviews:
    Dramatic Mirror 84:285, Aug 20, 1921
    New York Clipper 69:24, Aug 14, 1921
    New York Times p. 18, Aug 16, 1921
    Theatre Magazine 34:236, Oct 1921
    Weekly Review 5:215, Sep 3, 1921

Nobody Home (with Paul Rubens)
  Productions:
    Opened April 20, 1915 for 135 performances.
  Reviews:
    Dramatic Mirror 73:8, Apr 28, 1915
    Green Book 14:59-60, Jul 1915
                14:191-2, Jul 1915

Life (NY) 65:808, May 16, 1915
Theatre Magazine 21:280+, Jun 1915

Nobody's Business (with Frank Mandel)
Productions:
Opened October 22, 1923 for 40 performances.
Reviews:
New York Times p. 17, Oct 23, 1923
VIII, p. 1, Oct 28, 1923

Polly Preferred
Productions:
Opened January 11, 1923 for 184 performances.
Reviews:
New York Clipper 70:14, Jan 17, 1923
New York Times p. 13, Jan 12, 1923

Polly with a Past (with George Middleton)
Productions:
Opened September 8, 1917 for 315 performances.
Reviews:
Bookman 46:284-5, Nov 1917
Dramatic Mirror 77:5+, Sep 15, 1917
Green Book 18:774-8, Nov 1917
Life (NY) 70:466, Sep 20, 1917
New York Dramatic News 64:6, Sep 15, 1917
New York Times p. 7, Sep 7, 1917
II, p. 5, Sep 16, 1917
p. 13, Mar 3, 1921
Theatre Magazine 26:197+, Oct 1917

R.A.F. (see Golden Wings)

The Rule of Three
Productions:
Opened February 16, 1914 for 80 performances.
Reviews:
Bookman 39:145, Apr 1914
Dramatic Mirror 71:6, Feb 18, 1914
Green Book 11:776, May 1914
11:972-4, Jun 1914
11:1058-68, Jun 1914
Hearst 25:685-700, May 1914
Life (NY) 63:409, Mar 5, 1914
Munsey 51:585, Apr 1914
New York Dramatic News 59:20, Feb 21, 1914
New York Times p. 11, Feb 17, 1914
Theatre Magazine 19:170+, Apr 1914

Theatre (see entry under Maugham, W. Somerset)

Wages for Wives (see Chicken Feed)

BORCHERT, WOLFGANG

Outside the Door
Productions:
(Off Broadway) Opened February 1949 in repertory.
Reviews:
New York Times p. 33, Mar 2, 1949

BOURDET, EDOUARD

Best Sellers (Vient de Paraître)
Productions:
Adapted by Dorothy Cheston Bennett.   Opened May 3, 1933
for 53 performances.
Reviews:
Catholic World 137:338-9, Jun 1933
Nation 136:594, May 24, 1933
New Outlook 161:49, Jun 1933
New York Times p. 20, May 4, 1933
Stage 10:11, Jun 1933
Time 21:52, May 15, 1933
Vogue 81:60, Jun 15, 1933

The Captive
Productions:
Adapted by Arthur Hornblow, Jr. from La Prisonnière.
Opened September 29, 1926 for 160 performances.
Reviews:
American Mercury 9:502-3, Dec 1926
              10:373-5, Mar 1927
Bookman 64:479, Dec 1926
Dramatist 18:1327, Jan 1927
Independent 44:14+, Dec 1926
Life (NY) 88:23, Oct 21, 1926
Nation 123:408, Oct 20, 1926
New Republic 48:324, Nov 10, 1926
New York Times p. 23, Sep 30, 1926
Theatre Arts 10:810-11, Dec 1926
Theatre Magazine 45:22+, Feb 1927
Vanity Fair 27:69+, Dec 1926
Vogue 68:82, Dec 1926

*Margot
Reviews:
Theatre Arts 20:364-6, May 1936

The Other Rose
Productions:
Adapted by George Middleton.   Opened December 20, 1923
for 84 performances.
Reviews:
American Mercury 1:247, Feb 1924

New York Times p. 15, Dec 21, 1923
                VII, p. 1, Dec 30, 1923
Theatre Magazine 39:15, Feb 1924

La Prisonnière (see The Captive)

The Rubicon
  Productions:
    Adapted by Henry Baron. Opened February 21, 1922
      for 132 performances.
  Reviews:
    New York Clipper 70:22, May 8, 1922
    New York Times p. 13, Sep 22, 1922

The Sex Fable (The Weaker Sex) (Le Sexe Faible)
  Productions:
    English text by Jane Hinton. Opened October 20, 1931 for
      33 performances.
  Reviews:
    Catholic World 134:336-7, Dec 1931
    Commonweal 15:18-19, Nov 4, 1931
    Nation 133:525, Nov 11, 1931
    New York Times p. 26, Oct 21, 1931
    Outlook 159:312, Nov 4, 1931
    Vanity Fair 36:90+, Apr 1931
    Vogue 78:57+, Dec 15, 1931

Times Have Changed (Les Temps Difficiles)
  Productions:
    Adapted by Louis Bromfield. Opened February 15, 1935 for
      32 performances.
  Reviews:
    Catholic World 141:90-1, Apr 1935
    Commonweal 21:570, Mar 15, 1935
    New York Times p. 28, Feb 19, 1935
    Stage 12:24-5, Apr 1935
    Theatre Arts 19:254-6, Apr 1935
                19:471, Jun 1935
    Vanity Fair 44:37, May 1935

Viente de Paraître (see Best Sellers)

The Weaker Sex (see The Sex Fable)

BOWEN, JOHN

After the Rain
  Productions:
    Opened October 9, 1967 for 64 performances.
  Reviews:
    America 117:723-4, Dec 9, 1967
    Christian Century 84:1527-8, Nov 29, 1967

New York Theatre Critics' Reviews 1967:262, 264
New York Times p. 13, Sep 2, 1967
            p. 54, Oct 10, 1967
            II, p. 3, Oct 22, 1967
            p. 54, Nov 28, 1967
New Yorker 43:81, Oct 21, 1967
Newsweek 70:113, Oct 23, 1967
Saturday Review 50:46, Oct 28, 1967

Coffee Lace (see Little Boxes)

The Fall and Redemption of Man
    Productions:
        (Off Off Broadway) Season of 1974-75.
        (Off Off Broadway) Opened June 1974.
    No Reviews.

Little Boxes (Consists of The Coffee Lace and Trevor).
    Productions:
        (Off Broadway) Opened December 3, 1969 for 15 performances.
    Reviews:
        Nation 209:703, Dec 22, 1969
        New York Theatre Critics' Reviews 1969:135
        New York Times p. 71, Dec 4, 1969
                    II, p. 7, Dec 14, 1969
        New Yorker 45:116, Dec 13, 1969

Trevor
    Productions:
        (Off Off Broadway) Opened July 8, 1977.
    Reviews:
        (see Little Boxes)

BRECHT, BERTOLT

Arturo Ui
    Productions:
        Adapted by George Tabori. Opened November 11, 1963 for
            eight performances.
        Translated by George Tabori as The Resistible Rise of Arturo
            Ui. Opened December 22, 1968 for 14 performances in
            repertory.
    Reviews:
        Catholic World 198:263-4, Jan 1964
        Commonweal 79:314+, Dec 6, 1963
                    89:528, Jan 24, 1969
        Nation 197:403-4, Dec 7, 1963
                208:60, Jan 13, 1969
        New Republic 149:26, Dec 21, 1963
                    153:34, Aug 7, 1965
        New York Theatre Critics' Reviews 1963:203
                                        1968:123

New York Times p. 51, Nov 16, 1960
                II, p. 5, Dec 25, 1960
                p. 49, Nov 12, 1963
                II, p. 1, Nov 24, 1963
                p. 28, Aug 8, 1968
                p. 22, Aug 30, 1968
                p. 44, Dec 23, 1968
                p. 28, Aug 18, 1969
                p. 33, Jul 28, 1972
New Yorker 36:66-8, Jul 2, 1960
           44:59-60, Jan 4, 1969
Newsweek 62:71, Nov 25, 1963
         73:57, Jan 6, 1969
Saturday Review 46:24, Nov 30, 1963
                52:74, Jan 11, 1969
Time 93:65, Jan 3, 1969

Baal
Productions:
(Off Broadway) Adapted by Eric Bentley. Opened May 6, 1965 for 43 performances.
(Off Off Broadway) English version by Eric Bentley and Martin Esslin. Season of 1969-1970.
Reviews:
Commonweal 82:413-14, Jun 18, 1965
Nation 196:381, May 4, 1963
       200:625-8, Jun 7, 1965
New York Times p. 33, May 7, 1965
               II, p. 1, Jun 6, 1965
New Yorker 41:158+, May 15, 1965
Newsweek 65:81, Jun 7, 1965
Time 85:64, May 14, 1965

The Baby Elephant (see also The Elephant Calf)
Productions:
(Off Off Broadway) Opened January 1976.
No Reviews.

Brecht on Brecht (see entry under Tabori, George)

Caucasian Chalk Circle
Productions:
English version by Eric Bentley. Opened March 24, 1966 for 93 performances (Repertory Theatre of Lincoln Center).
Reviews:
America 114:603-4, Apr 23, 1966
Commentary 41:76-7, Jun 1966
Commonweal 84:177, Apr 29, 1966
Life 60:15, Apr 22, 1966
Nation 183:202, Sep 8, 1956
       202:436-7, Apr 11, 1966
New Republic 119:27-8, Sep 6, 1948
             154:30+, Apr 16, 1966

New York Times p. 35, Nov 1, 1961
p. 28, Mar 30, 1962
II, p. 3, Mar 20, 1966
p. 35, Mar 25, 1966
II, p. 1, Apr 10, 1966
III, p. 20, Mar 16, 1977
New Yorker 31:62-4, Jul 16, 1955
38:159-60, May 12, 1962
42:122, Apr 2, 1966
Newsweek 67:90-1, Apr 4, 1966
Saturday Review 44:39, Nov 18, 1961
49:53, Apr 1, 1966
4:36-7, Apr 30, 1977
Time 87:63, Apr 1, 1966
Vogue 147:54, Jun 1966

*The Days of the Commune
Reviews:
New York Times p. 44, Nov 20, 1956

Drums in the Night
Productions:
(Off Broadway) Adapted by Frank Jones. Opened May 17,
1967 for 69 performances.
Reviews:
New York Times p. 54, May 18, 1967
New Yorker 43:106, June 3, 1967

*Edward II
Reviews:
New York Times p. 58, May 2, 1968

The Elephant Calf (see also The Baby Elephant)
Productions:
(Off Off Broadway) Season of 1971-1972.
(Off Off Broadway) Translated by Eric Bentley. Opened
January 1975.
No Reviews.

An Evening of Brecht (Consists of The Informer, The Jewish Wife,
and In Search of Justice.)
Productions:
(Off Off Broadway) Opened August 27, 1976.
No Reviews.

The Exception and the Rule
Productions:
(Off Broadway) Opened February 10, 1962 for one performance.
(Off Broadway) Adapted by Eric Bentley. Opened May 20,
1965 for 141 performances.
(Off Off Broadway) Translated by Eric Bentley. Opened January 1975.
(Off Off Broadway) Opened October 21, 1976.

Reviews:
America 113:62, Jul 10, 1965
Commonweal 82:414, Jun 18, 1965
New York Times p. 19, Mar 21, 1965
II, p. 1, Jun 6, 1965
Newsweek 65:81, Jun 7, 1965

Galileo
Productions:
(Off Broadway) Translated by Charles Laughton. Opened
December 7, 1947 for six performances.
Adapted by Charles Laughton. Opened April 13, 1967 in rep-
ertory for 76 performances.
Reviews:
America 116:793-4, May 27, 1967
Catholic World 166:74, Oct 1947
Christian Century 84:657-8, May 17, 1967
Commonweal 47:255-6, Dec 19, 1947
Nation 204:603-4, May 8, 1967
New Republic 117:36, Dec 29, 1947
156:28-30, May 6, 1967
New York Theatre Critics' Reviews 1967:324
New York Times p. 21, Aug 1, 1947
p. 5, Jan 5, 1963
p. 25, Jan 26, 1967
p. 31, Apr 14, 1967
II, p. 1, Apr 23, 1967
II, p. 3, Apr 30, 1967
p. 34, Nov 27, 1968
p. 88, Dec 1, 1968
New Yorker 43:146, Apr 22, 1967
Newsweek 30:60, Dec 29, 1947
69:107, Apr 24, 1967
Reporter 36:50-2, May 18, 1967
Saturday Review 50:46, Apr 29, 1967
Theatre Arts 31:68-70, Dec 1947
32:12-13, Feb 1948
Time 89:93, Apr 21, 1967
Vogue 111:192, Apr 1, 1948
149:76, Jun 1967

The Good Woman of Setzuan
Productions:
Adapted by Eric Bentley. Opened December 18, 1956 for 24
performances.
(Off Broadway) Translated by Eric Bentley. Opened March
10, 1963 for 12 performances.
Translated by Ralph Manheim. Opened November 5, 1970
for 46 performances in repertory.
(Off Off Broadway) Opened February 1975.
(Off Off Broadway) English version by Eric Bentley. Opened
January 23, 1976.

Reviews:
  Catholic World 184:385-6, Feb 1957
  Christian Century 74:138, Jan 30, 1957
  Nation 184:27, Jan 5, 1957
      211:542, Nov 23, 1970
      222:189, Feb 14, 1976
  New Republic 163:20, Nov 28, 1970
      174:28, Mar 13, 1976
  New York Theatre Critics' Reviews 1956:161
      1970:169
  New York Times p. 41, Dec 19, 1976
      II, p. 1, Dec 30, 1956
      p. 51, Nov 6, 1970
      II, p. 1, Nov 15, 1970
      II, p. 7, Dec 6, 1970
      p. 24, Feb 4, 1975
      p. 28, Jan 27, 1976
      p. 28, Mar 24, 1976
  New Yorker 32:45-6, Dec 29, 1956
      46:141, Nov 14, 1970
      51:96-7, Feb 24, 1975
  Newsweek 76:74, Nov 16, 1970
  Saturday Review 40:24, Jan 5, 1957
      49:55, Jun 4, 1966
  Theatre Arts 41:26, Feb 1957

Guns of Carrar (see also Rifles of Mother Carrar)
  Productions:
    (Off Off Broadway) Opened December 9, 1968 for 2 perform-
    ances.
  Reviews:
    New York Times p. 53, Dec 19, 1968

*Der Hofmeister
  Reviews:
    New York Times p. 9, Aug 10, 1963
    Theatre Arts 47:58-9, Oct 1963

In Search of Justice (see An Evening of Brecht)

In the Jungle of Cities
  Productions:
    (Off Broadway) Translated by Gerhard Nellhaus. Opened De-
    cember 20, 1960 for 66 performances.
    (Off Broadway) Translated by Gerhard Nellhaus. Opened No-
    vember 2, 1961 for 80 performances.
    (Off Off Broadway) Translated by Anselm Hollo. Opened
    March 25, 1977.
  Reviews:
    Nation 192:18-19, Jan 7, 1961
    New Republic 142:30-1, Jan 9, 1961
    New York Times p. 39, Dec 21, 1960
        II, p. 1, Jan 15, 1961

New York Times II, p. 4, May 21, 1961
                p. 75, Mar 1, 1970
             III, p. 24, Apr 6, 1977
New Yorker 36:42-3, Dec 31, 1960
Theatre Arts 45:10-11+, Mar 1961

The Informer (see An Evening of Brecht)
    Productions:
        (Off Broadway) Season of 1938-1939.
    No Reviews.

The Jewish Wife   (see An Evening of Brecht)

Justice
    Productions:
        (Off Broadway) Season of 1938-1939.
    No Reviews.

Die Kleinbürgerhochzeit (The Wedding Feast)
    Productions:
        (Off Broadway) Opened November 24, 1970 for 10 perform-
        ances.
    Reviews:
        New York Times p. 25, Nov 25, 1970

Man Is Man
    Productions:
        (Off Broadway) Translated by Gerhard Nellhaus.   Opened
            September 18, 1962 for 175 performances.
    Reviews:
        Commonweal 77:72, Oct 12, 1962
        New Republic 147:26+, Oct 1, 1962
        New York Times p. 31, Sep 19, 1962
        New Yorker 39:98+, Sep 29, 1962

A Man's a Man
    Productions:
        (Off Broadway) Adapted by Eric Bentley.   Opened September
            19, 1962 for 175 performances.
        (Off Off Broadway) Eric Bentley version.   Season of 1970-
            1971.
    Reviews:
        America 107:862, Oct 6, 1962
        Commonweal 77:72, Oct 12, 1962
        Nation 195:207-8, Oct 6, 1962
        New Republic 147:26+, Oct 1, 1962
        New York Times p. 30, Sep 20, 1962
                        p. 13, Feb 13, 1971
                        p. 26, Mar 5, 1971
        New Yorker 38:98+, Sep 29, 1962
        Theatre Arts 47:67, Feb 1963
        Time 80:81, Sep 28, 1962

Master Puntila and His Valet Matti   (see Squire Puntila and His
            Servant)

The Measures Taken
    Productions:
        (Off Broadway) English version by Eric Bentley; music by
            Hans Eisler. Opened October 4, 1974 for 102 performances.
        (Off Off Broadway) Opened November 1975.
        (Off Off Broadway) Opened January 2, 1976.
    Reviews:
        Nation 219:445, Nov 2, 1974
               220:698-700, Jun 7, 1975
        New York Times p. 32, Oct 16, 1974
                       II, p. 5, Oct 27, 1974
        New Yorker 50:66+, Oct 28, 1974

Mother
    Productions:
        Based on a novel by Maxim Gorki.   Translated by Paul
            Peters.   Opened November 19, 1935 for 36 performances.
        (Off Broadway) Translated by Lee Baxandall; music by Hanns
            Eisler and the San Francisco Mime Troupe.   Opened No-
            vember 20, 1974 for 21 performances.
    Reviews:
        Catholic World 142:469, Jan 1936
        Commonweal 23:162, Dec 6, 1935
        Nation 141:659-60, Dec 4, 1935
        New Republic 85:175, Dec 18, 1935
        New York Times p. 26, Nov 20, 1935
                       p. 33, Nov 22, 1974
                       III, p. 1, Dec 1, 1974
        Theatre Arts 20:13-15, Jun 1936
        Time 26:68, Dec 2, 1935

Mother Courage and Her Children
    Productions:
        Adapted by Eric Bentley.   Opened March 28, 1963 for 52
            performances.
        Opened November 16, 1967 in repertory for 11 performances.
        (Off Off Broadway) Opened October 19, 1972.
        (Off Off Broadway) Opened December 1974.
        (Off Off Broadway) Translated by Ralph Manheim.   Opened
            April 1977.
    Reviews:
        Catholic World 197:143-4, May 1963
        Commonweal 78:141-2, Apr 26, 1963
        Nation 182:557-8, Jun 30, 1956
               196:314-15, Apr 13, 1963
        New Republic 148:35-6, Apr 13, 1963
                     152:29, Jun 26, 1965
        New York Theatre Critics' Reviews 1963:362
        New York Times p. 5, Mar 30, 1963
                       p. 51, Apr 1, 1963

New York Times p. 32, May 12, 1964
            p. 55, Nov 17, 1967
            p. 65, Feb 16, 1975
            p. 30, Feb 25, 1975
            p. 11, Apr 9, 1977
New Yorker 39:71, Apr 6, 1963
Newsweek 61:85, Apr 8, 1963
       85:80+, Apr 7, 1975
Reporter 28:39-40, May 9, 1963
       28:8, Jun 6, 1963
Saturday Review 46:20, Apr 13, 1963
Theatre Arts 26:251-2, Apr 1942
       33:26-7, Jun 1949
       46:19-22, Jun 1962
       47:14-15, May 1963
Time 81:56, Apr 5, 1963

The Private Life of the Master Race
  Productions:
    (Off Broadway) English version by Eric Bentley. Opened June 11, 1945.
    (Off Off Broadway) Opened March 1975.
  Reviews:
    Commonweal 42:262-3, Jun 29, 1945
    New Republic 112:871, Jun 25, 1945
       113:48, Jul 9, 1945
    New York Times p. 28, Jun 13, 1945
       II, p. 1, Jun 17, 1945
       p. 33, Jan 31, 1956

Puntila (see Squire Puntila and His Servant)

Puntila and the Hired Man (see Squire Puntila and His Servant)

The Resistible Rise of Arturo Ui (see Arturo Ui)

*The Rifles of Mother Carrar (see also Guns of Carrar)
  Reviews:
    New York Times p. 49, Mar 28, 1972

*Rise and Fall of the City of Mahagonny
  Reviews:
    Nation 218:349, Mar 16, 1974
    New York Times p. 51, Feb 13, 1974
       II, p. 1, Feb 17, 1974
    Newsweek 83:91, Mar 11, 1974

*St. Joan of the Stockyards
  Reviews:
    New York Times p. 45, Jun 12, 1964
    Newsweek 77:123, May 10, 1971

*Schweik in the Second World War
 Reviews:
  New York Times p. 18, May 23, 1959
            II, p. 17, Nov 12, 1967
  Saturday Review 50:71, Nov 25, 1967

*Squire Puntila and His Servant
 Reviews:
  Christian Century 82:1097, Sep 8, 1965
  New York Times p. 34, Nov 21, 1964
  Saturday Review 45:22, Jun 9, 1962
            4:36-7, Apr 30, 1977
  Time 89:83, Apr 21, 1967

Trumpets and Drums
 Productions:
  (Off Off Broadway) Translated by Rose and Martin Kastner;
    music by Erich Bulling. Opened Season of 1969-1970.
 Reviews:
  New York Times p. 52, Oct 13, 1969

The Tutor (see Der Hofmeister)

The Wedding Feast (see Die Kleinbürgerhochzeit)

BRIDIE, JAMES (OSBORNE H. MAVOR)

The Anatomist
 Productions:
  Opened October 24, 1932 for eight performances.
 Reviews:
  New York Times p. 24, Oct 25, 1932
  Theatre Arts 17:24, Jan 1933

Daphne Laureola
 Productions:
  Opened September 18, 1950 for 56 performances.
 Reviews:
  Catholic World 172:148, Nov 1950
  Christian Science Monitor Magazine p. 8, Sep 23, 1950
  Commonweal 52:630, Oct 6, 1950
  Nation 171:295, Sep 30, 1950
  New Republic 123:22, Oct 2, 1950
  New York Theatre Critics' Reviews 1950:272
  New York Times II, p. 1, Sep 17, 1950
            p. 38, Sep 19, 1950
            II, p. 1, Sep 24, 1950
            II, p. 1, Oct 15, 1950
  New Yorker 26:52+, Sep 30, 1950
  Newsweek 36:82, Oct 2, 1950
  Saturday Review 33:30-1, Oct 14, 1950
  Theatre Arts 34:11, Nov 1950
  Time 56:56, Oct 2, 1950

*Dr. Angelus
   Reviews:
      Theatre Arts 31:47, Nov 1947

*Mr. Bolfry
   Reviews:
      New York Times II, p. 1, Aug 22, 1943
      Theatre Arts 27:655, Nov 1943
            27:720-1, Dec 1943

*Mr. Gillie
   Reviews:
      New Republic 122:20, Jun 19, 1950
      New York Times p. 31, Mar 10, 1950
      Theatre Arts 34:28, Dec 1950

*The Queen's Comedy
   Reviews:
      New York Times II, p. 3, Sep 10, 1950

A Sleeping Clergyman
   Productions:
      Opened October 8, 1934 for 40 performances.
   Reviews:
      Catholic World 140:211, Nov 1934
      Commonweal 20:618, Oct 26, 1934
      Literary Digest 118:24+, Oct 20, 1934
      Nation 139:486-7, Oct 24, 1934
      New Republic 80:314, Oct 24, 1934
      New York Times p. 16, Oct 9, 1934
                IX, p. 2, Oct 28, 1934
      Stage 12:8, Nov 1934
      Theatre Arts 17:769-70, Oct 1933
             18:899, Dec 1934
      Time 24:38, Oct 22, 1934

Storm Over Patsy (see entry under Frank, Bruno)

*Susannah and the Elders
   Reviews:
      New York Times p. 37, Oct 19, 1959

Tobias and the Angel
   Productions:
      Opened April 28, 1937 for 22 performances.
      (Off Broadway) Opened May 1950 in repertory.
   Reviews:
      America 98:496, Jan 25, 1958
      Catholic World 186:308, Jan 1958
             186:471, Mar 1958
      Christian Century 74:1385, Nov 20, 1957
      Commonweal 26:78, May 14, 1937
      Nation 144:543-4, May 8, 1937

New York Times p. 16, Apr 29, 1937
p. 36, Apr 26, 1950
Theatre Arts 23:708, Oct 1939

BRIEUX, EUGENE

Accused
Productions:
English version by George Middleton. Opened September 29,
1925 for 95 performances.
Reviews:
Life (NY) 86:26, Oct 22, 1925
Nation 121:446-7, Oct 14, 1925
New York Times p. 20, Sep 30, 1925
VIII, p. 1, Oct 11, 1925
Theatre Magazine 42:16, Dec 1925

The Affinity
Productions:
Translated by Laurence Irving. Opened January 3, 1910 for
24 performances.
Reviews:
Dramatic Mirror 63:5, Jan 15, 1910
Forum 43:191, Feb 1910

The Americans in France
Productions:
Opened August 3, 1920 for 7 performances.
Reviews:
Current Opinion 68:488-94, Apr 1920
Dramatic Mirror p. 237, Apr 7, 1920
Hearst 38:78, Oct 1920
Independent 103:229, Aug 28, 1920
New York Clipper 68:78, Aug 11, 1920
New York Times p. 14, Aug 4, 1920
Theatre 32:185, Dec 1920
Weekly Review 3:95-6, Jul 28, 1920
3:215-16, Sep 8, 1920

Damaged Goods
Productions:
Opened March 14, 1913 for 66 performances.
Adapted by Henry Herbert. Translated by John Pollock.
Opened May 17, 1937 for 8 performances.
Reviews:
Blue Book 17:665-8, Aug 1913
Bookman 37:431, Jun 1913
Current Opinion 54:296-7, Apr 1913
Dial 54:288, Apr 1, 1913
Dramatic Mirror 69:6-7, Mar 19, 1913
69:5, Mar 26, 1913
69:6, Apr 16, 1913

Dramatist 6:525-7, Jan 1915
Everybody's Magazine 29:677-9, Nov 1913
Harper's Weekly 58:18-19, Oct 25, 1913
International 7:107, Apr 1913
Life (NY) 61:628, Mar 27, 1913
Munsey 50:93-4, Oct 1913
New York Times p. 13, Mar 15, 1913
               p. 27, Mar 18, 1937
Red Book 21:497-500, Jul 1913
Theatre Magazine 17:134, May 1913

The Letter of the Law (The Red Robe)
  Productions:
    Opened February 23, 1920 for 89 performances.
  Reviews:
    Dramatic Mirror 82:367, Feb 28, 1920
    Independent 101:382, Mar 13, 1920
    Nation 110:340-1, Mar 13, 1920
    New York Clipper 67:25, Jan 25, 1920
                     68:19, Mar 3, 1920
    New York Times V, p. 5, Feb 29, 1920
    Theatre Magazine 31:253, Apr 1920
    Weekly Review 2:264, Mar 13, 1920

Madame Pierre
  Productions:
    Adapted by Arthur Hornblow, Jr.   Opened February 15, 1922
      for 37 performances.
  Reviews:
    Bookman 55:179, Apr 1922
    Independent 108:264, Mar 11, 1922
    Nation 114:236, Mar 1, 1922
    New Republic 30:198-9, Apr 12, 1922
    New York Clipper 70:20, Feb 22, 1922
    New York Times p. 11, Feb 16, 1922
                   VI, p. 1, Feb 19, 1922
    Theatre Magazine 35:236, Apr 1922

Maternity
  Productions:
    Translated by Benjamin F. Blanchard.   Adapted by Richard
      Bennett.   Opened January 6, 1915 for 21 performances.
  Reviews:
    Bookman 40:639-40, Feb 1915
    Dramatic Mirror 73:8, Jan 13, 1915
    Dramatist 3:203-5, Oct 1911
    Green Book 13:768, Apr 1915
    New Republic 1:26, Jan 23, 1915
    New York Dramatic News 60:17, Jan 16, 1915
    New York Times p. 13, Jan 7, 1915
                   VII, p. 6, Jan 10, 1915
    North American Review 201:267-9, Feb 1915
    Theatre Magazine 21:56-7+, Feb 1915

The Red Robe (see Letter of the Law)

The Three Daughters of Monsieur Dupont
    Productions:
        Translated by Laurence Irving.   Opened April 13, 1910 for
            21 performances.
    Reviews:
        Bookman 31:419-20, Jun 1910
        Dramatic Mirror 63:7, Apr 23, 1910
        Hampton's Magazine 24:826-8, Jun 1910
        Life (NY) 55:767, Apr 28, 1910
        Pearson's Magazine 23:835-40, Jun 1910
        Theatre Magazine 11:131, May 1910

BRUCKNER, FERDINAND

Criminals
    Productions:
        (Off Broadway) Opened December 20, 1941 for 15 performances.
    Reviews:
        Current History ns1:568, Feb 1942
        New York Times p. 24, Dec 22, 1941
        Theatre Arts 26:86, Feb 1942

Gloriana (Elizabeth von England)
    Productions:
        Opened November 25, 1938 for 5 performances.
    Reviews:
        New York Times p. 18, Nov 26, 1938

Nathan the Wise
    Productions:
        Adapted from a play by Gotthold Ephraim Lessing.
        (Off Broadway) Season of 1941-1942 in repertory for 11 per-
            formances.
        Opened April 3, 1942 for 28 performances.
        (Off Broadway) Opened February 21, 1944 for 22 performances.
    Reviews:
        Catholic World 155:214-15, May 1942
        Commonweal 35:647-8, Apr 17, 1942
        New Yorker 18:31, Apr 11, 1942
        New York Theatre Critics' Reviews 1942:321
        New York Times p. 15, Mar 12, 1942
                     p. 18, Apr 4, 1942
                     p. 26, Feb 22, 1944
                     p. 29, Mar 7, 1962
                     p. 29, Mar 23, 1962
                     p. 45, Dec 10, 1966
        New Yorker 18:31, Apr 11, 1942
        Newsweek 19:68, Apr 13, 1942
        Theatre Arts 26:290, May 1942
        Time 39:57, Apr 13, 1942

BÜCHNER, GEORG

Danton's Death   (see also Danton's Tod)
Productions:
Translated by Geoffrey Dunlop. Songs by Marc Blitzstein.
Opened November 2, 1938 for 21 performances.
New English version by Herbert Blau. Opened October 21,
1965 for 46 performances in repertory.
(Off Off Broadway) Opened December 1974.
(Off Off Broadway) Opened May 26, 1977.
Reviews:
America 113:647-8, Nov 20, 1965
Catholic World 148:345, Dec 1938
Christian Century 82:1578, Dec 22, 1965
Commentary 41:55-6+, Jan 1966
Commonweal 29:104, Nov 18, 1938
            83:191-2, Nov 12, 1965
Nation 147:573-4, Nov 26, 1938
        182:538, Jun 23, 1956
        201:370-1, Nov 15, 1965
New Republic 97:100, Nov 30, 1938
              153:37-8, Nov 6, 1965
New York Theatre Critics' Reviews 1965:298
New York Times p. 26, Nov 3, 1938
                IX, p. 1, Nov 13, 1938
                p. 1, Oct 13, 1965
                p. 56, Oct 14, 1965
                II, p. 17, Oct 17, 1965
                p. 46, Oct 22, 1965
                II, p. 1, Oct 31, 1965
New Yorker 41:108+, Oct 30, 1965
Newsweek 12:28, Nov 14, 1938
          68:86-7, Nov 1, 1965
Reporter 34:43, Jan 13, 1966
Saturday Review 39:24, May 12, 1956
                 48:41, Nov 6, 1965
Theatre Arts 23:13-14+, Jan 1939
Time 32:61, Nov 14, 1938
      86:84, Oct 29, 1965
Vogue 146:146, Dec 1965

Danton's Tod   (see also Danton's Death)
Productions:
Opened December 20, 1927 for 15 performances.
Reviews:
Dial 84:260-1, Mar 1928
Life (NY) 91:19, Jan 5, 1928
New Republic 53:194-5, Jan 4, 1928
New York Times p. 28, Dec 21, 1927
                VIII, p. 1, Jan 1, 1928
                VIII, p. 3, Jan 1, 1928
Theatre Arts 12:80+, Feb 1928
Vogue 71:122+, Feb 1928

Leonce and Lena
  Productions:
    (Off Off Broadway) Season of 1968-1969.
  Reviews:
    Nation 202:26-7, Jan 3, 1966
    Newsweek 83:117, Apr 22, 1974

Woyzeck
  Productions:
    Opened April 5, 1966 in repertory for 8 performances.
    (Off Off Broadway) Translated by Susan Shantl. Adapted by
      Louis Simmon. Season of 1967-1968.
    (Off Broadway) Translated by Henry J. Schmidt. Adapted by
      Richard Reich. Opened May 25, 1971 for 8 performances.
    (Off Broadway) Opened December 5, 1972 for 7 performances.
    (Off Off Broadway) English version by Christopher Martin.
      Season of 1974-1975.
    (Off Broadway) Translated by Mira Rafalowicz. Opened
      March 24, 1976 for 22 performances.
  Reviews:
    Commonweal 90:264, May 16, 1969
    Nation 222:446, Apr 10, 1976
    New York Times p. 34, Apr 6, 1966
                    p. 36, Apr 15, 1971
                    p. 27, Apr 16, 1971
                    p. 33, May 26, 1971
                    p. 42, Dec 6, 1972
                    p. 58, Apr 13, 1975
                    II, p. 5, Mar 7, 1976
                    p. 43, Mar 25, 1976
                    II, p. 5, Apr 4, 1976
    New Yorker 52:96+, Apr 5, 1976
    Newsweek 67:96, Apr 18, 1966
    Saturday Review 52:24, May 17, 1969
    Time 87:68, Apr 15, 1966

BUECHNER, GEORG see BÜCHNER, GEORG

CAMUS, ALBERT

Caligula
  Productions:
    Adapted by Justin O'Brien. Opened February 16, 1960 for 38
      performances.
    (Off Off Broadway) Opened May 1975.
    (Off Off Broadway) Opened November 20, 1975.
  Reviews:
    America 102:775, Mar 26, 1960
    Christian Century 77:352-4, Mar 23, 1960
    Life 48:85-8, Mar 7, 1960
    Nation 190:213-14, Mar 5, 1960

New Republic 142:21-2, Feb 29, 1960
New York Theatre Critics' Reviews 1960:365
New York Times p. 31, Feb 17, 1960
                 II, p. 1, Feb 28, 1960
                     p. 53, Dec 10, 1971
                 II, p. 5, Dec 12, 1971
New Yorker 36:100+, Feb 27, 1960
Newsweek 55:90, Feb 29, 1960
Saturday Review 43:36, Mar 5, 1960
Theatre Arts 44:59, Apr 1960
Time 75:51, Feb 29, 1960

The Misunderstanding
    Productions:
        (Off Off Broadway) Opened October 9, 1975.
        (Off Off Broadway) Opened May 1976.
    No Reviews.

*Possessed
    Adapted from the novel by Dostoevski.
    Reviews:
        New Yorker 35:106-7, Mar 7, 1959
        Time 73:61, Feb 9, 1959
        Yale Review 48:634-40, Jun 1959

CAPEK, KAREL

Insect Comedy (see The World We Live In)

Komedie (see Makropoulos Secret)

Makropoulos Secret (Komedie)
    Productions:
        Adapted by Randal C. Burrell. Opened January 21, 1926 for
            88 performances.
        Adapted by Tyrone Guthrie. Opened December 3, 1957 for
            33 performances.
    Reviews:
        America 98:404, Jan 4, 1958
        Catholic World 186:386, Feb 1958
        Christian Century 75:17, Jan 1, 1958
        Commonweal 67:336-7, Dec 27, 1957
        Life (NY) 87:18, Feb 18, 1926
        Nation 185:483, Dec 21, 1957
        New York Theatre Critics' Reviews 1957:161
        New York Times p. 12, Jan 22, 1926
                       p. 52, Dec 4, 1957
        New Yorker 33:84-5, Dec 14, 1957
        Saturday Review 40:22, Dec 28, 1957
        Theatre Arts 42:26, Feb 1958
        Theatre Magazine 43:18, Apr 1926
        Time 70:45, Dec 16, 1957

The Mother
Productions:
English version by Paul Selver and Miles Mallen. Opened
April 25, 1939 for 4 performances.
Reviews:
Commonweal 30:76, May 12, 1939
Nation 148:539, May 6, 1939
New York Times p. 26, Apr 26, 1939
Newsweek 13:22, May 8, 1939
Theatre Arts 23:402, Jan 1939

R. U. R. (Rossom's Universal Robots)
Productions:
Opened October 9, 1922 for 184 performances.
English version by Paul Selver. Opened December 3, 1942
for 4 performances.
Reviews:
Bookman 56:478-80, Dec 1922
Catholic World 116:504-5, Jan 1923
Current Opinion 74:61-74, Jan 1923
Collier's 70:23, Dec 9, 1922
Drama 13:90-1, Dec 1922
Forum 68:973-4, Nov 1922
Independent 109:321-2, Nov 25, 1922
Life (NY) 80:20, Nov 2, 1922
Literary Digest 75:30-1, Nov 4, 1922
Nation 115:478, Nov 1, 1922
New Republic 32:251-2, Nov 1, 1922
New York Clipper 70:20, Oct 18, 1922
New York Theatre Critics' Reviews 1942:152
New York Times p. 16, Oct 10, 1922
VIII, p. 1, Oct 15, 1922
VIII, p. 1, Oct 22, 1922
p. 30, Dec 4, 1942
IV, p. 13, May 17, 1950
Newsweek 20:93, Dec 14, 1942
Saturday Review 136:79, Jul 21, 1923
Theatre Magazine 36:375, Dec 1922

The World We Live In (The Insect Comedy) (with Josef Capek)
Productions:
Adapted by Owen Davis. Opened October 31, 1922 for 111
performances.
Adapted by Owen Davis. Opened June 3, 1948 for 14 per-
formances.
Reviews:
Bookman 56:610-11, Jan 1923
Catholic World 116:501-3, Jan 1923
Commonweal 48:235, Jun 18, 1948
Drama 13:130-1, Jun 1923
Forum 110:20-2, Jul 1948
Independent 109:320-1, Nov 25, 1922
Living Age 313:617-20, Jun 3, 1922

Nation 115:556, Nov 22, 1922
New Republic 118:28-9, Jun 21, 1948
New York Clipper 70:20, Nov 8, 1922
New York Times p. 16, Nov 1, 1922
          p. 26, Jun 4, 1948
School and Society 67:478, Jun 26, 1948

CARROLL, PAUL VINCENT

The Coggerers
Productions:
(Off Broadway) Season of 1959-1960.
Reviews:
New York Times p. 33, Mar 23, 1960

*The Devil Came from Dublin
Reviews:
New York Times p. 27, Jun 3, 1955
Theatre Arts 35:66-7, Nov 1951

Kindred
Productions:
Opened December 26, 1939 for 16 performances.
Reviews:
Commonweal 31:266, Jan 12, 1940
New York Times p. 17, Dec 27, 1939
          IX, p. 1, Jan 7, 1940
Newsweek 13:34, Jun 19, 1939
          15:38, Jan 8, 1940
Theatre Arts 24:165-6, Mar 1940

The Old Foolishness
Productions:
Opened December 20, 1940 for 3 performances.
Reviews:
Commonweal 33:282-3, Jan 3, 1941
New York Theatre Critics' Reviews 1940:182
New York Times p. 20, Dec 21, 1940
New Yorker 16:30, Dec 28, 1940
Theatre Arts 25:97, Feb 1941

Shadow and Substance
Productions:
Opened January 26, 1938 for 274 performances.
(Off Broadway) Opened July 1, 1946 in repertory.
(Off Broadway) Season of 1953-1954.
Reviews:
America 102:254-5, Nov 31, 1959
Catholic World 146:724-5, Mar 1938
Commonweal 27:440, Feb 11, 1938
          27:525, Mar 4, 1938
Independent Woman 17:147, May 1938

Literary Digest 125:22, Feb 19, 1938
Nation 146:162, Feb 5, 1938
New Republic 94:45, Feb 16, 1938
New York Times p. 16, Jan 27, 1938
         X, p. 1, Feb 6, 1938
         X, p. 1, Apr 24, 1938
         IX, p. 3, Oct 23, 1938
         p. 38, Mar 14, 1956
         p. 42, Nov 4, 1959
         II, p. 3, Jan 24, 1960
Newsweek 11:24, Jan 31, 1938
One Act Play Magazine 1:942-3, Feb 1938
Stage 15:50, Feb 1938
     15:6+, Mar 1938
Scribner's Magazine 102:66, Sep 1937
Theatre Arts 22:167-8, Mar 1938
Time 31:38, Feb 7, 1938
Vogue 91:108, Mar 15, 1938

The Strings, My Lord, Are False
  Productions:
    Opened May 19, 1942 for 15 performances.
  Reviews:
    Commonweal 36:159, Jun 5, 1942
    Nation 154:637, May 30, 1942
    New York Theatre Critics' Reviews 1942:287
    New York Times p. 29, Mar 18, 1942
               p. 24, May 20, 1942
    New Yorker 18:32, May 30, 1942
    Newsweek 19:67, Jun 1, 1942
    Theatre Arts 26:659, Oct 1942

Things That Are Caesar's
  Productions:
    Opened October 17, 1932 for four performances.
  Reviews:
    New York Times p. 23, Oct 18, 1932

The Wayward Saint
  Productions:
    Opened February 17, 1955 for 21 performances.
  Reviews:
    America 92:629-30, Mar 12, 1955
    Catholic World 181:68, Apr 1955
    Commonweal 61:655, Mar 25, 1955
    Nation 180:226, Mar 12, 1955
    New York Theatre Critics' Reviews 1955:362
    New York Times p. 17, Feb 18, 1955
               II, p. 1, Feb 27, 1955
    New Yorker 31:67-70, Mar 5, 1955
    Newsweek 45:58-9, Feb 28, 1955
    Saturday Review 38:26, Mar 5, 1955
    Theatre Magazine 39:20+, May 1955
    Time 65:60, Feb 28, 1955

The White Steed
  Productions:
    Opened January 10, 1939 for 136 performances.
    (Off Broadway) Season of 1941-1942 in repertory.
  Reviews:
    Catholic World 148:727-8, Mar 1939
    Commonweal 29:386, Jan 27, 1939
    Nation 148:100-2, Jan 21, 1939
    New Republic 98:17, Feb 8, 1939
    New York Times p. 16, Jan 11, 1939
    Newsweek 12:20, Aug 29, 1938
              13:24-5, Jan 23, 1939
    North American Review 277, no. 2:371, Jun 1939
    One Act Play Magazine 2:673-4, Jan 1939
    Stage 16:10+, Feb 1929
    Theatre Arts 23:172-3, Mar 1939
    Time 33:20, Jan 23, 1939

The Wise Have Not Spoken
  Productions:
    (Off Broadway) Opened February 1954.
  Reviews:
    New York Times p. 35, Feb 11, 1954
    New Yorker 30:66, Feb 20, 1954
    Theatre Arts 30:356, Jun 1946

CASELLA, ALBERTO

Death Takes a Holiday
  Productions:
    Adapted by Walter Ferris.   Opened December 26, 1929 for
      180 performances.
    Adapted by Walter Ferris.   Opened February 16, 1931 for
      32 performances.
  Reviews:
    Catholic World 130:725-6, Mar 1930
    Commonweal 11:369, Jan 29, 1930
    Life (NY) 95:20, Jan 17, 1930
    Literary Digest 104:18, Jan 18, 1930
    Nation 138:342, Mar 21, 1934
    New Republic 61:275-6, Jan 29, 1930
    New York Times VIII, p. 2, Jan 5, 1930
                  p. 22, Jan 29, 1930
                  p. 29, Feb 17, 1931
    Saturday Review 151:832, Jun 27, 1931
                    157:391, Apr 7, 1931
    Theatre Arts 14:191-2, Mar 1930
    Vogue 75:122, Feb 15, 1930

CHAMBERS, C. HADDON

The Great Pursuit (The Idlers)
    Productions:
        Opened May 22, 1916 for 29 performances.
    Reviews:
        Book News 34:403, May 1916
        Dramatic Mirror 75:8, Apr 1, 1916
                       75:4, Apr 8, 1916
                       75:2, Apr 15, 1916
        Life (NY) 67:644, Apr 6, 1916
        Harper's Weekly 62:376, Apr 8, 1916
        Nation 102:366, Mar 30, 1916
        New York Dramatic News 63:13, Aug 19, 1916
        Theatre Magazine 23:274, May 1916

The Idlers   (see The Great Pursuit)

Passers-by
    Productions:
        Opened September 14, 1911 for 124 performances.
    Reviews:
        Blue Book 14:676-9, Feb 1912
        Bookman 34:239+, Nov 1911
        Dramatic Mirror 66:10, Sep 20, 1911
        Dramatist 3:212-14, Jan 1912
        Everybody's 25:822-4, Dec 1911
        Green Book Album 6:1197, Dec 1911
                         6:1205-6, Dec 1911
        Leslie's Weekly 113:356, Sep 28, 1911
        Life (NY) 67:644, Apr 6, 1916
        Munsey 46:277, Nov 1911
        Pearson 26:652-6, Nov 1911
        Red Book 18:369+, Dec 1911
        Theatre Magazine 13:117, Oct 1911

The Saving Grace
    Productions:
        Opened September 30, 1918 for 96 performances.
    Reviews:
        Bookman 50:163-4, Sep 1919
        Dramatic Mirror 79:543, Oct 12, 1918
        Forum 60:621, Nov 1918
        Green Book 20:954-7, Dec 1918
        Life (NY) 72:524-5, Oct 10, 1918
        Nation 105:602, Nov 29, 1917
        New York Dramatic News 65:6, Oct 12, 1918
        New York Times p. 11, Oct 1, 1918
        Theatre Magazine 28:277, Nov 1918

Tante
    Productions:
        Opened October 28, 1913 for 79 performances.

Reviews:
 Bookman 38:365, Dec 1913
 Book News 32:217, Dec 1913
 Dramatic Mirror 70:10, Nov 5, 1913
 Dramatist 5:441-2, Jan 1914
 Everybody's 30:257-60, Feb 1914
 Green Book 11:72-3, Jan 1914
 Life (NY) 62:838, Nov 13, 1913
 New York Dramatic News 58:21, Nov 8, 1913
 New York Times p. 11, Oct 29, 1913
   VII, p. 9, Nov 2, 1913
 Theatre Magazine 18:173-4, Dec 1913

The Thief
 Opened October 16, 1911 for 16 performances.
 No Reviews.

The Tyranny of Tears
 Productions:
 Opened September 29, 1913 for 32 performances.
 Reviews:
 Dramatic Mirror 70:6, Oct 1, 1913
 Dramatist 5:397-8, Oct 1913
 New York Times p. 13, Sep 30, 1913
 Theatre Magazine 18:143, Nov 1913

CHEKHOV, ANTON

The Anniversary (see also Another Evening with Chekhov)
 Productions:
 (Off Broadway) Season of 1960-1961.
 (Off Off Broadway) Season of 1972-1973.
 (Off Off Broadway) Opened March 1977.
 (Off Off Broadway) Opened April 15, 1977.
 Reviews:
 Nation 192:419, May 13, 1961
 New York Times p. 34, May 26, 1955
   p. 26, Apr 21, 1961

Another Evening with Chekhov (Consists of The Anniversary, A Summer in the Country, and Swan Song)
 Productions:
 (Off Off Broadway) Opened March 1, 1974.
 No Reviews.

A Bear
 Productions:
 Opened February 19, 1915 in repertory (Washington Square Players).
 Translated by Roy Temple House. Opened August 30, 1916 in repertory (Washington Square Players).
 Opened February 5, 1948 for 14 performances.

(Off Off Broadway) Opened March 24, 1976.
Reviews:
New York Times p. 29, Feb 6, 1948

The Boor (see also A Chekhov Portfolio)
    Productions:
    (Off Off Broadway) Season of 1972-1973.
    (Off Off Broadway) Opened October 14, 1975.
    (Off Off Broadway) Opened April 15, 1977.
No Reviews.

The Celebration
    Productions:
    (Off Off Broadway) Season of 1967-1968.
No Reviews.

A Chekhov Portfolio (Consists of On the Harmfulness of Tobacco,
        The Boor, Summer in the Country, and Swan Song)
    Productions:
    (Off Off Broadway) Opened January 16, 1975.
No Reviews.

The Cherry Orchard
    Productions:
    Opened January 1923 in repertory (Moscow Art Theatre).
    Opened November 1923 in repertory (Moscow Art Theatre).
    Translated by George Calderon. Opened March 5, 1928 for
        five performances.
    Translated by Constance Garnett. Opened October 15, 1928
        for 63 performances.
    Translated by Constance Garnett. Opened September 23, 1929
        for 14 performances.
    Translated by Constance Garnett. Opened March 6, 1933 for
        30 performances.
    Translated by Irina Skariatina. Opened January 25, 1944 for
        96 performances.
    Translated by Irina Skariatina. Opened January 1, 1945 for
        eight performances.
    (Off Broadway) Season of 1959-1960.
    (Off Broadway) Opened November 14, 1962 for 61 performances.
    Opened February 9, 1965 for 11 performances.
    Translated by Eva Le Gallienne. Opened March 19, 1968 for
        38 performances in repertory.
    Translated by J. P. Davis. Opened May 6, 1970 for five
        performances.
    (Off Off Broadway) Translated by Irene and Sonia Moore.
        Season of 1970-1971.
    (Off Broadway) Opened December 7, 1972 for 86 performances.
    (Off Off Broadway) Season of 1972-1973.
    (Off Off Broadway) Translated by Irene and Sonia Moore.
        Opened February 1975.
    (Off Off Broadway) Opened November 1, 1975.
    (Off Off Broadway) Opened January 22, 1976.

(Off Broadway) Opened April 2, 1976 for 56 performances.
(Off Off Broadway) Opened June 25, 1976.
New English version by Jean-Claude Van Itallie. Opened
February 17, 1977 for 62 performances.

Reviews:
America 94:167, Nov 5, 1955
      108:121-2, Jan 19, 1963
      118:551, Apr 20, 1968
      128:103, Feb 3, 1973
      136:241, Mar 19, 1977
Catholic World 129:78+, Apr 1929
      158:584-5, Mar 1944
Commonweal 17:693, Apr 19, 1933
      39:420, Feb 11, 1944
      63:223, Dec 2, 1955
Dance Magazine 51:37+, May 1977
Dramatist 6:590, Jul 1915
Independent 110:97-8, Feb 3, 1923
Life 16:101-2+, Feb 28, 1944
Literary Digest 99:27, Dec 8, 1928
Nation 127:461, Oct 31, 1928
      158:167, Feb 5, 1944
      186:522, Jun 7, 1958
      201:87-8, Aug 16, 1965
      216:157-8, Jan 29, 1973
      224:313-14, Mar 12, 1977
New Republic 110:180-1, Feb 7, 1944
      110:211, Feb 14, 1944
      133:30, Nov 21, 1955
      152:26-8, Feb 27, 1965
      176:28+, Mar 26, 1977
New York Clipper 70:14, Jan 31, 1923
New York Theatre Critics' Reviews 1944:276
      1968:307, 318
      1970:257
      1973:318
      1977:336
New York Times p. 18, Jan 23, 1923
      VII, p. 1, Feb 4, 1923
      p. 20, Mar 6, 1928
      VIII, p. 1, Mar 11, 1928
      p. 20, Mar 7, 1933
      IX, p. 2, Sep 7, 1941
      p. 22, Jan 26, 1944
      II, p. 1, Feb 6, 1944
      p. 16, Jan 2, 1945
      p. 10, Jun 23, 1945
      VI, p. 33, Mar 5, 1950
      p. 38, Oct 19, 1955
      p. 22, May 16, 1958
      p. 10, Apr 16, 1960
      p. 41, Apr 20, 1960
      p. 17, Jun 4, 1960

New York Times p. 49, Dec 15, 1961
p. 46, Nov 15, 1962
p. 29, Jun 18, 1964
p. 46, Feb 10, 1965
p. 15, Feb 12, 1965
p. 17, Aug 2, 1965
p. 41, Mar 20, 1968
II, p. 3, Apr 7, 1968
II, p. 3, Apr 14, 1968
p. 63, May 7, 1970
p. 21, Jan 12, 1973
II, p. 1, Jan 21, 1973
II, p. 1, Feb 4, 1973
p. 32, Jun 19, 1973
p. 56, Dec 26, 1974
p. 30, Apr 27, 1976
II, p. 1, Feb 13, 1977
II, p. 3, Feb 18, 1977
II, p. 1, Feb 27, 1977
p. 46, Mar 10, 1977
II, p. 3, Jul 1, 1977
New Yorker 38:118+, Nov 24, 1962
41:54+, Feb 20, 1965
44:104, May 30, 1968
48:59, Jan 20, 1973
53:54+, Feb 28, 1977
Newsweek 65:93-4, Feb 22, 1965
81:65, Jan 22, 1973
89:78-9, Feb 28, 1977
Scholastic 44:20, Apr 10, 1944
Theatre Arts 12:316, May 1928
18:199-202, Apr 1944
Time 43:94, Feb 7, 1944
101:56+, Jan 29, 1973
109:56, Feb 28, 1977
Vogue 72:98, Dec 8, 1928

A Country Scandal
Productions:
(Off Broadway) Translated and adapted by Alex Szogyi.
Opened May 5, 1960 for 203 performances.
(Off Broadway) Translated by Alex Szogyi. Opened September
25, 1975 for 28 performances.
Reviews:
America 103:362+, Jun 11, 1960
Nation 190:459-60, May 21, 1960
New York Times p. 21, May 6, 1960
II, p. 1, May 15, 1960
p. 24, Oct 8, 1975
New Yorker 36:94+, May 14, 1960
Saturday Review 43:26, May 28, 1960

*Don Juan in the Russian Manner
    Adapted by B. Ashmore.
  Reviews:
    New York Times p. 23, Apr 23, 1954

Fireworks on the James
  Productions:
    Translated by John Cournos. Adapted by Elizabeth McCormick
      from That Worthless Fellow Platonov. Opened May 14,
      1940 in repertory.
  Reviews:
    New York Times p. 30, May 15, 1940

I Forgot
  Productions:
    Opened February 16, 1935 for 53 performances (Moscow Art
      Players).
  Reviews:
    New York Times p. 24, Mar 12, 1935

Ivanoff
  Productions:
    Opened November 1923 in repertory (Moscow Art Theatre).
    (Off Broadway) Season of 1958-1959.
    Adapted by John Gielgud. Translated by Ariadne Nicolaeff.
      Opened May 3, 1966 for 47 performances.
    (Off Off Broadway) Translated by Alex Szogyi. Opened
      August 14, 1975.
    (Off Off Broadway) Opened April 24, 1976.
  Reviews:
    America 113:812-13, Jun 4, 1966
    Commonweal 69:496-7, Feb 6, 1959
             84:283, Jun 4, 1966
    Life 60:16, May 27, 1966
    Nation 202:661-2, May 30, 1966
    New Republic 123:21, Jul 3, 1950
    New York Times p. 23, Nov 27, 1923
                 II, p. 3, Oct 5, 1958
                 p. 42, Oct 8, 1958
                 II, p. 1, Oct 19, 1958
                 II, p. 1, May 3, 1966
                 p. 50, May 4, 1966
                 II, p. 1, May 15, 1966
                 p. 15, May 8, 1976
                 p. 25, Sep 18, 1976
                 II, p. 5, Sep 26, 1976
                 p. 38, Nov 25, 1976
    New Yorker 34:58+, Oct 18, 1958
               42:114, May 14, 1966
    Newsweek 67:98, May 16, 1966
    Saturday Review 41:26, Oct 25, 1958
               49:10, May 7, 1966
               49:47, May 21, 1966
    Time 87:75, May 13, 1966

The Marriage
  Productions:
    (Off Broadway) Season of 1936-1937.
  No Reviews.

The Marriage Proposal (see also The Proposal)
  Productions:
    (Off Broadway) Season of 1942-1943 in repertory.
    (Off Off Broadway) Season of 1972-1973.
    (Off Off Broadway) Opened May 1975.
    (Off Off Broadway) Opened February 1977.
    (Off Off Broadway) Opened April 15, 1977.
  Reviews:
    New York Times p. 51, Jun 28, 1966
    Theatre Arts 12:70-71, Jan 1928
    Theatre Magazine 47:46-8, May 1928

On the Harmfulness of Tobacco (see also A Chekhov Portfolio)
  Productions:
    Opened February 5, 1948 for 14 performances.
    (Off Broadway) Opened March 5, 1968 for 6 performances.
    Adapted by Bernard Bragg. Opened March 5, 1969 in reper-
      tory for 6 performances.
    (Off Off Broadway) Opened March 16, 1977.
  Reviews:
    New York Times p. 29, Feb 6, 1948
               p. 38, Apr 26, 1956
               p. 34, Mar 6, 1968
               p. 76, Mar 9, 1969

On the Hazards of Smoking Tobacco (see On the Harmfulness of
      Tobacco)

On the High Road (On the Highway)
  Productions:
    (Off Broadway) Season of 1960-1961.
  Reviews:
    Nation 192:419, May 13, 1961
    New York Times p. 26, Apr 21, 1961

Platonov
  Productions:
    (Off Off Broadway) Opened April 1975.
  No Reviews.

The Proposal (see also The Marriage Proposal)
  Productions:
    (Off Off Broadway) Opened March 24, 1976.
  No Reviews.

The Sea Gull
  Productions:
    Opened May 20, 1916 in repertory.

Opened April 9, 1929 for 31 performances.
Translated by Constance Garnett. Opened September 16, 1929 for 63 performances.
Opened February 25, 1930 for five performances.
Translated by Stark Young. Opened March 28, 1938 for 41 performances.
(Off Broadway) Season of 1952-1953.
Adapted by Mina Rostova, Kevin McCarthy, and Montgomery Clift. Opened May 11, 1954 for 40 performances.
(Off Broadway) Season of 1956-1957.
(Off Broadway) Translated by Alex Szogyi. Opened March 21, 1962 for 11 performances (APA Repertory).
Translated by Eva Le Gallienne. Opened April 5, 1964 for 16 performances (National Repertory Theatre).
(Off Broadway) Adapted by Gene Feist. Opened December 18, 1973 for 105 performances.
(Off Off Broadway) Opened December 5, 1974.
(Off Broadway) Opened January 8, 1975 for 42 performances.
(Off Off Broadway) Opened May 26, 1976.
(Off Off Broadway) Opened September 9, 1976.
(Off Off Broadway) Opened September 16, 1976.
(Off Off Broadway) Opened February 9, 1977.
Reviews:
America 91:257+, May 29, 1954
      96:310, Dec 8, 1956
Arts and Decoration 32:67, Nov 1929
Catholic World 130:1, Dec 1929
      147:214-15, May 1938
      179:307, Jul 1954
      184:227, Dec 1956
Commonweal 10:21, 564, May 8, Oct 2, 1929
      27:692, Apr 15, 1938
      60:269, Jun 18, 1954
      76:87, Apr 1962
Nation 129:366-7, Oct 2, 1929
      146:422-3, Apr 9, 1938
      178:469-70, May 29, 1954
      183:415, Nov 10, 1956
New Republic 7:175, Jun 17, 1916
      60:205, Oct 9, 1929
      94:305, Apr 13, 1938
      146:37, May 1962
New York Theatre Critics' Reviews 1954:327
      1964:298
New York Times p. 9, May 23, 1916
      p. 32, Apr 10, 1929
      p. 34, Sep 17, 1929
      p. 19, Mar 29, 1938
      p. 38, May 12, 1954
      II, p. 1, May 23, 1954
      p. 22, Jul 27, 1954
      p. 38, Oct 23, 1956
      p. 26, Jun 2, 1960

New York Times p. 33, Aug 24, 1960
               p. 84, Jan 8, 1961
               p. 42, Mar 22, 1962
               II, p. 1, Apr 1, 1962
               p. 36, Apr 6, 1964
               p. 27, Jul 25, 1968
               p. 47, Jan 24, 1974
               II, p. 5, Feb 3, 1974
               p. 43, Jul 8, 1974
               II, p. 5, Jan 5, 1975
               p. 49, Jan 9, 1975
               p. 22, Jan 31, 1975
               II, p. 7, Nov 23, 1975
               III, p. 8, Jan 21, 1977
               p. 36, Feb 22, 1977
New Yorker 30:70+, May 22, 1954
            38:115-16, Apr 7, 1962
            50:62, Jan 20, 1975
Newsweek 11:22, Apr 11, 1938
Saturday Review 37:22-3, May 29, 1954
Stage 15:10-11, May 1938
Theatre Arts 13:401-2, Jun 1929
           22:327-8, May 1938
           38:33, Aug 1954
           41:26, May 1957
Time 31:36-7, Apr 11, 1938
      63:71, May 24, 1954

Summer in the Country (see A Chekhov Portfolio; Another Evening
       with Chekhov)

The Swan Song (see also A Chekhov Portfolio; Another Evening
       with Chekhov)
Productions:
     (Off Broadway) Season of 1940-1941 in repertory.
     (Off Broadway) Season of 1943-1944 in repertory.
Reviews:
     New York Times p. 61, Mar 26, 1972

That Worthless Fellow Platonov (see Fireworks on the James)

Three Sisters
Productions:
     Opened January 1923 in repertory.
     Opened November 8, 1926 for 39 performances.
     (Off Broadway) Season of 1938-1939.
     Translated by Bernard Guilbert Guerney. Adapted by Samuel
       Rosen. Opened October 14, 1939 for nine performances.
     Opened December 21, 1942 for 123 performances.
     (Off Broadway) Season of 1954-1955.
     (Off Broadway) Season of 1959-1960.
     English version by Randall Jerrell. Opened June 22, 1964
       for 119 performances.

Opened February 11, 1965 for eight performances (Moscow
Art Theatre).
Opened October 9, 1969 in repertory for 11 performances.
Translated by Tyrone Guthrie and Leonid Kipnis. Opened
December 19, 1973 for seven performances.
Translated by Tyrone Guthrie. Opened November 4, 1975
for eight performances.
(Off Broadway) Translated by Stark Young. Opened April 26,
1977 for 24 performances.

Reviews:
America 102:55, Oct 10, 1959
        111:54, Jul 11, 1964
        121:145-6, Sep 6, 1969
Catholic World 156:597-8, Feb 1943
Commonweal 31:14, Oct 27, 1939
        37:326, Jan 15, 1943
        62:127, May 6, 1955
Current History 3:548, Feb 1943
Dial 82:79, Jan 1927
Fortune 107:808-16, May 1920
Harper's 231:32, Sep 1965
Life 14:33-5, Jan 4, 1943
Nation 123:488, Nov 10, 1926
        156:31, Jan 2, 1943
        180:293-4, Apr 2, 1955
        189:218-19, Oct 10, 1959
        199:37-9, Jul 27, 1964
        209:486, Nov 3, 1969
        224:634-6, May 21, 1977
New Republic 6:256-8, Jul 8, 1916
        100:369, Nov 1, 1939
        107:857, Dec 28, 1942
        132:22, Mar 21, 1955
        133:30, Nov 21, 1955
        152:26-8, Feb 27, 1965
        161:33, Nov 1, 1969
        162:31+, Mar 21, 1970
New York Theatre Critics' Reviews 1942:135
        1964:238
        1969:338
        1973:134
        1975:157
        1977:221
New York Times p. 12, Jan 30, 1923
        p. 24, Oct 27, 1926
        VIII, p. 1, Nov 7, 1926
        X, p. 3, Feb 13, 1938
        p. 23, Oct 16, 1939
        p. 18, Dec 14, 1942
        VII, p. 32, Dec 13, 1942
        p. 31, Dec 22, 1942
        VII, p. 1, Dec 27, 1942
        p. 13, Feb 26, 1955

New York Times II, p. 1, Mar 20, 1955
        p. 23, Aug 21, 1959
        p. 46, Sep 22, 1959
        II, p. 1, Oct 4, 1959
        p. 36, May 2, 1960
        p. 30, Jun 20, 1963
        p. 19, Jul 22, 1963
        p. 24, Jun 23, 1964
        II, p. 1, Jul 5, 1964
        p. 26, Jul 28, 1964
        p. 15, Feb 12, 1965
        p. 19, May 15, 1965
        p. 56, Mar 18, 1968
        p. 29, Aug 4, 1969
        II, p. 3, Aug 10, 1969
        II, p. 4, Aug 31, 1969
        p. 38, Oct 10, 1969
        II, p. 3, Oct 19, 1969
        p. 30, Feb 12, 1970
        II, p. 1, Feb 22, 1970
        p. 55, Dec 20, 1973
        p. 36, Nov 5, 1973
        II, p. 1, May 1, 1977
        II, p. 22, May 5, 1977
        II, p. 3, May 15, 1977
New Yorker 18:32, Jan 2, 1943
     35:96-8, Oct 3, 1959
     40:56, Jul 4, 1964
     41:96, Feb 27, 1965
     45:149, Oct 18, 1969
     49:42, Dec 31, 1973
     53:74, May 16, 1977
Newsweek 21:64, Jan 4, 1943
     64:45, Jul 6, 1964
     65:94, Feb 22, 1965
Saturday Review 46:34, Aug 24, 1963
     47:25, Jul 18, 1964
     52:20, Jul 5, 1969
     4:50-51, Jul 9, 1977
Theatre Arts 11:9-10, Jan 1927
     22:407-10, Jun 1938
     23:862-3, Dec 1939
     27:73-6, Feb 1943
     28:603-6, Oct 1943
     39:87, May 1955
     47:13, Aug 1963
Theatre Magazine 45:17-18, Jan 1927
Time 40:45-6+, Dec 2, 1942
     84:72, Jul 3, 1964
     95:68+, Feb 23, 1970
     109:99, May 16, 1977
Vogue 69:80+, Jan 1, 1927

A Tragedian in Spite of Himself
    Productions:
        Opened February 5, 1948 for 14 performances.
    Reviews:
        New York Times p. 29, Feb 6, 1948

Uncle Vanya
    Productions:
        Opened November 1923 in repertory (Moscow Art Theatre).
        Opened May 24, 1929 for two performances.
        Rose Caylor version. April 15, 1930 for 80 performances.
        Rose Caylor version. Sep 22, 1930 for 16 performances.
        Translated by Constance Garnett. Opened May 13, 1946 for
            five performances.
        (Off Broadway) Adapted by Stark Young. Season of 1955-1956.
        (Off Off Broadway) Translated by Constance Garnett. Season
            of 1970-1971.
        (Off Broadway) Adapted by Gene Feist. Opened January 24,
            1971 for 50 performances.
        Translated by Albert Todd and Mike Nichols. Opened June
            4, 1973 for 64 performances.
        (Off Off Broadway) Opened March 14, 1974.
        (Off Off Broadway) Opened February 1975.
        (Off Off Broadway) Opened January 15, 1976.
        (Off Off Broadway) Opened April 15, 1977.
        (Off Off Broadway) Adapted by Marlene Swartz. Opened April
            30, 1977.
    Reviews:
        America 94:646, Mar 10, 1956
        Catholic World 131:388-9, Jun 1930
                        163:357, Jul 1930
                        183:65, Apr 1956
        Christian Century 11:742-3, Apr 30, 1930
        Commonweal 44:166, May 31, 1946
                    67:75-6, Apr 20, 1956
        Life (NY) 95:16, May 9, 1930
        Nation 130:554+, May 7, 1930
                162:671, Jun 1, 1946
                182:147, Feb 18, 1956
                209:293, Sep 22, 1969
                216:827-8, Jun 25, 1973
        National Review 25:742, Jul 6, 1973
        New Republic 62:299-300, Apr 30, 1930
                    114:805, Jun 3, 1946
                    168:24+, Jun 30, 1973
        New York Theatre Critics' Reviews 1946:389
                                          1973:260
        New York Times p. 17, May 25, 1929
                        p. 26, Apr 16, 1930
                        II, p. 1, May 12, 1946
                        p. 18, May 14, 1946
                        II, p. 1, May 19, 1946
                        II, p. 3, Jan 29, 1956

New York Times p. 25, Feb 1, 1956
II, p. 1, Feb 12, 1956
VI, p. 29, Feb 12, 1956
VI, p. 34, Jun 24, 1956
p. 13, Feb 13, 1960
p. 19, Feb 14, 1960
p. 18, Jul 17, 1962
p. 16, Jul 2, 1963
II, p. 4, Aug 31, 1969
II, p. 7, Mar 15, 1970
p. 23, Jan 25, 1971
II, p. 29, Feb 21, 1971
p. 33, Mar 10, 1971
p. 16, Mar 27, 1971
p. 61, Mar 26, 1972
II, p. 1, Jun 3, 1973
p. 35, Jun 5, 1973
II, p. 1, Jun 10, 1973
p. 36, Jun 18, 1973
New Yorker 49:88, Jun 9, 1973
Newsweek 27:84, May 27, 1946
62:45, Aug 5, 1963
81:112, Jun 18, 1973
Saturday Review 29:32-4, Jun 1, 1946
39:24, Feb 18, 1956
52:20, Nov 15, 1969
Theatre Arts 14:460-1, Jun 1930
27:721-2, Dec 1943
Theatre Magazine 51:42-3+, Jun 1930
Time 47:66, May 27, 1946
67:48, Feb 13, 1956
97:52, Feb 22, 1971
101:70, Jun 18, 1973
Vogue 75:68-9, Jun 7, 1930

The Wedding
Productions:
Opened February 5, 1948 for 14 performances.
(Off Broadway) Season of 1960-1961.
Reviews:
New York Times p. 29, Feb 6, 1948
p. 26, Apr 21, 1961
p. 61, Mar 26, 1972
New Yorker 37:123, May 6, 1961

The Wood Demon
Productions:
(Off Broadway) Translated by Alex Szogyi. Season of 1966-1967 for 9 performances.
(Off Broadway) Translated by Ronald Hingley. Opened January 29, 1974 for 10 performances.
Reviews:
America 130:133, Feb 23, 1974

82 / CHEKHOV

Nation 218:222, Feb 16, 1974
New York Theatre Critics' Reviews 1974:370
New York Times p. 20, Sep 8, 1973
                II, p. 3, Jan 27, 1974
                p. 23, Jan 30, 1974
                II, p. 1, Feb 10, 1974
New Yorker 49:71, Feb 11, 1974
Time 103:95, Feb 18, 1974

CHIARELLI, LUIGI

La Maschera e il Volto (see The Mask and the Face)

The Mask and the Face (La Maschere e il Volto)
   Productions:
      Opened September 10, 1924 for 13 performances.
      Adapted by W. Somerset Maugham. Opened May 8, 1933
         for 40 performances.
   Reviews:
      Catholic World 137:337-8, Jun 1933
      Commonweal 18:107, May 26, 1933
      Nation 136:593-4, May 24, 1933
      New Outlook 161:48, Jun 1933
      New Republic 75:46-7, May 24, 1933
      New York Times p. 27, Sep 11, 1924
                   p. 18, Mar 20, 1933
      Stage 10:32-3, Jun 1933
         10:7-9, Jun 1933
      Time 21:52, May 15, 1933
      Vogue 81:39+, Jun 15, 1933

CHRISTIE, AGATHA

*Castle in the Air
   Adapted by A. Melville.
   Reviews:
      New York Times II, p. 3, Jan 8, 1950

*Go Back for Murder
   Reviews:
      New York Times p. 40, Mar 24, 1960

Hidden Horizon
   Productions:
      Opened September 19, 1946 for 12 performances.
   Reviews:
      New York Theatre Critics' Reviews 1946:340
      New York Times p. 42, Sep 20, 1946
      New Yorker 22:44, Sep 28, 1946

Love from a Stranger
    Productions:
        (Off Off Broadway) Opened October 15, 1974.
    No Reviews.

The Mousetrap
    Productions:
        (Off Broadway) Season of 1960-1961.
        (Off Off Broadway) Opened June 1975.
        (Off Off Broadway) Opened June 5, 1976.
        (Off Off Broadway) Opened February 26, 1977.
    Reviews:
        America 101:231, Apr 18, 1959
        New York Times p. 12, Sep 14, 1957
                     p. 46, Nov 7, 1960
                     II, p. 3, Nov 20, 1960
                     p. 60, Dec 10, 1964
                     p. 61, Nov 27, 1967
                     p. 51, Nov 27, 1969
                     p. 49, Nov 27, 1970
                     p. 83, Nov 26, 1972
                     p. 27, Nov 26, 1973
                     p. 40, Mar 25, 1974

The Patient
    Productions:
        (Off Off Broadway) Opened December 8, 1975.
    No Reviews.

The Rats
    Productions:
        (Off Off Broadway) Opened December 11, 1975.
    No Reviews.

The Spider's Web
    Productions:
        (Off Off Broadway) Opened January 15, 1974.
    Reviews:
        New York Times II, p. 3, Jan 9, 1955
                     p. 44, Jan 17, 1974

Ten Little Indians
    Productions:
        Opened June 27, 1944 for 426 performances.
        (Off Off Broadway) Opened March 1977.
    Reviews:
        New York Theatre Critics' Reviews 1944:160
        New York Times p. 21, Jun 28, 1944
        Newsweek 24:94, Jul 10, 1944
        Time 44:72, Jul 10, 1944

Witness for the Prosecution
  Productions:
    Opened December 16, 1954 for 645 performances.
    (Off Broadway) Opened March 4, 1966 for nine matinees
      (ANTA).
    (Off Off Broadway) Opened August 1975.
  Reviews:
    Catholic World 180:386-7, Feb 1955
    Collier's 135:6+, Apr 1, 1955
    New Republic 132:20, Mar 7, 1955
    New York Theatre Critics' Reviews 1954:216
    New York Times II, p. 3, Nov 15, 1953
                    p. 35, Dec 17, 1954
                    II, p. 1, Dec 26, 1954
                    p. 27, Jan 9, 1957
    Theatre Arts 39:14-15+, Mar 1955

CLAUDEL, PAUL

L'Annonce Faite à Marie   (see The Tidings Brought to Mary)

Break of Noon
  Productions:
    (Off Off Broadway) Season of 1976-1977.
  No Reviews.

Christophe Colomb
  Productions:
    Opened January 30, 1957
  Reviews:
    America 90:420-1, Jan 23, 1954
    Catholic World 185:67, Apr 1957
    Nation 184:147, Feb 16, 1957
    New Republic 136:20, Mar 18, 1957
    New York Theatre Critics' Reviews 1957:369
    New York Times II, p. 3, Nov 29, 1953
                      II, p. 7, Jan 20, 1957
                      p. 20, Jan 31, 1957
    New Yorker 29:74+, Oct 24, 1953
    Newsweek 49:67, Feb 11, 1957
    Saturday Review 40:22, Jan 26, 1957
    Theatre Arts 41:21, Apr 1957
    Time 69:70, Feb 11, 1957

*Coufontaine Trilogy (consists of The Hostage, Crusts, and The
          Humiliated Father)
  Reviews:
    New York Times p. 28, Nov 30, 1962

Crusts   (see Coufontaine Trilogy)

The Hostage   (see Coufontaine Trilogy)

Humiliated Father   (see Coufontaine Trilogy)

*Jeanne au Bûcher
  Reviews:
    New Yorker 30:56-8, Jul 10, 1954

Noontide (Partage de Midi)
  Productions:
    (Off Broadway) Adapted by Howard Hart.   Opened June 1,
      1961 for 70 performances.
  Reviews:
    America 105:471-3, Jun 24, 1961
    Commonweal 74:427-8, Jul 28, 1961
    New York Times II, p. 1, May 3, 1949
               p. 37, Jun 2, 1961
    New Yorker 37:94+, Jun 10, 1961
    Saturday Review 44:51, Jun 17, 1961

*Le Pain Dur
  Reviews:
    New York Times II, p. 3, May 1, 1949

*Le Partage Midi   (see Noontide)

*Satin Slipper
  Reviews:
    Saturday Review 28:13, Jun 30, 1945

*Tête d'or
  Reviews:
    New Yorker 44:100+, Mar 2, 1968

The Tidings Brought to Mary (L'Annonce Faite à Marie)
  Productions:
    (Off Broadway) Translated by L. M. Sill.   Opened December
      25, 1922 for 32 performances.
  Reviews:
    Commonweal 36:158, Jun 5, 1942
    Dial 62:98, Feb 8, 1917
         74:215-16, Feb 1923
    Freeman 6:472-3, Jan 24, 1923
    Nation 105:48, 175-6, Jul 12, 1917
           116:102, Jan 24, 1923
    New York Clipper 70:20, Jan 10, 1923
                     70:14, Jan 17, 1923
    New York Times p. 20, Dec 25, 1922
                   VII, p. 1, Dec 31, 1922
                   p. 24, May 21, 1942
                   IV, p. 2, May 24, 1942
                   p. 33, Apr 6, 1965
    Outlook 133:18-20, Jan 17, 1923

COCTEAU, JEAN

Antigone
Productions:
    (Off Broadway) Opened December 27, 1962 for 13 performances.
Reviews:
    New York Times p. 5, Dec 29, 1962
    New Yorker 38:77, Jan 12, 1963

*Azreal
Reviews:
    New York Times p. 9, Sep 16, 1946

*Bacchus
Reviews:
    New York Times p. 11, Dec 31, 1951

The Eagle Has Two Heads
Productions:
    Adapted by Ronald Duncan.   Opened March 19, 1947 for 29
        performances.
    (Off Broadway) Season of 1956-1957.
Reviews:
    Commonweal 45:613-14, Apr 4, 1947
    Harper's Bazaar 81:198-9, Feb 1941
    Nation 164:403+, Apr 5, 1947
    New Republic 116:38, Mar 31, 1947
    New York Theatre Critics' Reviews 1947:421
    New York Times p. 39, Mar 20, 1947
                   p. 18, Apr 4, 1947
                   p. 37, Dec 14, 1956
    New Yorker 23:52+, Mar 29, 1947
    Newsweek 29:84, Mar 31, 1947
    Saturday Review 30:40, Apr 12, 1947
    Theatre Arts 30:705-6, Dec 1946
                 31:45, May 1947
                 31:16+, May 1947
    Time 49:78, Mar 31, 1947

The Human Voice
Productions:
    (Off Off Broadway) Opened November 4, 1976.
No Reviews.

The Infernal Machine
Productions:
    Adapted by Albert Bermel.   Opened February 3, 1958 for
        40 performances.
    (Off Broadway) Season of 1953-1954.
    (Off Off Broadway) Opened February 6, 1976.
Reviews:
    America 98:614, Feb 22, 1958
    Catholic World 187:69, Apr 1958

Christian Century 75:283, Mar 5, 1958
New Republic 119:27, Jul 5, 1948
New York Theatre Critics' Reviews 1958:373
New York Times p. 22, Mar 22, 1954
              p. 33, Feb 4, 1958
New Yorker 30:163, Oct 9, 1954
          33:60-1, Feb 15, 1958
Theatre Arts 42:27, Apr 1958
Time 71:84+, Feb 17, 1958
     30:32-3, Dec 20, 1937

Intimate Relations (Les Parents Terribles)
  Productions:
    (Off Broadway) Translated by Charles Frank.   Opened Novem-
      ber 1, 1962 for 76 performances.
  Reviews:
    New York Times p. 27, Nov 2, 1962
                   II, p. 1, Nov 25, 1962
    New Yorker 38:148, Nov 10, 1962

La Machine Infernale   (see The Infernal Machine)

Opium
  Productions:
    Adapted by Roc Brynner from Opium-Journal of a Cure.
      Opened October 5, 1970 for 8 performances.
  Reviews:
    Nation 211:414, Oct 26, 1970
    New York Theatre Critics' Reviews 1970:212
    New York Times p. 58, Oct 6, 1970

Orphée
  Productions:
    (Off Broadway) Translated by Carl Wildman.   Opened
      December 27, 1962 for 13 performances.
    (Off Off Broadway) Opened June 13, 1975.
    (Off Off Broadway) Opened April 1976.
  Reviews:
    New York Times p. 5, Dec 29, 1962
    New Yorker 38:77, Jan 12, 1963

Les Parents Terribles   (see Intimate Relations)

*Typewriter
  Reviews:
    Commonweal 62:613, Sep 23, 1955
    New York Times p. 8, Jul 29, 1955

COLTON, JOHN

Drifting (with D. H. Andrews)
  Productions:

Opened January 2, 1922 for 63 performances.
Reviews:
Dramatic Mirror 95:17, Jan 7, 1922
New York Clipper 69:20, Jan 11, 1922
New York Times p. 20, Jan 3, 1922
VI, p. 1, Jan 22, 1922
Theatre Magazine 35:155+, Mar 1922

Nine Pine Street (with Carleton Miles)
Productions:
Opened April 27, 1933 for 28 performances.
Reviews:
Catholic World 137:336-7, Jun 1933
New Outlook 161:48, Jun 1933
New York Times p. 15, Apr 28, 1933
Newsweek 1:28, May 6, 1933
Stage 10:6+, Jun 1933
Time 21:52, May 8, 1933
Vogue 81:53+, Jun 1, 1933

Rain (with Clemence Randolph)
Based on W. Somerset Maugham's Miss Thompson.
Productions:
Opened November 7, 1922 for 648 performances.
Opened September 1, 1924 for 104 performances.
Opened February 12, 1935 for 47 performances.
(Off Broadway) Opened December 26, 1947 in repertory.
(Off Off Broadway) Season of 1969-1970.
(Off Broadway) Opened March 23, 1972 for 7 performances.
(Off Off Broadway) Opened May 21, 1977.
Reviews:
Bookman 56:611-12, Jan 1923
Catholic World 141:86-7, Apr 1935
Commonweal 21:513, Mar 1, 1935
Current Opinion 74:187-95, Feb 1923
Dramatist 14:1154, Apr 1923
Golden Book 22:106-7, Jul 1935
Hearst 43:93-5, Apr 1923
Life (NY) 80:18, Nov 30, 1922
Literary Digest 119:20, Feb 23, 1935
Nation 115:585-6, Nov 29, 1922
New Republic 33:349, Feb 21, 1923
New York Clipper 70:20, Nov 15, 1922
New York Times p. 18, Nov 8, 1922
VIII, p. 2, Feb 10, 1935
p. 24, Feb 13, 1935
VIII, p. 1, Feb 17, 1935
p. 15, Feb 2, 1948
p. 30, Mar 24, 1972
New York Times Magazine pp. 28-9, Nov 12, 1944
New Yorker 48:67, Apr 1, 1972
Theatre Arts 19:257, Apr 1935

Theatre Magazine 37:25, Jan 1923
37:28+, Feb 1923
Time 25:56, Feb 25, 1935

Saint Wench
Productions:
Opened January 2, 1933 for 12 performances.
Reviews:
New York Times p. 19, Jan 3, 1933
p. 18, Jan 13, 1933

Shanghai Gesture
Productions:
Opened February 1, 1926 for 206 performances.
Opened February 13, 1928 for 16 performances.
Reviews:
Bookman 63:215, Apr 1926
Life (NY) 87:21, Mar 4, 1926
New York Times p. 20, Feb 2, 1926
p. 26, Feb 14, 1928
Theatre Magazine 43:5+, Apr 1926
Vogue 67:134, Apr 1, 1926

COPEAU, JACQUES

Brothers Karamazov (with Jean Croue)
Productions:
Translated by Rosalind Ivan. Opened January 3, 1927 for
56 performances.
Reviews:
Bookman 65:71, Mar 1927
Current Opinion 64:178-83, Mar 1918
Independent 118:270, Mar 5, 1927
Nation 124:72, Jan 19, 1927
New Republic 49:247, Jan 19, 1927
New York Times p. 20, Jan 4, 1927
Vogue 67:81+, Mar 1, 1927

COWARD, NOEL

*Ace of Clubs
Reviews:
New York Times p. 7, Jul 8, 1950
II, p. 1, Aug 13, 1950

*After the Ball
Reviews:
New York Times p. 19, Jun 11, 1954
II, Jul 18, 1954

The Astonished Heart   (see Tonight at Eight-Thirty)

Bitter Sweet
    Productions:
        Opened November 5, 1929 for 159 performances.
        Opened May 7, 1934 for 16 performances.
    Reviews:
        American Mercury 19:117-18, Jan 1930
        Life (NY) 94:20, Nov 29, 1929
        New York Times p. 23, Nov 19, 1929
        Outlook 154:32, Jan 1, 1930
        Theatre Magazine 51:44-5, Jan 1930

Blithe Spirit
    Productions:
        Opened November 5, 1941 for 657 performances.
        Opened September 6, 1943 for 32 performances.
        (Off Broadway) Opened February 1952.
    Reviews:
        Catholic World 154:335-6, Dec 1941
        Commonweal 35:123-4, Nov 21, 1941
        Life 11:69-71, Sep 29, 1941
        Harper's Bazaar 75:76, Nov 1941
        Nation 153:491, Nov 15, 1941
        New Republic 105:701, Nov 24, 1941
        New York Times p. 13, Jul 3, 1941
                       IX, p. 1, Jul 13, 1941
                        p. 26, Nov 6, 1941
                        X, p. 1, Nov 16, 1941
                       IX, p. 3, Jan 11, 1942
                        p. 20, Apr 17, 1942
                       II, p. 1, Sep 12, 1943
                        p. 43, Mar 10, 1946
                        p. 17, Jun 5, 1946
                        p. 7, Feb 23, 1952
                       II, p. 5, Jul 18, 1976
        New Yorker 17:37, Nov 15, 1941
        Newsweek 18:57, Nov 17, 1941
        Theatre Arts 26:8-9, Jan 1942
        Theatre Magazine 37:28, Jan 1942
        Time 38:67, Nov 17, 1941

Come into the Garden Maude   (see Noel Coward in Two Keys)

Conversation Piece
    Productions:
        Opened October 23, 1934 for 55 performances.
    Reviews:
        Catholic World 140:340-1, Dec 1934
        Literary Digest 118:20, Nov 3, 1934
        New York Times p. 20, Feb 17, 1934
                        p. 38, Nov 19, 1957

Theatre Arts 18:899-90, Dec 1934
Time 24:30, Nov 5, 1934

Design for Living
 Productions:
  Opened January 24, 1933 for 135 performances.
 Reviews:
  Arts and Decoration 38:41, Mar 1933
  Catholic World 136:715-16, Mar 1933
  Commonweal 17:441, Feb 15, 1933
  Literary Digest 115:16, Feb 11, 1933
  Nation 136:187-8, Feb 15, 1933
  New Outlook 161:48, Mar 1933
  New Republic 73:350-2, Feb 8, 1933
  New York Times p. 32, Oct 12, 1933
  Player's Magazine 9:11, Mar-Apr 1933
  Stage 10:12, Feb 1933
  Theatre Arts 17:257-8, Apr 1933
  Time 21:21, Jan 20, 1933
  Vogue 81:72, Mar 15, 1933

Easy Virtue
 Productions:
  Opened December 7, 1925 for 147 performances.
 Reviews:
  Bookman 62:705, Feb 1926
  Nation 121:739-40, Dec 23, 1925
  New Republic 45:133-4, Dec 23, 1925
  New York Times p. 28, Dec 8, 1925
  Theatre Magazine 43:16+, Feb 1926
  Vogue 67:108, Feb 1, 1926

Fallen Angels
 Productions:
  Opened December 1, 1927 for 36 performances.
  Opened January 17, 1956 for 239 performances.
  (Off Off Broadway) Season of 1968-1969.
 Reviews:
  Catholic World 134:590-1, Feb 1932
  Commonweal 63:542, Feb 24, 1956
  Nation 182:125, Feb 11, 1956
  New York Theatre Critics' Reviews 1956:389
  New York Times p. 20, Dec 2, 1927
              p. 27, Jan 18, 1956
  New Yorker 31:58-60, Jan 28, 1956
  Newsweek 47:43-4, Feb 6, 1956
  Saturday Review 4:452, Dec 17, 1927
  Theatre Arts 40:17, Mar 1956
  Time 67:34, Jan 30, 1956

Family Album (see Tonight at Eight-Thirty)

Fumed Oak (see Tonight at Eight-Thirty)

Hands Across the Sea   (see Tonight at Eight-Thirty)

Hay Fever
 Productions:
  Opened October 5, 1925 for 49 performances.
  Opened December 29, 1931 for 95 performances.
  Opened November 9, 1970 for 24 performances.
  (Off Broadway) Opened July 30, 1976 for 14 performances.
  (Off Off Broadway) Opened January 22, 1977.
 Reviews:
  Bookman 62:478, Dec 1925
  Nation 121:468-9, Oct 21, 1925
       211:572, Nov 30, 1970
  New York Theatre Critics' Reviews 1970:151, 166
  New York Times p. 25, Oct 5, 1925
            VIII, p. 2, Dec 6, 1931
            p. 25, Dec 30, 1931
            p. 52, Oct 28, 1964
            p. 55, Nov 10, 1970
            II, p. 18, Nov 22, 1970
  New Yorker 40:200-1, Nov 21, 1964
         46:103, Nov 21, 1970
  Newsweek 76:137, Nov 23, 1970

*Island Fling
 Reviews:
  Theatre Arts 35:24-5+, Sep 1951

Look After Lulu
 Productions:
  Based on Georges Feydeau's Occupe-toi d'Amélie.   Opened
   March 3, 1959 for 3 performances.
  (Off Broadway) Opened April 2, 1965 for 9 performances.
 Reviews:
  America 100:726, Mar 21, 1959
  Catholic World 189:157, May 1959
  Commonweal 70:24-5, Apr 3, 1959
  Nation 188:262, Mar 21, 1959
  New York Theatre Critics' Reviews 1959:356
  New York Times p. 35, Mar 4, 1959
  New Yorker 35:80+, Mar 14, 1959
  Newsweek 53:90, Mar 16, 1959
  Theatre Arts 43:24+, May 1959
  Time 73:59, Mar 16, 1959

The Marquise
 Productions:
  Opened November 14, 1927 for 80 performances.
 Reviews:
  New York Times p. 26, Nov 15, 1927
  Saturday Review 4:452, Dec 17, 1927
  Theatre Magazine 47:38-9, Feb 1928
  Vogue 71:120, Jan 15, 1928

Noel Coward in Two Keys (consists of Come into the Garden and
     A Song at Twilight)
   Productions:
     Opened February 28, 1974 for 140 performances.
   Reviews:
     America 130:227-8, Mar 23, 1974
     Nation 218:380-1, Mar 23, 1974
     National Review 26:483-4, Apr 26, 1974
     New York Theatre Critics' Reviews 1974:356
     New York Times II, p. 1, Feb 24, 1974
                    p. 18, Mar 1, 1974
                    II, p. 1, Mar 10, 1974
                    p. 33, Mar 13, 1974
     New Yorker 50:102, Mar 11, 1974
     Newsweek 83:91, Mar 11, 1974
     Time 103:103, Mar 11, 1974

Nude with Violin
   Productions:
     Opened November 14, 1957 for 86 performances.
     (Off Off Broadway) Opened August 2, 1973.
   Reviews:
     America 98:355, Dec 14, 1957
     Catholic World 186:308, Jan 1958
     Christian Century 74:1449, Dec 4, 1957
     Commonweal 67:489, Feb 7, 1958
     Dance Magazine 32:9, Feb 1958
     Nation 185:416, Nov 30, 1957
     New York Theatre Critics' Reviews 1957:180
     New York Times p. 30, Sep 25, 1956
                    II, p. 3, Dec 2, 1956
                    p. 26, Jan 25, 1957
                    p. 36, Nov 15, 1957
                    p. 45, Jun 11, 1973
                    p. 14, Jun 16, 1973
     New Yorker 33:78-80, Nov 23, 1957
     Newsweek 50:84, Nov 25, 1957
     Reporter 17:35-6, Dec 12, 1957
     Saturday Review 40:23, Nov 30, 1957
     Theatre Arts 41:30-1, May 1957
                   42:20, Jan 1958
     Time 70:91, Nov 25, 1957

*Pacifica 1860
   Reviews:
     New York Times p. 30, Dec 20, 1946

*Peace in Our Time
   Reviews:
     New York Times p. 18, Jul 23, 1947
                    II, p. 2, Aug 24, 1947
                    VI, p. 48, Sep 14, 1947
     Theatre Arts 31:45, Nov 1947

Point Valaine
  Productions:
      Opened January 16, 1935 for 55 performances.
  Reviews:
      New Republic 81:363, Feb 6, 1935
      New York Times p. 22, Jan 17, 1935
                    VIII, p. 1, Feb 3, 1935
      Newsweek 5:26, Jan 26, 1935
      Player's Magazine 11:11, Mar-Apr 1935
      Theatre Arts 19:167+, Mar 1935
      Time 25:63, Jan 28, 1935

Present Laughter
  Productions:
      Opened October 29, 1946 for 158 performances.
      Opened January 31, 1958 for 6 performances.
      (Off Off Broadway) Season of 1970-1971.
  Reviews:
      Catholic World 164:261, Dec 1946
      Commonweal 45:116, Nov 15, 1946
      Life 21:116, Oct 28, 1946
      Nation 163:565, Nov 16, 1946
      New Republic 115:628, Nov 11, 1946
      New York Theatre Critics' Reviews 1946:283
      New York Times II, p. 9, May 9, 1943
                     II, p. 1, May 23, 1943
                     II, p. 1, Oct 27, 1946
                       p. 31, Oct 30, 1946
                     II, p. 3, Dec 1, 1946
                       p. 66, Jan 24, 1971
      New Yorker 22:56+, Nov 9, 1946
      Saturday Review 29:24-6+, Nov 23, 1946
      Theatre Arts 31:18, Jan 1947
      Time 41:65, May 10, 1943
           48:55, Nov 11, 1946
           105:68, Jun 9, 1975

Private Lives
  Productions:
      Opened January 27, 1931 for 256 performances.
      Opened October 4, 1948 for 248 performances.
      (Off Broadway) Opened May 19, 1968 for 9 performances.
      Opened December 4, 1969 for 204 performances.
      Opened February 6, 1975 for 92 performances.
      (Off Off Broadway) Opened June 5, 1976.
  Reviews:
      America 122:54, Jan 17, 1970
              127:470, Dec 2, 1972
      Arts and Decoration 35:83, Jul 1931
      Bookman 73:523, Jul 1931
      Catholic World 132:719-20, Mar 1931
                     168:160, Nov 1948
      Commonweal 91:409, Jan 9, 1970

Life (NY) 97:18, Feb 20, 1931
Life 25:64-5, Dec 27, 1948
Nation 132:165, Feb 11, 1931
      167:444, Oct 16, 1948
      209:704, Dec 22, 1969
National Review 20:705-6, Jul 16, 1968
New Republic 66:19, Feb 18, 1931
            119:27, Nov 1, 1948
New York Theatre Critics' Reviews 1948:209
                                     1969:166
                                     1975:360
New York Times p. 24, Jan 28, 1931
              p. 30, Oct 5, 1948
              II, p. 1, Nov 7, 1948
              p. 8, Jul 4, 1963
              p. 59, May 20, 1968
              p. 55, May 23, 1968
              p. 52, Dec 5, 1969
              II, p. 3, Dec 14, 1969
              p. 38, Feb 11, 1970
              p. 36, Oct 9, 1972
              p. 41, Aug 16, 1973
              p. 14, Feb 7, 1975
              II, p. 5, Feb 16, 1975
New Yorker 24:53, Oct 16, 1948
         45:115, Dec 13, 1969
         50:84, Feb 17, 1975
Newsweek 32:88, Oct 18, 1948
        74:117, Dec 15, 1969
        85:66, Feb 17, 1975
Outlook 157:234, Feb 11, 1931
Saturday Review 31:30-2, Oct 23, 1948
               52:36, Dec 20, 1969
Theatre Magazine 53:25, Apr 1931
Time 52:82, Oct 18, 1948
    94:84, Dec 12, 1969
    104:108+, Nov 25, 1974
Vogue 77:87+, Mar 15, 1931

Quadrille
   Productions:
     Opened November 3, 1954 for 150 performances.
   Reviews:
     America 92:283, Dec 4, 1954
     Catholic World 180:307, Jan 1955
     Commonweal 61:288, Dec 10, 1954
     Life 33:166, Oct 13, 1952
     Nation 179:450, Nov 20, 1954
     New York Theatre Critics' Reviews 1954:259
     New York Times p. 20, Jul 17, 1952
                        II, p. 3, Oct 12, 1952
                        II, p. 1, Apr 5, 1953
                        II, p. 1, Oct 31, 1954

New York Times p. 39, Nov 4, 1954
            II, p. 1, Nov 14, 1954
New Yorker 30:103, Nov 13, 1954
Newsweek 44:98, Nov 15, 1954
Saturday Review 37:27, Nov 27, 1954
Theatre Arts 38:20-5+, Nov 1954
            39:16+, Jan 1955
Time 64:62, Nov 15, 1954
Vogue 124:125, Dec 1954

Red Peppers (see also Tonight at Eight-Thirty)
    Productions:
        (Off Broadway) Season of 1960-1961.
        (Off Off Broadway) Opened April 1975.
        (Off Off Broadway) Opened January 28, 1977.
    Reviews:
        New York Times p. 8, Feb 21, 1948
                      p. 39, Apr 14, 1975

*Relative Values
    Reviews:
        New York Times p. 41, Nov 29, 1951
                    II, p. 7, Dec 9, 1951
        New Yorker 27:78+, Jan 19, 1952

Shadow Play (see Tonight at Eight-Thirty)

*Sigh No More
    Reviews:
        New York Times p. 15, Aug 24, 1945
                    II, p. 1, Sep 2, 1945

*A Song at Twilight (see also Noel Coward in Two Keys)
    Reviews:
        New York Times p. 86, Apr 17, 1966
        New Yorker 42:70, Jul 23, 1966
        Vogue 148:50, Aug 15, 1966

*South Sea Bubble
    Reviews:
        New York Times p. 37, Apr 26, 1956

*Still Life (see also Tonight at Eight-Thirty)
    Reviews:
        New York Times p. 33, Mar 11, 1958
                    II, p. 1, Mar 16, 1958

*Suite in Three Keys
    Reviews:
        New York Times p. 38, Apr 27, 1966

This Happy Breed
    Productions:
       (Off Broadway) Opened March 1952.
    Reviews:
       New York Times II, p. 1, May 9, 1943
                       II, p. 1, May 23, 1943
                       p. 23, Apr 4, 1952
       Time 41:65, May 10, 1943

This Was a Man
    Productions:
       Opened November 23, 1926 for 31 performances.
    Reviews:
       Bookman 64:734, Feb 1927
       New York Times p. 27, Nov 24, 1926
                     VIII, p. 1, Nov 28, 1926
       Theatre Magazine 45:15, Feb 1927
       Vogue 69:120, Jan 15, 1927

This Year of Grace
    Productions:
       Opened November 7, 1928 for 157 performances.
    Reviews:
       American Mercury 16:120-1, Jan 1929
       Dial 86:245, Mar 1929
       Life (NY) 92:11, Nov 30, 1928
       New Republic 57:15-17, Nov 21, 1928
       Theatre Magazine 49:60, Jan 1929
       Vogue 72:55, Dec 22, 1928

Tonight at Eight-Thirty (A Repertory of One-Act Plays)
    Productions:
       Opened November 24, 1936 for 118 performances.
          Plays presented included:
          The Astonished Heart
          Family Album
          Fumed Oak
          Hands Across the Sea
          Red Peppers
          Shadow Play
          Still Life
          Ways and Means
          We Were Dancing
       Opened February 20, 1948 for 26 performances. Plays presented included:
          Family Album
          Fumed Oak
          Hands Across the Sea
          Red Peppers
          Shadow Play
          Ways and Means
       Opened May 3, 1967 in repertory for 5 performances.
       (Off Off Broadway) Opened August 15, 1973.

Plays presented:
Fumed Oak
Still Life
Ways and Means
Reviews:
Catholic World 144:471-2, Jan 1937
      167:72-3, Apr 1948
Commonweal 25:193, Dec 11, 1936
     47:521, Mar 5, 1948
Nation 166:285, Mar 6, 1948
New Republic 89:217, Dec 16, 1936
New York Theatre Critics' Reviews 1948:329+
            1967:302
New York Times p. 17, Nov 25, 1936
      p. 23, Nov 28, 1936
      XII, p. 5, Dec 6, 1936
      p. 16, Mar 2, 1937
      p. 15, Aug 6, 1940
      IX, p. 1, Aug 11, 1940
      p. 8, Feb 21, 1948
      p. 34, May 4, 1967
      p. 27, Aug 18, 1973
New Yorker 24:50, Mar 6, 1948
Newsweek 8:20-2, Dec 5, 1936
Saturday Review 15:5, Dec 19, 1936
Stage 14:56-7, Dec 1936
Theatre Arts 21:18+, Jan 1937
Time 28:39, Dec 7, 1936
Vogue 111:150, Apr 1, 1948

The Vortex
Productions:
Opened September 16, 1925 for 157 performances.
Reviews:
Bookman 62:319, Nov 1925
Life (NY) 86:20, Oct 8, 1925
Nation 121:469, Oct 21, 1925
New Republic 44:177, Oct 7, 1925
New York Times p. 20, Sep 17, 1925
      VII, p. 1, Sep 27, 1925
Theatre Magazine 42:22, Jul 1925

*Waiting in the Wings
Reviews:
New York Times p. 31, Aug 9, 1960
      p. 40, Sep 8, 1960

Ways and Means (see Tonight at Eight-Thirty)

We Were Dancing (see Tonight at Eight-Thirty)

The Young Idea
Productions:
    Opened March 18, 1932 for 3 performances.
No Reviews.

DANE, CLEMENCE

A Bill of Divorcement
Productions:
    Opened October 10, 1921 for 173 performances.
Reviews:
    Bookman 54:376-7, Dec 1921
    Current Opinion 72:199-209, Feb 1922
    Dramatic Mirror 84:557, Oct 15, 1921
    Everybody's 46:92-8, Feb 1922
    Hearst 41:45-7+, Apr 1922
    Independent 107:110, Oct 29, 1921
    Leslie's Weekly 133:835-6, Dec 17, 1921
    Life (NY) 78:18, Nov 3, 1921
    Nation 113:545, Nov 9, 1921
    New Republic 27:198, Jul 13, 1921
              29:130, Dec 28, 1921
    New York Clipper 69:20, Oct 19, 1912
    New York Times p. 22, Oct 11, 1921
              VI, p. 1, Oct 16, 1921
              VI, p. 1, Oct 23, 1921
    Theatre Magazine 34:385-6, Dec 1921
              35:84+, Feb 1922

*Call Home the Heart
Reviews:
    New York Times p. 54, Apr 13, 1947

Come of Age (Music by Richard Addinsell)
Productions:
    Opened January 12, 1934 for 35 performances.
    Opened January 23, 1952 for 30 performances.
Reviews:
    Catholic World 138:731, Mar 1934
              174:463, Mar 1952
    Commonweal 55:445-6, Feb 8, 1952
    Literary Digest 117:23, Feb 24, 1934
    Nation 138:140, Jan 31, 1934
    New Outlook 163:49, Feb 1934
    New Republic 77:368, Feb 7, 1934
    New York Theatre Critics' Reviews 1952:382
    New York Times p. 16, Jan 13, 1934
              X, p. 6, Jan 21, 1934
              p. 22, Jan 24, 1952
              II, p. 1, Feb 3, 1952
    New Yorker 27:48+, Feb 2, 1952
    Newsweek 3:34, Jan 20, 1934

Saturday Review 10:476, Feb 10, 1934
35:23, Feb 9, 1952
Stage 11:9+, Feb 1934
Theatre Arts 18:170, Mar 1934
36:19+, Apr 1952
Time 59:40, Feb 4, 1952

*Cousin Muriel
Reviews:
New York Times X, p. 1, Mar 17, 1940

Granite
Productions:
Opened February 11, 1927 for 70 performances.
Opened January 13, 1936 for eight performances.
Reviews:
Independent 118:445+, Apr 23, 1927
Nation 124:250, Mar 30, 1927
142:138, Jan 29, 1936
New York Times p. 13, Feb 12, 1927
p. 24, Jan 14, 1936
Pictorial Review 37:51, Apr 1936

The Mariners
Productions:
Opened March 28, 1927 for 16 performances.
Reviews:
Bookman 65:450, Jun 1927
Life (NY) 89:21, Apr 14, 1927
Nation 124:405, Apr 13, 1927
New Republic 50:223-4, Apr 13, 1927
New York Times p. 22, Mar 29, 1927
VIII, p. 1, Apr 3, 1927
Vogue 69:84-5, May 15, 1927

The Way Things Happen
Productions:
Opened January 28, 1924 for 24 performances.
Reviews:
American Mercury 1:370-1, Mar 1924
Canadian Magazine 62:449-50, Apr 1924
Life (NY) 83:18, Feb 14, 1924
New York Times p. 17, Jan 29, 1924
VII, p. 1, Feb 3, 1924
Theatre Magazine 39:15, Apr 1924

Will Shakespeare
Productions:
Opened January 1, 1923 for 80 performances.
Reviews:
Bookman 57:53-4, Mar 1923
Current Opinion 74:315-23, Mar 1923
Independent 110:72-4, Jan 20, 1923

Literary Digest 71:24-5, Dec 24, 1921
Literary Review 3:497-8, Mar 3, 1923
Nation 116:102, Jan 24, 1923
New Republic 33:252-3, Jan 31, 1923
New York Clipper 70:20, Jan 10, 1923
New York Times p. 14, Jan 2, 1923
              VII, p. 1, Jan 21, 1923
North American Review 215:574-6, Apr 1922
Outlook 133:164-6, Jan 24, 1923
Theatre Magazine 35:158-61+, Mar 1922
              37:20, Mar 1923

D'ANNUNZIO, GABRIELE

La Citta Morta (Dead City)
    Productions:
        Opened November 29, 1923 in repertory for 2 performances.
    Reviews:
        Nation 104:414, Apr 4, 1918
        New York Times p. 14, Nov 28, 1923

Dead City (see La Citta Morta)

DE GHELDERODE, MICHEL

The Blind Men (see 3 by Ghelderode)

Christopher Columbus (see 3 by Ghelderode)

*The Chronicles of Hell
    Reviews:
        New York Times II, p. 12, Oct 19, 1969

Escurial
    Productions:
        (Off Broadway) Season of 1960-1961.
        (Off Broadway) Translated by George Hauger. Opened March
            5, 1968 for 6 performances.
        (Off Off Broadway) Opened June 25, 1975.
        (Off Broadway) Translated by George Hauger. Opened
            October 25, 1975.
    Reviews:
        New York Times p. 29, Oct 3, 1956
                       p. 13, Jul 22, 1960
                       p. 41, Apr 25, 1961
                       p. 22, May 5, 1961
                       p. 34, Mar 6, 1968

Hop, Signor
    Productions:
        (Off Broadway) Opened May 7, 1962 for 8 performances.

Reviews:
   Commonweal 76:259-60, Jun 1, 1962
   New York Times p. 45, May 8, 1962
   New Yorker 38:104+, May 19, 1962
   Theatre Arts 46:58, Aug 1962

Pantagleize
   Productions:
      Tr., Geo. Hauger. Opened Nov 30, 1967 in reper. for 59 perfor.
      Tr., Geo. Hauger. Opened Sep 3, 1968 in reper. for 9 perfor.
   Reviews:
      America 118:130-1, Jan 27, 1968
      Christian Century 85:332+, Mar 13, 1968
      Commonweal 84:470, Jan 19, 1968
      Nation 205:669-70, Dec 18, 1967
      New York Theatre Critics' Reviews 1967:208
      New York Times p. 54, Dec 1, 1967
                     II, p. 3, Dec 17, 1967
                        p. 45, Nov 2, 1971
      New Yorker 93:43, Dec 9, 1967
      Newsweek 70:97, Dec 11, 1967
      Reporter 38:36-7, Jan 11, 1968
      Saturday Review 51:26, Jan 6, 1968
      Theatre Arts 46:26-7, Aug 1962
      Time 90:96-7, Dec 8, 1967

School for Buffoons
   Productions:
      (Off Broadway) Translated by Kenneth S. White.   "Previewed"
         October 25, 1975.
      (Off Off Broadway) Opened June 25, 1975.
   No Reviews.

Strange Rider   (see 3 by Ghelderode)

Three Actors and Their Drama
   Productions:
      (Off Off Broadway) Opened February 7, 1977.
   No Reviews.

3 by Ghelderode (consists of The Blind Men, Strange Rider, and
            Christopher Columbus)
   Productions:
      (Off Broadway) Tr., Samuel Draper. Opened Nov 26, 1963.
   No Reviews.

The Women at the Tomb
   Productions:
      (Off Broadway) Season of 1960-1961.
   Reviews:
      New York Times p. 13, Jul 22, 1960
                     p. 41, Apr 25, 1961
                     p. 22, May 5, 1961

DE HARTOG, JAN

The Fourposter
  Productions:
    Opened October 24, 1951 for 632 performances.
    Opened January 5, 1955 for 15 performances.
  Reviews:
    America 92:463, Jan 29, 1955
    Catholic World 174:227, Dec 1951
                   180:468, Mar 1955
    Commonweal 55:118, Nov 9, 1951
    Life 31:125-6, Nov 26, 1951
    New Republic 132:22, Feb 7, 1955
    New York Theatre Critics' Reviews 1951:190
    New York Times p. 34, Oct 25, 1951
                   II, p. 1, Nov 25, 1951
                   p. 33, Apr 7, 1953
                   p. 23, Jan 6, 1955
    New Yorker 27:91, Nov 3, 1951
    Newsweek 38:64, Nov 5, 1951
    Saturday Review 35:27, Jul 5, 1952
    Theatre Arts 35:3, Dec 1951
                 36:21+, Jan 1952
                 39:91, Mar 1955
    Time 58:66, Nov 5, 1951

Skipper Next to God
  Productions:
    Opened January 4, 1948 for 6 performances.
  Reviews:
    Catholic World 166:458, Feb 1948
    Commonweal 47:372-3, Jan 23, 1948
    Life 24:86+, Mar 29, 1948
    New Republic 118:33, Jan 19, 1948
    New York Times p. 14, Jan 5, 1948
                   II, p. 1, Feb 1, 1948
    New Yorker 23:40, Feb 7, 1948
    School and Society 67:244-5, Mar 27, 1948

This Time Tomorrow
  Productions:
    Opened November 3, 1947 for 32 performances.
  Reviews:
    Catholic World 166:266-7, Dec 1947
    Commonweal 47:143, Nov 21, 1947
    Nation 165:568, Nov 22, 1947
    New Republic 117:32, Nov 17, 1947
    New York Theatre Critics' Reviews 1947:274
    New York Times p. 31, Nov 4, 1947
    New Yorker 23:57, Nov 15, 1947
    Newsweek 30:85, Nov 17, 1947
    School and Society 66:420-1, Nov 29, 1947
    Theatre Arts 31:17, Nov 1947
    Time 50:87, November 17, 1947

DELANEY, SHELAGH

The Lion in Love
  Productions:
    (Off Broadway) Opened April 25, 1963 for 6 performances.
  Reviews:
    America 108:63-4+, Jul 13, 1963
    New York Times p. 10, Dec 31, 1960
                  p. 30, Apr 23, 1963
                  p. 28, Apr 26, 1963
    New Yorker 39:90+, May 4, 1963
    Newsweek 61:83, May 6, 1963
    Theatre Arts 47:64-5, Jun 1963
    Time 81:76, May 3, 1963

A Taste of Honey
  Productions:
    Opened October 4, 1960 for 376 performances.
  Reviews:
    Catholic World 193:127-8, May 1961
    Commonweal 74:496, Sep 8, 1961
    Ebony 16:71-4, Feb 1961
    Horizon 3:102-3, Mar 1961
    Nation 188:461-2, May 16, 1959
           191:334+, Oct 29, 1960
    New Republic 143:22, Oct 17, 1960
    New York Theatre Critics' Reviews 1960:225
    New York Times p. 24, Feb 12, 1959
                  II, p. 3, Mar 15, 1959
                  p. 46, Oct 5, 1960
                  II, p. 1, Nov 6, 1960
                  p. 43, May 17, 1961
    New Yorker 34:97-8, Feb 7, 1959
               36:73, Oct 15, 1960
    Newsweek 56:102, Oct 17, 1960
    Reporter 23:46, Nov 24, 1960
    Saturday Review 43:22, Oct 22, 1960
    Theatre Arts 43:16-17+, May 1959
                 44:10-11, Dec 1960
    Time 76:54, Oct 17, 1960

DE MONTHERLANT, HENRI

*Cardinal of Spain
  Reviews:
    New York Times p. 16, Dec 22, 1960
    New Yorker 36:94, Jan 21, 1961

*Master of Santiago
  Reviews:
    Theatre Arts 41:93, May 1957

Port-Royal
 Productions:
  (Off Broadway) Season of 1959-1960.
 Reviews:
  America 93:155-6, May 7, 1955
  New York Times II, p. 3, Feb 27, 1955
         p. 41, Apr 26, 1960
  New Yorker 30:54-5, Jan 1, 1955
  Newsweek 55:84, May 2, 1960

*Queen after Death
 Reviews:
  New York Times p. 33, Mar 13, 1956

La Reine Morte
 Productions:
  Opened February 15, 1966 in repertory for 8 performances.
 Reviews:
  New Republic 141:31, Aug 24, 1959
  New York Times p. 52, Feb 16, 1966

DE MUSSET, ALFRED

Un Caprice
 Productions:
  Opened November 15, 1955 for 8 performances in repertory.
 No Reviews.

Lorenzaccio
 Productions:
  Opened October 14, 1958 in repertory.
  (Off Broadway) Translated by Renaud C. Bruce. Opened
   March 12, 1965 for 9 performances.
 Reviews:
  New York Theatre Critics' Reviews 1958:270
  New York Times p. 44, Oct 15, 1958
  Time 72:84, Oct 27, 1958

*No Trifling with Love
 Reviews:
  America 102:305+, Nov 28, 1959
  Nation 189:427, Dec 5, 1959
  New York Times p. 55, Nov 10, 1959
         p. 35, Mar 5, 1968
  New Yorker 35:117, Nov 21, 1959

On Ne Badine Pas Avec L'Amour (see No Trifling with Love)

Whims
 Productions:
  Opened October 4, 1915 in repertory.
 Reviews:
  Bookman 42:647+, Feb 1916

        Dramatic Mirror 74:8, Nov 13, 1915
                        74:4, Dec 25, 1915
        Green Book 15:301, Feb 1916
        New York Times p. 13, Nov 10, 1915

DE PORTO-RICHE, GEORGES

Amoureuse
    Productions:
        (Off Off Broadway) Opened January 16, 1976.
    No Reviews.

Lover's Luck
    Productions:
        Tr., Ralph Roeder. Opened Aug 30, 1916 in repertory.
    Reviews:
        Dramatic Mirror 76:7, Oct 7, 1916
        New York Times p. 9, Oct 3, 1916
                        II, p. 6, Oct 8, 1916

DEVAL, JACQUES

Another Love
    Productions:
        Translated and adapted by George Oppenheimer. Opened
        March 19, 1934 for 16 performances.
    Reviews:
        New York Times p. 26, Mar 20, 1934

Bathsheba
    Productions:
        Opened March 26, 1947 for 29 performances.
    Reviews:
        Catholic World 165:168, May 1947
        Commonweal 45:647, Apr 11, 1947
        New Republic 116:42, Apr 7, 1947
        New York Theatre Critics' Reviews 1947:415
        New York Times p. 40, Mar 27, 1947
        New Yorker 23:50, Apr 5, 1947
        Newsweek 29:80, Apr 7, 1947
        Time 49:77, Apr 7, 1947

Boudoir
    Productions:
        Opened February 7, 1941 for 11 performances.
    Reviews:
        New York Theatre Critics' Reviews 1941:388
        New York Times p. 18, Feb 8, 1941

*Errand for Bernice
    Reviews:
        Theatre Arts 29:14, Jan 1945

*Et l'Enfer Isabelle
Reviews:
New York Times p. 13, Sep 21, 1963

Her Cardboard Lover
Productions:
Adapted by Valerie Wyngate and P. G. Wodehouse. Opened
March 21, 1927 for 100 performances.
Reviews:
Bookman 65:447, Jun 1927
Dial 82:535, Jun 1927
Life (NY) 89:31, Apr 7, 1927
Nation 124:380, Apr 6, 1927
New Republic 50:194-5, Apr 6, 1927
New York Times p. 30, Mar 22, 1927
Vogue 69:84, May 15, 1927

Lorelei
Productions:
Opened November 29, 1938 for 7 performances.
Reviews:
Catholic World 148:472, Jan 1939
Nation 147:637, Dec 10, 1938
Newsweek 12:24, Dec 12, 1938
New York Times p. 21, Nov 30, 1938
Theatre Arts 23:95-6, Feb 1939

Mademoiselle
Productions:
Adapted by Grace George. Opened October 18, 1932 for
103 performances.
Reviews:
Arts and Decoration 38:57, Dec 1932
Catholic World 136:336-7, Dec 1932
Commonweal 17:49, Nov 9, 1932
Nation 135:465, Nov 9, 1932
New Outlook 161:47, Dec 1932
New Republic 73:128-9, Dec 14, 1932
New York Times p. 22, Oct 19, 1932
Stage 10:28-9, Dec 1932
Theatre Arts 17:17-18, Jan 1933
Vanity Fair 39:53, Jan 1933

Oh, Brother!
Productions:
Opened January 19, 1945 for 23 performances.
Reviews:
New York Theatre Critics' Reviews 1945:195
New York Times p. 26, Jun 20, 1945
New Yorker 21:32, Jun 30, 1945

Tonight in Samarkand (with Lorenzo Semple, Jr.)
Productions:

Opened February 16, 1955 for 29 performances.
Reviews:
    America 92:657, Mar 19, 1955
    Catholic World 181:66-7, Apr 1955
    Nation 180:226, Mar 12, 1955
    New York Theatre Critics' Reviews 1955:365
    New York Times p. 22, Feb 17, 1955
    New Yorker 31:50, Feb 26, 1955
    Newsweek 45:58, Feb 28, 1955
    Saturday Review 38:26, Mar 5, 1955
    Theatre Arts 39:15+, May 1955
    Time 65:60, Feb 28, 1955

Tovarich
    Productions:
        English version by Robert E. Sherwood. Opened October 15, 1936 for 356 performances.
        Adapted by Robert E. Sherwood. Opened May 14, 1952 for 15 performances.
        (Off Off Broadway) Opened February 1975.
    Reviews:
        Catholic World 144:335-6, Dec 1936
                      175:309, Jul 1952
        Commonweal 25:20, Oct 30, 1936
                56:224, Jun 6, 1952
        Life 3:22-3, Dec 20, 1937
        Literary Digest 122:22, Oct 31, 1936
        Nation 143:530, Oct 31, 1936
        New Republic 89:21, November 4, 1936
        New York Theatre Critics' Reviews 1952:281
        New York Times p. 19, Apr 25, 1935
                      IX, p. 1, May 19, 1935
                      p. 35, Sep 29, 1936
                      IX, p. 2, Oct 4, 1936
                      X, p. 1, Oct 15, 1936
                      p. 31, Oct 16, 1936
                      X, p. 1, Oct 25, 1936
                      X, p. 2, Apr 25, 1937
                      p. 39, May 15, 1952
        Newsweek 8:40, Oct 24, 1936
               10:30, Dec 20, 1937
        Saturday Review 35:26, May 31, 1952
        Theatre Arts 19:481, Jul 1935
                 20:919-23, Dec 1936
                 36:82, Jul 1952
        Time 28:47, Oct 26, 1936
             31:29, Jan 3, 1938

A Weak Woman
    Productions:
        Adapted by Ernest Boyd. Opened January 26, 1926 for 49 performances.

Reviews:
    Bookman 63:216-17, Apr 1926
    New York Times p. 16, Jan 27, 1926

DRINKWATER, JOHN

Abraham Lincoln
    Productions:
    Opened December 15, 1919 for 193 performances.
    Opened October 21, 1929 for eight performances.
    Reviews:
    Arts and Decoration 12:264, Feb 1920
    Bookman 50:551-5, Feb 1920
    Collier's 65:13+, Feb 7, 1920
    Current Opinion 67:93-7, Aug 1919
        68:351-2, Mar 1920
    Dramatist 10:974-5, Oct 1919
    Everybody's 42:66-7, Apr 1920
    Hearst 37:38-9+, Mar 1920
    Independent 101:86, Jan 17, 1920
        101:170-1, Jan 31, 1920
    Life 20:77-8+, Apr 8, 1946
    Life (NY) 74:1070-1, Dec 25, 1919
    Literary Digest 59:29-30, Dec 28, 1918
        61:28-9, Jun 28, 1919
        64:30-2, Jan 3, 1920
        64:33-4, Mar 6, 1920
    Living Age 300:623-6, Mar 8, 1919
        304:790-2, Mar 27, 1920
        310:493-4, Aug 20, 1921
    Nation 109:292-3, Aug 30, 1919
        110:858-9, Jan 3, 1920
    New Republic 20:268-9, Oct 1, 1919
        21:148, Dec 31, 1919
    New York Dramatic Mirror 81:2023, Jan 1, 1920
    New York Times IV, p. 2, Jul 6, 1919
        p. 18, Dec 16, 1919
        VIII, p. 21, Dec 21, 1919
        IX, p. 1, Apr 28, 1940
        X, p. 1, May 5, 1940
    North American 210:824-36, Dec 1919
    Outlook 123:537-8, Dec 24, 1919
    Review 1:710-11, Dec 27, 1919
    Theatre Magazine 31:89+, Feb 1920
    Time 47:50, Feb 25, 1946
    Touchstone 6:269-75, Feb 1920

Bird in Hand
    Productions:
    Opened April 4, 1929 for 500 performances.
    Opened November 10, 1930 for 65 performances.
    Opened October 19, 1942 for eight performances.

Reviews:
American Mercury 17:249, Jun 1929
Catholic World 129:203-4, May 1929
Commonweal 10:50, May 15, 1929
Life (NY) 93:20, Apr 26, 1929
Nation 128:514, Apr 24, 1929
155:458, Oct 31, 1942
New York Theatre Critics' Reviews 1942:200
New York Times p. 28, Apr 5, 1929
X, p. 1, Apr 14, 1929
p. 6, Nov 11, 1930
p. 24, Oct 20, 1942
'Outlook 151:670, Apr 24, 1929
Theatre Magazine 50:43, Aug 1929
Vogue 73:104, Jun 8, 1929

A Man's House
Productions:
(Off Broadway) April 1 through April 18, 1943.
Reviews:
Commonweal 37:616, Apr 9, 1943
New York Times p. 10, Apr 3, 1943
II, p. 2, Apr 4, 1943

Mary Stuart
Productions:
Opened March 21, 1921 for 40 performances.
Reviews:
Arts and Decoration 15:23, May 1921
Bookman 53:277-8, May 1921
Current Opinion 70:631-40, May 1921
Drama 11:266-7, 297, May 1921
11:265-6, May 1921
Dramatic Mirror 83:527, Mar 26, 1921
Independent 105:329, Apr 2, 1921
Life (NY) 77:500, Apr 7, 1921
Nation 112:564-6, Apr 13, 1921
New Republic 26:162, Apr 6, 1921
New York Clipper 69:23, Mar 30, 1921
New York Times p. 15, Mar 22, 1921
Outlook 128:12-13, May 4, 1921
Players Magazine 25:119, Feb 1949
Review 4:322-4, Apr 6, 1921
Saturday Review 134:502, Oct 7, 1921
Theatre Magazine 33:318, 320, May 1921
33:401, 416, Jun 1921
Weekly Review 4:323-4, Apr 6, 1921
Yale Review 11:425-6, Jan 1922

Robert E. Lee
Productions:
Opened November 20, 1923 for 15 performances.

Reviews:
   American Mercury 1:118, Jan 1924
   Current Opinion 75:317-31, Sep 1923
   Dial 76:612, Dec 1923
   Life (NY) 82:18, Dec 13, 1923
   Literary Digest 78:30-1, Sep 8, 1923
                79:30-1, Dec 1, 1923
   New York Times III, p. 15, Aug 16, 1923
   Theatre Magazine 38:12, Sep 1923
                39:5+, Jan 1924

DUERRENMATT, FRIEDRICH

*An Angel Comes to Babylon
  Reviews:
   New York Times p. 15, Sep 29, 1962

Die Ehe des Herrn Mississippi (see also The Marriage of Mr.
     Mississippi)
  Productions:
   (Off Broadway) Opened November 19, 1969 for 6 performances.
  Reviews:
   New York Times p. 60, Nov 20, 1969

Fools Are Passing Through
  Productions:
   (Off Broadway) Season of 1957-1958.
  Reviews:
   New York Times p. 24, Apr 3, 1958

*Frank V
  Reviews:
   Nation 196:57, Jan 19, 1963
   New Yorker 38:103, Jan 12, 1963

The Jackass
  Productions:
   Adapted from a radio script. (Off Broadway) Season of
    1959-1960.
  Reviews:
   New York Times p. 39, Mar 24, 1960
                p. 20, Mar 25, 1960

The Marriage of Mr. Mississippi (see also Die Ehe des Herrn
     Mississippi)
  Productions:
   (Off Off Broadway) Opened February 1, 1974.
  Reviews:
   New York Times p. 27, Feb 20, 1974

The Physicists
  Productions:
    Adapted by James Kirkup. Opened October 14, 1964 for 55
      performances.
    (Off Off Broadway) Opened March 1975.
  Reviews:
    Christian Century 80:301-2, Mar 6, 1963
    Commonweal 81:237-8, Nov 13, 1964
    Life 57:89-90, Nov 20, 1964
    Nation 196:380, May 4, 1963
         199:340, Nov 9, 1964
    New York Theatre Critics' Reviews 1964:193
    New York Times p. 52, Oct 14, 1964
                  II, p. 1, Oct 25, 1964
                     p. 36, Feb 14, 1977
    Newsweek 64:102, Oct 26, 1964
    Saturday Review 47:31, Oct 31, 1964
    Time 84:67, Oct 23, 1964
    Vogue 144:152, Dec 1964

Play Strindberg
  Productions:
    Based on Strindberg's The Dance of Death. Translated by
      James Kirkup. (Off Broadway) Opened June 3, 1971
      for 65 performances.
  Reviews:
    Nation 213:380, Oct 18, 1971
    New York Theatre Critics' Reviews 1971:221
    New York Times p. 20, Jun 4, 1971
                  II, p. 1, Jun 13, 1971
    New Yorker 47:84, Jun 12, 1971

*Portrait of a Planet
  Reviews:
    New Republic 168:23, Mar 17, 1973

Romulus
  Productions:
    Adapted by Gore Vidal. Opened January 10, 1962 for 69
      performances.
  Reviews:
    America 106:772-3, Mar 10, 1962
    Christian Century 79:233, Feb 21, 1962
    Nation 194:106-7, Feb 3, 1962
    National Review 12:173-4, Mar 13, 1962
    New Republic 146:20+, Jan 29, 1962
    New York Theatre Critics' Reviews 1962:380
    New York Times p. 24, Aug 25, 1960
                  p. 27, Jan 11, 1962
                  p. 25, Mar 2, 1962
                  p. 29, Apr 30, 1964
    New Yorker 37:63, Jan 20, 1962
    Newsweek 59:50, Jan 22, 1962

Saturday Review 45:29, Jan 27, 1962
Theatre Arts 46:62-3, Mar 1962
Time 79:68+, Jan 19, 1962

The Visit
Productions:
Adapted by Maurice Valency. Opened May 5, 1958 for 189
performances.
Adapted by Maurice Valency. Opened March 8, 1960 for 16
performances.
(Off Off Broadway) Adapted by Maurice Valency. Opened
April 19, 1968 for 9 performances.
Opened November 25, 1973 for 32 performances.
Reviews:
America 99:299, May 31, 1958
Catholic World 187:312, Jul 1958
Christian Century 75:668-9, Jun 4, 1958
Commonweal 68:377-9, Jul 11, 1958
Life 44:91-4, Jun 2, 1958
Nation 186:455-6, May 17, 1958
217:668, Dec 17, 1973
New Republic 170:33, Jan 5, 1974
New York Theatre Critics' Reviews 1958:294
1973:163
New York Times p. 40, May 6, 1958
II, p. 1, May 18, 1958
II, p. 1, Sep 7, 1958
p. 38, Mar 9, 1960
p. 13, Jun 25, 1960
p. 41, Sep 13, 1967
p. 59, May 13, 1973
p. 43, Nov 26, 1973
II, p. 1, Dec 2, 1973
p. 36, Dec 26, 1973
New Yorker 34:87, May 17, 1958
36:118+, Mar 19, 1960
49:111, Dec 10, 1973
Reporter 18:27, Jun 12, 1958
Saturday Review 41:30-1, May 24, 1958
Theatre Arts 42:17+, May 1958
Time 71:83, May 19, 1958
102:86+, Dec 10, 1973

DUMAS, ALEXANDRE, fils

Camille
Productions:
Opened December 5, 1910 in repertory.
Opened June 19, 1911 in repertory.
Opened December 4, 1916 in repertory.
Opened December 24, 1917 for 56 performances.

Translated by Henriette Metcalf. Opened January 26, 1931
for 57 performances.
New version by Edna and Delos Chappell and Robert Edmund
Jones. Opened November 1, 1932 for 15 performances.
Translated by Henriette Metcalf. Opened December 4, 1935
in repertory for 7 performances.
(Off Off Broadway) Opened May 2, 1973.
(Off Broadway) Adapted by Charles Ludlam. Opened May 13,
1974 for 113 performances.
Reviews:
Book News 36:255-6, Mar 1918
Catholic World 133:83-4, Apr 1931
Collier's 47:21, Aug 21, 1911
Commonweal 13:637-8, Apr 8, 1931
Dramatic Mirror 78:5, Jan 5, 1918
Green Book 19:401-2+, Mar 1918
Green Book Album 5:614-21, Mar 1911
Life 1:64, Nov 23, 1936
Modern Language Notes 49:472-6, Nov 1934
Nation 135:512-13, Nov 23, 1932
New Outlook 161:47, Dec 1932
New Republic 66:19, Feb 18, 1931
              73:214-15, Jan 4, 1933
New York Times IV, p. 5, Dec 23, 1917
               p. 13, Dec 25, 1917
               VIII, p. 2, Jan 25, 1931
               p. 21, Jan 27, 1931
               VIII, p. 1, Feb 15, 1931
               p. 23, Oct 28, 1932
               p. 23, Nov 2, 1932
               p. 21, Jul 31, 1935
               p. 33, Sep 19, 1956
               p. 24, May 4, 1973
               p. 31, May 14, 1974
               II, p. 1, Jul 14, 1974
Outlook 157:234, Feb 11, 1931
Theatre Arts 17:15-16, Jan 1933
Theatre Magazine 6:64+, Mar 1906
                 27:85, Feb 1918
                 53:26, Apr 1931
Vogue 77:108+, Mar 15, 1931
      80:75, Dec 15, 1932

La Dame aux Camélias (see Camille)

Kean (see The Royal Box)

The Lady of the Camellias (see Camille)

The Royal Box
    Productions:
        Adapted by Charles Coghlan from Kean. Opened November
        20, 1928 for 39 performances.

Reviews:
    Dramatic Mirror 69:7, Mar 26, 1913
    Life (NY) 92:13, Dec 14, 1928
    New York Times p. 32, Nov 21, 1928

The Three Guardsmen
    Productions:
    (Off Broadway) Opened February 1936.
    Reviews:
    New York Times p. 21, Feb 17, 1936

DUNSANY, LORD (E. J. M. D. PLUNKETT)

The Gods of the Mountains
    In repertory. November 1916 and January 1919.
    Reviews:
    Bookman 44:471+, Jan 1917
    Dramatic Mirror 76:7, Dec 9, 1916
                    80:231, Feb 15, 1919
    Forum 51:782-90, May 1914
    New York Times p. 11, Nov 28, 1916
                    II, p. 6, Dec 3, 1916
                    IV, p. 2, Jan 26, 1919
                    p. 36, May 25, 1950
    North American Review 205:134, Jan 1917

The Golden Doom
    In repertory. November 1916 and January 1919.
    Reviews:
    Bookman 44:476, Jan 1917
    Dramatic Mirror 80:231, Feb 15, 1919
    New York Times p. 9, Dec 5, 1916

If
    Productions:
    Opened October 25, 1927 for 27 performances.
    Reviews:
    Life (NY) 90:25, Nov 17, 1925
    New York Times p. 26, Oct 26, 1927
                    IX, p. 1, Oct 30, 1927
    Saturday Review 4:320, Nov 19, 1927
    Theatre Magazine 47:40, Jan 1928

King Argimenes
    In repertory. November 1916 and January 1919.
    Reviews:
    Bookman 44:473-4, Jan 1917
    Dramatic Mirror 80:231, Feb 15, 1919
    New York Times p. 9, Dec 19, 1916

The Laughter of the Gods
    In repertory. January 15, 1919.

Reviews:
Dramatic Mirror 80:160, Feb 1, 1919
Nation 108:132, Jan 25, 1919
New York Dramatic News 65:8, Jan 25, 1919
New York Times p. 11, Jan 16, 1919
                    IV, p. 2, Jan 26, 1919

A Night at an Inn
Productions:
Opened April 15, 1918 for 16 performances.
Opened May 9, 1930 for one performance.
Reviews:
Bookman 44:470+, Jan 1917
Current Opinion 60:411, Jun 1916
                    63:91-4, Aug 1917
Dramatic Mirror 78:584, Apr 27, 1918
                    83:1073, Jun 25, 1921
Independent 106:17, Jul 23, 1921
New York Times p. 11, Apr 16, 1913
Theatre Magazine 24:18+, Jul 1916

The Queen's Enemies
Productions:
Opened December 18, 1916 in repertory.
Reviews:
Bookman 44:471+, Jan 1917
Dramatic Mirror 76:7, Nov 25, 1916
New York Times p. 9, Nov 15, 1916
                    II, p. 6, Nov 19, 1916

The Tents of the Arabs
In repertory. January 15, 1919.
Reviews:
Dramatic Mirror 80:374, Mar 15, 1919
Life (NY) 73:416, Mar 13, 1919
New York Times p. 9, Mar 4, 1919
Theatre Magazine 29:207-8, Apr 1919

DURRENMATT, FRIEDRICH (see Duerrenmatt, Friedrich)

DYER, CHARLES

Rattle of a Simple Man
Productions:
Opened April 17, 1963 for 94 performances.
Reviews:
New York Theatre Critics' Reviews 1963:340
New York Times p. 39, Apr 18, 1963
New Yorker 39:82, Apr 27, 1963
Saturday Review 46:23, May 4, 1963
Theatre Arts 47:10-11, Jun 1963
Time 81:58, Apr 26, 1963

Staircase
  Productions:
    Opened January 10, 1968 for 61 performances.
    (Off Off Broadway) Opened April 3, 1975.
  Reviews:
    Commonweal 87:592, Feb 16, 1968
    Nation 206:156, Jan 29, 1968
    New York Theatre Critics' Reviews 1968:390
    New York Times p. 41, Jan 11, 1968
                  II, p. 3, Jan 21, 1968
    New Yorker 43:82, Jan 20, 1968
    Newsweek 71:96, Jan 22, 1968
    Saturday Review 51:41, Jan 27, 1968
    Time 91:66, Jan 19, 1968
    Vogue 151:104, Mar 1, 1968

ECHEGARY, JOSE

Maria Rosa
  Productions:
    Translated by Angel Guimera. English version by Walter
        Gillpatrick and Guido Marburg. Opened January 19, 1914
        for 48 performances.
  Reviews:
    Bookman 39:61-2, Mar 1914
    Dramatic Mirror 71:7, Jan 21, 1914
    Green Book 11:695, Apr 1914
    Harper's Weekly 58:27, Feb 14, 1914
    Life (NY) 63:232, Feb 5, 1914
    Munsey 51:580-83, Apr 1914
    New York Times p. 9, Jan 20, 1914
    Theatre Magazine 19:114-5, Mar 1914

ELIOT, T. S.

The Cocktail Party
  Productions:
    Opened January 21, 1950 for 409 performances.
    Opened October 7, 1968 for 44 performances (A. P. A.
        Phoenix).
    (Off Off Broadway) Opened October 1974.
    (Off Off Broadway) Opened November 21, 1975.
  Reviews:
    America 119:445-7, Nov 9, 1968
    American Mercury 70:557-8, May 1950
    Catholic World 170:466, Mar 1950
                  171:469-70, Sep 1950
    Christian Science Monitor Magazine p. 6, May 27, 1950
    Commonweal 51:463, Feb 3, 1950
                51:507-8, Feb 17, 1950
    Fortnightly 174 (ns 168):391-8, Dec 1950

Life 27:16+, Sep 26, 1949
Nation 170:94-5, Jan 28, 1950
New Republic 122:30, Feb 13, 1950
New York Theatre Critics' Reviews 1950:376
                                       1968:219
New York Times p. 28, Aug 23, 1949
                II, p. 2, Sep 11, 1949
                p. 17, Jan 23, 1950
                II, p. 1, Jan 29, 1950
                VI, p. 14, Jan 29, 1950
                II, p. 1, Apr 16, 1950
                p. 33, May 4, 1950
                II, p. 2, May 7, 1950
                II, p. 3, May 21, 1950
                II, p. 3, Dec 17, 1950
                p. 42, Oct 8, 1968
                II, p. 1, Oct 20, 1968
New Yorker 25:47, Jan 28, 1950
            26:26-9, Apr 1, 1950
            44:159, Oct 19, 1968
Newsweek 35:66, Jan 30, 1950
Saturday Review 33:28-30, Feb 4, 1950
                33:48, Feb 11, 1950
School and Society 72:180-2, Sep 16, 1950
Theatre Arts 34:8, May 1950
           34:10, Apr 1950
Time 54:58, Sep 5, 1949
      55:37, Jan 30, 1950
      92:72+, Oct 18, 1968

The Confidential Clerk

Productions:
    Opened February 11, 1954 to 117 performances.
Reviews:
    America 90:608+, Mar 6, 1954
    Catholic World 179:68-9, Apr 1954
    Commentary 17:367-72, Apr 1954
    Commonweal 59:475-6, Feb 12, 1954
                    59:599, Mar 19, 1954
    Life 36:56-8+, Feb 1, 1954
    Nation 178:184+, Feb 27, 1954
    New Republic 129:17-18, Sep 21, 1953
                    130:22, Feb 22, 1954
                    131:124-5, Nov 22, 1954
    New York Theatre Critics'Reviews 1954:370
    New York Times p. 20, Dec 22, 1952
                    p. 22, Aug 26, 1953
                    p. 21, Aug 27, 1953
                    II, p. 2, Aug 30, 1953
                    II, p. 3, Oct 11, 1953
                    II, p. 1, Feb 7, 1954
                    p. 22, Feb 12, 1954
                    II, p. 1, Feb 21, 1954

New York Times Magazine pp. 36-7, Sep 6, 1953
                      p. 16, Feb 21, 1954
New Yorker 29:110-11, Oct 10, 1953
           30:62+, Feb 20, 1954
Newsweek 43:94, Feb 22, 1954
Saturday Review 36:26-8, Aug 29, 1953
                36:44-6, Sep 12, 1953
                37:26-8, Feb 27, 1954
Theatre Arts 37:81-2, Nov 1953
             38:22-3, Apr 1954
             38:22-5, May 1954
Time 63:80+, Feb 22, 1954
Vogue 123:130-1, Mar 1, 1954

*The Elder Statesman
  Reviews:
    Life 45:108, Nov 24, 1958
    New York Times p. 21, Aug 20, 1958
                   p. 35, Aug 26, 1958
                   II, p. 3, Aug 31, 1958
    New Yorker 34:168, Nov 1, 1958
    Saturday Review 41:30-1, Sep 13, 1958
    Time 72:43+, Sep 8, 1958

The Family Reunion
  Productions:
    (Off Broadway) Opened December, 1947 (On Stage).
    (Off Broadway) Opened October 1950 in repertory.
    Opened October 20, 1958 for 20 performances.
    (Off Broadway) Opened November 20, 1967 for 3 performances (Equity Theatre).
  Reviews:
    America 100:174, Nov 8, 1958
    Catholic World 188:331, Jan 1959
    Christian Century 75:1380-2, Nov 26, 1958
    Commonweal 69:232-4, Nov 28, 1958
    Nation 148:676, Jun 10, 1939
           187:347, Nov 8, 1958
    New Republic 98:384-5, May 3, 1939
    New York Theatre Critics' Reviews 1958:255
    New York Times X, p. 1, Apr 9, 1939
                   p. 9, Nov 29, 1947
                   p. 13, Jun 9, 1956
                   p. 39, Oct 21, 1958
                   II, p. 1, Oct 26, 1958
                   p. 26, Dec 10, 1960
    New Yorker 34:99-101, Nov 1, 1958
    One Act Play Magazine 3:82, Jan 1940
    Reporter 19:35, Nov 27, 1958
    Saturday Review 19:12, Apr 1, 1939
                    41:25, Nov 8, 1958
    Theatre Arts 41:23-4, May 1957
                 42:64, Dec 1958

Time 72:48, Nov 3, 1958
Yale Review 28:836-8, Summer, 1939

Murder in the Cathedral
Productions:
Opened March 20, 1936 for 38 performances.
Opened February 16, 1938 for 21 performances.
(Off Broadway) Opened February 1959 in repertory.
(Off Off Broadway) Opened January 14, 1977.
Reviews:
Catholic World 143:209-11, May 1936
Christian Century 52:1636, Dec 18, 1935
Commonweal 23:636, Apr 3, 1936
              27:524, Mar 4, 1938
Forum 95:346-7, Jun 1936
Life 19:123-7, Oct 1, 1945
Nation 141:417, Oct 9, 1935
       142:459-60, Apr 8, 1936
New Republic 85:290, Jan 15, 1936
             86:253, Apr 8, 1936
             94:101, Mar 2, 1938
New York Times p. 12, Nov 2, 1935
               IX, p. 1, Feb 16, 1936
               p. 13, Mar 21, 1936
               IX, p. 1, Mar 29, 1936
               p. 16, Feb 17, 1938
               XI, p. 1, Feb 20, 1938
               II, p. 1, Apr 26, 1953
               p. 12, Mar 22, 1958
               p. 38, Jun 21, 1966
New Yorker 29:87, May 2, 1953
Newsweek 7:26, Mar 28, 1936
Saturday Review 12:10-11, Oct 12, 1935
                49:41, Jul 9, 1966
Stage 13:97, Nov 1935
Theatre Arts 20:25-6, Jan 1936
             20:341-3, May 1936
             22:254-5, Apr 1938
Time 31:34, Feb 28, 1938
Yale Review 25:427-9, Winter 1936

Sweeney Agonistes
Productions:
(Off Broadway) Opened March 1952.
Reviews:
New Republic 127:17-18, Dec 8, 1952
Theatre Arts 37:12-13+, Feb 1953
Time 60:69, Dec 22, 1952

ENGLAND, BARRY

Conduct Unbecoming
  Productions:
    Opened October 12, 1970 for 144 performances.
  Reviews:
    America 124:47, Jan 16, 1971
    Nation 211:444, Nov 2, 1970
    National Review 23:324, Mar 23, 1971
    New Republic 163:20+, Nov 7, 1970
    New York Times Critics' Reviews 1970:187
    New York Times p. 14, Jul 26, 1969
                    p. 50, Oct 13, 1970
                    II, p. 6, Oct 25, 1970
                    p. 13, Feb 13, 1971
    New Yorker 46:129, Oct 24, 1970
    Newsweek 76:86, Oct 26, 1970
    Saturday Review 53:12, Oct 31, 1970
    Time 96:93-4, Oct 26, 1970

ERVINE, ST. JOHN

Boyd's Daughter
  Productions:
    Opened October 11, 1940 for three performances.
  Reviews:
    American Mercury 51:485-6, Dec 1940
    New York Theatre Critics' Reviews 1940:256
    New York Times p. 20, Oct 12, 1940
    Time 36:71, Oct 21, 1940

The First Mrs. Fraser
  Productions:
    Opened December 28, 1929 for 352 performances.
    Opened November 5, 1947 for 38 performances.
  Reviews:
    American Mercury 19:245-7, Feb 1930
    Commonweal 120:593, Feb 1930
                166:266, Dec 1947
    Life (NY) 95:20, Jan 17, 1930
              95:18, Jun 6, 1930
    Nation 165:603, Nov 29, 1947
    New Republic 117:35, Nov 24, 1947
    New York Theatre Critics' Reviews 1947:267
    New York Times II, p. 1, Nov 2, 1947
                    p. 36, Nov 6, 1947
    New Yorker 23:54, Nov 15, 1947
    Newsweek 30:84, Nov 17, 1947
    Saturday Review 148:13, Jul 6, 1929
    School and Society 66:422, Nov 29, 1947
    Theatre Arts 14:114-15, Feb 1930
                 14:200, Mar 1930

Theatre Magazine 51:8, Mar 1930
                 52:32+, Jul 1930
Time 50:87, Nov 17, 1947
Vogue 75:118, Feb 15, 1930

Jane Clegg

Productions:
     Opened February 23, 1920 for 112 performances.
Reviews:
     Dial 60:472, May 11, 1916
     Dramatic Mirror 76:15, Aug 5, 1916
                    82:363, Feb 28, 1920
     Forum 63:489, Apr-May 1920
     Independent 101:382, Mar 13, 1920
     Life (NY) 75:462, Mar 11, 1920
     Nation 101:755-6, Dec 23, 1915
              110:376-7, Mar 20, 1920
     New Republic 22:61, Mar 10, 1920
     New York Clipper 68:19, Mar 3, 1920
     New York Times p. 14, Feb 25, 1920
                    V, p. 5, Feb 29, 1920
                    V, p. 6, Mar 28, 1920
     Outlook 126:182, Sep 29, 1920
     Theatre Magazine 31:265+, Apr 1920
     Weekly Review 2:289, Mar 20, 1920

John Ferguson

Productions:
     Opened May 13, 1919 for 177 performances.
     Opened July 10, 1933 for 54 performances.
Reviews:
     Bookman 53:527+, Aug 1921
     Catholic World 137:593-4, Aug 1933
     Commonweal 18:309, Jul 21, 1933
     Current Opinion 67:24-8, Jul 1919
     Dial 60:472, May 11, 1916
     Drama 23:466-7, Aug 1916
     Forum 62:375-6, Sep 1919
     Life (NY) 73:948, May 29, 1919
     Nation 102:202, Feb 17, 1916
              108:842-3, May 24, 1919
     New York Times p. 18, May 13, 1919
                   IV, p. 2, May 18, 1919
                   p. 15, Jul 11, 1933
     Touchstone 5:304-8, Jul 1919
     Theatre Magazine 30:13+, Jul 1919
     Weekly Review 1:87, Jun 7, 1919

The Magnanimous Lover

Productions:
     Opened February 4, 1913 in repertory.
Reviews:
     Dramatic Mirror 69:7, Feb 12, 1913

Everybody's Magazine 28:679, May 1913
Munsey 49:149-50, Apr 1913

Mary, Mary, Quite Contrary
Productions:
Opened September 11, 1923 for 86 performances.
Reviews:
Canadian Magazine 61:428-9, Sep 1923
Current Opinion 75:573-86, Nov 1923
Dramatist 14:1181-2, Oct 1923
Nation 117:331, Sep 26, 1923
New York Times p. 14, Sep 12, 1923
VII, p. 1, Sep 16, 1923
Overland Monthly 85:115, Apr 1927
Theatre Magazine 38:17+, Nov 1923

Mixed Marriage
Productions:
Opened Feburary 4, 1913 in repertory.
Opened December 14, 1920 for 124 performances.
Reviews:
Bookman 52:564, Feb 1921
Collier's 67:19, Jan 15, 1921
Dramatic Mirror 66:6, Dec 20, 1911
p. 1192, Dec 18, 1920
Everybody's Magazine 28:678-9, May 1913
Life (NY) 77:24, Jan 6, 1921
Nation 112:21, Jan 5, 1921
New York Clipper 68:30, Dec 29, 1930
New York Times p. 18, Dec 15, 1920
Outlook 127:49-50, Jan 12, 1921
Theatre Magazine 33:107, Feb 1921
Touchstone 8:355-60, Feb 1921
Weekly Review 3:658-9, Dec 29, 1920
4:55, Jan 19, 1921

*Private Enterprise
Reviews:
Theatre Arts 32:33-4, Feb 1948

The Wonderful Visit (with H. G. Wells)
Productions:
Opened February 12, 1924 for 56 performances.
Reviews:
American Mercury 1:502-3, Apr 1924
Dramatist 15:1207-8, Apr 1924
Living Age 308:789-92, Mar 26, 1921
New York Times p. 17, Feb 13, 1924
Theatre Magazine 39:19, May 1924

FABBRI, DIEGO

Between Two Thieves
    Productions:
        (Off Broadway) Season of 1959-1960.
    Reviews:
        America 102:718+, Mar 12, 1960
        New York Times p. 23, Feb 12, 1960

*La Bugiarda
    Reviews:
        New York Times p. 50, Mar 20, 1972

The Liar
    Productions:
        (Off Off Broadway) Opened September-October 1975.
    No Reviews.

FEYDEAU, GEORGES

A Bird in the Hand
    Productions:
        (Off Off Broadway) Translated and adapted by Edward Stern
            and Ann Ward Stern. Opened October 19, 1976.
    Reviews:
        New York Times p. 58, Oct 28, 1976

Breakfast in Bed
    Productions:
        Adapted by Willard Mack and Howard Booth. Opened
            February 3, 1920 for 75 performances.
    Reviews:
        Dramatic Mirror 82:258, Feb 14, 1920
        Dramatist 12:1043, Jan 1921
        New York Clipper 68:21, Feb 11, 1920
        New York Times p. 12, Feb 4, 1920

Chemin de Fer
    Productions:
        Adapted by Suzanne Grossman and Paxton Whitehead. Opened
            November 26, 1973 for 42 performances.
    Reviews:
        Nation 217:668-9, Dec 17, 1973
        New York Theatre Critics' Reviews 1973:160
        New York Times p. 48, Nov 27, 1973
                        II, p. 1, Dec 2, 1973
        New Yorker 49:111, Dec 10, 1973
        Time 102:96, Dec 17, 1973

*The Chemmy Circle
 Reviews:
    New York Times p. 17, Aug 10, 1968
    Saturday Review 51:49, Aug 24, 1968

Dear Departed Mother-in-Law (see Feu la Mère de Madame)

Le Dindon
 Productions:
    Opened March 7, 1961 in repertory for 6 performances.
 Reviews:
    New York Times p. 38, Mar 8, 1961
    New Yorker 37:124+, Mar 18, 1961

Feu la Mère de Madame (Dear Departed Mother-in-Law)
 Productions:
    Opened January 30, 1957 in repertory.
 Reviews:
    New York Theatre Critics' Reviews 1957:351
    New York Times p. 31, Feb 12, 1957
    Theatre Arts 41:82, Apr 1957

Un Fil a la Patte
 Productions:
    Opened February 17, 1966 in repertory for 8 performances.
 Reviews:
    New York Times p. 25, Feb 18, 1966

A Flea in Her Ear
 Productions:
    Translated by Barnett Shaw. Opened October 3, 1969 in
       repertory for 11 performances.
    (Off Off Broadway) Opened November 24, 1976.
 Reviews:
    Nation 209:451, Oct 27, 1969
    New Republic 161:33, Nov 1, 1969
    New York Theatre Critics' Reviews 1969:249
    New York Times II, p. 5, Oct 29, 1967
                  p. 59, Oct 30, 1967
                  p. 25, Oct 4, 1969
                  II, p. 9, Oct 12, 1969
                  p. 61, Dec 19, 1976
    New Yorker 45:86+, Oct 11, 1969
    Newsweek 74:125, Oct 13, 1969

Hotel Paradiso (with Maurice Desvallières)
 Productions:
    Adapted by Peter Glenville. Opened April 11, 1957 for
       108 performances.
    (Off Broadway) Season of 1959-1960.
    (Off Off Broadway) Opened April 1975.

Reviews:
Catholic World 185:228, Jun 1957
Commonweal 66:154, May 10, 1957
Life 42:122-4, May 13, 1957
Nation 184:377, Apr 27, 1957
New York Theatre Critics' Reviews 1957:298
New York Times p. 34, May 3, 1956
               p. 22, Apr 12, 1957
               II, p. 1, Apr 21, 1957
New Yorker 33:81, Apr 20, 1957
Newsweek 49:69, Apr 22, 1957
Saturday Review 39:30, Oct 13, 1956
               40:26, Apr 6, 1957
Theatre Arts 41:17, Jun 1957
Time 69:90, Apr 22, 1957
Vogue 129:85, Apr 15, 1957

Keep Your Eyes on Emily (see Occupe-toi d'Amélie)

The Lady from Lobster Square
Productions:
Opened April 4, 1910 for 24 performances.
Reviews:
Dramatic Mirror 63:5, Apr 16, 1910
Life (NY) 55:681, Apr 14, 1910

Lady from Maxim's
Productions:
(Off Off Broadway) Adapted by Jon Carlson and Gene Feist.
Season of 1969-1970.
Reviews:
New York Times p. 41, Jun 1, 1970

Le Main Passe (see The Chemmy Circle)

Occupe-toi d'Amélie (Keep Your Eyes on Emily) (see also Noel
Coward's Look after Lulu)
Productions:
Opened November 24, 1952 for four performances.
Reviews:
Nation 175:562, Dec 13, 1952
New York Theatre Critics' Reviews 1952:183
New York Times p. 35, Nov 25, 1952
Saturday Review 35:26, Dec 13, 1952

*Ruling the Roost
Reviews:
New York Times p. 45, Sep 5, 1972

There's One in Every Marriage
Productions:
Adapted by Suzanne Grossman and Paxton Whitehead. Opened
January 3, 1972 for 16 performances.

Reviews:
America 126:75, Jan 22, 1972
Nation 214:125, Jan 24, 1972
New York Theatre Critics' Reviews 1972:394
New York Times p. 28, Jan 4, 1972
    II, p. 1, Jan 16, 1972
New Yorker 47:70, Jan 15, 1972
Saturday Review 55:24, Jan 22, 1972
Time 99:47, Jan 17, 1972

FRANK, BRUNO

*Nina
 Reviews:
  Theatre Arts 19:832-3, Nov 1935

Storm over Patsy
 Productions:
  Adapted by James Bridie. Opened March 8, 1937 for 48
   performances.
 Reviews:
  Catholic World 145:86, Apr 1937
  Commonweal 25:584, Mar 19, 1937
  Literary Digest 123:28, Mar 20, 1938
  Nation 144:333, Mar 20, 1937
  New Republic 90:210, Mar 24, 1937
  New York Times p. 26, Mar 9, 1937
  Newsweek 9:21, Mar 20, 1937
  Theatre Arts 21:340+, May 1937
  Time 29:59, Mar 22, 1937

Twelve Thousand
 Productions:
  Adapted by William A. Drake. Opened May 12, 1928 for
   64 performances.
 Reviews:
  American Mercury 14:121-2, May 1928
  Outlook 149:23, May 2, 1928
  Nation 126:356, Mar 28, 1928
  New York Times p. 23, Mar 13, 1928
     IX, p. 1, Mar 18, 1928
  Theatre Arts 12:318, May 1928
  Theatre Magazine 47:76, May 1928
  Vogue 71:136, May 1, 1928

Young Madame Conti
 Productions:
  Adapted by Hubert Griffith and Benn W. Levy. Opened
   March 31, 1937 for 22 performances.
 Reviews:
  Catholic World 145:213, May 1937
  Commonweal 25:726, Apr 23, 1937

Literary Digest 123:21, Apr 17, 1937
New York Times p. 18, Apr 1, 1937
Newsweek 9:25, Apr 10, 1937
Theatre Arts 21:348-9, May 1937
Time 29:27, Apr 12, 1937

FREEMAN, DAVID E.

Battering Ram
    Productions:
        (Off Off Broadway) Opened April 24, 1975.
    No Reviews.

Creeps
    Productions:
        (Off Broadway) Opened December 4, 1973 for 15 performan-
        ces.
    Reviews:
        Nation 217:734, Dec 31, 1973
        New York Theatre Critics' Reviews 1973:144
        New York Times p. 75, Nov 18, 1973
                      p. 52, Dec 5, 1973
                      II, p. 5, Dec 16, 1973
        New Yorker 49:99, Dec 17, 1973
        Time 102:96, Dec 17, 1973

You're Gonna Be Alright, Jamie Boy
    Productions:
        (Off Off Broadway) Opened May 1977.
    No Reviews.

FRIEL, BRIAN

Crystal and Fox
    Productions:
        (Off Broadway) Opened April 23, 1973 for 24 performances.
    Reviews:
        New York Times p. 35, Apr 24, 1973

Faith Healer
    Productions:
        (Off Off Broadway) Opened June 1976.
    No Reviews.

The Freedom of the City
    Productions:
        Opened February 17, 1974 for 9 performances.
    Reviews:
        America 130:175, Mar 9, 1974
        Nation 218:315-16, Mar 9, 1974
        New York Theatre Critics' Reviews 1974:359

New York Times p. 54, Mar 1, 1973
                p. 32, Feb 18, 1974
                p. 27, Feb 27, 1974
New Yorker 50:68, Mar 4, 1974

Losers (see Lovers)

Lovers (Consists of Winners and Losers)
    Productions:
    Opened July 25, 1968 for 148 performances.
    (Off Off Broadway) Opened April 2, 1976.
    Reviews:
    America 119:140, Aug 31, 1968
    Commonweal 88:597, Sep 6, 1968
    Life 65:10, Aug 30, 1968
    New York Theatre Critics' Reviews 1968:254
    New York Times II, p. 1, Sep 24, 1967
                    p. 21, Jul 26, 1968
                    II, p. 1, Aug 4, 1968
                    p. 43, Nov 26, 1968
                    II, p. 36, Dec 1, 1968
                    p. 26, Jan 28, 1975
    New Yorker 44:65, Aug 3, 1968
    Newsweek 72:65, Aug 5, 1968
    Saturday Review 51:46, Aug 10, 1968
    Time 92:49, Aug 2, 1968

The Loves of Cass McGuire
    Productions:
    Opened October 6, 1966 for 20 performances.
    Reviews:
    Commonweal 85:106, Oct 28, 1966
    New York Theatre Critics' Reviews 1966:274
    New York Times p. 36, Oct 7, 1966
                    p. 52, Oct 13, 1966
                    II, p. 1, p. 16, Jun 4, 1967
    New Yorker 42:118+, Oct 15, 1966
    Newsweek 68:98, Oct 17, 1966
    Saturday Review 49:73, Oct 22, 1966
    Time 88:93, Oct 14, 1966

The Mundy Scheme
    Productions:
    Opened December 11, 1969 for 4 performances.
    Reviews:
    New York Theatre Critics' Reviews 1969:161
    New York Times p. 75, Dec 12, 1969

Philadelphia, Here I Come!
    Productions:
    Opened February 16, 1966 for 326 performances.
    (Off Off Broadway) Opened November 12, 1975.

Reviews:
America 114:364, Mar 12, 1966
Catholic World 203:319-20, Aug 1966
Commonweal 83:668-9, Mar 11, 1966
Nation 202:309-10, Mar 14, 1966
New York Theatre Critics' Reviews 1966:367
New York Times p. 28, Feb 17, 1966
II, p. 3, Mar 6, 1966
p. 59, Nov 21, 1966
p. 29, Jan 12, 1975
p. 22, Nov 19, 1975
New Yorker 42:71, Feb 26, 1966
Newsweek 67:87, Feb 28, 1966
Saturday Review 49:54, Mar 5, 1966
Time 87:101, Feb 25, 1966
Vogue 147:109, Apr 1, 1966

Winners (see also Lovers)
Productions:
(Off Off Broadway) Opened June 13, 1975.
(Off Off Broadway) Opened June 16, 1976.
(Off Off Broadway) Opened December 13, 1976.
No Reviews.

FRISCH, MAX

Andorra
Productions:
English version by George Tabori. Opened February 9,
1963 for nine performances.
Reviews:
Christian Century 79:1098, Sep 12, 1962
New Republic 148:28-9, Mar 9, 1963
New York Theatre Critics' Reviews 1963:380
New York Times p. 5, Feb 11, 1963
p. 7, Feb 25, 1963
New Yorker 38:114, Feb 16, 1963
Newsweek 61:60, Feb 25, 1963
Saturday Review 46:29, Mar 2, 1963
Time 81:75, Feb 22, 1963

Biedermann und die Brandstifer (see The Firebugs)

*Chinese Wall
Reviews:
Saturday Review 49:40, May 28, 1966

The Firebugs
Productions:
(Off Broadway) Adapted by Mordecai Gorelik. Opened
February 11, 1963 for eight performances.

(Off Broadway) Translated by Mordecai Gorelik. Opened
July 1, 1968 for 8 performances.
(Off Broadway) Opened November 26, 1969 as Biedermann und
die Brandstifer for 6 performances.
(Off Off Broadway) Adapted by Lou Trapani. Opened February
18, 1974.
(Off Off Broadway) Opened March 1975.
Reviews:
New Republic 148:29, Mar 9, 1963
New York Times p. 7, Feb 13, 1963
           p. 41, Nov 22, 1963
           p. 36, Jul 2, 1968
           p. 15, Jul 4, 1968
           p. 14, Jul 5, 1968
           p. 52, Nov 27, 1969
           p. 38, Mar 27, 1975
New Yorker 39:114, Feb 23, 1963
Newsweek 61:60, Feb 25, 1963
Saturday Review 46:29, Mar 2, 1963
Time 81:75, Feb 22, 1963

The Great Rage of Philip Hotz (see Die Grosse Wut des Philip
     Hotz)

Die Grosse Wut des Philip Hotz
Productions:
(Off Broadway) Opened November 26, 1969 for 6 performances.
(Off Off Broadway) Opened May 28, 1976 as The Great Rage
of Philip Hotz.
Reviews:
New York Times p. 52, Nov 27, 1969

A House in Berlin
Productions:
(Off Broadway) Opened December 1950 in repertory.
Reviews:
New York Times p. 32, Dec 27, 1950

Philip Hotz (see Die Grosse Wut des Philip Hotz)

*Public Prosecutor Is Sick of It All
Reviews:
Saturday Review 1:55, Mar 1973

FRY, CHRISTOPHER

*The Boy with a Cart
Reviews:
New York Times p. 19, Apr 5, 1954
           p. 20, Apr 16, 1954
           II, p. 1, Apr 25, 1954
Saturday Review 37:32, May 1, 1954

*Curtmantle
  Reviews:
    New York Times p. 44, Sep 5, 1962
    Time 77:84, Mar 10, 1961

The Dark Is Light Enough
  Productions:
    Opened February 23, 1955 for 69 performances.
  Reviews:
    America 922:657+, Mar 19, 1955
    Catholic World 181:65, Apr 1955
    Commonweal 62:78, Apr 22, 1955
    Life 38:105-6, Apr 11, 1955
    Nation 180:226, Mar 12, 1955
    New York Theatre Critics' Reviews 1955:357
    New York Times p. 12, May 1, 1954
               II, p. 3, Feb 6, 1955
               p. 20, Feb 24, 1955
               II, p. 1, Mar 16, 1955
    New Yorker 30:58+, May 29, 1954
               31:67, Mar 5, 1955
    Newsweek 45:85, Mar 7, 1955
    Saturday Review 37:39, Apr 3, 1954
               38:26, Mar 12, 1955
    Theatre Arts 39:72-5, Feb 1955
               39:26+, Mar 1955
               39:17+, May 1955
    Time 65:92, Mar 7, 1955

The Firstborn
  Productions:
    Opened April 30, 1958 for 38 performances.
  Reviews:
    America 99:243-4, May 17, 1958
    Catholic World 187:310, Jul 1958
    Christian Century 74:201, Feb 13, 1957
                  75:646, May 28, 1958
    Commonweal 68:205-6, May 23, 1958
    Nation 186:456, May 17, 1958
    New York Theatre Critics' Reviews 1958:303
    New York Times p. 22, Jan 30, 1952
               p. 29, Jan 7, 1957
               p. 35, May 1, 1958
               II, p. 1, May 11, 1958
               p. 16, Jul 4, 1958
    New Yorker 34:83-4, May 10, 1958
    Saturday Review 41:29, May 17, 1958
    Time 71:66, May 12, 1958

The Lady's Not for Burning
  Productions:
    Opened November 8, 1950 for 151 performances.
    (Off Broadway) Season of 1956-1957.

(Off Off Broadway) Season of 1974-1975.
Reviews:
America 96:656, Mar 9, 1957
Catholic World 172:306, Jan 1951
Christian Science Monitor Magazine p. 4, Nov 18, 1950
Commonweal 53:196, Dec 1, 1956
Life 29:141-2+, Nov 27, 1950
Nation 171:466, Nov 18, 1950
New Republic 123:22, Nov 27, 1950
New York Theatre Critics' Reviews 1950:213
New York Times p. 42, Nov 9, 1950
                II, p. 1, Nov 26, 1950
                p. 34, Apr 4, 1951
                p. 26, Feb 22, 1957
                p. 13, Jan 31, 1959
                p. 51, Aug 22, 1972
New Yorker 26:77, Nov 18, 1950
Newsweek 36:96, Nov 20, 1950
Saturday Review 33:46+, Dec 2, 1950
School and Society 73:180-1, Mar 24, 1951
Theatre Arts 35:13, Jan 1951
Time 56:58, Nov 20, 1950

A Phoenix Too Frequent
    Productions:
    Opened April 26, 1950 for 5 performances.
    (Off Off Broadway) Season of 1970-1971.
Reviews:
    Catholic World 171:227, Jun 1950
    Christian Science Monitor Magazine p. 9, May 6, 1950
    Commonweal 52:152, May 19, 1950
    Nation 170:457, May 13, 1950
    New Republic 122:21, May 15, 1950
    New York Theatre Critics' Reviews 1950:303
    New York Times p. 36, Apr 27, 1950
                   p. 13, Oct 10, 1953
                   p. 33, Mar 11, 1958
                   II, p. 1, Mar 16, 1958
    New Yorker 26:52, May 6, 1950
    Newsweek 35:80, May 8, 1950
    Theatre Arts 34:15, Jul 1950

A Sleep of Prisoners
    Productions:
    Opened October 16, 1951 for 31 performances.
Reviews:
    Catholic World 174:226, Dec 1951
    Commonweal 55:92, Nov 2, 1951
    Life 31:73-5+, Nov 12, 1951
    Nation 173:381, Nov 3, 1951
    New Republic 124:23, Jun 11, 1951
                 125:22, Nov 12, 1951
    New York Theatre Critics' Reviews 1951:207

New York Times p. 46, May 16, 1951
VI, p. 58, May 20, 1951
II, p. 1, Oct 14, 1951
p. 36, Oct 17, 1951
II, p. 1, Oct 28, 1951
p. 21, Jan 2, 1952
p. 10, Jan 15, 1955
New Yorker 27:66, Oct 27, 1951
Newsweek 38:84, Oct 29, 1951
Saturday Review 34:60+, Nov 17, 1951
35:22, Mar 1, 1952
School and Society 74:406-7, Dec 22, 1951
Survey 87:527, Dec 1951
Theatre Arts 35:3, Dec 1951
36:20, Jan 1952
Time 57:70-1, May 28, 1951
58:38, Oct 29, 1951

*Thor, with Angels
Reviews:
Christian Century 73:1453, Dec 12, 1956
Commonweal 65:175, Nov 16, 1956
New York Times p. 29, Oct 15, 1956

Tiger at the Gates (see entry under Giraudoux, Jean)

Venus Observed
Productions:
Opened February 13, 1952 for 86 performances.
Reviews:
Catholic World 175:69, Apr 1952
Commonweal 55:543, Mar 7, 1952
Nation 174:237, Mar 8, 1952
New Republic 122:21-2, Jun 5, 1950
126:23, Mar 3, 1952
New York Theatre Critics' Reviews 1952:364
New York Times p. 34, Jan 19, 1950
p. 27, Jan 24, 1950
II, p. 1, Feb 10, 1952
p. 24, Feb 14, 1952
II, p. 1, Feb 24, 1952
New Yorker 25:85, Feb 11, 1950
26:58+, Feb 23, 1952
Newsweek 39:95, Feb 25, 1952
Saturday Review 35:20-2, Mar 1, 1952
35:26, May 10, 1952
School and Society 75:183-4, Mar 22, 1952
Theatre Arts 34:29, Dec 1950
36:18-19, Apr 1952
Time 59:80, Feb 25, 1952

*Yard of Sun
  Reviews:
    Time 96:56, Aug 10, 1970

FUGARD, ATHOL

The Blood Knot
  Productions:
    (Off Broadway) Opened March 1, 1964 for 240 performances.
    (Off Off Broadway) Opened February 11, 1976.
    (Off Off Broadway) Opened May 25, 1977.
  Reviews:
    America 110:552, Apr 18, 1964
    Nation 198:334-5, Mar 30, 1964
    New York Times p. 30, Mar 3, 1964
                   p. 44, May 27, 1964
                   p. 50, Sep 17, 1964
                   p. 26, Mar 2, 1976
                   p. 85, Nov 28, 1976
    New Yorker 40:110+, Mar 14, 1964
    Newsweek 63:97, Mar 16, 1964
    Time 83:73, Mar 13, 1964
    Vogue 143:62, May 1964

Boesman and Lena
  Productions:
    (Off Broadway) Opened June 22, 1970 for 205 performances.
    (Off Off Broadway) Opened January 19, 1977.
  Reviews:
    Commonweal 93:47-8, Oct 9, 1970
    Nation 211:285, Sep 28, 1970
    New Republic 163:16+, Jul 25, 1970
    New York Theatre Critics' Reviews 1970:201
    New York Times p. 42, Jun 22, 1970
                   p. 35, Jun 23, 1970
                   II, p. 1, Jul 5, 1970
                   p. 6, Jul 6, 1970
                   II, p. 1, Jul 12, 1970
                   III, p. 22, Feb 2, 1977
    New Yorker 46:57, Jul 4, 1970
               52:68, Feb 7, 1977
    Newsweek 76:78, Jul 6, 1970
    Saturday Review 53:53, Sep 19, 1970
    Time 96:63, Jul 13, 1970

Hello and Goodbye
  Productions:
    (Off Off Broadway) Opened November 11, 1968 for 2 per-
      formances.
    (Off Broadway) Opened September 18, 1969 for 45 per-
      formances.

Reviews:
    Nation 209:517-18, Nov 10, 1969
    New Republic 161:24, Oct 11, 1969
    New York Theatre Critics' Reviews 1969:202
    New York Times p. 36, Nov 13, 1968
                      p. 54, Sep 19, 1969
    New Yorker 45:97, Sep 27, 1969
    Newsweek 74:106, Sep 29, 1969
    Saturday Review 52:26, Oct 11, 1969

The Island (with John Kani and Winston Ntshona)
    Productions:
    Opened November 24, 1974 for 52 performances.
    Reviews:
    America 131:415, Dec 21, 1974
    Commonweal 101:330, Jan 17, 1975
    Nation 219:637-8, Dec 14, 1974
    New Republic 171:16+, Dec 21, 1974
    New York Theatre Critics' Reviews 1974:169
    New York Times p. 37, Nov 25, 1974
                    II, p. 5, Dec 1, 1974
                        p. 30, Dec 17, 1974
                        p. 29, Apr 1, 1975
    New Yorker 50:69, Dec 9, 1974
    Newsweek 84:98, Dec 2, 1974
    The Progressive 39:40, Apr 1975

People Are Living There
    Productions:
    (Off Broadway) Opened November 18, 1971 for 20 per-
        formances.
    Reviews:
    Nation 213:605, Dec 6, 1971
    New York Theatre Critics' Reviews 1971:155
    New York Times p. 35, Nov 19, 1971
    Newsweek 78:121, Dec 6, 1971

Sizwe Banzi Is Dead (with John Kani and Winston Ntshona)
    Productions:
    Opened November 13, 1974 for 159 performances.
    Reviews:
    America 131:415, Dec 21, 1974
    Commonweal 101:330, Jan 17, 1975
    Nation 219:637-8, Dec 14, 1974
    New Republic 171:16+, Dec 21, 1974
    New York Theatre Critics' Reviews 1974:171
    New York Times p. 56, Nov 14, 1974
                    II, p. 7, Nov 24, 1974
                    II, p. 5, Dec 1, 1974
                        p. 30, Dec 17, 1974
                        p. 29, Apr 1, 1975
    New Yorker 50:131, Nov 25, 1974
    Newsweek 84:98, Dec 2, 1974
    The Progressive 39:40, Apr 1975

GALSWORTHY, JOHN

A Bit of Love
  Productions:
    Opened May 12, 1925 for 4 performances.
  Reviews:
    Dial 59:328, Oct 14, 1915
    Dramatic Mirror 73:5, Jun 23, 1915
    Nation 101:298, Jun 5, 1915
          101:25, Jul 1, 1915
          120:635-6, Jun 3, 1925
    New Republic 3:210, Jun 26, 1915
    New York Times p. 24, May 13, 1925

Escape
  Productions:
    Opened October 26, 1927 for 173 performances.
  Reviews:
    American Mercury 13:118-20, Jan 1928
    Catholic World 126:379-80, Dec 1927
    Dial 84:82, Jan 1928
    Dramatist 19:1363, Jan 1928
    Independent 119:606, Dec 17, 1927
    Life (NY) 90:25, Nov 17, 1927
    Living Age 330:673-6, Sep 25, 1926
              331:340-5, Nov 15, 1926
    Nation 125:311-12, Nov 16, 1927
    New Republic 52:311-12, Nov 9, 1927
    New York Times p. 33, Oct 27, 1927
                  IX, p. 1, Nov 6, 1927
    Outlook 147:308, Nov 9, 1927
    Saturday Review 4:299-300, Nov 12, 1927
    Theatre Arts 12:14-15, Jan 1928
    Vogue 70:66, Dec 15, 1927

The Fugitive
  Productions:
    Opened May 19, 1917 for 56 performances.
  Reviews:
    Book News 35:257, May 1917
    Dramatic Mirror 77:7, Mar 14, 1917
    Dramatist 5:459, Apr 1914
    Green Book 17:971-5, Jun 1917
    Harper's Weekly 61:263, Sep 11, 1915
    Life (NY) 69:526, Mar 29, 1917
    Nation 104:380, Mar 29, 1917
    New York Times VIII, p. 5, Apr 1, 1917
    Theatre Magazine 25:277+, May 1917
    Yale Review 11:298-303, Jan 1922

Justice
  Productions:
    Opened April 3, 1916 for 104 performances.

Reviews:
    American Mercury 70:585-99, Sep 1910
                   70:819-31, Oct 1910
    Book News 34:432-3, Jun 1916
    Bookman 43:340-2, Jun 1916
    Current Opinion 60:324-8, May 1916
    Dramatic Mirror 75:8, Apr 8, 1916
    Dramatist 2:128, Jun 1911
            7:676, Apr 1916
    Everybody's Magazine 35:122-4, Jul 1916
    Green Book 15:969-77, Jun 1916
    Harper's Weekly 62:440, Apr 22, 1916
    Hearst 30:165-7+, Sep 1916
    Literary Digest 52:1220-1, Apr 29, 1916
    Nation 102:419-20, Apr 13, 1916
           122:429-30, Apr 30, 1916
    New Republic 6:294, Apr 15, 1916
    New York Dramatic News 62:17, Apr 8, 1916
    New York Times p. 11, Apr 4, 1916
               II, p. 8, Apr 9, 1916
               II, p. 7, Apr 16, 1916
               II, p. 8, Apr 23, 1916
    Outlook 132:246-8, May 31, 1916
    Stage 14:72, Aug 1937
    Theatre Arts 19:415, Jun 1935
    Theatre Magazine 14:89-90, Sep 1911
                   23:273, May 1916
                   23:296-7+, May 1916
                   24:77, Aug 1916

The Little Man
   Productions:
    Opened February 12, 1917 for 56 performances.
   Reviews:
    Dramatic Mirror 77:7, Feb 24, 1917
    New Republic 10:106, Feb 24, 1917
    New York Times p. 9, Feb 13, 1917
    Theatre Magazine 25:215+, Apr 1917

Loyalties
   Productions:
    Opened September 27, 1922 for 220 performances.
   Reviews:
    Bookman 56:477-8, Dec 1922
           63:161-5, Apr 1926
    Catholic World 116:507-9, Jan 1923
    Current Opinion 73:750-5+, Dec 1922
    Dramatist 13:1134-8, Oct 1922
    Everybody's Magazine 48:96-103, Feb 1923
    Fortnightly Review 118:349-52, Aug 1922
    Forum 68:975-6, Nov 1922
           68:1039-41, Dec 1922
    Hearst 42:85+, Dec 1922

Independent 110:32-4, Jan 6, 1923
Life (NY) 80:18, Oct 19, 1922
Nation 115:420, Oct 18, 1922
New Republic 32:277-8, Nov 8, 1922
New York Clipper 70:21, Oct 4, 1922
New York Times p. 18, Sep 28, 1922
      VI, p. 1, Oct 8, 1922
      III, p. 4, Jan 14, 1923
Theatre Magazine 36:370-1+, Dec 1922
      37:28+, Jan 1923

Mob
Productions:
  Opened October 1920
Reviews:
  Bookman 53:274-5, May 1921
  Dramatic Mirror p. 683, Oct 16, 1920
  Dramatist 6:510-12, Oct 1914
  New Republic 1:27-8, Nov 7, 1914
  New York Clipper 68:29, Oct 27, 1920
  New York Times p. 18, Oct 11, 1920
  Theatre Magazine 32:422, Dec 1920
  Weekly Review 3:426-7, Nov 3, 1920
  Yale Review 4:623, Apr 1915

Old English
Productions:
  Opened December 23, 1924 for 183 performances.
Reviews:
  American Mercury 4:244, Feb 1925
  Current Opinion 78:316-23, Mar 1925
  Dramatist 16:1249-50, Jan 1925
  Nation 120:49-50, Jan 14, 1925
  New York Times p. 11, Dec 24, 1924
      p. 21, Feb 10, 1925
  Theatre Magazine 40:16+, Mar 1925
      42:26+, Jul 1925

The Pigeon
Productions:
  Opened March 12, 1912 for 64 performances.
  Opened February 2, 1922 for 92 performances.
Reviews:
  Blue Book 15:478-80, Jul 1912
  Book News 31:287, Dec 1912
  Bookman 35:243, May 1912
  Dramatic Mirror 67:6, Mar 13, 1912
  Green Book 7:970, May 1912
  Independent 72:617-19, Mar 21, 1912
  Life (NY) 59:588, Mar 21, 1912
  Munsey 47:283, May 1912
  Nation 114:196, Feb 15, 1922
  New York Clipper 70:20, Feb 8, 1922

New York Dramatic News 55:14-15, Mar 16, 1912
New York Times p. 13, Feb 3, 1922
Red Book 19:370+, Jun 1912
Theatre Magazine 15:106-7, Apr 1912
Yale Review 1:690-3, Jul 1912

The Roof
Productions:
Opened October 30, 1931 for 28 performances.
Reviews:
Catholic World 134:333, Dec 1931
New York Times p. 22, Oct 31, 1931
Theatre Arts 16:19, Jan 1932

The Silver Box
Productions:
Opened January 17, 1928 for 23 performances.
Reviews:
Dramatist 2:158, Apr 1911
Life (NY) 91:21, Feb 2, 1928
New York Times p. 23, Jan 18, 1928
Theatre Magazine 7:114+, May 1907
Vogue 71:94+, Mar 15, 1928

The Skin Game
Productions:
Opened October 20, 1920 for 176 performances.
Reviews:
Bookman 51:659, Aug 1920
          53:275, May 1921
Current Opinion 69:649-56, Nov 1920
Drama 12:122+, Jan 1922
Dramatic Mirror p. 795, Oct 30, 1920
Dramatist 11:1011-12, Jul 1920
Fortnightly Review 113:961-5, Jun 1920
Forum 65:242-4, Feb 1921
Independent 104:213, Nov 13, 1920
Life (NY) 76:872-3, Nov 11, 1920
Literary Digest 67:30, Nov 6, 1920
Living Age 305:494-5, May 22, 1920
Nation 111:539, Nov 10, 1920
New York Clipper 68:29, Oct 27, 1920
New York Times p. 11, Oct 21, 1920
          VI, p. 1, Oct 31, 1920
Theatre Magazine 33:7+, Jan 1921
Weekly Review 3:454-5, Nov 10, 1920

Strife
Productions:
Opened November 17, 1909 in repertory.
Reviews:
Bookman 30:461, Feb 1910

Current Literature 48:81-3, Jan 1910
48:537-45, May 1910
Dramatic Mirror 62:5, Nov 27, 1909
Forum 43:70, Jan 1910
Green Book 3:391-2, Feb 1910
Hampton 24:272, Feb 1910
Life (NY) 54:855, Dec 9, 1909
Literary Digest 39:1013, Dec 4, 1909
Metropolitan Magazine 31:816-17, Mar 1910
Nation 89:520, Nov 25, 1909
Pearson 22:229-31, Aug 1909
Theatre Magazine 11:2+, Jan 1910

Windows
Productions:
Opened October 8, 1923 for 48 performances.
Reviews:
Bookman 58:441, Dec 1923
Dramatist 14:1167-8, Jul 1923
Freeman 8:186, Oct 31, 1923
Life (NY) 82:18, Oct 25, 1923
Nation 117:469-70, Oct 24, 1923
New York Times p. 17, Oct 9, 1923
VIII, p. 1, Oct 24, 1923
Theatre Magazine 38:16-17, Dec 1923

GARCIA-LORCA, FEDERICO

*Belissa in the Garden
Reviews:
Saturday Review 35:50, Nov 21, 1953

Bitter Oleander (see Blood Wedding)

Blood Wedding (Bitter Oleander)
Productions:
Translated by José A. Weissman. Opened February 11,
1935 for 24 performances.
(Off Broadway) Opened February 1949 in repertory.
(Off Broadway) Season of 1957-1958.
(Off Off Broadway) Season of 1972-1973.
(Off Off Broadway) Opened January 18, 1973.
(Off Off Broadway) Opened March 6, 1975.
(Off Off Broadway) Opened May 1977.
Reviews:
Catholic World 169:65, Apr 1949
Commonweal 49:542-3, Mar 11, 1949
62:473, Aug 12, 1955
Forum 111:164, Mar 1949
Nation 168:221, Feb 19, 1949
New Republic 82:78, Feb 27, 1935
120:27, Feb 21, 1949

New York Times p. 24, Feb 12, 1935
                II, p. 1, Jan 30, 1949
                p. 16, Feb 7, 1949
                p. 35, Apr 1, 1958
Saturday Review 21:21, Jan 15, 1940
School and Society 69:155, Feb 26, 1949
Theatre Arts 19:248+, Apr 1935
              33:24, May 1949
Vanity Fair 44:43, Apr 1935

Bodas de Sangre   (see Blood Wedding)

Dona Rosita La Sotera
    Productions:
    (Off Off Broadway) Season of 1969-70.
    No Reviews.

The House of Bernarda Alba
    Productions:
    Translated by James Graham-Lujan and Richard L. O'Connell.
        Opened January 7, 1951 for 17 performances.
    (Off Off Broadway) Opened March 1977.
    Reviews:
    Christian Science Monitor Magazine p. 8, May 20, 1950
    Commonweal 53:398, Jan 26, 1951
                62:475, Aug 12, 1955
    Nation 172:66, Jan 20, 1951
    New Republic 124:22, Feb 5, 1951
    New York Theatre Critics' Reviews 1951:395
    New York Times p. 14, Jan 8, 1951
                   p. 23, Nov 25, 1963
                   p. 39, Feb 28, 1972
    New Yorker 26:54+, Jan 20, 1951
    School and Society 73:100-1, Feb 17, 1951
    Theatre Arts 35:17, Mar 1951

If Five Years Pass
    Productions:
    (Off Broadway) Opened April 6, 1945.
    (Off Broadway) Opened May 10, 1962 for 22 performances.
    Reviews:
    Commonweal 42:17, Apr 20, 1945
                42:71, May 4, 1945
    New York Times p. 37, May 11, 1962
    Theatre Arts 46:57, Aug 1962

*Love of Don Perlimplin
    Reviews:
    Saturday Review 36:50, Nov 21, 1953

*Mariana Pineda
    Reviews:
    Nation 184:508, Jun 8, 1957

The Shoemaker's Prodigious Wife
Productions:
   (Off Broadway) Opened June 1949 in repertory.
Reviews:
   New York Times p. 38, Jun 15, 1949

Yerma
Productions:
   Translated by W. S. Merwin. Opened December 8, 1966 in
      repertory for 60 performances.
   (Off Off Broadway) English version by James Graham-Lujan
      and Richard L. O'Connell. Season of 1970-71.
   (Off Broadway) Opened October 17, 1972 for 16 performances.
Reviews:
   Nation 204:30, Jan 2, 1967
          215:444-5, Nov 6, 1972
   New Republic 156:41-2, Jan 7, 1967
                168:25-6, May 12, 1973
   New York Theatre Critics' Reviews 1966:210
   New York Times p. 60, Dec 9, 1966
                  p. 50, Apr 20, 1971
                  II, p. 1, May 7, 1972
                  p. 56, Oct 19, 1972
   New Yorker 48:119, Oct 28, 1972
   Newsweek 68:106, Dec 19, 1966
   Saturday Review 49:68, Dec 24, 1966
                   55:80, Nov 11, 1972
   Time 88:87, Dec 16, 1966

GENET, JEAN

The Balcony
Productions:
   (Off Broadway) Translated by Bernard Frechtman. Opened
      March 30, 1960 for 672 performances.
   (Off Off Broadway) Opened January 2, 1976.
   (Off Broadway) English version by Terry Hands and Barbara
      Wright. Opened December 4, 1976 for 43 performances.
Reviews:
   Christian Century 77:546-8, May 4, 1960
   Nation 185:18, Jul 6, 1957
          190:282-3, Mar 26, 1960
   New Republic 142:21-2, Mar 28, 1960
   New York Times p. 41, Apr 23, 1957
                  p. 21, Mar 4, 1960
                  II, p. 1, Mar 20, 1960
                  p. 46, Dec 14, 1976
   New Yorker 36:116+, Mar 12, 1960
   Saturday Review 43:34, Mar 26, 1960
   Time 75:54+, Apr 18, 1960

The Blacks
Productions:
  (Off Broadway) Translated by Bernard Frechtman.   Opened
     May 4, 1961 for 1,408 performances.
  (Off Off Broadway) Opened February 1977.
Reviews:
  America 105:671, Aug 26, 1961
  Catholic World 194:62-4, Oct 1961
  Christian Century 78:744-5, Jun 14, 1961
  Ebony 17:47-8+, Sep 1962
  Nation 192:447-8, May 20, 1961
  New Republic 144:21-2, May 29, 1961
  New York Times p. 23, May 5, 1961
                 II, p. 1, May 14, 1961
                 p. 37, Sep 25, 1963
                 II, p. 3, May 3, 1964
                 p. 44, May 30, 1973
  New Yorker 37:93-4, May 13, 1961
  Newsweek 57:68, May 15, 1961
  Saturday Review 44:29, Jun 3, 1961
  Theatre Arts 45:8-9, Jul 1961
  Time 77:64, May 12, 1961
  Yale Review 55:209-26, Dec 1965

Deathwatch
Productions:
  (Off Broadway) Season of 1958-1959.
  (Off Broadway) Opened February 11, 1962 in repertory.
  (Off Off Broadway) Opened September 1975.
  (Off Off Broadway) Opened October 1975.
Reviews:
  New York Times p. 25, Mar 7, 1957
                 p. 34, Oct 10, 1958
                 p. 20, Sep 12, 1975
                 II, p. 5, Sep 21, 1975
  Saturday Review 41:28, Nov 1, 1958

The Maids
Productions:
  (Off Broadway) Translated by Bernard Frechtman.   Opened
     November 14, 1963 for 62 performances.
  (Off Off Broadway) Translated by Bernard Frechtman.
     Season of 1974-1975.
  (Off Off Broadway) Opened April 1977.
Reviews:
  Commonweal 62:398-9, Jul 22, 1955
  Nation 180:469-70, May 28, 1955
  New York Times p. 29, Nov 15, 1963
  New Yorker 39:143-4+, Nov 23, 1963

*Les Paravents   (see also The Screens)
    Reviews:
       New York Times p. 36, Apr 22, 1966
                    II, p. 5, May 22, 1966
                       p. 19, Oct 8, 1966
       New Yorker 42:180-1, Oct 1, 1966

The Screens   (see also Les Paravents)
    Productions:
       Translated by Minos Volanakis.
       (Off Broadway) Opened November 30, 1971 for 28
          performances.
    Reviews:
       Nation 213:701-2, Dec 27, 1971
       New York Theatre Critics' Reviews 1971:152
       New York Times p. 53, Dec 13, 1971
                    II, p. 3, Dec 19, 1971
       Newsweek 78:58, Dec 20, 1971
       Time 98:55, Dec 27, 1971

GERALDY, PAUL

Aimer   (see To Love)

The Nest (Les Noces d'Argent)
    Productions:
       Adapted by Grace George.   Opened January 28, 1922 for
          161 performances.
    Reviews:
       Bookman 55:180, Apr 1922
       Independent 108:265, Mar 11, 1922
       Life (NY) 79:18, Mar 2, 1922
       New York Clipper 70:20, Feb 8, 1922
       New York Times p. 20, Feb 2, 1922
       Theatre Magazine 35:215+, Apr 1922

She Had to Know
    Productions:
       Adapted by Grace George.   Opened February 2, 1925 for
          80 performances.
    Reviews:
       Life (NY) 85:18, Feb 26, 1925
       Nation 120:192-3, Feb 18, 1925
       New York Times p. 25, Feb 3, 1925
       Theatre Magazine 41:16, Apr 1925

To Love (Aimer)
    Productions:
       Translated by Grace George.   Opened October 17, 1922
          for 55 performances.

Reviews:
    Dramatist 13:1135-6, Oct 1922
    Forum 68:1041-3, Dec 1922
    Nation 115:506-7, Nov 8, 1922
    New York Clipper 70:20, Oct 25, 1922
    New York Times p. 16, Oct 18, 1922
    Theatre Magazine 36:371, Dec 1922

GHELDERODE, MICHEL DE see DE GHELDERODE, MICHEL

GIDE, ANDRE

Le Procès (see The Trial)

The Trial (Le Procès) (with Jean-Louis Barrault)
  Productions:
    Based on Kafka's novel. Opened November 17, 1952 for
    4 performances.
    (Off Broadway) Season of 1964-1965 for 9 performances.
  Reviews:
    Christian Science Monitor Magazine p. 9, May 6, 1950
    Nation 175:500, Nov 29, 1952
    New York Theatre Critics' Reviews 1952:194
    New York Times p. 36, Nov 18, 1952
              p. 33, May 21, 1966
    Saturday Review 35:41, Dec 6, 1952

GIRAUDOUX, JEAN

Amphitryon 38
  Productions:
    Adapted by S. N. Behrman. Opened November 1, 1937
    for 153 performances.
  Reviews:
    Catholic World 146:338-9, Dec 1937
    Commonweal 27:78, Nov 12, 1937
    Life 3:70, Jul 1937
    Literary Digest 1:35, Nov 20, 1935
    Nation 145:539, Nov 13, 1937
    New Republic 93:44, Nov 17, 1937
              94:132, Mar 9, 1938
    New York Times p. 32, November 2, 1937
              XI, p. 1, Nov 7, 1937
              p. 18, Jun 23, 1971
    Newsweek 10:20-1, Jul 3, 1937
             10:22, Nov 8, 1937
    Scribner's Magazine 102:66+, Oct 1937
    Stage 15:46-9, Oct 1937
        15:94, Nov 1937
        15:44-5, Jan 1938

Theatre Arts 21:924, Dec 1937
Time 30:25, Nov 8, 1937

The Apollo of Bellac
 Productions:
  (Off Off Broadway) Opened January 12, 1976.
 Reviews:
  New York Times p. 12, May 29, 1954
          II, p. 1, Jun 6, 1954
            p. 39, Apr 10, 1957
            p. 17, Mar 7, 1958

*L'Appolon de Marsac
 Reviews:
  Theatre Arts 31:25, Nov 1947

Duel of Angels
 Productions:
  Adapted by Christopher Fry.   Opened April 19, 1960 for
   51 performances.
 Reviews:
  America 103:266, May 14, 1960
  Christian Century 77:672-3, Jun 1, 1960
  Life 48:95, May 16, 1960
  Nation 190:411-12, May 7, 1960
  New York Theatre Critics' Reviews 1960:287
  New York Times p. 42, Apr 20, 1960
          II, p. 1, May 1, 1960
            p. 24, Jul 14, 1960
  New Yorker 36:83, Apr 30, 1960
  Newsweek 55:54, May 2, 1960
  Saturday Review 43:26, May 7, 1960
  Time 75:78, May 2, 1960

The Enchanted   (see also Intermezzo)
 Productions:
  Adapted by Maurice Valency.   Opened January 18, 1950
   for 45 performances.
  (Off Broadway) Opened June 1951.
 Reviews:
  Catholic World 170:469, Mar 1950
  Commonweal 51:486, Feb 10, 1950
  New Republic 122:30, Feb 13, 1950
  New York Theatre Critics' Reviews 1950:387
  New York Times p. 34, Jan 19, 1950
           p. 41, Apr 23, 1958
           p. 39, Oct 13, 1971
  New Yorker 25:50, Jan 28, 1950
  Newsweek 35:67, Jan 30, 1950
  School and Society 71:118-19, Feb 25, 1950
  Theatre Arts 34:17+, Mar 1950
  Time 55:37, Jan 30, 1950

*Folie de Chaillot
　　Reviews:
　　　　New York Times p. 17, Dec 20, 1945

*For Lucretia
　　Reviews:
　　　　Nation 178:489-90, Jun 5, 1954
　　　　New Yorker 29:85, Dec 19, 1953

La Guerre de Troie n'Aura Pas Lieu　(see Tiger at the Gates)

Hiatus　(see Intermezzo)

Intermezzo　(see also The Enchanted)
　　Productions:
　　　　Opened January 30, 1957 in repertory.
　　　　(Off Off Broadway) Adapted by Paul Giovanni as Hiatus.
　　　　　　Season of 1967-1968.
　　Reviews:
　　　　Catholic World 185:68, Apr 1957
　　　　Commonweal 136:21, Mar 18, 1957
　　　　New York Theatre Critics' Reviews 1957:345
　　　　New York Times p. 20, Feb 15, 1957
　　　　Theatre Arts 41:82, Apr 1957

Judith
　　Productions:
　　　　(Off Broadway) English version by John K. Savacool.
　　　　　　Opened March 24, 1965 for 79 performances.
　　Reviews:
　　　　Nation 200:403-4, Apr 12, 1965
　　　　New Republic 152:23-4, Apr 10, 1965
　　　　New York Times p. 25, Jun 21, 1962
　　　　　　　　　　　p. 42, Mar 25, 1965
　　　　　　　　　　　II, p. 1, Apr 4, 1965
　　　　New Yorker 41:86, Apr 3, 1965
　　　　Reporter 32:38-40, May 6, 1965
　　　　Saturday Review 48:58, Apr 10, 1965
　　　　Time 85:79, Apr 9, 1965
　　　　Vogue 145:68, Jun 1965

The Madwoman of Chaillot
　　Productions:
　　　　Adapted by Maurice Valency.　Opened December 27, 1948
　　　　　　for 368 performances.
　　　　Adapted by Maurice Valency.　Opened June 13, 1950 for
　　　　　　17 performances.
　　　　(Off Broadway) Opened May 1952.
　　　　(Off Broadway) Season of 1953-1954.
　　　　(Off Broadway) Opened March 22, 1970 for 7 performances.
　　Reviews:
　　　　Catholic World 168:401, Feb 1949
　　　　Commonweal 49:351, Jan 14, 1949

Forum 111:93-4, Feb 1949
House and Garden 95:186, Apr 1949
Life 26:64+, Jan 24, 1949
Nation 168:53, Jan 8, 1949
New Republic 120:28, Jan 17, 1949
New York Theatre Critics' Reviews 1948:104
New York Times p. 18, Dec 28, 1948
            II, p. 1, Jan 9, 1949
            VI, p. 6, Mar 13, 1949
            II, p. 1, Sep 11, 1949
            p. 41, Jun 14, 1950
            p. 10, Feb 17, 1951
            II, p. 3, Mar 4, 1951
            II, p. 3, Apr 15, 1951
            p. 48, Mar 23, 1970
            p. 20, Mar 27, 1970
New Yorker 21:46-8, Feb 9, 1946
            24:48+, Jan 8, 1949
            46:64, Apr 4, 1970
Newsweek 33:72, Jan 10, 1949
Saturday Review 32:32-4, Jan 15, 1949
School and Society 69:82-4, Jan 29, 1949
Theatre Arts 33:14-17, Mar 1949
            33:57-92, Nov 1949
            41:67-8+, Mar 1957
Time 53:36, Jan 10, 1949
Vogue 107:168, Mar 1, 1946
            112:150-51, Mar 1, 1949

Ondine
     Productions:
         Adapted by Maurice Valency.   Opened February 18, 1954
            for 157 performances.
         (Off Broadway) Season of 1960-1961.
     Reviews:
         America 90:664+, Mar 20, 1954
         Catholic World 179:67-8, Apr 2, 1954
         Commonweal 59:649-50, Apr 2, 1954
         Life 36:60-2+, Mar 8, 1954
         Look 18:88+, Apr 20, 1954
         Nation 178:206, Mar 6, 1954
         New Republic 130:21, Mar 8, 1954
         New York Theatre Critics' Reviews 1954:362
         New York Times II, p. 1, Feb 14, 1954
                      VI, p. 15, Feb 14, 1954
                      p. 23, Feb 19, 1954
                      II, p. 1, Feb 28, 1954
         New Yorker 30:74+, Feb 27, 1954
         Newsweek 43:71, Mar 1, 1954
         Saturday Review 37:26-7, Mar 13, 1954
         Theatre Arts 38:18-20, May 1954
         Time 63:76, Mar 1, 1954

Pour Lucrèce (see For Lucretia)

Siegfried
    Productions:
        Translated by Philip Carr. Opened October 20, 1930 for
        23 performances.
    Reviews:
        Bookman 72:513-14, Jan 1931
        Catholic World 132:337, Dec 1930
        Commonweal 13:49, Nov 12, 1930
        Nation 131:506, Nov 5, 1930
        New York Times p. 34, Oct 21, 1930
        Vogue 76:134+, Dec 8, 1930
        Yale Review 20:816-17, Summer 1931

Song of Songs
    Productions:
        (Off Broadway) Season of 1958-1959.
    Reviews:
        New York Times p. 31, Oct 29, 1958.

Tiger at the Gates
    Productions:
        Translation by Christopher Fry. Opened October 3, 1955
        for 217 performances.
        (Off Broadway) Season of 1959-1960.
        Adapted by Christopher Fry. Opened February 29, 1968 in
        repertory for 44 performances.
        Opened April 20, 1977 for 13 performances.
    Reviews:
        America 94:258+, Nov 26, 1955
              118:422, Mar 30, 1968
        Catholic World 182:223-4, Dec 1955
        Christian Century 85:730-1, May 29, 1968
        Commonweal 63:200-1, Nov 25, 1955
                   88:49-50, Mar 29, 1968
        Life 39:164-5, Oct 17, 1955
        Living Age 349:457-8, Jan 1936
        Nation 181:348, Oct 22, 1955
        New Republic 133:22, Oct 24, 1955
        New York Theatre Critics' Reviews 1955:264
        New York Times p. 27, Jun 3, 1955
                       II, p. 1, Jun 12, 1955
                       VI, p. 21, Sep 11, 1955
                       II, p. 3, Oct 2, 1955
                       p. 40, Oct 4, 1955
                       II, p. 1, Oct 23, 1955
                       VI, p. 28, Oct 30, 1955
                       p. 30, Mar 1, 1968
                       II, p. 3, Mar 10, 1968
        New Yorker 31:61, Jul 30, 1955
                   31:76+, Oct 15, 1955
                   44:130+, Mar 9, 1968

Newsweek 46:103, Oct 17, 1955
            71:105-6, Mar 11, 1968
Reporter 13:42, Oct 20, 1955
Saturday Review 38:27, Oct 22, 1955
Theatre Arts 20:361-3, May 1936
            39:22, Dec 1955
Time 66:51-2, Oct 17, 1955
        91:71, Mar 8, 1968
Vogue 125:136-7+, Mar 1, 1955

*The Virtuous Island
    Reviews:
        Life 37:117-18, Dec 13, 1954
        New York Times p. 39, Apr 10, 1957

GORKI, MAXIM

At the Bottom   (see also Night Lodging and The Lower Depths)
    Productions:
        Adapted by William L. Laurence. Opened January 9, 1930
            for 72 performances.
    Reviews:
        New York Times p. 24, Jan 10, 1930
        Outlook 154:229, Feb 5, 1930
        Theatre Arts 14:190+, Mar 1930
        Theatre Magazine 51:48, Mar 1930
        Vogue 75:70+, Mar 1, 1930

*Children of the Sun
    Reviews:
        New York Times p. 56, Dec 11, 1963

*Country People
    Reviews:
        Nation 210:157, Feb 9, 1970
        New York Times p. 35, Jan 19, 1970
        Newsweek 75:74, Jan 26, 1970
        Saturday Review 53:24, Feb 7, 1970

*The Courageous One
    Reviews:
        New York Times p. 33, Jan 21, 1958
                    II, p. 1, Feb 2, 1958

Enemies
    Productions:
        English version by Jeremy Brooks and Kitty Hunter-Blair.
        Opened November 9, 1972 for 44 performances in repertory.
    Reviews:
        Nation 215:538-40, Nov 27, 1972
        New Republic 167:24+, Dec 16, 1972
        New York Theatre Critics' Reviews 1972:196

New York Times II, p. 1, Nov 5, 1972
p. 47, Nov 10, 1972
II, p. 1, Nov 19, 1972
New Yorker 48:69, Nov 18, 1972
Newsweek 80:89, Nov 20, 1972

The Lower Depths (see also Night Lodging and At the Bottom)
Productions:
Opened January 1923 in repertory.
Opened November 1923 in repertory (Moscow Art Theatre).
(Off Broadway) Season of 1938-1939 in repertory.
(Off Broadway) Season of 1956-1957.
(Off Broadway) Translated by Alex Szogyi. Opened March 30,
1964 for 52 performances.
(Off Off Broadway) Opened November 13, 1969 for 12
performances.
(Off Broadway) Adapted by Alex Szogyi. Opened October 23,
1972 in repertory for 6 performances.
(Off Off Broadway) Opened October 1975.
(Off Off Broadway) Opened December 1, 1976.
Reviews:
Arts and Decoration 32:75, Mar 1930
Commonweal 11:342, Jan 22, 1930
Nation 198:404, Apr 20, 1964
New York Times p. 16, Jan 16, 1923
p. 29, Oct 3, 1956
p. 30, Mar 31, 1964
II, p. 1, Apr 12, 1964
p. 72, Dec 16, 1971
p. 35, Aug 28, 1972
p. 42, Oct 25, 1972
p. 20, Feb 19, 1975
New Yorker 40:95-7, Apr 11, 1964
Outlook 154:229, Feb 5, 1930

The Mother (see entry under Brecht, Bertolt)

Night Lodging (see also The Lower Depths and At the Bottom)
Productions:
Opened December 22, 1919 for 14 performances.
Reviews:
Current Opinion 68:195-7, Feb 1920
Nation 110:49-50, Jan 1920
New Republic 21:173, Jan 7, 1920
New York Times p. 12, Dec 23, 1919
VIII, p. 2, Dec 28, 1919

The Red Devil
Productions:
(Off Off Broadway) Opened November 5, 1975.
No Reviews.

Summerfolk
  Productions:
    (Off Broadway) English version by Jeremy Brooks and Kitty
      Hunter-Blair. Opened February 5, 1975 for 13 perform-
      ances.
  Reviews:
    America 132:219, Mar 22, 1975
    Nation 220:380-1, Mar 29, 1975
    New York Theatre Critics' Reviews 1975:335
    New York Times p. 27, Feb 6, 1975
                 II, p. 5, Feb 16, 1975
                 p. 20, Feb 19, 1975
    New Yorker 51:95-6, Feb 24, 1975
    Newsweek 85:66, Feb 17, 1975

*Yegor Bulichov
  Reviews:
    New York Times p. 27, Jan 12, 1971

The Zykovs
  Productions:
    Opened April 10, 1975.
  Reviews:
    New York Times p. 28, Apr 15, 1975
    New Yorker 51:103, Apr 21, 1975

GRANVILLE-BARKER, HARLEY

Anatol (see entry under Schnitzler, Arthur)

Deburau (see entry under Guitry, Sacha)

Dr. Knock (see entry under Romains, Jules)

A Hundred Years Old (see entry under Quintero, Serafin and
            Joaquin Alvarez)

The Kingdom of God (see entry under Martinez-Sierra, Gregorio)

The Lady from Alfaqueque (with Helen Granville-Barker)
  Productions:
    Opened January 14, 1929 for 17 performances.
  Reviews:
    Dial 86:246, Mar 1929
    New York Times p. 22, Jan 15, 1929

The Madras House
  Productions:
    Opened October 29, 1921 for 80 performances.
  Reviews:
    Dial 72:114, Jan 1922
    Dramatic Mirror 84:701, Nov 12, 1921

Independent 107:164, Nov 12, 1921
Nation 113:574-5, Nov 16, 1921
New York Times p. 18, Oct 31, 1921
          VI, p. 1, Nov 6, 1921
Theatre Magazine 35:98, Feb 1922
         35:151, Mar 1922

The Morris Dance
   Productions:
     Based on novel by Robert Louis Stevenson and Lloyd Osbourne.
     Opened February 13, 1917 for 23 performances.
   Reviews:
     Dramatic Mirror 77:7, Feb 17, 1917
     Life (NY) 69:312, Feb 22, 1917
     Nation 104:222, Feb 22, 1917
     New York Drama News 64:6, Feb 17, 1917
     New York Times p. 7, Feb 12, 1917
     Theatre Magazine 25:213, Apr 1917

Pan and the Young Shepherd
   Productions:
     Adapted from the play by Maurice Hewlett. Opened March 18,
     1918 for 32 performances.
   Reviews:
     Dramatic Mirror 78:7, Mar 30, 1918
     Life (NY) 71:558, Apr 4, 1918
     New York Times p. 9, Mar 19, 1918
     Theatre Magazine 27:288+, May 1918

Prunella   (see entry under Housman, Laurence)

The Romantic Young Lady   (see entry under Martinez-Sierra,
      Gregorio)

A Sunny Morning   (see entry under Quintero, Serafin and Joaquin
      Alvarez)

*Waste
   Reviews:
     American Playwright 3:161-6, Mar 1914
     Dramatist 3:259-60, Jul 1912
     Theatre Arts 21:106-7, Feb 1937

The Women Have Their Way   (see entry under Quintero, Serafin
      and Joaquin Alvarez)

GRAY, SIMON

Butley
   Productions:
     Opened October 31, 1972 for 135 performances.

Reviews:
America 127:418, Nov 18, 1972
Nation 215:538, Nov 27, 1972
New Republic 167:22, Nov 25, 1972
New York Theatre Critics' Reviews 1972:200
New York Times II, p. 1, Apr 23, 1972
            p. 28, Oct 27, 1972
            II, p. 1, Oct 29, 1972
            p. 54, Nov 1, 1972
            II, p. 1, Nov 5, 1972
            II, p. 1, Jan 28, 1973
New Yorker 48:130, Nov 11, 1972
Newsweek 80:96, Nov 13, 1972
Saturday Review 55:92, Dec 2, 1972
Time 100:82, Nov 13, 1972

*Dutch Uncle
Reviews:
New York Times p. 41, Mar 28, 1969

*The Idiot
Reviews:
New York Times p. 18, Jul 17, 1970
            p. 39, Jul 30, 1970

Otherwise Engaged
Productions:
Opened February 2, 1977 for 135 performances.
Reviews:
America 136:148, Feb 19, 1977
Commentary 63:75, Apr 1977
Nation 224:219-21, Feb 19, 1977
New Republic 176:20-1, Feb 26, 1977
New York Theatre Critics' Reviews 1977:378
New York Times II, p. 5, Aug 17, 1975
            p. 33, Aug 18, 1975
            II, p. 7, Jan 30, 1977
            p. 28, Feb 3, 1977
            III, p. 17, Feb 9, 1977
            II, p. 7, Feb 13, 1977
            III, p. 3, Feb 25, 1977
            II, p. 1, Jul 17, 1977
            III, p. 3, Aug 5, 1977
New Yorker 52:53, Feb 14, 1977
Newsweek 89:66, Feb 14, 1977
Psychology Today 11:28, Jun 1977
Saturday Review 4:46-7, Mar 19, 1977
Time 107:80, Apr 19, 1976
        109:85, Feb 14, 1977

Wise Child
Productions:
Opened January 27, 1972 for 4 performances.

Reviews:
New York Theatre Critics' Reviews 1972:378
New York Times p. 22, Jan 28, 1972
    II, p. 1, Feb 6, 1972
New Yorker 47:69, Feb 5, 1972

GREENE, GRAHAM

Carving a Statue
Productions:
(Off Broadway) Opened April 30, 1968 for 12 performances.
Reviews:
New York Times p. 25, Sep 18, 1964
    p. 43, May 1, 1968

The Complaisant Lover
Productions:
Opened November 1, 1961 for 101 performances.
Reviews:
Christian Century 78:1532, Dec 20, 1961
Commonweal 75:233-4, Nov 24, 1961
Nation 193:437, Nov 25, 1961
New York Theatre Critics' Reviews 1961:184
New York Times p. 28, Jun 19, 1959
    II, p. 3, Oct 29, 1961
    p. 43, Nov 2, 1961
New Yorker 35:80, Aug 29, 1959
    37:117-18, Nov 11, 1961
Newsweek 58:95, Nov 13, 1961
Reporter 25:62, Dec 7, 1961
Saturday Review 42:25, Jul 4, 1959
    44:36, Dec 2, 1961
Theatre Arts 43:22, Dec 1959
    46:15+, Jan 1962
Time 73:53-4, Jun 29, 1959
    78:66, Nov 10, 1961

The Living Room
Productions:
Opened November 17, 1954 for 22 performances.
(Off Broadway) Opened November 21, 1962 for 23
    performances.
Reviews:
America 90:600-2, Mar 6, 1954
    92:386-7, Jan 8, 1955
    93:433-5, Jul 30, 1955
Catholic World 177:406-10, Sep 1953
Commonweal 59:477-8, Feb 12, 1954
    61:278, Dec 10, 1954
    61:333, Dec 24, 1954
    61:354-5, Dec 31, 1954
    71:123-4, Oct 30, 1959

Commonweal 77:316-17, Dec 14, 1962
Nation 177:138, Aug 15, 1953
    179:496-7, Dec 4, 1954
New Republic 131:22, Dec 13, 1954
New York Theatre Critics' Reviews 1954:251
New York Times p. 41, Nov 18, 1954
        II, p. 1, Nov 28, 1954
        p. 43, Nov 22, 1962
New Yorker 29:69, Jul 18, 1953
    30:156+, Oct 23, 1954
    30:86, Nov 27, 1954
Newsweek 44:92, Nov 29, 1954
Saturday Review 36:24, Aug 1, 1953
    37:24-5, Dec 18, 1954
Theatre Arts 39:12+, Feb 1955
Time 64:50, Nov 29, 1954
    64:55, Dec 20, 1954

The Potting Shed
  Productions:
    Opened January 29, 1957 for 143 performances.
    (Off Broadway) Opened October 19, 1962 for nine
      performances.
    (Off Broadway) Season of 1958-1959.
  Reviews:
    America 96:594-5, Feb 23, 1957
        97:168-70, May 4, 1957
        97:293, Jun 8, 1957
    Catholic World 185:66, Apr 1957
        186:210-13, Dec 1957
    Christian Century 74:262, Feb 27, 1957
    Commonweal 65:613-14, Mar 15, 1957
    Life 42:65-6+, Apr 1, 1957
    Nation 184:146, Feb 16, 1957
    New York Theatre Critics' Reviews 1957:372
    New York Times p. 32, Jan 30, 1957
              II, p. 1, Feb 10, 1957
              II, p. 3, Mar 16, 1958
              p. 49, Nov 3, 1958
              p. 29, Aug 22, 1974
    New Yorker 32:70+, Feb 9, 1957
    Newsweek 49:67, Feb 11, 1957
    Reporter 16:41, Mar 7, 1957
    Saturday Review 40:26-7, Feb 16, 1957
    Theatre Arts 41:15, Apr 1957
    Time 69:70, Feb 11, 1957

GREGORY, LADY

Coats
  Productions:
    Opened February 4, 1913 in repertory (The Irish Players).

Reviews:
    Dramatic Mirror 69:7, Mar 5, 1913
    New York Times p. 13, Mar 4, 1913

Damer's Gold
    Productions:
        Opened February 4, 1913 in repertory (The Irish Players).
    Reviews:
        Dramatic Mirror 69:6-7, Feb 19, 1913

The Dragon
    Productions:
        Opened March 25, 1929 for five performances.
    Reviews:
        New York Times p. 34, Mar 26, 1929
        Weekly Review 3:321, Oct 13, 1920

The Gaol Gate (The Jail Gate)
    Productions:
        Opened November 20, 1911 in repertory (The Irish Players).
        Opened February 4, 1913 in repertory (The Irish Players).
    Reviews:
        Dramatic Mirror 66:6, Dec 6, 1911

Hyacinth Halvey
    Productions:
        Opened November 20, 1911 in repertory (The Irish Players).
    Reviews:
        Dramatic Mirror 66:7, Dec 20, 1911

The Image
    Productions:
        Opened November 20, 1911 in repertory (The Irish Players).
    Reviews:
        Dramatic Mirror 66:6, Dec 27, 1911

The Jackdaw
    Productions:
        Opened November 20, 1911 in repertory (The Irish Players).
        Opened February 4, 1913 in repertory (The Irish Players).
    Reviews:
        Dramatic Mirror 69:7, Feb 12, 1913

The Jail Gate   (see The Gaol Gate)

The Rising of the Moon
    Productions:
        Opened November 20, 1911 in repertory (The Irish Players).
        Opened February 4, 1913 in repertory (The Irish Players).
        Opened October 21, 1932 in repertory (Irish Repertory
            Company).
        (Off Broadway) Season of 1936-1937.
        (Off Broadway) Opened April 1, 1938.

(Off Off Broadway) Opened April 2, 1976.
Reviews:
American Playwright 1:24, Jan 1912
Dramatic Mirror 66:7, Nov 22, 1911
New York Times p. 25, Oct 21, 1932
p. 13, Feb 15, 1937

Spreading the News
Productions:
Opened November 20, 1911 in repertory (The Irish Players).
Opened February 4, 1913 in repertory (The Irish Players).
Reviews:
Dramatic Mirror 66:7, Nov 22, 1911
Green Book 7:636, Mar 1912
New York Times p. 27, Dec 27, 1954

The Travelling Man
Productions:
Opened December 26, 1916 for two performances.
Reviews:
Dramatic Mirror 77:7, Jan 6, 1917

The Workhouse Ward
Productions:
Opened November 20, 1911 in repertory (The Irish Players).
Opened February 4, 1913 in repertory (The Irish Players).
(Off Broadway) Season of 1936-1937.
Reviews:
Catholic World 189:243, Jun 1959
Dramatic Mirror 66:6, Dec 6, 1911
New York Times p. 13, Feb 15, 1937
p. 15, Apr 11, 1959
New Yorker 35:82-3, Apr 18, 1959

GRIFFITHS, TREVOR

Comedians
Productions:
Opened November 28, 1976 for 145 performances.
Reviews:
America 135:472, Dec 25, 1976
Commentary 63:74, Apr 1977
Nation 223:670, Dec 18, 1976
New York Theatre Critics' Reviews 1976:102
New York Times II, p. 5, Nov 21, 1976
III, p. 1, Nov 26, 1976
p. 34, Nov 29, 1976
III, p. 3, Dec 3, 1976
II, p. 1, Dec 5, 1976
II, p. 3, Dec 5, 1976
New Yorker 52:134, Dec 6, 1976

Newsweek 88:97-8, Dec 13, 1976
Time 107:82, Apr 19, 1976
108:88+, Dec 13, 1976

GUITRY, SACHA

The Comedian
‾‾Productions:
Adapted by David Belasco. Opened March 13, 1923 for
87 performances.
Reviews:
Dial 74:635-6, Jun 1923
Hearst 44:85-7+, Jul 1923
Life (NY) 81:20, Apr 5, 1923
New York Clipper 71:14, Mar 21, 1923
New York Times p. 14, Mar 14, 1923
VIII, p. 1, Mar 25, 1923
Theatre Magazine 37:14+, May 1923

Deburau
‾‾Productions:
Adapted by Harley Granville-Barker. Opened December 23,
1920 for 189 performances.
Reviews:
Bookman 52:566-7, Feb 1921
Collier's 67:19, Jan 22, 1921
Dramatic Mirror 83:11, Jan 1, 1921
Dramatist 12:1070-1, Jul 1921
Fortune 116:1034-44, Dec 1921
Hearst 39:21-3+, Apr 1921
Life (NY) 77:64, Jan 13, 1921
New Republic 27:51, Jan 8, 1921
New York Clipper 68:18, Dec 29, 1920
New York Times VI, p. 1, Dec 19, 1920
p. 14, Dec 14, 1920
VI, p. 3, Jan 2, 1921
VI, p. 9, Jan 9, 1921
VI, p. 1, Jan 16, 1921
VI, p. 1, Jan 30, 1921
Outlook 127:249-50, Feb 16, 1921
Theatre Magazine 33:81-2+, Feb 1921
33:172-3+, Mar 1921
Weekly Review 4:39-40, Jan 12, 1921

Don't Listen, Ladies
‾‾Productions:
Translated by Stephen Powys. Opened December 28, 1948
for 15 performances.
Reviews:
New York Theatre Critics' Reviews 1948:100
New York Times p. 16, Dec 29, 1948
New Yorker 24:52, Jan 8, 1949

Newsweek 33:72, Jan 10, 1949
Theatre Arts 33:17, Mar 1949
Time 53:36, Jan 10, 1949

The Grand Duke
  Productions:
    Translated by A. Abdullah. Opened November 1, 1921 for
      131 performances.
  Reviews:
    Dramatic Mirror 84:665, Nov 5, 1921
    Dramatist 13:1087-8, Jan 1922
    Hearst 41:17-19+, Feb 1922
    Independent 107:165, Nov 12, 1921
    Life (NY) 78:18, Nov 24, 1921
    New Republic 28:352, Nov 16, 1921
    New York Clipper 69:20, Nov 9, 1921
    New York Times p. 20, Nov 2, 1921
                    VI, p. 1, Nov 17, 1921
    Theatre Magazine 35:25+, Jan 1922

*Limping Devil
  Reviews:
    New York Times p. 36, Jan 22, 1948

Mozart (Music by Reynaldo Hahn)
  Productions:
    English version by Ashley Dukes. Prologue by Brian Hooker.
      Opened November 22, 1926 for 32 performances.
  Reviews:
    Arts and Decoration 24:55, Apr 1926
    Nation 124:46, Jan 12, 1927
    New York Times p. 26, Nov 23, 1926
                    p. 16, Dec 28, 1926
    Vogue 69:122, Jan 15, 1927
          69:126, Feb 1927

Pasteur
  Productions:
    Adapted by Arthur Hornblow, Jr. Opened March 12, 1923
      for 16 performances.
  Reviews:
    New York Clipper 71:14, Mar 14, 1923
    New York Times p. 19, Mar 13, 1923
                    VII, p. 1, Mar 18, 1923
    Science ns56:12, Jul 7, 1922
    Theatre Magazine 37:5+, May 1923

Sleeping Partners
  Productions:
    Opened October 5, 1918 for 161 performances.
  Reviews:
    Dramatic Mirror 79:579, Oct 19, 1918
    Life (NY) 72:562, Oct 17, 1918

New York Dramatic News 65:7, Oct 12, 1918
New York Times p. 11, Oct 7, 1918
      IV, p. 2, Oct 13, 1918
      p. 16, Aug 8, 1940
Theatre Magazine 28:347, Dec 1918

HAMILTON, PATRICK

Angel Street (Gas Light)
  Productions:
    Opened December 5, 1941 for 1,295 performances.
    Opened January 22, 1948 for 14 performances.
    (Off Broadway) Opened 1948 in repertory.
    Opened December 26, 1975 for 52 performances.
  Reviews:
    Commonweal 47:424, Feb 6, 1948
    Nation 153:649, Dec 20, 1941
    New Republic 118:34, Feb 9, 1948
    New York Theatre Critics' Reviews 1941:182
    New York Times p. 15, Dec 6, 1941
             II, p. 1, Jul 9, 1944
             p. 26, Jan 23, 1948
             p. 12, Dec 27, 1975
             II, p. 7, Jan 11, 1976
    New Yorker 23:40, Jan 31, 1948
    Newsweek 18:72, Dec 15, 1941
    Theatre Arts 26:77, 87, Feb 1942
    Time 38:73, Dec 15, 1941
    Vogue 99:60-61, Feb 15, 1942

The Duke in Darkness
  Productions:
    Opened January 24, 1944 for 24 performances.
  Reviews:
    Commonweal 39:420, Feb 11, 1944
    New York Theatre Critics' Reviews 1944:279
    New York Times VIII, p. 1, Oct 18, 1942
             p. 15, Jan 25, 1944
    Theatre Arts 28:208, Apr 1944

Gas Light (see Angel Street)

Rope's End (Rope)
  Productions:
    Opened September 19, 1929 for 100 performances.
  Reviews:
    Catholic World 120:467-8, Jan 1930
    Literary Digest 103:18-19, Oct 19, 1929
    New York Times p. 34, Sep 20, 1929
    Review of Reviews 80:158, Dec 1929
    Theatre Magazine 50:74, Nov 1929
    Vogue 74:154, Nov 9, 1929

HAMPTON, CHRISTOPHER

A Doll's House (see entry under Ibsen, Henrik)

Hedda Gabler (see entry under Ibsen, Henrik)

The Philanthropist
   Productions:
     Opened March 15, 1971 for 72 performances.
   Reviews:
     America 124:540, May 22, 1971
     Nation 211:252, Sep 21, 1970
         212:442, Apr 5, 1971
     New York Theatre Critics' Reviews 1971:329
     New York Times p. 20, Aug 5, 1970
          p. 59, Sep 10, 1970
          II, p. 1, Jan 17, 1971
          p. 47, Mar 16, 1971
          II, p. 1, Mar 28, 1971
          II, p. 28, Apr 25, 1971
          p. 20, May 15, 1971
     New Yorker 47:83, Mar 27, 1971
     Newsweek 77:109, Mar 29, 1971
     Saturday Review 54:22, Apr 3, 1971
     Time 97:67, Mar 29, 1971

Savages
   Productions:
     (Off Off Broadway) Opened February 24, 1977.
   Reviews:
     America 129:443, Dec 8, 1973
     New Yorker 53:66+, Mar 14, 1977
     Newsweek 84:91, Sep 9, 1974

Total Eclipse
   Productions:
     (Off Broadway) Opened February 23, 1974 for 32 performances.
   Reviews:
     Nation 218:348, Mar 16, 1974
     New York Theatre Critics' Reviews 1974:291
     New York Times p. 42, Sep 13, 1968
     New Yorker 50:102+, Mar 11, 1974
     Newsweek 83:103+, Mar 25, 1974

When Did You Last See My Mother?
   Productions:
     (Off Broadway) Opened January 4, 1967 for 11 performances
      in repertory.
   Reviews:
     New York Times p. 27, Jan 5, 1967

HARTOG, JAN DE see DE HARTOG, JAN

HARWOOD, H. M.

Billeted (with F. Tennyson Jesse)
    Productions:
        Opened December 25, 1917 for 79 performances.
        Opened May 9, 1922 for 23 performances.
    Reviews:
        Dramatic Mirror 78:7, Jan 5, 1918
        Green Book 19:393+, Mar 1918
        Nation 105:379, Oct 4, 1917
        New York Times p. 7, Dec 26, 1917
                        IV, p. 8, Jan 6, 1918
        Theatre Magazine 27:73+, Feb 1918
                        36:32, Jul 1922

The Black Mask (with F. Tennyson Jesse)
    Productions:
        Opened September 27, 1913 in repertory (The Princess
            Players).
    Reviews:
        Bookman 38:364, Dec 1913
        Dramatic Mirror 70:6, Oct 15, 1913
        Green Book 10:1062-3, Dec 1913
        Theatre Magazine 18:143, Nov 1913

Cynara (with R. F. Gore-Browne)
    Productions:
        Opened November 2, 1931 for 210 performances.
    Reviews:
        Arts and Decoration 36:62, Jan 1932
        Catholic World 134:333-4, Dec 1931
        Commonweal 15:270, Jan 6, 1932
        New York Times p. 31, Nov 3, 1931
        Outlook 159:376, Nov 18, 1931
        Sketch Book 9:20, Jan 1932
        Theatre Arts 16:21, Jan 1932
        Theatre Guild Magazine 9:3-4, Dec 1931
                        9:2, Jan 1932
        Town and Country 86:46-7, Dec 1931
        Vanity Fair 37:74, Jan 1932
        Vogue 79:82, Jan 15, 1932

A Kiss of Importance (with André Picard)
    Productions:
        Adapted by Arthur Hornblow, Jr. Opened December 1, 1930
            for 24 performances.
    Reviews:
        Life (NY) 96:18-19, Dec 19, 1930
        New York Times p. 31, Dec 2, 1930

Lady Jane (The Old Folks at Home)
    Productions:
        Opened September 10, 1934 for 40 performances.

Reviews:
Catholic World 140:90-1, Oct 1934
Golden Book 20:506+, Nov 1934
Literary Digest 118:20, Sep 22, 1934
Nation 139:364, Sep 26, 1934
New York Times p. 24, Sep 11, 1934
Theatre Arts 18:817, Nov 1934
Vanity Fair 43:49-50, Nov 1934

The Man in Possession
Productions:
Opened November 1, 1930 for 98 performances.
Reviews:
Catholic World 132:338-9, Dec 1930
Commonweal 13:329, Jan 21, 1931
Life (NY) 96:15, Nov 21, 1930
New York Times VIII, p. 4, Oct 12, 1930
p. 19, Nov 3, 1930
Theatre Magazine 53:25-6, Jan 1931
Vogue 77:88, Jan 1, 1931

The Old Folks at Home   (see Lady Jane)

The Pelican (with F. Tennyson Jesse)
Productions:
Opened September 21, 1925 for 65 performances.
Reviews:
Bookman 62:320, Nov 1925
New York Times p. 23, Sep 22, 1925
VII, p. 1, Sep 27, 1925
Theatre Magazine 42:18, Nov 1925

A Pin to See the Peepshow (with F. Tennyson Jesse)
Productions:
Opened September 27, 1953 for one performance.
Reviews:
New York Theatre Critics' Reviews 1953:278
New York Times p. 17, Sep 18, 1953
II, p. 1, Nov 8, 1953
New Yorker 29:79, Sep 26, 1953
Newsweek 42:90, Sep 28, 1953
Theatre Arts 37:19, Nov 1953

A Pinch Hitter
Productions:
Opened January 1, 1922 for 17 performances.
Reviews:
Life (NY) 79:18, Jun 22, 1922
New York Clipper 70:24, Jun 7, 1922
Theatre Magazine 36:71+, Aug 1922

Please Help Emily
Productions:
    Opened August 14, 1916 for 40 performances.
Reviews:
    Dramatic Mirror 76:8-9, Aug 19, 1916
    Dramatist 8:741-2, Oct 1916
    Nation 103:183, Aug 24, 1916
    New York Dramatic News 63:3+, Aug 19, 1916
    New York Times p. 7, Aug 15, 1916
    Theatre Magazine 24:138, Sep 1916

HAUPTMANN, GERHART

The Assumption of Hannele (see Hannele)

Before Sundown (Before Sunset)
Productions:
    (Off Broadway) Opened March 6, 1962 for 14 performances.
Reviews:
    New York Times p. 43, Mar 14, 1962

*Hamlet at Wittenberg
Reviews:
    Modern Language Review 32:595-7, Oct 1937
    Theatre Arts 20:361-3, May 1936

Hannele (The Assumption of Hannele)
Productions:
    Opened April 11, 1910 for 16 performances.
    Opened February 15, 1924 for three performances.
Reviews:
    American Mercury 1:503, Apr 1924
    Bookman 31:417-18, Jun 1910
    Dramatic Mirror 63:7, Apr 23, 1910
    Green Book 2:1245-6, Jun 1910
    Hampton 24:829-30, Jun 1910
    Independent 112:106, Feb 16, 1924
    Life (NY) 55:766, Apr 28, 1910
    New Republic 38:21, Feb 27, 1924
    New York Times p. 16, Feb 16, 1924
    Theatre Magazine 11:139-41, May 1910

Die Ratten (The Rats)
Productions:
    Opened April 12, 1966 for 8 performances.
Reviews:
    New York Times p. 36, Apr 13, 1966

Rose Bernd
Productions:
    Opened September 26, 1922 for 87 performances.

Reviews:
    Dial 73:584-5, Nov 1922
    Forum 68:974-5, Nov 1922
    Life (NY) 80:18, Oct 19, 1922
    Nation 115:392-4, Oct 11, 1922
        115:440, Oct 25, 1922
    New Republic 32:251-2, Nov 1, 1922
    New York Times p. 17, Sep 27, 1922
    Theatre Arts 17:27-8, Jan 1933
    Theatre Magazine 36:375, Dec 1922

The Weavers
    Productions:
        Translated by Mary Morrison.   Opened December 14, 1915
            for 87 performances.
    Reviews:
        Book News 34:323-4, Mar 1916
        Bookman 42:647, 650, Feb 1916
        Collier's 57:24, May 13, 1916
        Craftsman 20:531, Aug 1911
        Current Opinion 60:178-9, Mar 1916
        Dramatic Mirror 74:8, Dec 25, 1915
        Dramatist 7:654-6, Jan 1916
        Harper's Weekly 62:16, Jun 1, 1916
        Hearst 29:372-4, 386, May 1916
        Life (NY) 66:1282, Dec 30, 1915
        Nation 101:786, Dec 30, 1915
            115:392-4, Oct 11, 1922
        New Republic 5:200, Dec 25, 1915
        New York Times p. 15, Dec 15, 1915
        North American Review 203:289, Feb 1916
        Survey 35:372, Jan 1, 1916
        Theatre Magazine 23:64, Feb 1916

HEBBLE, FRIEDRICH

Judith
    Productions:
        (Off Broadway) Opened Season of 1947-1948 in repertory.
    No Reviews.

HEIJERMANS, HERMANN

The Devil to Pay
    Productions:
        Translated by Caroline Heijermans-Houwink and Lilian
            Saunders.   Opened December 3, 1925 for 11 performances.
    Reviews:
        New York Times p. 26, Dec 4, 1925
                IX, p. 4, Dec 13, 1925

The Good Hope
  Productions:
    Translated by Lilian Saunders and Caroline Heijermans-
      Houwink. Opened October 18, 1927 for 49 performances.
  Reviews:
    Canadian Forum 12:198, Feb 1932
    Nation 125:185, Nov 2, 1927
    New Republic 52:285, Nov 2, 1927
    New York Times p. 24, Oct 19, 1927
                    VIII, p. 1, Oct 23, 1927
    Outlook 147:340, Nov 16, 1927
    Saturday Review 4:275-6, Nov 5, 1927
    Theatre Arts 11:895+, Dec 1927
    Theatre Magazine 47:70, Jan 1928
    Vogue 70:116, Dec 15, 1927

HOCHHUTH, ROLF

The Deputy
  Productions:
    Adapted by Jerome Rothenberg. Opened February 26, 1964
      for 316 performances.
  Reviews:
    America 108:730-1, May 25, 1963
            109:70, Jul 20, 1963
            109:187, Aug 24, 1963
            109:570-3+, Nov 9, 1963
            110:139-40, Jan 25, 1964
            110:304-5, Mar 7, 1964
            110:499, Apr 11, 1964
            110:341-2, Mar 14, 1964
            110:400, Mar 28, 1964
            110:495-6, Apr 4, 1964
    Catholic World 197:380-5, Sep 1963
                   199:135-6, May 1964
    Christian Century 80:980-1, Aug 7, 1963
                      80:1269-70, Oct 16, 1963
                      81:349, Mar 11, 1964
                      81:507-8, Apr 22, 1964
    Commonweal 79:647-62, Feb 28, 1964
               79:749-51, Mar 20, 1964
               80:174-6, May 1, 1964
    Life 56:28D, Mar 13, 1964
    Nation 197:287-8, Nov 2, 1963
           198:277-8, Mar 16, 1964
           198:270-2, Mar 16, 1964
    New Republic 150:23-5, Mar 14, 1964
    New York Theatre Critics' Reviews 1964:332
    New York Times p. 7, Feb 23, 1963
                   p. 36, Apr 28, 1963
                   II, p. 3, May 5, 1963
                   p. 13, Jul 5, 1963

New York Times p. 46, Sep 10, 1963
            p. 41, Sep 26, 1963
            p. 19, Sep 27, 1963
            p. 15, Jan 25, 1964
            II, p. 1, Feb 23, 1964
            p. 23, Feb 25, 1964
            p. 26, Feb 27, 1964
            p. 18, Feb 28, 1964
            VII, p. 1, Mar 1, 1964
            II, p. 1, Mar 8, 1964
            p. 37, Jun 19, 1964
New Yorker 39:54+, Dec 28, 1963
          40:118, Mar 7, 1964
Newsweek 61:65, Mar 11, 1963
        63:78-9, Mar 2, 1964
        63:78-9, Mar 9, 1964
Reporter 30:46+, Jan 30, 1964
       30:40+, Apr 9, 1964
Saturday Evening Post 237:36+, Feb 29, 1964
Saturday Review 47:16, Mar 14, 1964
              47:41-2, Mar 21, 1964
Time 82:75-6, Nov 1, 1963
    83:50, Mar 6, 1964
U. S. News and World Report 56:60, Mar 16, 1964
Vogue 143:54, Apr 15, 1964

*Guerillas
  Reviews:
    Nation 211:124-6, Aug 17, 1970
    New York Times p. 91, May 17, 1970
    Newsweek 75:105, Jun 1, 1970

*Midwife
  Reviews:
    Newsweek 79:106, May 22, 1972

The Representative (see The Deputy)

Soldiers
  Productions:
    Translated by Robert D. MacDonald. Opened May 1, 1968
      for 22 performances.
  Reviews:
    America 118:752-4, Jun 8, 1968
           119:140, Aug 31, 1968
    Commonweal 88:182-4, Apr 26, 1968
              88:335, May 31, 1968
    Life 64:12, Jun 7, 1968
    Nation 205:700-1, Dec 25, 1967
        206:678, May 20, 1968
    New York Theatre Critics' Reviews 1968:279, 285
    New York Times p. 14, Oct 10, 1967
                p. 37, Oct 11, 1967

New York Times p. 88, Mar 3, 1968
              II, p. 1, Mar 10, 1968
              p. 58, May 2, 1968
              II, p. 3, May 12, 1968
              p. 54, May 13, 1968
New York Times Magazine pp. 48-9+, Nov 19, 1967
New Yorker 44:83-4, May 11, 1968
           71:105, Mar 11, 1968
           71:109, May 13, 1968
Reporter 38:38-9, May 30, 1968
Saturday Review 50:27+, Dec 2, 1967
              51:32+, May 18, 1968
Time 90:82, Oct 20, 1967
     91:72+, May 10, 1968
Vogue 151:158, May 1968

Der Stellvertreter (see The Deputy)

The Vicar (see The Deputy)

The Vicar of Christ (see The Deputy)

HOCHWALDER, FRITZ

Crown Colony
    Productions:
        (Off Broadway) Translated by Richard Conlin. Season of
           1946-7 in repertory.
    No Reviews.

The Strong Are Lonely
    Productions:
        Adapted by Eva Le Gallienne. Opened September 29, 1953
           for 7 performances.
    Reviews:
        America 95:265, Jun 9, 1956
        Catholic World 178:146, Nov 1953
        Commonweal 59:60-1, Oct 23, 1953
        Nation 177:317, Oct 17, 1953
        New Republic 129:20, Oct 26, 1953
        New York Theatre Critics' Reviews 1953:269
        New York Times II, p. 1, Sep 27, 1953
                   p. 38, Sep 30, 1953
        New Yorker 29:72-4, Oct 10, 1953
        Saturday Review 36:36, Oct 17, 1953
        Theatre Arts 37:17, Dec 1953
        Time 62:50, Oct 12, 1953

*Sur la Terre Comme au Ciel
    Reviews:
        America 89:221, May 23, 1953

HOPKINS, JOHN

Economic Necessity
  Productions:
    (Off Off Broadway) Opened March 25, 1976.
  No Reviews.

Find Your Way Home
  Productions:
    Opened January 2, 1974 for 135 performances.
  Reviews:
    America 130:33, Jan 19, 1974
    Nation 218:187-8, Feb 9, 1974
    New Republic 170:22, Jan 26, 1974
    New York Theatre Critics' Reviews 1974:398
    New York Times p. 43, Jan 3, 1974
              II, p. 3, Jan 13, 1974
    New Yorker 49:58, Jan 14, 1974
    Time 103:42+, Jan 14, 1974

*This Story of Yours
  Reviews:
    New York Times p. 60, Dec 14, 1968

HOUGHTON, STANLEY

Fancy Free
  Productions:
    Opened March 14, 1913 in repertory for 115 performances.
  Reviews:
    Blue Book 17:438-9, Jul 1913
    Bookman 37:310-11, May 1913
    Dramatic Mirror 69:6, Mar 19, 1913

Hindle Wakes (Fanny Hawthorne)
  Productions:
    Opened December 9, 1912 for 32 performances.
    Opened May 11, 1922 for 36 performances.
  Reviews:
    American Playwright 2:5, Jan 1913
    Bookman 36:641, Feb 1913
    Colliers 50:7, Dec 28, 1912
    Current Opinion 55:169-72, Sep 1913
    Dramatist 4:323, Jan 1913
    Everybody's Magazine 28:394-7, Mar 1913
    Green Book 9:249, Feb 1913
    Life (NY) 60:2492-3, Dec 19, 1912
    McClure's Magazine 40:64-5+, Mar 1913
    New York Times p. 22, May 12, 1922

Red Book 21:115, May 1913
Theatre Magazine 17:2-3, Jan 1913

Phipps
Productions:
Opened September 27, 1913 in repertory.
Opened October 17, 1914 in repertory.
Reviews:
Dramatic Mirror 72:8, Oct 28, 1914
Green Book 13:125, Jan 1915
Theatre Magazine 20:267, Dec 1914

The Younger Generation
Productions:
Opened September 25, 1913 for 60 performances.
Reviews:
Bookman 38:266, Nov 1913
Dramatic Mirror 70:6, Oct 1, 1913
Dramatist 5:396, Oct 1913
Everybody's 29:809, Dec 1913
Life (NY) 62:612, Oct 9, 1913
New York Times p. 11, Sep 26, 1913
Theatre Magazine 18:145, Nov 1913

HOUSMAN, LAURENCE

*Jacob
Reviews:
New York Times VIII, p. 1, Jun 14, 1942

Prunella (with Harley Granville-Barker and J. Moorat)
Productions:
Opened October 27, 1913 for 104 performances.
Reviews:
American Mercury 77:33-4, Mar 1914
Bookman 38:363, Dec 1913
Current Opinion 56:24-8, Jan 14, 1914
Dramatic Mirror 70:6, Oct 29, 1913
Everybody's Magazine 30:264, Feb 1914
Green Book 11:71-2, Jan 1914
            11:165-6, Jan 1914
Harper's Bazaar 49:37+, Mar 1914
International 7:364+, Dec 1913
Leslie's Weekly 117:495, Nov 20, 1913
Life (NY) 62:790-1, Nov 6, 1913
Literary Digest 47:944-5, Nov 15, 1913
Munsey 50:726-7, Jan 1914
New York Times p. 9, Oct 27, 1913
Theatre Magazine 18:174-5+, Dec 1913

Victoria Regina
  Productions:
    Opened December 26, 1935 for 517 performances.
    Opened October 3, 1938 for 87 performances.
  Reviews:
    Catholic World 142:598-9, Feb 1936
    Commonweal 23:301, Jan 10, 1936
    Harper's 172:1-2, Apr 1936
    Literary Digest 121:19, Jan 11, 1936
    Life 4:62-4, Apr 11, 1938
    Nation 142:83-4, Jan 15, 1936
    New Republic 85:286, Jan 15, 1936
    New York Times p. 25, Sep 5, 1935
                   p. 30, Dec 13, 1935
                   p. 15, Dec 27, 1935
                   IX, p. 1, Jan 5, 1936
                   p. 20, Oct 4, 1938
    Newsweek 6:25, Dec 28, 1935
    Pictorial Review 37:50, Apr 1936
    Scholastic 29:3-5+, Oct 3, 1936
    Stage 13:41-3, Jan 1936
          13:6, Feb 1936
    Theatre Arts 20:86+, Feb 1936
                 20:467, Dec 1936
                 22:386, May 1938
    Time 26:22, Dec 30, 1935
    Vogue 89:70-1+, May 15, 1937

HUGO, VICTOR

Clair de Lune
  Productions:
    Dramatized by Michael Strange from Victor Hugo's The Man
      Who Laughed. Opened April 18, 1921 for 64 performances.
  Reviews:
    Bookman 53:381, Jun 1921
    Current Opinion 71:55-63, Jul 1921
    Dramatic Mirror 83:697, Apr 23, 1921
    Dramatist 12:1069-70, Jul 1921
    Life (NY) 77:648, May 5, 1921
    Nation 112:672, May 4, 1921
    New Republic 26:299, May 4, 1921
    New York Clipper 69:19, Apr 27, 1921
    New York Times VI, p. 1, Apr 10, 1921
                   p. 15, Apr 19, 1921
                   VI, p. 1, Apr 24, 1921
    Review 4:444-6, May 7, 1921
    Theatre Magazine 33:417+, Jun 1921
                     34:92, Aug 1921

Gil Blas
    Productions:
        (Off Broadway) Opened season of 1957-58.
    Reviews:
        New York Times p. 16, Dec 14, 1957

The Man Who Laughed (see Clair de Lune)

Marie Tudor
    Productions:
        Opened October 21, 1958 in repertory.
        (Off Off Broadway) Opened November 6, 1975.
    Reviews:
        New York Times Critics' Reviews 1958:252
        New York Times p. 39, Oct 22, 1958

Ruy Blas (see Gil Blas)

HUXLEY, ALDOUS

The Devils of Loudon (see John Whiting's The Devils)

Genius and the Goddess (with Beth Wendel in collaboration with
        Alec Coppell)
    Productions:
        Opened December 10, 1957 for seven performances.
    Reviews:
        New York Theatre Critics' Reviews 1957:153
        New York Times p. 41, Dec 11, 1957
        New Yorker 33:42-3, Dec 21, 1957
        Saturday Review 40:22, Dec 28, 1957
        Theatre Arts 42:24, Feb 1958

The Giaconda Smile
    Productions:
        Opened October 7, 1950 for 41 performances.
    Reviews:
        Catholic World 172:226, Dec 1950
        Christian Science Monitor Magazine p. 11, Oct 14, 1950
        Commonweal 53:61-2, Oct 27, 1950
        Nation 171:371, Oct 21, 1950
        New Republic 123:22, Nov 6, 1950
        New York Times II, p. 1, Oct 1, 1950
                        p. 21, Oct 9, 1950
                        II, p. 1, Oct 15, 1950
        New Yorker 26:52, Oct 14, 1950
        Newsweek 36:84+, Oct 16, 1950
        Theatre Arts 34:13, Dec 1950
        Time 56:53, Oct 16, 1950

IBSEN, HENRIK

Brand
  Productions:
    (Off Off Broadway) Translated by Michael Meyer.   Season of
      1970-1971.
  Reviews:
    Modern Language Notes 51:99-106, Feb 1936
    New York Times p. 18, Apr 12, 1974
    New Yorker 35:79, May 30, 1959

*Cataline
  Reviews:
    Theatre Arts 20:170, Mar 1936

A Doll's House
  Productions:
    Opened April 29, 1918 for 32 performances.
    Adapted by Thornton Wilder.   Opened December 27, 1937
      for 144 performances.
    (Off Broadway) Season of 1943-1944 in repertory.
    (Off Broadway) Season of 1955-1956.
    (Off Broadway) Adapted by Carmel Ross.   Translated by R.
      Farquharson Sharpe.   Opened February 2, 1963 for 66
      performances.
    Adapted by Christopher Hampton.   Opened January 13, 1971
      for 111 performances.
    (Off Off Broadway) Opened September 1974.
    Adapted by Christopher Hampton.   Opened March 5, 1975
      for 56 performances.
    (Off Off Broadway) Opened September 24, 1976.
  Reviews:
    America 124:318-19, Mar 27, 1971
            132:303-4, Apr 19, 1975
    Catholic World 146:596-7, Feb 1938
    Dramatic Mirror 78:656, May 11, 1918
    Green Book 20:11-13, Jul 1918
    Life 70:10, Mar 12, 1971
    Literary Digest 125:22-3, Jan 15, 1938
    Living Age 320:415-16, Mar 1, 1924
    Nation 146:53-4, Jan 8, 1938
           212:154-6, Feb 1, 1971
           220:348-9, Mar 22, 1975
    New Republic 93:338, Jan 26, 1938
                 164:24+, Mar 13, 1971
                 172:22+, Mar 29, 1975
    New York Theatre Critics' Reviews 1971:390
                                      1975:318
    New York Times p. 13, Apr 30, 1918
                   IV, p. 8, May 5, 1918
                   p. 28, Dec 28, 1937
                   p. 32, Nov 15, 1954
                   p. 29, May 8, 1956

New York Times p. 5, Feb 4, 1963
p. 34, Dec 25, 1970
p. 45, Jan 14, 1971
II, p. 1, Jan 24, 1971
II, p. 1, Feb 7, 1971
p. 45, Nov 2, 1971
p. 44, Mar 6, 1975
II, p. 1, Mar 16, 1975
II, p. 5, Apr 6, 1975
New Yorker 38:68+, Feb 9, 1963
46:66-7, Jan 23, 1971
51:92, Mar 17, 1975
Newsweek 11:28, Jan 10, 1938
61:56, Feb 18, 1963
77:66-7, Mar 1, 1971
85:61-5, Mar 17, 1975
One-Act Play Magazine 1:845-7, Jan 1938
Player's Magazine 14:12, Sep-Oct 1937
Saturday Review 2:48, Apr 19, 1975
Scribner's Magazine 103:71, Mar 1938
Stage 15:55, Feb 1938
Theatre Arts 20:170, Mar 1936
22:92+, Feb 1938
22:384, May 1938
47:12-13, Apr 1963
Theatre Magazine 12:41-4, Aug 1910
27:358, Jun 1918
Time 31:32, Jan 10, 1938
97:48, Jan 25, 1971
105:73, Mar 17, 1975
Vogue 157:114+, Mar 1, 1971

An Enemy of the People
  Productions:
    November 1923 in repertory (Moscow Art Theatre).
    Opened October 3, 1927 for 127 performances.
    Opened November 5, 1928 for 16 performances.
    Opened February 15, 1937 for 16 performances.
    Adapted by Arthur Miller. Opened December 28, 1950
      for 36 performances.
    (Off Broadway) Adapted by Arthur Miller. Season of 1958-
      1959.
    (Off Off Broadway) Adapted by Arthur Miller. Opened
      February 9, 1968 for 9 performances.
    Adapted by Arthur Miller. Opened March 11, 1971 for 54
      performances.
  Reviews:
    Catholic World 172:387, Feb 1951
    Christian Science Monitor Magazine p. 6, Jan 6, 1951
    Commonweal 53:374, Jan 19, 1951
    Independent 104:1, Oct 2, 1920
    Nation 125:430-1, Oct 19, 1927
    144:249, Feb 27, 1937

Nation 172:18, Jan 6, 1951
New Republic 90:139, Mar 10, 1937
      124:22, Jan 22, 1951
New York Theatre Critics' Reviews 1950:154
      1971:334
New York Times p. 25, Dec 4, 1923
      p. 32, Oct 4, 1927
      p. 19, Feb 16, 1937
      II, p. 3, Dec 24, 1950
      p. 14, Dec 29, 1950
      II, p. 1, Jan 7, 1951
      p. 24, Feb 26, 1958
      p. 24, Feb 5, 1959
      p. 26, Mar 12, 1971
      II, p. 3, Mar 21, 1971
      p. 32, Jun 29, 1975
New Yorker 26:44, Jan 13, 1951
      34:68+, Feb 14, 1959
Newsweek 37:67, Jan 8, 1951
Outlook 147:279, Nov 2, 1927
Saturday Review 42:34, Feb 21, 1959
School and Society 73:105, Feb 17, 1951
Theatre Arts 11:884+, Dec 1927
      35:15, Mar 1951
Theatre Magazine 46:42, Dec 1927
Time 57:31, Jan 8, 1951
Vogue 70:172, Dec 1, 1927
Weekly Review 3:274, Sep 29, 1920

Ghosts
   Productions:
     Opened March 4, 1912 for 4 performances.
     Opened April 20, 1915 for 2 performances.
     Translated by William Archer. May 7, 1917 in repertory
      (Washington Square Players).
     Opened February 7, 1919 for 1 performance.
     Opened Winter 1922 for 21 performances.
     November 29, 1923 in repertory for 2 performances.
     Opened March 16, 1926 for 34 performances.
     Translated by William Archer, revised by Harrison Grey
      Fishe. Opened January 10, 1927 for 24 performances.
     Opened May 23, 1933 for 6 performances.
     (Off Broadway) Season of 1934-1935 in repertory.
     (Off Broadway) Opened October 2, 1935.
     Opened December 12, 1935 for 81 performances.
     Translated by Eva Le Gallienne. Opened February 24, 1948
      for 10 performances.
     (Off Broadway) Opened June 1951.
     (Off Broadway) Opened September 1951.
     (Off Broadway) Adapted by Carmel Ross. Translated by R.
      Farquharson Sharpe. Opened September 21, 1961 for
      216 performances.

(Off Broadway) Adapted by Gene Feist. Opened March 13,
   1973 for 89 performances.
(Off Off Broadway) Opened April 26, 1974.
(Off Off Broadway) Season of 1974-1975 (Jean Cocteau).
(Off Off Broadway) Season of 1974-1975 (Time & Space Ltd.)
(Off Broadway) Translated by Rolfe Fjelde. Opened March 6,
   1975 in repertory for 37 performances.
(Off Off Broadway) Opened November 1975.
(Off Off Broadway) Adapted by Marlene Swartz. Opened
   September 18, 1976.
Reviews:
   America 106:29, Oct 7, 1961
   American Mercury 10:376, Mar 1927
   Bookman 65:205, Apr 1927
   Catholic World 142:601, Feb 1936
   Commonweal 23:244, Dec 27, 1935
                75:94, Oct 20, 1961
   Dramatic Mirror 73:8, Apr 1, 1915
                   77:7, May 19, 1917
                   80:304, Mar 1, 1919
   Dramatist 17:1322, Oct 1926
   Life (NY) 69:892, May 17, 1917
   Nation 166:256, Feb 28, 1948
          193:459, Dec 2, 1961
   New Republic 11:83, May 19, 1917
                85:230, Jan 1, 1936
                145:30-1, Oct 9, 1961
   New York Theatre Critics' Reviews 1948:343
                                     1973:253
   New York Times p. 4, Apr 16, 1915
                  p. 9, May 8, 1917
                  p. 13, Feb 8, 1919
                  p. 12, Feb 7, 1922
                  p. 14, Nov 7, 1923
                  VII, p. 1, Jan 16, 1927
                  p. 24, May 24, 1933
                  p. 30, Dec 13, 1935
                  p. 28, May 12, 1936
                  IX, p. 1, Jun 23, 1940
                  p. 31, Feb 17, 1948
                  p. 29, Sep 22, 1961
                  p. 35, Apr 4, 1973
                  II, p. 3, Apr 22, 1973
                  p. 46, Apr 3, 1975
                  II, p. 5, Apr 13, 1975
                  II, p. 5, May 11, 1975
   New Yorker 37:120+, Sep 30, 1961
   Newsweek 6:39, Dec 21, 1935
   Theatre Arts 20:97-8, Feb 1936
                45:59-60, Nov 1961
   Theatre Magazine 25:340, Jun 1917
                    29:144, Mar 1919

Time 26:32, Dec 23, 1935
78:88, Oct 6, 1961
101:90, May 7, 1973

Hedda Gabler
  Productions:
    Opened April 8, 1918 for 24 performances.
    Opened May 16, 1924 for 8 performances.
    Translated by William Archer. Opened January 26, 1926
      for 59 performances.
    Translated by Julie Le Gallienne and Paul Leyssac. Opened
      March 26, 1928 for 15 performances.
    Opened February 2, 1929 for 25 performances.
    Opened November 16, 1936 for 32 performances.
    Translated by Ethel Borden and Mary Cass Canfield. Opened
      January 29, 1942 for 12 performances.
    Translated by Eva Le Gallienne. Opened February 24, 1948
      for 15 performances.
    (Off Broadway) Opened October 1950 in repertory.
    (Off Broadway) Season of 1955-1956.
    (Off Broadway) Translated by Michael Meyer. Opened
      November 9, 1960 for 340 performances.
    (Off Broadway) Opened Janaury 16, 1970 for 81 performances.
    Adapted by Christopher Hampton. Opened February 17, 1971
      for 56 performances.
    (Off Off Broadway) Opened October 1973.
    (Off Off Broadway) Opened November 23, 1973.
    (Off Off Broadway) Opened February 20, 1974.
    (Off Off Broadway) Opened April 24, 1974.
    (Off Off Broadway) English version by Christopher Martin.
      Season of 1974-1975.
    (Off Broadway) Translated by William Archer. Opened
      September 20, 1975 for 48 performances.
  Reviews:
    America 124:318-19, Mar 27, 1971
    Catholic World 144:469, Jan 1937
    Commonweal 9:460, Feb 20, 1929
              21:207, Dec 14, 1934
              25:134, Nov 27, 1936
              35:417, Feb 13, 1942
              74:304-5, Jun 16, 1961
    Dramatic Mirror 78:585, Apr 17, 1918
                    78:548, Apr 20, 1918
                    p. 635, Oct 9, 1920
    Forum 52:765-9, Nov 1914
    Green Book 6:1211-18, Dec 1911
    Life 70:10, Mar 12, 1971
    Nation 139:720, Dec 19, 1934
           143:641-2, Nov 28, 1936
           154:202, Feb 14, 1942
           191:462-3, Dec 10, 1960
           211:253, Sep 21, 1970
           212:314, Mar 8, 1971

National Review 22:852, Aug 11, 1970
New Republic 14:359, Apr 20, 1918
         39:49, Jun 4, 1924
         45:356-7, Feb 17, 1926
         106:204, Feb 9, 1942
         106:238, Feb 16, 1942
         143:39, Nov 28, 1960
         164:24+ , Mar 13, 1971
New York Theatre Critics' Reviews 1942:358+
                                1948:327
                                1971:364
New York Times IV, p. 6, Apr 14, 1918
                p. 18, May 17, 1924
                p. 30, Mar 27, 1928
                p. 20, Feb 4, 1929
                p. 34, Nov 17, 1936
                p. 22, Jan 30, 1942
                p. 27, Feb 25, 1948
                p. 61, Nov 10, 1960
                p. 24, Nov 25, 1960
                p. 39, Jun 5, 1968
                p. 78, Jan 18, 1970
                II, p. 3, Jan 25, 1970
                p. 28, Jun 12, 1970
                II, p. 1, Jun 21, 1970
                p. 12, Jul 18, 1970
                p. 30, Feb 18, 1971
                II, p. 1, Feb 28, 1971
                II, p. 3, Mar 7, 1971
                p. 36, May 8, 1974
                p. 25, Apr 9, 1975
                p. 42, Apr 24, 1975
New Yorker 36:94+ , Nov 19, 1960
         38:175-6, Dec 15, 1962
         47:84-5, Feb 27, 1971
         50:44-5, Oct 28, 1974
Newsweek 8:19, Nov 28, 1936
        77:66-7, Mar 1, 1971
Outlook 151:299, Feb 20, 1929
Review 1:525-6, Oct 25, 1919
Saturday Review 44:27, Jan 28, 1961
Theatre Arts 21:11, Jan 1937
         26:226, Apr 1942
         27:50-1, Jan 1943
         45:72, Jan 1961
Theatre Magazine 27:287, May 1918
              27:349, Jun 1918
              43:14-15, Apr 1926
              47:65, Jun 1928
Time 94:58, Dec 19, 1969
      95:70, Jun 22, 1970
      96:45, Jul 20, 1970
      97:67, Mar 1, 1971

Time 105:62, May 5, 1975
Vogue 73:104, Mar 30, 1929
Weekly Review 3:427-8, Nov 3, 1920

John Gabriel Borkman
    Productions:
        Opened April 1, 1915 for 3 performances.
        Translated by Eva Le Gallienne. Opened January 29, 1926
           for 7 performances.
        Opened November 9, 1926 for 15 performances.
        Opened November 12, 1946 for 21 performances.
        (Off Broadway) Adapted by Gene Feist. Opened December 30,
           1976 for 43 performances.
    Reviews:
        Catholic World 164:360, Jan 1947
        Commonweal 45:167, Nov 29, 1946
        Current Opinion 58:408-9, Jun 1915
        Dramatic Mirror 73:8, Apr 21, 1915
        Harper's Weekly 60:419, May 1, 1915
        Life 21:109, Dec 21, 1946
        Nation 163:629, Nov 30, 1946
           220:286, Mar 8, 1975
        New Republic 2:285, Apr 17, 1915
           115:726, Dec 2, 1946
        New York Theatre Critics' Reviews 1946:263
        New York Times p. 13, Apr 14, 1915
                 p. 13, Jan 30, 1926
                 p. 24, Nov 10, 1926
                 p. 33, Nov 13, 1946
                 p. 13, Dec 9, 1950
                 p. 57, Nov 26, 1959
                 p. 47, Jan 20, 1977
                 II, p. 5, Jan 30, 1977
                 III, p. 16, Feb 9, 1977
        New Yorker 22:57, Nov 23, 1946
        Newsweek 29:94, Nov 25, 1946
        Review 2:494+, May 8, 1920
        Saturday Review 29:30, Nov 30, 1946
        Theatre Arts 31:23+, Jan 1947
        Theatre Magazine 21:281, Jun 1915
        Time 48:55, Nov 25, 1946

The Lady from the Sea
    Productions:
        November 6, 1911 in repertory.
        Opened March 18, 1929 for 24 performances.
        Opened May 1, 1934 for 15 performances.
        Opened August 7, 1950 for 16 performances.
        (Off Broadway) Season of 1956-1957.
        (Off Off Broadway) Opened September 18, 1973.
        Translated by Michael Meyer. Opened March 18, 1976
           for 77 performances.

Reviews:
Bookman 35:362+, Dec 1911
Catholic World 139:344-5, Jun 1934
         172:69-70, Oct 1950
Commonweal 9:626-7, Apr 3, 1929
Dramatic Mirror 66:7, Nov 15, 1911
Life (NY) 58:902, Nov 23, 1911
Nation 171:174, Aug 19, 1950
      222:445-6, Apr 10, 1976
New Republic 36:309-11, Nov 14, 1923
        79:22, May 16, 1934
        123:23, Aug 28, 1950
        174:20-1, Apr 10, 1976
New York Theatre Critics' Reviews 1976:322
New York Times p. 36, Mar 19, 1929
       p. 25, May 2, 1934
       II, p. 1, Sep 9, 1945
       p. 23, Aug 8, 1950
       p. 49, Dec 13, 1956
       p. 63, Sep 20, 1973
       p. 21, Mar 19, 1976
       II, p. 1, Mar 28, 1976
New Yorker 49:112, Oct 8, 1973
      52:62+, Mar 29, 1976
Theatre Magazine 14:186, Dec 1911
Time 107:67, Mar 29, 1976

League of Youth
  Productions:
    (Off Off Broadway) Adapted by Arthur Reel. Opened
    November 28, 1976.
  Reviews:
    New York Times p. 10, Feb 5, 1977

Little Eyolf
  Productions:
    Opened April 18, 1910 for 48 performances.
    Opened February 2, 1926 for 8 performances.
    (Off Broadway) Translated by R. V. Forslund. Opened
    March 16, 1964 for 33 performances.
  Reviews:
    Bookman 31:416-17, Jun 1910
    Collier's 45:34, May 7, 1910
    Dramatic Mirror 63:8, Apr 30, 1910
    Hampton 24:828, Jun 1910
    Harper's Weekly 54:24, May 21, 1910
    Life (NY) 55:766, Apr 28, 1910
    Metropolitan Magazine 32:532-3, Jul 1910
    Nation 198:355-6, Apr 6, 1964
    New Republic 45:356-7, Feb 17, 1926
    New York Times p. 22, Feb 3, 1926
                p. 31, Mar 17, 1964

New Yorker 40:138, Mar 28, 1964
Theatre Magazine 11:201, Jun 1910

The Master Builder
  Productions:
    Opened November 10, 1925 for 76 performances (Eva Le
      Gallienne).
    Opened November 1, 1926 for 29 performances.
    Week of September 16, 1929 in repertory.
    (Off Broadway) Season of 1940-1941 in repertory.
    (Off Broadway) Opened June 1950 in repertory.
    (Off Broadway) Season of 1953-1954.
    (Off Broadway) Season of 1954-1955.
    Adapted by Max Faber. Opened March 1, 1955 for 40
      performances.
    (Off Broadway) Translated by Michael Meyer. Opened
      October 17, 1971 for 64 performances.
    (Off Off Broadway) Opened October 4, 1975.
  Reviews:
    America 93:25-6, Apr 2, 1955
    Catholic World 122:663-4, Feb 1926
              181:68, Apr 1955
    Commonweal 62:127, May 6, 1955
    Nation 123:513-14, Nov 17, 1926
           180:246, Mar 19, 1955
    New Republic 132:27-8, Mar 14, 1955
                 165:24+, Nov 6, 1971
    New York Theatre Critics' Reviews 1955:349
                                      1971:208
    New York Times p. 27, Nov 11, 1925
                   VIII, p. 1, Nov 15, 1925
                   p. 35, Nov 2, 1926
                   p. 19, May 26, 1950
                   II, p. 3, Feb 20, 1955
                   p. 23, Mar 2, 1955
                   II, p. 1, Mar 20, 1955
                   p. 42, Dec 18, 1957
                   p. 50, Jun 10, 1964
                   p. 26, Jun 22, 1968
                   p. 46, Oct 18, 1971
                   II, p. 5, Dec 19, 1971
                   p. 52, Oct 15, 1973
                   II, p. 3, May 29, 1977
                   p. 12, Jul 16, 1977
    New Yorker 31:64+, Mar 12, 1955
               47:103-4, Oct 30, 1971
    North American Review 196:254-63, Aug 1912
    Review 2:65, Jun 17, 1920
    Saturday Review 38:30, Apr 2, 1955
    Theatre Arts 39:87, May 1955

Peer Gynt
Productions:
Translated by William Archer and Charles Archer. Opened
February 5, 1923 for 120 performances.
English version by Paul Green. Opened January 28, 1951
for 32 performances.
English version by Norman Ginsburg. Opened January 12,
1960 for 32 performances.
(Off Broadway) Translated by Michael Meyer. Opened
July 8, 1969 for 19 performances.
(Off Off Broadway) Opened April 23, 1976.
Reviews:
Bookman 57:192-3, Apr 1923
Catholic World 172:464, Mar 1951
Commonweal 53:468-9, Feb 16, 1951
Dial 74:420-1, Apr 1923
Dramatist 13:1120-21, Jul 1922
Freeman 7:16-17, Mar 14, 1923
Independent 110:141-2, Feb 17, 1923
Literary Digest 76:30-1, Mar 3, 1923
Modern Language Notes 29:233-9, Dec 1914
Nation 116:258, Feb 28, 1923
       172:139-40, Feb 10, 1951
       190:106, Jan 30, 1960
New Republic 34:46-7, Mar 7, 1923
             124:22-3, Mar 5, 1951
             142:21, Feb 1, 1960
New York Clipper 71:14, Feb 14, 1923
New York Theatre Critics' Reviews 1951:373
                                  1960:393
New York Times p. 14, Feb 6, 1923
               VII, p. 1, Feb 11, 1923
               II, p. 1, Oct 1, 1944
               p. 15, Jan 29, 1951
               II, p. 1, Feb 4, 1951
               p. 21, Jan 13, 1960
               II, p. 1, Jan 24, 1960
               p. 33, Sep 27, 1962
               II, p. 1, Jul 6, 1969
               p. 56, Jul 17, 1969
               p. 12, Dec 23, 1970
               p. 64, Jan 18, 1976
New Yorker 26:61, Feb 10, 1951
           35:72+, Jan 23, 1960
Saturday Review 52:35-6, Aug 2, 1969
School and Society 73:184, Mar 24, 1951
Theatre Arts 19:908-9, Dec 1935
             29:147, Mar 1945
             35:14, Apr 1951
Theatre Magazine 37:15+, Apr 1923
Time 44:70, Sep 18, 1944

Pillars of Society
  Productions:
    Opened March 28, 1910 for 16 performances.
    Opened October 14, 1931 for 2 performances.
    (Off Broadway) Opened February 1951 in repertory.
  Reviews:
    Bookman 31:414-17, Jun 1910
    Commonweal 14:639-40, Oct 28, 1931
    Dramatic Mirror 63:6, Apr 9, 1910
                    69:6-7, Feb 12, 1913
    Everybody's 22:849-50, Jun 1910
    Green Book 3:1244-5, Jun 1910
    Life (NY) 55:680-1, Apr 14, 1910
    Metropolitan Magazine 32:401, Jun 1910
    New York Times p. 17, Oct 15, 1931
    Theatre Arts 15:989-90, Dec 1931
    Theatre Magazine 11:129-33+, May 1910

Rosmersholm
  Productions:
    Translated by Charles Archer. Opened May 5, 1925 for
      30 performances.
    Translated by Eva Le Gallienne. Opened December 2, 1935
      for 8 performances.
    (Off Broadway) Translated by Carmel Ross. Opened April
      11, 1962 for 119 performances.
    (Off Broadway) Opened December 3, 1974 for 32 performances.
    Translated by Rolf Fjelde. Opened May 6, 1977.
  Reviews:
    Bookman 61:578-9, Jul 1925
    Commonweal 23:218, Dec 20, 1935
                76:175+, May 11, 1962
    Nation 120:579-80, May 20, 1925
           194:407-8, May 5, 1962
           220:26-7, Jan 11, 1975
    New Republic 146:20-2, Apr 30, 1962
    New York Theatre Critics' Reviews 1974:122
    New York Times p. 27, May 6, 1925
                   p. 32, Dec 3, 1935
                   p. 11, Nov 23, 1946
                   p. 42, Apr 12, 1962
                   II, p. 1, Apr 22, 1962
                   p. 33, Apr 6, 1973
                   p. 49, Dec 16, 1974
    New Yorker 38:85-7, Apr 21, 1962
    Theatre Arts 46:59+, Jun 1962
    Yale Review 5:120-1, Oct 1915

Two By Ibsen (A Doll's House and Hedda Gabler, adapted by
      Christopher Hampton. See individual plays.)

The Vikings of Helgeland (Vikings)
   Productions:
      Opened May 12, 1930 for 8 performances.
   Reviews:
      Commonweal 12:109, May 28, 1930
      Nation 130:633, May 28, 1930
      New Republic 63:42-3, May 28, 1930
      New York Times p. 27, May 13, 1930
      Theatre Arts 12:638-41, Sep 1928
      Theatre Magazine 52:42, Jul 1930

When We Dead Awaken
   Productions:
      (Off Broadway) Opened April 18, 1966 for 8 performances.
      (Off Off Broadway) Opened April 12, 1973.
   Reviews:
      New York Times p. 37, Apr 19, 1966
                     p. 59, Nov 9, 1971
                     p. 20, Feb 1, 1977
      Review 1:568, Nov 8, 1919

The Wild Duck
   Productions:
      Opened March 11, 1918 for 32 performances.
      Opened February 24, 1925 for 103 performances.
      Translated by William Archer. Opened November 19, 1928
         for 80 performances.
      Opened April 16, 1938 for 3 performances.
      Adapted by Max Faber. Opened December 26, 1951 for
         15 performances.
      Translated by Eva Le Gallienne. Opened January 11, 1967
         for 45 performances in repertory.
      (Off Off Broadway) Opened November 6, 1975.
   Reviews:
      America 116:265, Feb 18, 1967
      Bellman 24:604-6, Jun 1, 1918
      Bookman 61:337, May 1925
             62:678-81, Feb 1926
      Catholic World 174:464, Mar 1952
      Commonweal 55:349, Jan 11, 1952
      Dial 78:430-3, May 1925
      Dramatic Mirror 78:5, Mar 23, 1918
      Green Book 19:969+, Jun 1918
      Life (NY) 71:474-5, Mar 21, 1918
               85:18, Mar 19, 1925
               92:13, Dec 14, 1928
      Nation 106:328-9, Mar 21, 1918
            120:299, Mar 18, 1925
            204:156-7, Jan 30, 1967
      New Republic 9:356, Jan 27, 1917
                  14:238, Mar 23, 1918
                  42:70-1, Mar 11, 1925
                  126:23, Jan 21, 1952

New York Theatre Critics' Reviews 1951:128
                                    1967:389
New York Times p. 11, Mar 12, 1918
               IV, p. 12, Mar 17, 1918
               p. 17, Nov 19, 1928
               p. 16, Apr 16, 1938
               p. 17, Dec 27, 1951
               p. 49, Jan 12, 1967
               II, p. 8, Jan 22, 1967
               p. 50, May 2, 1972
               p. 32, Jun 19, 1973
New Yorker 42:69, Jan 21, 1967
Saturday Review 50:48, Jan 28, 1967
Theatre Arts 15:634-7, Aug 1931
            36:70, Mar 1952
Theatre Magazine 27:217, Apr 1918
Time 59:44, Jan 7, 1952
    89:70-1, Jan 20, 1967

IONESCO, EUGENE

*Air Walker
    Reviews:
    Time 81:34, Jan 4, 1963

*Amédée, or How to Disentangle Yourself
    Adapted by D. Prouse and D. Clauyel.
    Reviews:
    New York Times p. 27, Nov 1, 1955

The Bald Soprano
    Productions:
    (Off Broadway) Season of 1958-1959.
    (Off Broadway) Translated by Donald M. Allen. Opened
        September 17, 1963, for 40 performances.
    (Off Off Broadway) Season of 1971-1972.
    Reviews:
    Catholic World 187:387, Aug 1958
    Nation 187:59, Aug 2, 1958
    New York Times p. 39, Jun 4, 1958
                   p. 30, Jan 16, 1962
                   p. 35, Sep 18, 1963
                   p. 36, Feb 6, 1964
    New Yorker 39:94+, Sep 28, 1963
    Newsweek 62:60, Sep 30, 1963

Bedlam Galore (see Plays by Eugene Ionesco)

La Cantatrice Chauve (see The Bald Soprano)

The Chairs (see also Les Chaises)
  Productions:
    Translated by Donald T. Watson.   Opened January 9, 1958
      for 22 performances.
  Reviews:
    Catholic World 186:469, Mar 1958
    Christian Century 75:137, Jan 29, 1958
    Nation 195:17, Jul 6, 1957
    New York Theatre Critics' Reviews 1958:397
    New York Times p. 20, Jan 10, 1958
    New Yorker 33:68, Jan 18, 1958
    Newsweek 51:84, Jan 20, 1958
    Saturday Review 41:26, Jan 25, 1958
    Theatre Arts 42:14, Mar 1958
    Time 71:42, Jan 20, 1958

Les Chaises (see also The Chairs)
  Productions:
    (Off Broadway) Opened May 5, 1970 for 8 performances.
  Reviews:
    New York Times p. 49, May 6, 1970
    New Yorker 46:105, May 16, 1970

*Comment s'en de'Barrasser
  Reviews:
    Nation 185:439, Dec 7, 1957

Exit the King
  Productions:
    Translated by Donald Watson.
    Opened January 9, 1968 in repertory for 47 performances.
    (Off Broadway) Opened April 15, 1974 for 9 performances.
  Reviews:
    America 109:512-14, Nov 2, 1963
    Christian Century 85:332+, Mar 13, 1968
    Nation 196:57-8, Jan 19, 1963
          206:155-6, Jan 29, 1968
    New York Theatre Critics' Reviews 1968:384, 394
    New York Times p. 19, Sep 13, 1963
                   p. 48, Jan 10, 1968
                   II, p. 1, Jan 21, 1968
                   p. 35, Apr 17, 1974
                   XXII, p. 20, Apr 3, 1977
    Newsweek 38:102, Jan 12, 1963
             43:82+, Jan 20, 1968
             71:96, Jan 22, 1968
    Reporter 38:46+, Feb 22, 1968
    Saturday Review 51:41, Jan 27, 1968
    Theatre Arts 48:31-2, Jan 1964
    Time 91:67, Jan 19, 1968

For Two or More (see Plays by Eugene Ionesco)

Foursome   (see Plays by Eugene Ionesco)

How to Disentangle Yourself   (see Amédée, or How to Disentangle
     Yourself)

*Hunger and Thirst
     Reviews:
     New York Times p. 28, Jan 19, 1965

L'Impromtu   (see Plays by Eugene Ionesco)

Jack, or the Submission
     Productions:
     (Off Broadway) Season of 1958-1959.
     (Off Off Broadway) Opened December 6, 1975.
     Reviews:
     Nation 187:59, Aug 2, 1958
     New York Times p. 39, Jun 4, 1958

La Jeune Fille à Marier
     Productions:
     (Off Broadway) Opened May 5, 1970 for 8 performances.
     Reviews:
     New York Times p. 49, May 6, 1970
     New Yorker 46:105, May 16, 1970

The Killer
     Productions:
     (Off Broadway) Translated by Donald Watson.   Opened
          March 22, 1960 for 16 performances.
     (Off Broadway) Opened February 11, 1962 in repertory.
     Reviews:
     New York Times p. 24, Mar 21, 1960
                    p. 33, Mar 23, 1960
                    II, p. 1, Apr 3, 1960
     New Yorker 36:82+, Apr 2, 1960
     Saturday Review 43:37, Apr 9, 1960

The Killing Game
     Productions:
     (Off Off Broadway) Opened November 1, 1975.
     No Reviews.

La Lacune
     Productions:
     (Off Broadway) Opened May 5, 1970 for 8 performances.
     Reviews:
     New York Times p. 49, May 6, 1970
     New Yorker 46:105, May 16, 1970

The Leader   (see Plays by Eugene Ionesco)

The Lesson
    Productions:
        Translated by Donald Watson. Opened January 9, 1958 for
           22 performances.
        (Off Broadway) Translated by Donald M. Allen. Opened
           September 17, 1963 for 40 performances.
        (Off Off Broadway) Opened October 6, 1973.
        (Off Off Broadway) Opened May 26, 1976.
        (Off Off Broadway) Opened October 1, 1976.
    Reviews:
        Catholic World 186:468-9, Mar 1958
        Christian Century 75:137, Jan 29, 1958
        Nation 196:87, Jan 25, 1958
        New York Theatre Critics' Reviews 1958:397
        New York Times p. 29, Oct 3, 1956
                   p. 20, Jan 10, 1958
                   p. 35, Sep 18, 1963
                   p. 36, Feb 6, 1964
        New Yorker 33:68, Jan 18, 1958
                  39:96, Sep 28, 1963
        Newsweek 51:84, Jan 20, 1958
        Saturday Review 41:26, Jan 25, 1958
        Theatre Arts 42:14, Mar 1958
        Time 71:42, Jan 20, 1958

*Macbett
    Reviews:
        America 128:399-400, Apr 28, 1973
        Nation 216:701-2, May 28, 1973
        New York Times p. 22, Jan 18, 1972
                   p. 45, Feb 9, 1972
        Newsweek 81:94, Jun 4, 1973

The New Tenant
    Productions:
        (Off Broadway) Season of 1959-1960.
        (Off Broadway) Translated by Donald Watson. Opened
           May 24, 1964 for 32 performances.
    Reviews:
        Nation 185:439, Dec 7, 1957
        New York Times p. 40, May 28, 1964
                   p. 27, Aug 11, 1970

Le Nouveau Locataire (see The New Tenant)

*Pedestrian in the Air
    Reviews:
        New York Times p. 33, Mar 4, 1964
        Newsweek 63:96-7, Mar 16, 1964
        Saturday Review 49:53, Feb 5, 1966

Le Pieton de l'Air (see Pedestrian in the Air)

*Plays by Eugene Ionesco (Consists of Foursome, The Leader,
    L'Impromtu, Bedlam Galore, and For Two or More)
  Reviews:
    New York Times p. 34, Mar 8, 1965

Rhinoceros
  Productions:
    Translated by Derth Prouse. Opened January 9, 1961
      for 240 performances.
    Translated by Derth Prouse. Opened September 18, 1961
      for 16 performances.
    (Off Off Broadway) Opened September 17, 1976.
  Reviews:
    America 104:576-7, Jan 28, 1961
            104:593-5, Feb 4, 1961
    Américas 17:6-10, Feb 1965
    Catholic World 192:380-1, Mar 1961
    Christian Century 78:274, Mar 1, 1961
    Nation 192:85-6, Jan 28, 1961
    National Review 10:157-8, Mar 11, 1961
    New Republic 144:22-3, Jan 30, 1961
    New York Theatre Critics' Reviews 1961:397
    New York Times p. 41, Nov 2, 1959
                  p. 90, Jan 24, 1960
                  p. 15, Apr 30, 1960
                  II, p. 1, Jan 8, 1961
                  p. 27, Jan 10, 1961
                  II, p. 1, Jan 22, 1961
    New Yorker 36:103, May 28, 1960
               36:66+, Jan 21, 1961
    Newsweek 57:57, Jan 23, 1961
    Saturday Review 44:51, Jan 21, 1961
    Theatre Arts 45:9-10, Mar 1961
    Time 75:56, May 23, 1960
         77:77, Jan 20, 1961

Le Roi se Meurt (see Exit the King)

The Shepherd's Chameleon
  Productions:
    (Off Broadway) Season of 1960-1961.
  Reviews:
    New York Times p. 41, Nov 30, 1960

*La Soif et la Faim
  Reviews:
    New York Times p. 47, Mar 2, 1966
                  p. 27, Mar 3, 1966
    New Yorker 42:101-2, Jul 16, 1966

Submission (see Jack, or the Submission)

*Le Tableau
  Reviews:
    New York Times p. 34, Sep 4, 1963

*Triumph of Death
  Reviews:
    Time 95:64, Feb 16, 1970

Victims of Duty
  Productions:
    (Off Broadway) Season of 1959-1960.
    (Off Broadway) Translated by Donald Watson. Opened
      May 24, 1964 for 32 performances.
    (Off Broadway) Translated by Donald Watson. Opened
      March 5, 1968 for 6 performances as part of a bill
      called The Victims.)
  Reviews:
    New York Times p. 26, Jan 20, 1960
                   p. 40, May 28, 1964
                   p. 34, Mar 6, 1968
    New Yorker 40:88-9, Jun 6, 1964

*Wipe-Out Games
  Reviews:
    New York Times II, p. 14, Apr 25, 1971

ISHERWOOD, CHRISTOPHER see AUDEN, W. H.

JEROME, HELEN

*Jane Eyre
  Reviews:
    New York Times X, p. 2, Jan 3, 1937
                   X, p. 2, Jan 24, 1937
                   X, p. 1, Feb 7, 1937
    Saturday Review 15:18, Feb 13, 1937
    Stage 14:45-6, Jan 1937

Pride and Prejudice
  Productions:
    Opened November 5, 1935 for 219 performances.
  Reviews:
    Catholic World 142:341-2, Dec 1935
                   144:469-71, Jan 1937
    Commonweal 23:106, Nov 22, 1935
               25:220, Dec 18, 1936
    Literary Digest 120:20, Nov 16, 1935
    Nation 141:603-4, Nov 20, 1935
    New Republic 85:134, Dec 11, 1935
    New York Times p. 19, Oct 23, 1935
                   X, p. 1, Nov 3, 1935

New York Times p. 32, Nov 6, 1935
                    IX, p. 2, Nov 10, 1935
                    IX, p. 1, Nov 17, 1935
Newsweek 6:19, Nov 16, 1935
Stage 13:7-8, Dec 1935
Theatre Arts 20:7-9+, Jan 1936
Time 26:40, Nov 18, 1935
Vanity Fair 45:44+, Jan 1937

JOB, THOMAS

Barchester Towers
    Productions:
    Opened November 30, 1937 for 40 performances.
    Reviews:
    Catholic World 146:469-70, Jan 1938
    Commonweal 27:220, Dec 17, 1937
    New Republic 93:170-1, Dec 15, 1937
    New York Times p. 26, Nov 19, 1937
                    XI, p. 3, Nov 28, 1937
                    p. 27, Dec 1, 1937
    Newsweek 10:31, Dec 13, 1937
    Stage 15:54+, Jan 1938
    Theatre Arts 22:8+, Jan 1938
    Time 30:57, Dec 13, 1937

Guilty (see Therese)

Land's End
    Productions:
    Opened December 11, 1946 for 5 performances.
    Reviews:
    New York Theatre Critics' Reviews 1946:222
    New York Times p. 37, Dec 12, 1946
    New Yorker 22:41, Dec 21, 1946
    Theatre Arts 31:16, Feb 1947

Therese (Guilty)
    Productions:
    Opened October 9, 1945 for 96 performances.
    Reviews:
    Catholic World 162:168, Nov 1945
    Commonweal 43:45, Oct 26, 1945
    Life 19:57-60, Oct 22, 1945
    Nation 161:413, Oct 20, 1945
    New Republic 113:573, Oct 29, 1945
    New York Theatre Critics' Reviews 1945:146
    New York Times p. 24, Oct 10, 1945
                    II, p. 1, Oct 28, 1945
    New Yorker 21:46, Oct 20, 1945
    Newsweek 26:93, Oct 22, 1945
    Saturday Review 28:22-4, Oct 20, 1945

Theatre Arts 29:683-4, Dec 1945
Time 46:70, Oct 22, 1945

Uncle Harry
    Productions:
        Opened May 20, 1942 for 430 performances.
    Reviews:
        Catholic World 155:471-2, Jul 1942
        Independent Woman 21:378, Dec 1942
        Life 12:45-6+, Jun 29, 1942
        New York Theatre Critics' Reviews 1942:284
        New York Times p. 24, May 21, 1942
        New Republic 106:798, Jun 8, 1942
        Newsweek 17:67, Jun 1, 1942
        Theatre Arts 26:421-2, Jul 1942
        Time 39:34, Jun 1, 1942

JOHNSTON, DENIS

*Golden Cuckoo
    Reviews:
        Newsweek 14:30, Jul 31, 1939
        Theatre Arts 24:243, Apr 1940

The Moon in the Yellow River
    Productions:
        Opened February 29, 1932 for 40 performances.
        (Off Broadway) Opened February 6, 1961 for 48 performances.
    Reviews:
        Arts and Decoration 37:46, May 1932
        America 104:768, Mar 11, 1961
        Bookman 74:665, Mar 1932
        Catholic World 135:74, Apr 1932
        Commonweal 15:550, Mar 16, 1932
        Nation 134:319, Mar 16, 1932
                192:193-4, Mar 4, 1961
        New Republic 70:127, Mar 16, 1932
        New York Times p. 19, Mar 1, 1932
                    VIII, p. 1, Mar 13, 1932
                    II, p. 3, Feb 5, 1961
                    p. 40, Feb 7, 1961
        New Yorker 37:93-4, Feb 18, 1961
        Outlook 160:229, Apr 1932
        Theatre Arts 16:354, May 1932
                45:84, Apr 1961
        Theatre Guild Magazine 9:36-8, Apr 1932
        Vanity Fair 38:26, 66, Jun 1932
        Vogue 79:61, 88, May 1, 1932

The Old Lady Says "No!"
    Productions:
        Opened February 17, 1948 for 8 performances.

Reviews:
Catholic World 167:72, Apr 1948
Commonweal 47:520, Mar 5, 1948
New Republic 118:24, Mar 1, 1948
New York Theatre Critics' Reviews 1948:342
New York Times p. 35, Feb 18, 1948
             II, p. 1, Feb 22, 1948
New Yorker 24:49, Feb 28, 1948
Time 51:63, Mar 1, 1948

JONES, HENRY ARTHUR

Cock O' the Walk
  Productions:
    Opened December 27, 1915 for 72 performances.
  Reviews:
    American Mercury 81:90, May 1916
    Bookman 42:651, Feb 1916
    Collier's 57:24, May 13, 1916
    Dramatic Mirror 74:11, Oct 16, 1915
                  75:8, Jan 1, 1916
    Dramatist 7:614, Oct 1915
    Green Book 15:442-3, Mar 1916
    Harper's Weekly 61:427, Oct 30, 1915
    Nation 102:26-7, Jan 6, 1916
    New York Dramatic News 62:19, Jan 1, 1916
    Theatre Magazine 23:64, 67, Feb 1916

The Goal
  Productions:
    In repertory beginning October 17, 1914. (Princess Players.)
    (Off Broadway) Opened season of 1940-1941 in repertory.
  Reviews:
    Bookman 40:416, Dec 1914
    Dramatic Mirror 72:8, Oct 28, 1914
    Green Book 13:124, Jan 1915

The Liars
  Productions:
    Opened November 9, 1915 in repertory.
  Reviews:
    Dramatic Mirror 74:8, Nov 20, 1915
    Harper's Weekly 61:515, Nov 27, 1915
    Life (NY) 66:1008-9, Nov 25, 1915
    Nation 101:605, Nov 18, 1915
    New York Times p. 13, Nov 10, 1915

The Lie
  Productions:
    Opened December 24, 1914 for 172 performances.
  Reviews:
    Bookman 40:638-9, Feb 1915

Book News 33:303-4, Feb 1915
Current Opinion 58:99, Feb 1915
Dramatic Mirror 73:8, Jan 6, 1915
Dramatist 6:552-5, Apr 1915
Green Book 13:567-8, Mar 1915
Hearst 28:126-9, Aug 1915
Life (NY) 65:68-9, Jan 14, 1915
Munsey 54:324+, Mar 1915
Nation 99:783, Dec 31, 1914
New Republic 1:25, Jan 16, 1915
New York Times p. 11, Dec 25, 1914
Theatre Magazine 21:56, 59, Feb 1915

Lydia Gilmore
Productions:
Opened February 1, 1912 for 12 performances.
Reviews:
American Playwright 1:42, Feb 1912
Bookman 35:170, Apr 1912
Dramatic Mirror 67:6-7, Feb 7, 1912
Everybody's 26:681, Mar 1912
Green Book 7:799, Apr 1912
Life (NY) 59:348, Feb 15, 1912
Munsey 47:126-7, Apr 1912
Theatre Magazine 15:74+, Mar 1912

Mary Goes First
Productions:
Opened November 2, 1914 for 32 performances.
Reviews:
American Playwright 3:392, Dec 1914
Bookman 40:414, Dec 1914
Dramatic Mirror 72:8, Nov 11, 1914
Dramatist 6:515, Oct 1914
Life (NY) 64:904, Nov 19, 1914
Nation 99:530, Oct 29, 1914
99:587, Nov 12, 1914
New York Times I, p. 7, Nov 4, 1914
Theatre Magazine 20:300, Dec 1914

Mrs. Dane's Defense
Productions:
Opened February 6, 1928 for 16 performances.
Reviews:
Green Book 7:305-10, Feb 1912
New York Times p. 30, Feb 7, 1928
Theatre Arts 31:28+, Mar 1947
Theatre Magazine 47:48, Apr 1928

We Can't Be as Bad as All That
Productions:
Opened December 30, 1910 for 19 performances.

Reviews:
Bookman 23:607, Feb 1911
Canadian Magazine 36:476-8, Mar 1911
Columbian 3:1079-81, Mar 1911
Dramatic Mirror 65:11, Jan 4, 1911
Life (NY) 57:124, Jan 12, 1911
Munsey 44:710, Feb 1911
Red Book 16:949-52, Mar 1911
Theatre Magazine 13:35-7, Feb 1911

JOYCE, JAMES

Exiles
Productions:
Opened February 19, 1925 for 41 performances.
(Off Broadway) Opened season of 1956-57.
(Off Off Broadway) Opened season of 1971-72.
(Off Broadway) Opened May 19, 1977 for 36 performances.
Reviews:
American Mercury 4:501, Apr 1925
Life (NY) 85:20, Mar 12, 1925
Nation 107:430-1, Oct 12, 1918
120:272, Mar 11, 1925
184:281, Mar 30, 1957
224:732-3, Jun 11, 1977
New Republic 16:318-19, Oct 12, 1918
New York Times p. 20, Feb 20, 1925
p. 27, Mar 13, 1957
II, p. 1, Mar 24, 1957
p. 42, Nov 19, 1970
III, p. 3, May 20, 1977
New Yorker 53:84+, May 30, 1977

KAISER, GEORG

From Morn to Midnight
Productions:
Translated by Ashley Dukes. Opened May 14, 1922 in repertory.
Opened June 26, 1922 for 24 performances.
(Off Off Broadway) Translated and adapted by John Teta and Irma Bartenieff. Opened May 24, 1973.
Reviews:
Bookman 55:598, Aug 1922
Dial 73:116-17, Jul 1922
Dramatist 14:1141, Jan 1923
Nation 114:726, Jun 14, 1922
New Republic 31:189, Jul 12, 1922
New York Times p. 41, Dec 7, 1948
Theatre Magazine 36:71, 94, Aug 1922

Gas
Productions:
(Off Broadway) Season of 1943-44 in repertory.
(Off Broadway) Opened August 18, 1947 in repertory.
Reviews:
Drama 16:164+, Feb 1926

Morning to Midnight (see From Morn to Midnight)

Oktobertag (see The Phantom Lover)

The Phantom Lover (Oktobertag)
Productions:
Translated by Herman Bernstein and Adolph E. Meyer.
Opened September 4, 1928 for 15 performances.
Reviews:
Life (NY) 92:11, Sep 21, 1928
New York Times p. 25, Sep 5, 1928

*Raft of the Medusa
Reviews:
Theatre Arts 33:28-9, Jun 1949

*Der Soldat Tanaka
Reviews:
Theatre Arts 26:251, Apr 1942

KAPEK, KAREL see CAPEK, KAREL

KATAYEV, VALENTIN

A Million Torments
Productions:
(Off Broadway) Translated and adapted by Charles Malamuth.
Opened January 15, 1936.
Reviews:
New York Times p. 24, Jan 16, 1936

Squaring the Circle
Productions:
Adapted by Dimitri Ostrow. Translated by Charles Malamuth
and Eugene Lyons. Opened October 3, 1935 for 108
performances.
Reviews:
Catholic World 142:213, Nov 1935
Literary Digest 120:23, Aug 31, 1935
Nation 141:490, Oct 23, 1935
141:590, Nov 20, 1935
Newsweek 6:29, Oct 12, 1935
New York Times X, p. 3, Sep 22, 1935
X, p. 3, Sep 29, 1935

New York Times IX, p. 2, Sep 7, 1941
Saturday Review 12:16, Oct 12, 1935
Theatre Arts 18:418, Jun 1934
             19:900, Dec 1935
Time 26:45, Oct 14, 1935
Vanity Fair 45:68, Dec 1935

KIPPHARDT, HEINAR

The Case of J. Robert Oppenheimer   (see In the Matter of J.
    Robert Oppenheimer)

In the J. Robert Oppenheimer Affair   (see In the Matter of J.
    Robert Oppenheimer)

In the Matter of J. Robert Oppenheimer
   Productions:
      Translated by Ruth Spiers.
      Opened March 6, 1969 for 64 performances.
      Opened June 26, 1969 for 108 performances.
   Reviews:
      America 120:430-31+, Apr 5, 1969
      Commonweal 90:46-8, Mar 28, 1969
      Life 66:16, Apr 25, 1969
      Nation 208:379-80, Mar 24, 1969
      New York Theatre Critics' Reviews 1969:339
      New York Times p. 27, Nov 3, 1964
                  p. 56, Dec 15, 1964
                  p. 52, Dec 27, 1964
                  p. 55, May 27, 1968
                  p. 31, Jun 7, 1968
                  II, p. 1, Jun 9, 1968
                  p. 36, Mar 6, 1969
                  p. 28, Mar 7, 1969
                  II, p. 1, Mar 16, 1969
                  II, p. 4, May 25, 1969
                  p. 32, Sep 13, 1969
      New Yorker 45:131, Mar 15, 1969
      Newsweek 64:93, Nov 16, 1964
             73:133, Mar 17, 1969
      Saturday Review 51:18, Jul 6, 1968
               52:72, Mar 22, 1969
      Time 84:70, Nov 20, 1964
         93:66, Mar 14, 1969
      Vogue 146:296-8+, Sep 1, 1965

KNOTT, FREDERICK

Dial "M" for Murder
   Productions:
      Opened October 29, 1952 for 522 performances.

(Off Off Broadway) Opened June 1975.
Reviews:
Catholic World 176:229, Dec 1952
Commonweal 57:164, Nov 21, 1952
Life 33:73-6, Nov 10, 1952
Nation 175:454, Nov 15, 1952
New York Theatre Critics' Reviews 1952:215
New York Times p. 41, Oct 14, 1952
              II, p. 3, Oct 26, 1952
              p. 41, Oct 30, 1952
              II, p. 1, Nov 30, 1952
              II, p. 4, Dec 14, 1952
              II, p. 1, Nov 8, 1953
              II, p. 3, Nov 15, 1953
              p. 27, Jan 9, 1957
              p. 12, Feb 8, 1958
Newsweek 40:94, Nov 10, 1952
Saturday Review 35:30, Nov 15, 1952
              36:5, Aug 1, 1953
Theatre Arts 37:22-3, Jan 1953
              37:66-7, Jun 1953
Time 60:71, Nov 10, 1952

*Mr. Fox of Venice
Reviews:
New York Times p. 28, Apr 16, 1959

Wait until Dark
Productions:
Opened February 2, 1966 for 373 performances.
Reviews:
Look 30:112-13+, May 17, 1966
New York Theatre Critics' Reviews 1966:376
New York Times p. 21, Feb 3, 1966
              II, p. 1, Feb 7, 1966
Newsweek 67:88, Feb 14, 1966
Saturday Review 49:52-3, Feb 19, 1966
Time 87:66, Feb 11, 1966

Write Me a Murder
Productions:
Opened October 26, 1961 for 196 performances.
Reviews:
America 106:375, Dec 9, 1961
New York Theatre Critics' Reviews 1961:194
New York Times II, p. 3, Oct 22, 1961
              p. 28, Oct 27, 1961
New Yorker 37:126+, Nov 4, 1961
Newsweek 58:69, Nov 6, 1961
Saturday Review 44:39, Nov 18, 1961
Theatre Arts 46:12-13, Jan 1962
Time 78:44, Nov 3, 1961

KOPS, BERNARD

*Dream of Peter Mann
Reviews:
New York Times p. 40, Sep 6, 1960

The Hamlet of Stepney Green
Productions:
(Off Broadway) Season of 1958-59.
Reviews:
Christian Century 76:83, Jan 21, 1959
New York Times p. 21, Nov 14, 1958
New Yorker 34:102-3, Nov 22, 1958

LABICHE, EUGENE

The Straw Hat
Productions:
Adapted by Paul Tulane and Agnes Hamilton James.   Opened
October 14, 1926 for 57 performances.
Reviews:
New York Times p. 23, Jun 16, 1926

LAWLER, RAY

Summer of the 17th Doll
Productions:
Opened January 22, 1958 for 29 performances.
(Off Broadway) Opened February 20, 1968 for 40 performances.
Reviews:
Commonweal 67:540, Feb 21, 1958
Nation 185:19, Jul 6, 1957
    186:126, Feb 8, 1958
    206:356, Mar 11, 1968
New York Theatre Critics' Reviews 1958:389
New York Times II, p. 1, Jan 19, 1958
    p. 23, Jan 23, 1958
    p. 52, Oct 14, 1959
    p. 59, Feb 21, 1968
    II, p. 3, Mar 3, 1968
New Yorker 33:53, Jul 13, 1957
    33:53, Feb 1, 1958
    44:82+, Mar 2, 1968
Newsweek 51:54, Feb 3, 1958
    71:56, Mar 4, 1968
Reporter 18:36-7, Mar 6, 1958
Saturday Review 41:27, Feb 8, 1958
    51:26, Mar 9, 1968
Theatre Arts 42:18-19, Apr 1958
Time 71:76+, Feb 3, 1958

*The Unshaven Cheek
 Reviews:
     New York Times p. 38, Aug 20, 1963

LENORMAND, HENRI RENE

The Failures
 Productions:
     Translated by Winifred Katzin.   Opened November 19, 1923
         for 40 performances.
 Reviews:
     American Mercury 1:116, Jan 1924
     Drama 14:133, Jan 1924
     Freeman 8:376, Dec 26, 1923
     Life (NY) 82:18, Dec 13, 1923
     Nation 117:692, Dec 12, 1923
     New Republic 37:46, Dec 5, 1923
     New York Times p. 20, Nov 23, 1923
                         VIII, p. 1, Dec 2, 1923
                         p. 30, Jan 6, 1959
     New Yorker 34:72, Jan 17, 1959
     Theatre Magazine 39:16, Feb 1924

Fear (with Jean D'Augugan)
 Productions:
     Opened March 14, 1913 in repertory.
     Opened September 27, 1913 in repertory.
 Reviews:
     Blue Book 17:436-7, Jul 1913
     Bookman 37:312, May 1913
     Dramatic Mirror 69:6, Mar 19, 1923
     Red Book 21:310+, Jun 1913

Man and His Phantoms
 Productions:
     Opened November 10, 1924 in repertory.
 No Reviews.

Time Is a Dream
 Productions:
     Opened in the Fall of 1923 for nine performances.
 Reviews:
     Nation 118:540, May 7, 1924
     New Republic 38:287, May 7, 1924

LEVY, BENN W.

Art and Mrs. Bottle
 Productions:
     Opened November 18, 1930 for 50 performances.
     (Off Broadway) Opened October 19, 1945 in repertory.

Reviews:
Arts and Decoration 34:80, Feb 1931
Catholic World 132:462, Jan 1931
Commonweal 13:159, Dec 10, 1930
Drama 21:12, Feb 1931
Life (NY) 96:18, Dec 19, 1930
New York Times p. 19, Nov 19, 1930
Theatre Magazine 53:26, Jan 1931
Vogue 77:82, Feb 1, 1931

Clutterbuck
Productions:
Opened December 3, 1949 for 218 performances.
Reviews:
Catholic World 170:386, Feb 1950
Nation 169:629, Dec 24, 1949
New Republic 122:21, Jan 2, 1950
New York Theatre Critics' Reviews 1949:205
New York Times p. 29, Dec 5, 1949
p. 34, Aug 9, 1950
New Yorker 25:54, Dec 10, 1949
Newsweek 34:79, Dec 12, 1949
Theatre Arts 34:11, Feb 1950
Time 54:83, Dec 12, 1949

The Devil Passes
Productions:
Opened January 4, 1932 for 96 performances.
(Off Broadway) Opened Season of 1938-39 in repertory.
Reviews:
Catholic World 134:589-90, Feb 1932
Commonweal 15:329-30, Jan 20, 1932
Literary Digest 112:15, Jan 23, 1932
Nation 134:126, Jan 1927
New York Times p. 20, Jan 5, 1932
Outlook 160:86, Jan 20, 1932
Theatre Arts 16:193-4, Mar 1936
Theatre Guild Magazine 9:35, Feb 1932

If I Were You (with Paul Hervey Fox)
Productions:
Opened January 24, 1938 for 8 performances.
Reviews:
Nation 146:162, Feb 5, 1938
New York Times p. 24, Jan 25, 1938

A Man with Red Hair
Productions:
Adapted from Hugh Walpole's novel. Opened November 8,
1928 for 20 performances.
Reviews:
Life (NY) 91:31, Apr 5, 1928
New York Times p. 22, Nov 9, 1928

Mrs. Moonlight
  Productions:
    Opened September 29, 1930 for 321 performances.
  Reviews:
    Catholic World 133:204, Nov 1930
    Commonweal 13:274, Jan 7, 1931
    New York Times p. 24, Sep 30, 1930
                   p. 21, Nov 21, 1952

Rape of the Belt
  Productions:
    Opened November 5, 1960 for 5 performances.
  Reviews:
    New York Theatre Critics' Reviews 1960:179
    New York Times p. 46, Nov 7, 1960
    New Yorker 36:104, Nov 12, 1960

*Return to Tyassi
  Reviews:
    New York Times p. 31, Dec 1, 1950

Springtime for Henry
  Productions:
    Opened December 9, 1931 for 199 performances.
    Opened May 1, 1933 for 16 performances.
    Opened March 14, 1951 for 53 performances.
  Reviews:
    Arts and Decoration 36:56, Feb 1932
    Bookman 74:563, Jan-Feb 1932
    Catholic World 134:588, Feb 1932
                   173:147, May 1951
    Commonweal 15:215, Dec 23, 1931
                53:646, Apr 6, 1951
    Life 21:86, Aug 5, 1946
    Nation 133:732, 734 Dec 30, 1931
           172:285, Mar 24, 1951
    New Republic 69:189-90, Dec 30, 1931
    New York Theatre Critics' Reviews 1951:315
    New York Times p. 29, Dec 10, 1931
                   p. 20, May 2, 1933
                   p. 16, Feb 27, 1940
                   II, p. 1, Jul 27, 1947
                   II, p. 3, Mar 11, 1951
                   p. 36, Mar 15, 1951
    New Yorker 27:56, Mar 24, 1951
    Outlook 159:535, Dec 23, 1931
    Theatre Arts 35:21, May 1951
    Time 36:62, Jul 22, 1940
         57:67, Mar 26, 1951
    Vogue 79:58-9, Feb 1, 1932

This Woman Business
    Productions:
        Opened December 7, 1926 for 47 performances.
    Reviews:
        New York Times p. 25, Dec 8, 1926

Topaze (see entry under Pagnol, Marcel)

The Tumbler
    Productions:
        Opened February 24, 1960 for 5 performances.
    Reviews:
        New York Theatre Critics' Reviews 1960:349
        New York Times p. 32, Feb 25, 1960
        New Yorker 36:123-4, Mar 1960

Young Madame Conti (see entry under Frank, Bruno)

LONSDALE, FREDERICK

Another Love Story
    Productions:
        Opened October 12, 1943 for 104 performances.
    Reviews:
        New York Theatre Critics' Reviews 1943:260
        New York Times p. 29, Oct 13, 1929
        New Yorker 19:34, Oct 23, 1943
        Newsweek 22:110, Oct 25, 1923
        Theatre Arts 27:707, Dec 1943

Aren't We All?
    Productions:
        Opened May 21, 1923 for 32 performances.
        Opened April 13, 1925 for 16 performances.
    Reviews:
        New York Clipper 71:14, May 30, 1923
        New York Times p. 14, May 22, 1923
        Theatre Magazine 38:14-15, Aug 1923
                            38:26+, Sep 1923

Canaries Sometimes Sing
    Productions:
        Opened October 20, 1930 for 24 performances.
    Reviews:
        Life (NY) 96:17, Nov 7, 1930
        New York Times p. 34, Oct 21, 1930
        Nation 131:506, Nov 5, 1930

The Day after Tomorrow
    Productions:
        Opened October 26, 1950 for 12 performances.

Reviews:
  Christian Science Monitor Magazine p. 6, Nov 4, 1950
  Commonweal 53:140, Nov 17, 1950
  New York Theatre Critics' Reviews 1950:227
  New York Times p. 25, Oct 27, 1950
  New Yorker 26:76, Nov 4, 1950
  Newsweek 36:89, Nov 6, 1950
  Theatre Arts 35:10, Jan 1951
  Time 56:57, Nov 6, 1950

The Fake
  Productions:
  Opened October 6, 1924 for 88 performances.
  Reviews:
  Life (NY) 84:18, Oct 23, 1924
  New York Times p. 26, Oct 7, 1924
  Theatre Magazine 39:62, Dec 1924

Foreigners
  Productions:
  Opened December 5, 1939 for seven performances.
  Reviews:
  Nation 149:688, Dec 16, 1939
  New York Times p. 30, Dec 6, 1939
  Newsweek 14:35, Dec 18, 1939

The High Road
  Productions:
  Opened September 10, 1928 for 144 performances.
  Reviews:
  American Mercury 15:375-6, Nov 1928
  Catholic World 128:213-14, Nov 1928
  Life (NY) 92:17, Sep 28, 1928
  Nation 127:328, Oct 3, 1928
  New York Times p. 31, Sep 11, 1928
  Outlook 150:864, Sep 26, 1928
  Theatre Magazine 48:46-8, Nov 1928
  Vogue 72:108+, Oct 27, 1928

The Last of Mrs. Cheyney
  Productions:
  Opened November 9, 1925 for 385 performances.
  Reviews:
  Dial 80:166, Feb 1926
  New York Times p. 23, Nov 10, 1925
  Theatre Magazine 43:15, Jan 1926
  Vogue 67:63, Jan 1, 1926

On Approval
  Productions:
  Opened October 18, 1926 for 96 performances.
  Reviews:
  Life (NY) 88:23, Nov 11, 1926

New York Times p. 27, Oct 19, 1926
                 VIII, p. 1, Mar 1, 1942
Theatre Magazine 44:74, Dec 1926

Once Is Enough
   Productions:
     Opened February 15, 1938 for 105 performances.
   Reviews:
     Catholic World 147:83-4, Apr 1938
     Commonweal 27:524, Mar 4, 1938
     Nation 146:253, Feb 26, 1938
     New Republic 94:101, Mar 2, 1938
     New York Times p. 17, Jan 28, 1938
                   p. 16, Feb 16, 1938
     Newsweek 11:32, Feb 28, 1938
     One Act Play Magazine 1:1025, Mar 1938
     Theatre Arts 22:250+, Apr 1938
     Time 31:35, Feb 28, 1938

Spring Cleaning
   Productions:
     Opened November 9, 1923 for 251 performances.
   Reviews:
     Life (NY) 82:18, Nov 29, 1923
     Nation 117:615, Nov 28, 1923
     New York Times p. 16, Nov 10, 1923
                  VIII, p. 1, Nov 18, 1923
     Theatre Magazine 39:17+, Jan 1924
                       39:26+, Jan 1924

*The Way Things Go
   Reviews:
     Christian Science Monitor Magazine p. 4, Mar 18, 1950
     New York Times p. 19, Mar 3, 1950
                  II, p. 3, Mar 12, 1950

The Woman of It
   Productions:
     Opened January 14, 1913 for 15 performances.
   Reviews:
     Dramatic Mirror 69:6, Jan 22, 1913
     Life (NY) 61:240, Jan 30, 1913
     Munsey 48:1017, Mar 1913
     New York Dramatic News 57:22, Jan 25, 1913
     New York Times p. 13, Jan 15, 1913

LORCA, FEDERICO GARCIA see GARCIA-LORCA, FEDERICO

LUKE, PETER

Hadrian VII
~~Productions:~~
  Based on the works of Fr. Rolphe (Baron Corvo). Opened
    January 8, 1969 for 359 performances.
Reviews:
  America 120:70-72, Jan 18, 1969
          120:231-2, Feb 22, 1969
  Atlantic 223:62-5, Mar 1969
  Commonweal 89:588-9, Feb 7, 1969
  Nation 208:124-5, Jan 27, 1969
  National Review 21:168, Feb 25, 1969
  New Republic 160:32-4, Jan 25, 1969
  New York Times Critics' Reviews 1969:391
  New York Times p. 14, Jul 4, 1969
               p. 41, Dec 27, 1969
               p. 22, Jan 9, 1969
               II, p. 1, Jan 19, 1969
               II, p. 6, May 11, 1969
               p. 20, Sep 20, 1969
  New Yorker 44:66+, Aug 3, 1968
             44:72, Jan 18, 1969
  Newsweek 73:80, Jan 20, 1969
  Saturday Review 50:40-41, Jan 25, 1969
  Time 91:53, May 31, 1968
       93:68-9, Jan 17, 1969
  Vogue 153:54, Feb 15, 1969

McCARTHY, JUSTIN HUNTLEY

If I Were King
~~Productions:~~
  Opened September 22, 1913 in repertory.
  Opened April 29, 1916 for 33 performances.
Reviews:
  Dramatic Mirror 75:8, May 6, 1916
  Life (NY) 67:902, May 11, 1916
  New York Times p. 13, Sep 25, 1913

MAETERLINCK, MAURICE

The Betrothal
~~Productions:~~
  Translated by Alexander Teixeira de Mattos. Opened
    November 18, 1918 for 120 performances.
Reviews:
  Canadian Magazine 53:438, Sep 1919
  Current Opinion 66:23-6, Jan 1919
  Dramatic Mirror 79:831, Dec 7, 1918
  Dramatist 10:927, Jan 1919

Independent 96:210, Nov 16, 1918
Life (NY) 72:900, Dec 12, 1918
Literary Digest 59:28-9, Dec 7, 1918
Nation 107:671-2, Nov 10, 1918
New Republic 17:313, Jan 11, 1919
New American 209:117, Jan 1919
New York Times p. 11, Nov 19, 1918
VIII, p. 8, Dec 1, 1918
Theatre Magazine 29:17, 21, Jan 1919

The Blue Bird
Productions:
Opened October 1, 1910 in repertory.
Opened September 15, 1911 for 19 performances.
Opened December 24, 1923 for 33 performances.
Reviews:
Blue Book 12:631-4, Jan 1911
Bookman 33:137, Apr 1911
Canadian Magazine 36:288, Jan 1911
Collier's 46:24+, Oct 22, 1910
Current Literature 49:548-50, Nov 1910
Dramatic Mirror 64:8, Oct 5, 1910
65:7, Feb 8, 1911
66:11, Sep 20, 1911
Everybody's 24:119-20, Jan 1911
Green Book 4:1218, Dec 1910
Harper's 54:20, Oct 29, 1910
Independent 71:1300, Dec 14, 1911
Literary Digest 41:645, Oct 15, 1910
Life (NY) 56:616, Oct 13, 1910
New England Magazine 43:36-42, Sep 1910
New York Times p. 13, Dec 26, 1923
VII, p. 1, Dec 30, 1923
Pearson 24:522-7, Oct 1910
Play Book 1:3-6, Sep 1913
Review of Reviews 42:689, Dec 1910
Theatre Arts 7:29-40, Jan 1923
Theatre Magazine 12:130, Nov 1910

The Burgomaster of Belgium
Productions:
Opened March 24, 1919 for 32 performances.
Reviews:
Dramatist 10:942, Apr 1919
Forum 61:627-8, May 1919
Life (NY) 73:614, Apr 10, 1919
Nation 108:511, Apr 5, 1919
108:578, Apr 12, 1919
Theatre Magazine 29:200, Apr 1919
29:273-4, May 1919

The Death of Tintagiles
  Productions:
      Translated by Philip Moeller. Opened August 30, 1916 in
        repertory (Washington Square Players).
  Reviews:
      Dramatic Mirror 59:20, Mar 21, 1914
                      77:7, Feb 24, 1917
      Theatre Magazine 25:213, 223, Apr 1917

Interior
  Productions:
      Opened February 19, 1915 in repertory.
      Opened October 4, 1915 in repertory.
  Reviews:
      Dramatic Mirror 73:8, Feb 24, 1915
      New York Times p. 11, Oct 19, 1915

The Intruder
  Productions:
      Opened September 26, 1916 for 31 performances.
  Reviews:
      Dramatic Mirror 76:7, Oct 7, 1916
      Life (NY) 68:626-7, Oct 12, 1916
      Nation 103:330, Oct 5, 1916
      Theatre Magazine 24:283, Nov 1916
      Vogue 72:156, Sep 15, 1928
      Yale Review 5:122-3, Oct 1915

Mary Magdalene
  Productions:
      Opened December 5, 1910 for 16 performances.
  Reviews:
      Bookman 23:602-4, Feb 1911
      Collier's 46:24, Jan 7, 1911
      Current Literature 49:667-9, Dec 1910
      Dramatist 2:121, Jan 1911
      Dramatic Mirror 64:7, Dec 7, 1910
      Everybody's 24:408-13, Mar 1911
      Independent 70:150, Jan 19, 1911
      Life (NY) 56:1108, Dec 15, 1910
      Literary Digest 41:1202-3, Dec 24, 1910
      Nation 91:374, Oct 20, 1910
      New England Magazine 43:485-91, Jan 1911
      Red Book 16:753-8, Feb 1911
      Theatre Magazine 13:2-3, Jan 1911

A Miracle of Saint Anthony
  Productions:
      Opened February 19, 1915 in repertory (Washington Square
        Players).
      Translated by Ralph Roeder. Opened August 30, 1916 in
        repertory (Washington Square Players).

Reviews:
Nation 107:131, Aug 3, 1918
New York Times p. 15, May 8, 1915
Theatre Magazine 21:282+, Jun 1915

Pelleas and Melisande
Productions:
Opened December 4, 1923 for 13 performances.
Reviews:
Life (NY) 82:18, Dec 27, 1923
Nation 117:747, Dec 26, 1923
New Republic 37:123, Dec 26, 1923
New York Times p. 23, Dec 5, 1923
                  IX, p. 1, Dec 16, 1923
                  p. 38, Feb 20, 1957
                  II, p. 8, Mar 17, 1957
Theatre Magazine 39:14-15, Feb 1924

Sister Beatrice
Productions:
Opened March 14, 1910 in repertory.
Opened June 19, 1911 for 1 performance in repertory.
Reviews:
Blue Book 13:926-7, Sep 1911
Bookman 31:412-14, Jun 1910
Cosmopolitan 49:77-8, Jun 1910
Dramatic Mirror 63:7, Mar 26, 1910
                  65:7, Jun 21, 1911
Everybody's 22:841-9, Jun 1910
Green Book 3:1243-4, Jun 1910
Life (NY) 55:516, Mar 24, 1910
Pearson 23:692-4, May 1910
Theatre Magazine 11:186, 188, Jun 1910
                  11:98-9, Apr 1910

MARCEAU, FELICIEN

The Egg
Productions:
Translated by Robert Schlitt.   Opened January 8, 1962
    for eight performances.
Reviews:
Nation 184:554, Jun 22, 1957
New Republic 146:20+, Jan 29, 1962
New York Theatre Critics' Reviews 1962:384
New York Times p. 23, Jan 9, 1962
New Yorker 33:66, Jun 29, 1957
            37:63, Jan 20, 1962
Newsweek 59:50, Jan 22, 1962
Saturday Review 43:35, Dec 10, 1960
                45:29, Jan 27, 1962
Time 79:68, Jan 19, 1962

The Good Soup
    Productions:
        Adapted by Garson Kanin.   Opened March 2, 1960 for 21
        performances.
    Reviews:
        America 103:27, Apr 2, 1960
        Nation 190:262, Mar 19, 1960
        New York Theatre Critics' Reviews 1960:330
        New York Times p. 26, Mar 3, 1960
        New Yorker 36:113-14, Mar 12, 1960
        Saturday Review 43:26-7, Mar 19, 1960
        Theatre Arts 43:14, Jul 1959
        Time 75:73, Mar 14, 1960

MARCEL, GABRIEL

Colombyre
    Productions:
        (Off Broadway) Opened January 1951 in repertory.
    Reviews:
        New York Times p. 13, Dec 15, 1951

MARCUS, FRANK

Keyholes
    Productions:
        (Off Off Broadway) Opened November 20, 1973.
    No Reviews.

The Killing of Sister George
    Productions:
        Opened October 5, 1966 for 205 performances.
    Reviews:
        Christian Century 84:16-17, Jan 4, 1967
        Commonweal 85:106, Oct 28, 1966
        Esquire 66:8+, Nov 1966
        Life 61:6, Dec 2, 1966
        Nation 203:459-60, Oct 31, 1966
        National Review 19:100, Jan 24, 1967
        New York Theatre Critics' Reviews 1966:277
        New York Times p. 28, Jun 18, 1965
                     p. 57, Oct 6, 1966
                     II, p. 1, Oct 16, 1966
                     p. 50, Mar 28, 1967
        Newsweek 68:98+, Oct 17, 1966
        Reporter 35:62-3, Nov 17, 1966
        Saturday Review 49:72-3, Oct 22, 1966
        Time 88:93, Oct 14, 1966
        Vogue 148:99, Nov 15, 1966

*Mrs. Mouse, Are You Within?
Reviews:
New York Times II, p. 26, Jun 2, 1968
p. 45, Jul 8, 1968
II, p. 1, Jul 28, 1968

Notes on a Love Affair
Productions:
(Off Off Broadway) Season of 1974-75.
Reviews:
New York Times p. 61, Mar 26, 1972
II, p. 4, Apr 16, 1972

MARTINEZ-SIERRA, GREGORIO

The Cradle Song
Productions:
Translated by John G. Underhill. Opened January 24, 1927
for 57 performances.
Opened the week of September 16, 1929 in repertory.
Opened October 6, 1930 in repertory.
(Off Broadway) Season of 1955-56.
Reviews:
America 94:342, Dec 17, 1955
Bookman 65:207, Apr 1927
Catholic World 124:812-13, Mar 1927
182:385, Feb 1956
Commonweal 63:457-8, Feb 3, 1956
Dramatic Mirror 83:427, Mar 5, 1921
Independent 105:281, Mar 19, 1921
Nation 112:411, Mar 16, 1921
124:243-4, Mar 2, 1927
New Republic 50:274, Apr 27, 1927
51:18, May 25, 1927
134:20, Jun 2, 1956
New York Clipper Vol. 69: Mar 16, 1921
New York Times p. 18, Jan 25, 1927
VIII, p. 1, Jan 30, 1927
p. 32, Dec 2, 1955
Outlook 145:231-2, Feb 23, 1927
Theatre Arts 28:342, Jun 1944
Theatre Magazine 33:340, May 1921
Vogue 69:138, 140, Mar 15, 1927
Weekly Review 4:280, Mar 23, 1921

The Kingdom of God
Productions:
English version by Helen and Harley Granville-Barker.
Opened December 20, 1928 for 92 performances.
Reviews:
Dial 86:350-51, Apr 1929
Life (NY) 93:23, Jan 18, 1929

Literary Digest 100:21-2, Jan 12, 1929
Nation 128:52, Jan 7, 1929
New Republic 57:245-7, Jan 16, 1929
New York Times X, p. 1, Oct 14, 1928
                   IX, p. 2, Oct 21, 1928
                   VIII, p. 1, Dec 30, 1928
Theatre Magazine 49:49, Mar 1929
Vogue 73:71, 106, Feb 16, 1929

The Road to Happiness (with Eduardo Marquina)
    Productions:
        Opened May 2, 1927 for 16 performances in repertory.
    Reviews:
        New Republic 50:354-5, May 18, 1927

The Romantic Young Lady
    Productions:
        English version by Helen and Harley Granville-Barker.
        Opened May 4, 1926 for 25 performances.
    Reviews:
        Bookman 63:589-90, Jul 1926
        Nation 122:561, May 9, 1926
        New Republic 47:59-60, Jun 2, 1926
        New York Times p. 24, May 5, 1926
        Theatre Magazine 44:5, 15, Jul 1926
        Vogue 68:69, Jul 1, 1926

Spring in Autumn
    Productions:
        Adapted by Blanche Yurka and Nene Belmonte. Opened
        October 24, 1933 for 41 performances.
    Reviews:
        Commonweal 19:75, Nov 17, 1933
        New Outlook 162:46, Dec 1933
        New York Times p. 22, Oct 25, 1933

MASEFIELD, JOHN

The Faithful
    Productions:
        Opened October 13, 1919 for 49 performances.
    Reviews:
        Dial 60:77, Jan 20, 1916
        Drama 21:155, Feb 1916
        Dramatist 10:968, Oct 1919
        Living Age 301:719, Jun 21, 1919
        Nation 101:604, Nov 18, 1915
              109:591, Nov 8, 1919
        New Republic 4:312, Oct 23, 1915
                     20:326, Nov 12, 1919
        New York Times p. 14, Oct 14, 1919
        Review 1:545, Nov 1, 1919

Saturday Review 120:139, Aug 7, 1915
Theatre Arts 4:67, Jan 1920

The Tragedy of Nan (Nan)
    Productions:
        Opened January 13, 1913 for one performance.
        Opened February 17, 1919 for four performances.
    Reviews:
        Dramatic Mirror 69:67, Jan 22, 1913
                        77:4, Aug 25, 1917
                        77:28, Sep 22, 1917
                        82:362, Feb 28, 1920
        Dramatist 7:687-8, Apr 1916
        Independent 72:1158-60, May 30, 1912
        Life (NY) 75:414, Mar 4, 1920
        Living Age 274:778, Sep 28, 1912
        New York Dramatic Mirror 69:67, Jan 22, 1913
        Theatre Magazine 31:271-2, Apr 1920

MAUGHAM, W. SOMERSET

The Breadwinner
    Productions:
        Opened September 22, 1931 for 55 performances.
    Reviews:
        Commonweal 134:209, Nov 1931
        Life (NY) 98:19, Oct 9, 1931
        New Republic 68:209, Oct 7, 1931
        New York Times p. 19, Sep 23, 1931
        Outlook 159:182, Oct 7, 1931
        Theatre Arts 15:990, Dec 1931
        Theatre Magazine 53:30, Feb 1931

Caesar's Wife
    Productions:
        Opened November 24, 1919 for 81 performances.
    Reviews:
        Dramatic Mirror 80:1861, 1863, Dec 4, 1919
        Independent 101:86, Jan 17, 1920
        New York Times p. 9, Nov 25, 1919
        Review 1:688, Dec 20, 1919
        Theatre Magazine 31:19, Jan 1920

The Camel's Back
    Productions:
        Opened November 13, 1923 for 15 performances.
    Reviews:
        Life (NY) 82:50, Dec 6, 1923
        Nation 117:615, Nov 20, 1923
        New York Times p. 19, Nov 14, 1923
                        VIII, p. 1, Nov 18, 1923

Caroline
  Productions:
    Opened September 29, 1916 for 45 performances.
  Reviews:
    Dramatic Mirror 76:7, Sep 30, 1916
    Nation 102:364, Mar 30, 1916
         103:331, Oct 5, 1916
    New York Times p. 11, Feb 27, 1916
                   p. 9, Sep 21, 1916
                   II, p. 4, Sep 24, 1916
    Theatre Magazine 24:273, 283, Nov 1916

The Circle
  Productions:
    Opened September 12, 1921 for 175 performances.
    Opened April 18, 1938 for 72 performances.
    (Off Broadway) Opened March 26, 1974 for 96 performances.
  Reviews:
    Bookman 54:232, Nov 1921
    Catholic World 147:346-7, Jun 1938
    Commonweal 28:48, May 6, 1938
    Current Opinion 71:463-72, Oct 1921
    Dramatic Mirror 84:412, Sep 17, 1921
    Dramatist 12:1079, Oct 1921
    Everybody's Magazine 46:91, Jan 1922
    Hearst 40:61, Dec 1921
    Independent 106:137, Sep 24, 1921
    Nation 113:356, Sep 28, 1921
           146:512-3, Apr 30, 1938
    New Republic 28:161, Oct 5, 1921
    New York Clipper 69:17, Sep 21, 1921
    New York Theatre Critics' Reviews 1974:281
    New York Times VI, p. 1, Aug 14, 1921
                   p. 12, Sep 13, 1921
                   p. 24, Apr 19, 1938
                   p. 50, Apr 18, 1974
                   II, p. 1, Apr 28, 1974
    New Yorker 50:64, Apr 29, 1974
              52:73-4, Aug 30, 1976
    Newsweek 11:26, Apr 25, 1938
    Review 5:275, Sep 24, 1921
    Theatre Arts 29:167-9, Mar 1945
    Theatre Magazine 34:300+, Nov 1921
                     34:316, Nov 1921
    Time 31:26, May 2, 1938

The Constant Wife
  Productions:
    Opened November 29, 1926 for 233 performances.
    Opened December 8, 1951 for 138 performances.
    Opened April 4, 1975 for 32 performances.

Reviews:
  Bookman 64:733, Feb 1927
  Catholic World 174:392, Feb 1952
  Commonweal 55:299, Dec 28, 1951
  Dial 82:169, Feb 1927
  Dramatist 18:1339, Apr 1907
  Life (NY) 88:19, Dec 16, 1926
  Nation 124:21, Jan 5, 1927
  New Republic 49:108, Dec 15, 1926
                126:22, Jan 7, 1952
  New York Theatre Critics' Reviews 1951:149
                                      1975:272
  New York Times p. 11, Dec 31, 1926
                 p. 34, Dec 10, 1951
                 II, p. 3, Dec 16, 1951
                 p. 28, Apr 15, 1975
                 p. 43, Apr 16, 1975
                 II, p. 5, Apr 20, 1975
                 II, p. 5, Apr 27, 1975
  New Yorker 27:22, Dec 15, 1951
             51:81, Apr 28, 1975
  Newsweek 38:69, Dec 17, 1951
           85:85, Apr 28, 1975
  Saturday Review 34:18-19, Dec 29, 1951
  School and Society 75:326, May 24, 1952
  Theatre Magazine 45:16, Feb 1927
                   45:26+, Mar 1927
  Time 58:76, Dec 17, 1951
       105:95, Apr 28, 1975
  Vogue 69:118, Feb 1, 1927

East of Suez
  Productions:
  Opened September 21, 1922 for 100 performances.
  Reviews:
  Dramatist 14:1140, Jan 1923
  New York Clipper 70:21, Oct 4, 1922
  New York Times p. 16, Sep 22, 1922
  Theatre Magazine 36:380+, Dec 1922
                   36:299, Nov 1922

The Explorer
  Productions:
  Opened May 7, 1912 for 23 performances.
  Reviews:
  American Playwright 1:190, Jun 1912
  Green Book Album 8:123, Jul 1912
  Life (NY) 59:1073, May 23, 1912
  Theatre Magazine 15:171, Jun 1912

For Services Rendered
  Productions:
  Opened April 12, 1923 for 21 performances.

Reviews:
    Catholic World 137:208-10, May 1933
    Commonweal 17:719, Apr 26, 1933
    New Outlook 161:46, May 1933
    Nation 136:511-12, May 3, 1933
    New York Times p. 15, Apr 13, 1933
    Newsweek 1:28, Apr 22, 1933
    Stage 10:7, May 1933
         10:16, May 1933
    Theatre Arts 17:416, Jun 1933
    Time 21:21, Apr 24, 1933

*Lady Frederick
    Reviews:
    Green Book Album 1:928-64, May 1909
    New York Times p. 57, Sep 17, 1970
    Theatre Arts 31:30, Mar 1947

The Land of Promise
    Productions:
    Opened December 25, 1913 for 76 performances.
    Reviews:
    American Playwright 3:39-42, Feb 1914
    Bookman 38:609, Feb 1914
    Dramatist 5:419, Jun 1914
    Green Book Album 11:414, Mar 1914

The Letter
    Productions:
    Opened September 26, 1927 for 104 performances.
    Reviews:
    Dial 84:166-7, Feb 1928
    Dramatist 19:1361-2, Jan 1927
    Independent 119:482, Nov 12, 1927
    Life (NY) 90:23, Oct 13, 1927
    New Republic 52:207-8, Oct 12, 1927
    New York Times p. 30, Sep 27, 1927
    Outlook 147:181-2, Oct 12, 1927
    Saturday Review 4:193-4, Oct 15, 1927
    Theatre Magazine 46:28, 30, 56, Nov 1927
    Vogue 70:166, Nov 15, 1927

The Mask and the Face (see entry under Chiarelli, Luigi)

Mrs. Dot
    Productions:
    Opened January 24, 1910 for 72 performances.
    Reviews:
    Collier's 44:34, Feb 12, 1910
    Dramatic Mirror 63:6, Feb 5, 1910
    Dramatist 1:89, Jul 1910
    Life (NY) 55:245, Feb 10, 1910

The Noble Spaniard
    Productions:
        Opened September 20, 1909 for 40 performances.
    Reviews:
        Forum 42:439, Nov 1909
        Life (NY) 54:476, Oct 7, 1909
        New York Dramatic Mirror 62:7, Oct 2, 1909
        Theatre Magazine 10:137, 160, Nov 1909

On My Coral Islands
    Productions:
        (Off Off Broadway) Opened December 9, 1976.
    No Reviews.

Our Betters
    Productions:
        Opened May 12, 1917 for 112 performances.
        Opened February 20, 1928 for 128 performances.
        (Off Off Broadway) Opened December 1975.
    Reviews:
        Dial 84:439-40, May 1928
        Green Book 17:964-71, Jun 1917
        Life 91:19, Mar 15, 1928
            69:486, Mar 22, 1917
        Nation 104:350, Mar 22, 1917
        New Republic 10:200, Mar 17, 1917
        New York Times p. 9, Mar 13, 1917
                      VIII, p. 5, Mar 25, 1917
                      p. 18, Feb 21, 1928
                      IX, p. 1, Mar 4, 1928
        Outlook 148:383, Mar 7, 1928
        Vogue 71:94-5, Apr 15, 1928

Penelope
    Productions:
        Opened December 13, 1909 for 48 performances.
    Reviews:
        Collier's 44:34, Feb 23, 1910
        Dramatic Mirror 62:5, Dec 25, 1909
        Forum 43:189, Feb 1910
        Theatre Magazine 11:12, Jan 1910

*Perfect Gentleman
    Reviews:
        Theatre Arts 39:49-64, Nov 1955

Rain   (see entry under Colton, John)

The Sacred Flame
    Productions:
        Opened November 19, 1928 for 24 performances.
        Opened October 6, 1952 for 24 performances.

Reviews:
  Life (NY) 92:9, Dec 28, 1928
  Nation 175:365, Oct 18, 1952
  New York Theatre Critics' Reviews 1952:249
  New York Times p. 28, Nov 20, 1928
            p. 35, Oct 8, 1952
  New Yorker 28:82, Oct 18, 1952
  Outlook 150:1275, Dec 5, 1928
  Saturday Review 35:28-9, Oct 25, 1952
  Time 60:56, Oct 20, 1952

Sheppey
  Productions:
    Opened April 18, 1944 for 23 performances.
  Reviews:
    Commonweal 40:60-1, May 5, 1944
    Nation 158:521, Apr 29, 1940
    New York Theatre Critics' Reviews 1944:209
    New York Times p. 27, Apr 19, 1944
    New Yorker 20:44, Apr 29, 1944
    Saturday Review 156:327-8, Sep 23, 1933
    Theatre Arts 18:101, Feb 1934
              28:335-6, Jun 1944
    Time 43:58, May 1, 1944

Smith
  Productions:
    Opened September 5, 1910 for 112 performances.
  Reviews:
    Bookman 32:349, Dec 1910
    Harper's Weekly 54:13, Nov 19, 1910
    Life (NY) 56:434, Sep 15, 1910
    New York Dramatic Mirror 64:11, Sep 14, 1910
    Theatre Magazine 12:98, 107, Oct 1920

Theatre (with Guy Bolton)
  Productions:
    Opened November 12, 1941 for 69 performances.
  Reviews:
    Catholic World 154:473, Jan 1942
    Commonweal 35:144, Nov 28, 1941
    New Republic 105:762, Dec 8, 1941
    New York Theatre Critics' Reviews 1941:226
    New York Times p. 34, Nov 13, 1941
    Theatre Arts 26:15, Jan 1942

Too Many Husbands
  Productions:
    Opened October 8, 1919 for 102 performances.
  Reviews:
    Dramatic Mirror 80:1654, Oct 23, 1919
    Nation 109:548, Oct 25, 1919
    New York Times p. 16, Oct 19, 1919
              VIII, p. 3, Oct 19, 1919

MAURIAC, FRANCOIS

Asmodée (see Intruder)

The Egoists
  Productions:
    (Off Broadway) Season of 1959-1960.
  Reviews:
    America 102:139, Oct 31, 1959
    New York Times p. 52, Oct 14, 1959

*Intruder
  Translated by Sir Basil Bartlett.
  Reviews:
    Commonweal 68:77-9, Apr 18, 1958
    Theatre Arts 23:465, Jul 1939

MAVOR, OSBORNE H. see BRIDIE, JAMES

MILNE, A. A.

Ariadne (Business First)
  Productions:
    Opened February 23, 1925 for 48 performances.
  Reviews:
    Living Age 324:562-71, Mar 7, 1925
    New York Times p. 17, Feb 27, 1925

Belinda
  Productions:
    Opened May 6, 1918 for 32 performances.
  Reviews:
    Dramatic Mirror 78:692, May 18, 1918
    Green Book 20:6-9, Jul 1918
    Life (NY) 71:802, May 16, 1918
    New York Dramatic News 65:6, May 11, 1918
    New York Times p. 11, May 7, 1918
    Theatre Magazine 27:355+, Jun 1918

Business First (see Ariadne)

The Dover Road
  Productions:
    Opened December 23, 1921 for 204 performances.
  Reviews:
    Arts and Decoration 16:278, Feb 1922
    Bookman 55:61, Mar 1922
    Everybody's 46:157, May 1922
    Fortune 118:339, Aug 1922
    Independent 108:41-3, Jan 14, 1922
    Life (NY) 79:18, Jan 12, 1922

New York Clipper 69:20, Dec 28, 1921
New York Times p. 7, Dec 24, 1921
Theatre Magazine 35:360, Jun 1922
                35:143+, Mar 1922

Give Me Yesterday (Success)
    Productions:
        Opened March 4, 1931 for 72 performances.
    Reviews:
        Arts and Decoration 35:57, May 1931
        Catholic World 133:80-1, Apr 1931
        Commonweal 13:694, Apr 22, 1931
        Life (NY) 97:25, Mar 21, 1931
        Nation 132:306, Mar 18, 1931
        New York Times p. 39, Mar 3, 1931
                       p. 32, Mar 5, 1931
                       IX, p. 1, Mar 15, 1931
        Outlook 157:411, Mar 18, 1931
        Theatre Arts 15:372-3, May 1931
        Vogue 77:59+, May 1, 1931

The Great Broxopp
    Productions:
        Opened November 15, 1921 for 66 performances.
    Reviews:
        Dramatic Mirror 84:736, Nov 19, 1921
        Independent 108:43, Jan 14, 1922
        New York Clipper 69:20, Nov 23, 1921
        New York Times p. 22, Nov 16, 1921
                       VI, p. 1, Nov 27, 1921
        Theatre Magazine 35:128, Feb 1922

The Ivory Door
    Productions:
        Opened October 18, 1927 for 310 performances.
    Reviews:
        Life (NY) 90:23, Nov 10, 1927
        New York Times p. 24, Oct 19, 1927
        Outlook 147:465, Dec 14, 1927
        Saturday Review 4:320, Nov 19, 1927
        Theatre Magazine 47:38, Jan 1928

The Lucky One
    Productions:
        Opened November 20, 1922 for 40 performances.
    Reviews:
        Life (NY) 80:18, Dec 14, 1922
        Nation 115:671, Dec 13, 1922
        New York Clipper 70:20, Nov 29, 1922
        New York Times p. 15, Nov 21, 1922
                       VIII, p. 1, Dec 3, 1922
        Theatre Magazine 37:19, Jan 1923

Meet the Prince (To Have the Honor)
Productions:
Opened February 25, 1929 for 96 performances.
Reviews:
Catholic World 129:85, Apr 1929
Commonweal 9:544-5, Mar 13, 1929
New York Times p. 30, Feb 26, 1929
X, p. 1, Mar 10, 1929
Outlook 151:423, Mar 13, 1929

Michael and Mary
Productions:
Opened December 13, 1929 for 246 performances.
Reviews:
Drama 20:138, Feb 1930
Life (NY) 95:20, Jan 3, 1930
New York Times p. 23, Dec 14, 1929
Outlook 154:32, Jan 1, 1930
Nation 130:52, Jan 8, 1930
Theatre Magazine 51:45-6, Feb 1930
Vogue 75:118, Feb 15, 1930

Miss Marlowe at Play
Productions:
(Off Broadway) Opened March 1940 in repertory.
No Reviews.

Mr. Pim Passes By
Productions:
Opened February 28, 1921 for 124 performances.
Opened April 18, 1927 for 36 performances.
Reviews:
Bookman 65:573, Jul 1927
Current Opinion 70:755-84, Jun 1921
Dramatic Mirror 83:428, Mar 5, 1921
Independent 105:281, Mar 19, 1921
Life (NY) 77:390, Mar 17, 1921
Nation 112:411, Mar 16, 1921
New York Clipper 69:23, Mar 9, 1921
New York Times p. 18, Mar 1, 1921
p. 24, Apr 19, 1927
VIII, p. 1, May 22, 1927
Outlook 127:627, Apr 20, 1921
Theatre Magazine 33:319+, May 1921
34:152+, Sep 1921
Weekly Review 4:280, Mar 23, 1921

The Perfect Alibi
Productions:
Opened November 27, 1928 for 255 performances.
Reviews:
Bookman 68:685, Feb 1929
Commonweal 10:104, May 29, 1929

Life (NY) 92:9, Dec 28, 1928
New York Times p. 24, Nov 28, 1928
Outlook 150:1355, Dec 19, 1928

The Romantic Age
Productions:
Opened November 14, 1922 for 31 performances.
Reviews:
Life (NY) 80:18, Dec 14, 1922
New York Clipper 70:20, Nov 22, 1922
New York Times II, p. 1, Mar 19, 1922
Weekly Review 3:603, Dec 15, 1920

Sarah Simple
Productions:
(Off Broadway) Opened November 16, 1940 in repertory.
Reviews:
New York Times p. 26, Nov 15, 1940
                p. 22, Nov 18, 1940

Success (see Give Me Yesterday)

They Don't Mean Any Harm
Productions:
Opened February 23, 1932 for 15 performances.
Reviews:
New York Times p. 25, Feb 24, 1932
Theatre Arts 16:363-4, May 1932
Theatre Guild 9:9, Apr 1932

To Have the Honor (see Meet the Prince)

The Truth About Blayds
Productions:
Opened March 14, 1922 for 108 performances.
Opened April 11, 1932 for 24 performances.
Reviews:
Bookman 55:387-8, Jun 1922
Catholic World 135:210, May 1932
Commonweal 16:49-50, May 11, 1922
Current Opinion 72:629-39, May 1922
Dramatist 13:1101-2, Apr 1922
Everybody's 47:76-82, Aug 1922
Independent 108:462-3, May 13, 1922
Life (NY) 79:20, Apr 6, 1922
Literary Digest 73:30-1, May 13, 1922
Nation 114:376, Mar 29, 1922
        134:497-8, Apr 27, 1932
New Republic 30:198-9, Apr 12, 1922
New York Clipper 70:22, Mar 22, 1922
New York Times p. 22, Mar 15, 1922
                VI, p. 1, Mar 26, 1922
                p. 25, Apr 12, 1932

Theatre Magazine 35:306-7, May 1922
36:156+, Sep 1922

The Ugly Duckling
Productions:
(Off Off Broadway) Opened February 13, 1976.
No Reviews.

MOLNAR, FERENC

Carnival
Productions:
Translated by Melville Baker.   Opened December 29, 1924
for 32 performances.
Reviews:
Drama 15:97, Feb 1925
Life (NY) 85:18, Jan 22, 1925
Nation 120:75, Jan 21, 1925
New York Times VIII, p. 2, Nov 30, 1924
p. 15, Dec 30, 1924
Theatre Magazine 40:15, Mar 1925

Delicate Story
Productions:
English text by Gilbert Miller.   Opened December 4, 1940
for 29 performances.
Reviews:
Catholic World 152:470-1, Jan 1941
Nation 151:641, Dec 21, 1940
New York Theatre Critics' Reviews 1940:199
New York Times p. 32, Dec 5, 1940
Newsweek 16:66, Dec 16, 1940
Stage 1:9, Dec 1940
Theatre Arts 25:97, Feb 1941
Time 36:72, Dec 16, 1940

Fashions for Men
Productions:
English version by Benjamin Glazer.   Opened December 5,
1922 for 86 performances.
Reviews:
Bookman 56:747-9, Feb 1923
Dramatist 14:1161, Apr 1923
Life (NY) 80:18, Dec 28, 1922
New York Clipper 70:20, Dec 13, 1922
New York Times p. 22, Dec 6, 1922
VII, p. 1, Dec 24, 1922
III, p. 4, Jan 14, 1923

The Glass Slipper
Productions:
Opened October 19, 1925 for 65 performances.

Reviews:
  Bookman 62:594, Jan 1926
  Life (NY) 86:20, Nov 12, 1925
  Nation 121:550-51, Nov 11, 1925
  New York Times p. 29, Oct 20, 1925
                     VIII, p. 2, Oct 25, 1925

The Good Fairy
  Productions:
    English text by Jane Hinton.   Opened November 24, 1931
      for 151 performances.
    English text by Jane Hinton.   Opened November 17, 1932
      for 68 performances.
  Reviews:
    Arts and Decoration 36:56, Feb 1932
    Bookman 74:565, Jan 1932
    Catholic World 134:469, Jan 1932
    Commonweal 15:187-8, Dec 16, 1931
    Nation 133:678, Dec 16, 1931
    New York Times p. 17, Nov 25, 1931
                    p. 22, Nov 18, 1932
    Outlook 159:470, Dec 9, 1931
    Theatre Arts 16:97-8, Feb 1932
    Theatre Guild Magazine 9:3-4, Jan 1932
    Vogue 79:82, Jan 15, 1932

The Guardsman   (see also Where Ignorance Is Bliss)
  Productions:
    Opened October 13, 1924 for 248 performances.
  Reviews:
    American Mercury 3:501-2, Dec 1924
    Dial 77:440-41, Nov 1924
    Living Age 323:68-78, Oct 4, 1924
    Nation 119:501, Nov 5, 1924
    New York Times p. 23, Oct 14, 1924
                    VI, p. 16, Nov 11, 1945
                    II, p. 15, Aug 17, 1969
                    p. 17, Mar 29, 1975
    Theatre Magazine 39:15, Dec 1924

Launzi
  Productions:
    Adapted by Edna St. Vincent Millay.   Opened October 10,
      1923 for 13 performances.
  Reviews:
    Life (NY) 82:20, Nov 1, 1923
    Nation 117:470, Oct 24, 1923
    New Republic 36:230-1, Oct 24, 1923
    New York Times p. 16, Oct 11, 1923
    Theatre Magazine 38:16, Dec 1923

Liliom
  Productions:
    Opened April 20, 1921 for 83 performances.
    Adapted by Benjamin Glazer. Opened October 26, 1932
      for 35 performances.
    Adapted by Benjamin Glazer. Opened March 25, 1940
      for 56 performances.
  Reviews:
    Bookman 53:414-15, Jul 1921
    Catholic World 136:463-4, Jan 1933
                   151:210-11, May 1940
    Commonweal 17:75, Nov 16, 1932
               31:514, Apr 5, 1940
    Current Opinion 71:187-97, Aug 1921
    Drama 11:308-10, Jun 1921
    Dramatic Mirror 83:733, Apr 30, 1921
                    84:485, Oct 1, 1921
    Everybody's 45:57-64, Oct 1921
    Hearst 40:25-7+, Aug 1921
    Life (NY) 77:648, May 5, 1921
    Literary Digest 69:24-5, May 21, 1921
    Nation 112:695, May 11, 1921
           150:497, Apr 6, 1940
    National Magazine 50:519, Mar-Apr 1922
    New Republic 26:299, May 4, 1921
                 102:473, Apr 8, 1940
    New York Clipper 69:19, Apr 27, 1921
    New York Theatre Critics' Reviews 1940:354
    New York Times p. 18, Apr 21, 1921
                   VI, p. 1, Apr 21, 1921
                   VII, p. 1, May 1, 1921
                   VI, p. 1, May 27, 1921
                   p. 23, Oct 27, 1932
                   p. 17, Mar 26, 1940
                   IX, p. 1, Mar 31, 1940
                   VI, p. 72, Feb 5, 1956
                   p. 12, Feb 18, 1956
    New Yorker 16:30, Apr 6, 1940
    Newsweek 15:34, Apr 8, 1940
    Outlook 128:153-4, May 25, 1921
    Player's Magazine 16:20-3, Jan 1940
    Poet Lore 35:43-7, Mar 1924
    Theatre Arts 17:14-15+, Jan 1933
                 24:315-16, May 1940
    Theatre Magazine 34:5+, Jul 1921
                     34:220-6, Oct 1921
    Time 35:38, Apr 8, 1940
    Vogue 95:66, May 1, 1940
    Weekly Review 4:444-5, May 7, 1921

Mima
  Productions:
    Adapted by David Belasco from Molnar's The Red Mill.

Opened December 12, 1928 for 180 performances.
Reviews:
American Mercury 16:249, Feb 1929
Bookman 68:686, Feb 1929
Catholic World 128:593-4, Feb 1929
Life (NY) 93:23, Jan 18, 1929
New York Times p. 24, Dec 13, 1928
                    VIII, p. 1, Dec 23, 1928
Scientific American 140:244-5, Mar 1929
Theatre Magazine 49:49, Feb 1929
Vogue 73:118, Feb 2, 1929

Miracle in the Mountains
    Productions:
    Opened April 25, 1947 for 3 performances.
    Reviews:
    New York Theatre Critics' Reviews 1947:387
    New York Times p. 10, Apr 26, 1947
    New Yorker 23:54+, May 3, 1927
    Newsweek 29:86, May 5, 1947
    Time 49:76, May 5, 1947

Olympia
    Productions:
    English version by Sidney Howard. Opened October 16,
    1928 for 39 performances.
    Reviews:
    Dial 85:534-5, Dec 1928
    Life (NY) 92:17, Nov 9, 1928
    New York Times p. 26, Oct 17, 1928
    Theatre Magazine 48:47+, Dec 1928
    Vogue 72:146, Dec 8, 1928

One, Two, Three
    Productions:
    Opened September 29, 1930 for 40 performances.
    Reviews:
    Catholic World 132:209, Nov 1930
    Commonweal 12:610, Oct 15, 1930
    Life (NY) 96:19, Oct 17, 1930
    New York Times p. 24, Sep 30, 1930
    Vanity Fair 35:90, Dec 1930

The Phantom Rival (see also Tale of the Wolf)
    Productions:
    Opened October 6, 1914 for 127 performances.
    Reviews:
    American Playwright 3:363-6, Nov 1914
    American Mercury 79:84, Feb 1915
    Bookman 40:255-6, Nov 1914
    Book News 33:127-8, Nov 1914
    Collier's 54:9, Jan 2, 1915
    Current Opinion 57:400-404, Dec 1914

Dramatic Mirror 72:8, Oct 14, 1914
Green Book 12:1059-60, Dec 1914
McClure's 44:23-6, Jan 1915
Nation 99:476-7, Oct 15, 1914
New York Dramatic News 60:18, Oct 17, 1914
North American Review 200:934-6, Dec 1914
Theatre Magazine 20:209+, Nov 1914

The Play's the Thing
  Productions:
    Adapted by P. G. Wodehouse. Opened November 3, 1926
      for 260 performances.
    Adapted by P. G. Wodehouse. Opened April 9, 1928
      for 24 performances.
    Adapted by P. G. Wodehouse. Opened April 28, 1948
      for 244 performances.
    (Off Broadway) Adapted by P. G. Wodehouse. Opened
      January 9, 1973 for 64 performances.
    Adapted by P. G. Wodehouse. Opened May 7, 1973 for
      87 performances.
    (Off Off Broadway) Adapted by P. G. Wodehouse. Opened
      July 26, 1974.
    (Off Off Broadway) Adapted by P. G. Wodehouse. Opened
      November 26, 1976.
  Reviews:
    Catholic World 167:264-5, Jun 1948
    Dial 82:76, Jan 1927
    Life 24:85-6+, May 24, 1948
    Life (NY) 88:22, Nov 25, 1926
    Nation 123:540, Nov 24, 1926
      166:557-8, May 15, 1948
    New Republic 118:34, May 17, 1948
    New York Theatre Critics' Reviews 1948:283
                                      1973:278
    New York Times p. 25, Nov 4, 1926
                   VIII, p. 1, Nov 14, 1926
                   p. 32, Apr 16, 1928
                   p. 19, Apr 29, 1948
                   II, p. 1, May 9, 1948
                   II, p. 1, May 16, 1948
                   p. 42, Feb 1, 1973
                   II, p. 1, Feb 11, 1973
                   p. 38, May 8, 1973
                   p. 47, May 26, 1973
                   p. 25, Jul 26, 1974
    New Yorker 24:54, May 8, 1948
    Newsweek 31:77, May 10, 1948
    Theatre Arts 32:13+, Jun 1948
    Theatre Magazine 45:14-15, Jan 1927
                     45:26+, Feb 1927
    Time 51:81, May 10, 1948
    Vanity Fair 27:42, Jan 1927

The Red Mill   (see Mima)

Still Life
    Productions:
        (Off Off Broadway) Opened December 1974.
    No Reviews.

The Swan
    Productions:
        Translated by Melville Baker.   Opened October 23, 1923
            for 255 performances.
    Reviews:
        Classic 18:46+, Jan 1924
        Current Opinion 76:58-64, Jan 1924
        Freeman 8:281-2, Nov 28, 1923
        Life (NY) 82:20, Nov 15, 1923
        New York Times p. 14, Aug 27, 1924
                        p. 16, Aug 17, 1954
        Theatre Magazine 38:14-15, Dec 1923

A Tale of the Wolf   (see also The Phantom Rival)
    Productions:
        Opened October 7, 1925 for 13 performances.
    Reviews:
        New York Times p. 31, Oct 8, 1925
                       IX, p. 1, Oct 18, 1925

There Is a Play Tonight
    Productions:
        (Off Broadway) Season of 1960-61.
    Reviews:
        New York Times p. 24, Feb 16, 1961

The Violet
    Productions:
        Opened September 29, 1930 for 40 performances.
    Reviews:
        Catholic World 132:209, Nov 1930
        Commonweal 12:610, Oct 15, 1930
        Life (NY) 96:19, Oct 17, 1930
        New York Times p. 24, Sep 30, 1930
        Vanity Fair 35:90, Dec 1930

Where Ignorance Is Bliss
    Productions:
        English version by Philip Littell.   Opened September 3,
            1913 for 8 performances.
    Reviews:
        American Playwright 2:278-9, Sep 1913
        Bookman 38:136, Oct 1913
        Dramatic Mirror 70:6, Sep 10, 1913
        Everybody's Magazine 29:686, Nov 1913
        Harper's Weekly 58:26, Sep 20, 1913

New York Dramatic News 58:18-19, Sep 13, 1913
New York Times p. 9, Sep 4, 1913
Smart Set 49:145-7, Nov 1913
Theatre Magazine 18:115, Oct 1913

MONTHERLANT, HENRI DE see DE MONTHERLANT, HENRI

MORLEY, ROBERT

Edward, My Son (with Noel Langley)
Productions:
Opened September 30, 1948 for 260 performances.
Reviews:
Catholic World 168:159, Nov 1948
Commonweal 49:12-13, Oct 15, 1948
Forum 110:351-2, Dec 1948
Life 25:111-14, Oct 18, 1948
Nation 167:501, Oct 30, 1948
New Republic 119:26, Oct 18, 1948
New York Theatre Critics' Reviews 1948:219
New York Times p. 30, Oct 1, 1948
                 II, p. 1, Oct 10, 1948
                 p. 39, Apr 13, 1949
New York Times Magazine pp. 48-9, Oct 3, 1948
New Yorker 24:60+, Oct 9, 1948
Newsweek 32:84, Oct 11, 1948
Saturday Review 31:26-8, Oct 16, 1948
School and Society 68:303, Oct 30, 1948
Theatre Arts 31:35-6, Oct 1947
             33:14, Jan 1949
Time 52:78, Oct 11, 1948
Vogue 112:183, Dec 1948

Short Story
Productions:
(Off Broadway) Opened March 13, 1940 in repertory.
No Reviews.

MUNRO, C. K.

At Mrs. Beam's
Productions:
Opened April 26, 1926 for 59 performances.
Reviews:
Bookman 63:587-8, Jul 1926
Nation 122:540, May 12, 1926
New Republic 46:361-2, May 12, 1926
New York Times p. 24, Apr 26, 1926
Overland Monthly 85:115, Apr 1927

Theatre Magazine 44:16, Jul 1926
Vogue 68:68, Jul 1, 1926

Beau-Strings
  Productions:
    Opened April 26, 1926 for 24 performances.
  Reviews:
    Bookman 63:587-8, Jul 1926
    New York Times p. 22, Apr 27, 1926
    Theatre Magazine 44:16, Jul 1926
    Vogue 68:68, Jul 1, 1926

The Watched Pot
  Productions:
    (Off Broadway) Opened October 28, 1947 in repertory.
  Reviews:
    New York Times p. 31, Oct 29, 1947

MURRAY, T. C.

Autumn Fire
  Productions:
    Opened October 26, 1926 for 71 performances.
  Reviews:
    Independent 117:621, Nov 27, 1926
    New York Times p. 25, Oct 27, 1926
    Theatre Magazine 45:16+, Jan 1927

Birthright
  Productions:
    Opened November 20, 1911 in repertory (Irish Players).
    Opened February 4, 1913 in repertory (Irish Players).
    Season of 1919-1920.
    Opened October 21, 1932 in repertory (Irish Repertory
      Company).
  Reviews:
    American Playwright 1:25-6, Jan 1912
    Dramatic Mirror 66:7, Nov 22, 1911
                     69:7, Feb 12, 1913
                     82:1098, May 29, 1920
    Green Book 7:462-3+, Mar 1912
    Life (NY) 75:1089, Jun 10, 1920
    New York Times p. 14, May 25, 1920
                   p. 25, Nov 4, 1932

Maurice Harte
  Productions:
    Opened February 4, 1913 in repertory (Irish Players).
  Reviews:
    Dramatic Mirror 69:6-7, Feb 19, 1913
    Everybody's 28:679-80, May 1913
    New York Times p. 5, Feb 14, 1913

Spring
    Productions:
        Opened in the Fall of 1934 for two performances in
           repertory (Abby Theatre Players).
    No Reviews.

NESTROY, JOHANN

Einen Jux Will Er Sich Machen (He Wants To Have a Good Time)
    Productions:
        Opened April 2, 1968 for 6 performances.
    Reviews:
        New York Times p. 41, Apr 3, 1968

He Wants to Have a Good Time (see Einen Jux Will Er Sich
      Machen)

The Merchants of Yonkers
    Productions:
        Adapted by Thornton Wilder. Opened December 28, 1938
           for 39 performances.
    Reviews:
        Catholic World 148:599-600, Feb 1939
        Commonweal 29:330, Jan 13, 1939
        Nation 148:74, Jan 14, 1939
        New York Times p. 30, Dec 13, 1938
                    IX, p. 3, Dec 18, 1938
                    p. 14, Dec 29, 1938
                    IX, p. 1, Jan 8, 1939
        Newsweek 13:32, Jan 9, 1939
        Theatre Arts 23:173-4, Mar 1939
        Time 33:25, Jan 9, 1939

NICHOLS, PETER

A Day in the Death of Joe Egg
    Productions:
        Opened February 1, 1968 for 154 performances.
        (Off Off Broadway) Opened January 1975.
        (Off Off Broadway) Opened February 12, 1976.
    Reviews:
        America 118:330-1, Mar 9, 1968
        Commentary 45:76, Apr 1968
        Commonweal 87:718-20, Mar 15, 1968
        Life 63:106+, Nov 24, 1967
        Nation 206:247-9, Feb 19, 1968
        New York Theatre Critics' Reviews 1968:358, 362
        New York Times p. 26, Feb 2, 1968
                    p. 22, Feb 3, 1968
                    II, p. 1, Feb 11, 1968
                    p. 43, Apr 27, 1968

New York Times p. 1, Jun 19, 1968
New Yorker 43:84, Aug 19, 1967
        43:86, Feb 10, 1968
Newsweek 71:89, Feb 12, 1968
Reporter 38:44, Mar 7, 1968
Saturday Review 51:26, Feb 17, 1968
Time 91:75, Mar 15, 1968
Vogue 150:70, Oct 15, 1967
      151:44, Mar 15, 1968

*Forget-Me-Not-Lane
  Reviews:
    New York Times p. 27, Aug 17, 1971
             p. 97, Apr 8, 1973
             II, p. 1, Apr 22, 1973
    Newsweek 81:87, Apr 30, 1973

Joe Egg (see A Day in the Death of Joe Egg)

The National Health
  Productions:
    Opened October 10, 1974 for 53 performances.
  Reviews:
    America 131:349, Nov 30, 1974
    Catholic World 212:314-15, Mar 1971
    Nation 219:444-5, Nov 2, 1974
    New Republic 171:32+, Nov 2, 1974
    New York Theatre Critics' Reviews 1974:218
    New York Times p. 75, Oct 19, 1969
             p. 50, Apr 7, 1974
             II, p. 14, Apr 14, 1974
             p. 28, Oct 11, 1974
             p. 35, Oct 18, 1974
             II, p. 7, Oct 20, 1974
             II, p. 5, Nov 10, 1974
    New Yorker 50:6, Oct 21, 1974
    Newsweek 83:117, Apr 22, 1974
    Time 104:90+, Oct 21, 1974

NICHOLS, ROBERT

Wings Over Europe (with Maurice Browne)
  Productions:
    Opened December 10, 1928 for 90 performances.
    (Off Broadway) Opened January 29, 1948 for 7 performances
      in repertory.
    (Off Broadway) Opened February 1949 in repertory.
  Reviews:
    American Mercury 16:247-8, Feb 1929
    Catholic World 128:589-90, Feb 1929
    Dial 86:170-71, Feb 1929
    Life (NY) 93:23, Jan 19, 1923

Literary Digest 99:19-20, Dec 29, 1928
Nation 127:721-2, Dec 26, 1928
New Republic 57:163-4, Dec 26, 1928
New York Times p. 35, Dec 11, 1928
                III, p. 4, Dec 6, 1928
Outlook 151:224, Feb 6, 1929
Review of Reviews 79:158, Feb 1929
Theatre Arts 13:84-7, Feb 1929
Theatre Magazine 49:49-51, Feb 1929
                49:30-31+, Mar 1929
Vogue 73:58-9+, Feb 2, 1929

OBEY, ANDRE

Boubouroche (with Denys Amiel)
    Productions:
    Opened November 28, 1921 for 41 performances.
    Reviews:
    Nation 113:736, Dec 21, 1921
    New York Clipper 69:20, Dec 7, 1921
    New York Times p. 20, Nov 29, 1921

Hoboes in Heaven (with G. M. Martens and Claude Arrieu)
    Productions:
    (Off Broadway) Opened October 23, 1947 for 23 performances.
    Reviews:
    Commonweal 47:120, Nov 14, 1947

Lucrèce
    Productions:
    Translated by Thornton Wilder. Musical setting by Deems
        Taylor.
    Opened December 20, 1932 for 31 performances.
    Reviews:
    American Review 5:97-105, Apr 1935
    Arts and Decorations 38:56, Feb 1933
    Catholic World 136:586-7, Feb 1933
    Commonweal 17:301, Jan 11, 1933
    Literary Digest 115:15, Jan 7, 1933
    Nation 136:47-8, Jan 11, 1933
    New Outlook 161:49, Feb 1933
    New Republic 73:268-9, Jun 18, 1933
    New York Times p. 22, Nov 30, 1932
                    III, p. 3, Dec 4, 1932
                    p. 22, Dec 21, 1932
                    IX, p. 1, Jan 1, 1933
    Saturday Review 9:375, Jan 14, 1933
    Stage 10:6-7+, Jan 1933
            10:7-8, Feb 1933
            17:179-80, Mar 1933
    Vogue 81:72, Feb 15, 1933

Noah
  Productions:
    Adapted by Arthur Wilmurt. Music by Louis Horst. Opened
      February 13, 1935 for 45 performances.
    (Off Broadway) Opened June 7, 1946 for 2 performances
      in repertory.
    (Off Broadway) Opened March 1950 in repertory.
    (Off Broadway) Opened season of 1954-55.
    (Off Broadway) Opened season of 1959-60.
  Reviews:
    American Review 4:572-87, Mar 1935
    Catholic World 141:88-9, Apr 1935
    Commonweal 21:513, Mar 1, 1935
    Nation 140:259-60, Feb 27, 1935
    New Republic 82:105, Mar 6, 1935
    New York Times p. 25, Feb 14, 1935
                  VIII, p. 2, Mar 3, 1935
                  IX, p. 1, Aug 4, 1935
                  p. 16, Aug 10, 1935
                  p. 26, Oct 9, 1935
                  p. 32, Nov 6, 1935
                  XI, p. 6, Dec 1, 1935
                  p. 32, Oct 11, 1954
    Newsweek 5:26, Feb 23, 1935
    Player's Magazine 23:15, Sep-Oct 1946
    Saturday Review 38:24, Jan 29, 1955
    Stage 12:115-16, Mar 1935
    Theatre Arts 19:253-4+, Apr 1935
                 19:734+, Oct 1935
    Time 25:56-7, Feb 25, 1935

The Wife with the Smile (with Denys Amiel)
  Productions:
    Opened November 28, 1921 for 41 performances.
  Reviews:
    Bookman 54:572-3, Feb 1922
    Nation 113:735-6, Dec 21, 1921
    New York Clipper 69:20, Dec 7, 1921
    New York Times p. 20, Nov 29, 1921
                  VII, p. 1, Dec 4, 1921

O'CASEY, SEAN

Bedtime Story
  Productions:
    Opened April 15, 1959 for 37 performances.
    (Off Off Broadway) Opened February 9, 1976.
    (Off Off Broadway) Opened March 1976.
  Reviews:
    New York Times p. 35, May 8, 1952
                  p. 21, Apr 1, 1957
                  p. 33, Mar 11, 1958

New York Times II, p. 1, Mar 16, 1958
           p. 28, Apr 16, 1959
           II, p. 1, Apr 26, 1959
Theatre Arts 43:9, Jun 1959

*The Bishop's Bonfire
  Reviews:
  Atlantic 196:96, Oct 1955
  New York Times p. 22, Mar 1, 1955
              II, p. 3, Mar 6, 1955
                 p. 22, Jul 27, 1961
  Time 65:58, Mar 14, 1955

Cock-a-Doodle Dandy
  Productions:
  (Off Broadway) Season of 1958-1959.
  Opened January 20, 1969 for 40 performances.
  (Off Off Broadway) Opened February 18, 1976.
  Reviews:
  America 120:232, Feb 22, 1969
  Nation 187:416, Nov 29, 1958
         208:187-9, Feb 10, 1969
  New York Theatre Critics' Reviews 1969:388
  New York Times p. 29, Dec 12, 1949
              p. 26, Feb 1, 1950
              p. 26, Nov 4, 1955
              p. 40, Oct 7, 1958
              II, p. 1, Nov 9, 1958
              p.. 39, Nov 13, 1958
              II, p. 1, Nov 23, 1958
              p. 35, Sep 2, 1959
              p. 43, Sep 8, 1959
              p. 40, Jan 21, 1969
              II, p. 1, Feb 2, 1969
              p. 26, Mar 2, 1976
  New Yorker 34:100-2, Nov 22, 1958
            44:44+, Feb 1, 1969
  Newsweek 52:78, Nov 24, 1958
  Saturday Review 38:37, Nov 19, 1955
                 41:37, Dec 6, 1958
  Theatre Arts 42:22-4, Nov 1958
              43:9, Jan 1959
  Time 72:83, Nov 24, 1958
       93:72, Jan 31, 1969
  Vogue 153:112, Mar 1, 1969

*Drums of Father Ned
  Reviews:
  Saturday Review 42:22, May 9, 1959

The End of the Beginning
  Productions:
  (Off Off Broadway) Opened March 1976.
  No Reviews.

Figuro in the Night
    Productions:
        (Off Broadway) Opened October 30, 1962 for one performance
        (ANTA Matinee).
    Reviews:
        New York Times p. 33, Oct 31, 1962

*Hall of Healing
    Reviews:
        New York Times p. 35, May 8, 1952

Juno and the Paycock
    Productions:
        Opened March 15, 1926 for 74 performances.
        Opened December 19, 1927 for 40 performances.
        Opened October 21, 1932 in repertory (Irish Repertory
          Company).
        Opened November 23, 1934 for 9 performances.
        Opened December 6, 1937 for 8 performances.
        Opened January 16, 1940 for 105 performances.
        (Off Broadway) Opened July 1, 1946 in repertory.
        (Off Broadway) Opened June 23, 1947 in repertory.
        (Off Broadway) Season of 1954-1955.
        (Off Off Broadway) Opened March 1977.
    Reviews:
        Arts and Decoration 25:64, May 1926
        Bookman 63:343-4, May 1926
        Catholic World 150:730-1, Mar 1940
        Commonweal 31:327, Feb 2, 1940
        Dial 84:259-60, Mar 1928
        Drama 18:67-70, Dec 1927
        Independent 116:580, May 15, 1926
        Living Age 321:869-70, May 3, 1924
        Nation 122:348, Mar 31, 1926
        New York Theatre Critics' Reviews 1940:415+
        New York Times p. 22, Mar 10, 1926
                   VIII, p. 1, Mar 21, 1926
                   p. 32, Dec 20, 1927
                   p. 24, Oct 20, 1932
                   p. 32, Dec 7, 1937
                   p. 24, Jan 17, 1940
                   IX, p. 1, Jan 21, 1940
                   IX, p. 1, Jan 28, 1940
                   p. 20, Feb 24, 1955
                   p. 41, May 6, 1964
                   p. 40, Aug 3, 1966
                   p. 23, Mar 5, 1973
                   II, p. 7, Nov 24, 1974
                   II, p. 5, Dec 29, 1974
        Theatre Arts 10:286+, May 1926
                  24:154+, Mar 1940
        Theatre Magazine 43:15, May 1926
        Time 35:36, Jan 29, 1940

Time 104:95+, Nov 18, 1974
Vogue 67:98+, May 15, 1926
71:87+, Feb 15, 1928

The Moon Shines on Kylenamoe
Productions:
(Off Broadway) Opened October 30, 1962 for one performance
(ANTA Matinee).
Reviews:
New York Times p. 33, Oct 31, 1962

The Plough and the Stars
Productions:
Opened November 28, 1927 for 32 performances.
Opened November 12, 1934 for 13 performances.
Opened October 7, 1937 for four performances (Abbey
Theatre Players).
(Off Broadway) Opened January 1950 in repertory.
(Off Broadway) Opened Spring of 1953.
Opened December 6, 1960 for 32 performances.
Opened January 4, 1973 for 44 performances.
(Off Broadway) Opened November 16, 1976 for 15 perform-
ances.
Reviews:
America 91:481, Aug 14, 1954
American Mercury 9:245-6, Oct 1926
Catholic World 192:320, Feb 1961
Commonweal 21:122, Nov 23, 1934
Dial 84:58, Feb 28, 1958
Literary Digest 95:20-1, Dec 24, 1927
123:23, Jan 16, 1937
Living Age 328:693-4, Mar 27, 1926
122:21-2, Sep 19, 1936
Nation 125:718, Dec 21, 1927
144:194, Feb 13, 1937
176:353, Apr 25, 1953
191:510, Dec 24, 1960
216:122-4, Jan 22, 1973
National Review 25:216, Feb 16, 1973
New York Theatre Critics' Reviews 1960:147
1973:397
1976:83
New York Times p. 30, Nov 29, 1927
X, p. 1, Dec 4, 1927
p. 32, Dec 20, 1927
p. 22, Nov 13, 1934
p. 26, Oct 8, 1937
II, p. 2, Mar 12, 1950
II, p. 1, Apr 2, 1950
p. 14, Apr 6, 1956
II, p. 1, Dec 4, 1960
p. 56, Dec 7, 1960
p. 19, Jan 5, 1973

New York Times II, p. 1, Jan 14, 1973
II, p. 1, Oct 24, 1976
p. 58, Nov 18, 1976
New Yorker 36:96-8, Dec 17, 1950
48:59, Jan 13, 1973
Newsweek 9:30, Jan 23, 1937
81:41, Jan 15, 1973
Outlook 148:187, Feb 1, 1928
Queen's Quarterly 34:420-9, Apr - Jun 1927
Saturday Review 4:427, Dec 10, 1927
36:25, Jun 6, 1953
Theatre Arts 12:91-3, Feb 1928
45:11, Feb 1961
Theatre Magazine 47:58, Feb 1928
Time 29:45, Feb 1, 1937
76:63, Dec 19, 1960
101:56, Jan 29, 1973
Vogue 71:100, Feb 1, 1928

Pound on Demand
Productions:
    Opened December 19, 1946 for 40 performances.
    Opened April 15, 1959 for 37 performances.
Reviews:
    New Republic 116:42, Jan 6, 1947
    New York Theatre Critics' Reviews 1946:217
    New York Times p. 28, Apr 16, 1959
        p. 1, Apr 26, 1959
    Newsweek 28:71, Dec 30, 1946
    Theatre Arts 43:9, Jun 1959

Purple Dust
Productions:
    (Off Broadway) Season of 1956-1957.
Reviews:
    Catholic World 184:469-70, Mar 1957
    Nation 184:65, Jan 19, 1957
    New York Times p. 15, Dec 28, 1956
        II, p. 1, Jan 6, 1957
    Newsweek 49:67, Jan 21, 1957
    Saturday Review 40:48, Jan 19, 1957

Red Roses for Me
Productions:
    Opened December 28, 1955 for 29 performances.
    (Off Broadway) Opened November 27, 1961 for 176
        performances.
Reviews:
    America 94:459-60, Jan 21, 1956
    Commonweal 182:387, Feb 1956
    Nation 181:555-6, Dec 24, 1955
        182:39, Jan 14, 1956
    New Republic 134:21, Jan 30, 1956

New York Theatre Critics' Reviews 1955:182
New York Times II, p. 2, Mar 10, 1946
           p. 35, Apr 26, 1951
           II, p. 4, Dec 25, 1955
           p. 15, Dec 29, 1955
           II, p. 1, Jan 8, 1956
           p. 26, Feb 11, 1961
           p. 41, Nov 28, 1961
New Yorker 31:62+, Jan 14, 1956
        37:162+, Dec 9, 1961
Saturday Review 39:20, Jan 14, 1956
Theatre Arts 28:256, Apr 1944
        30:355, Jun 1946
        40:15, Mar 1956
Time 67:51, Jan 9, 1956

The Shadow of a Gunman
Productions:
(Off Broadway) Opened June 1951.
Opened November 20, 1958 for 52 performances.
Opened January 12, 1959 for 48 performances.
(Off Broadway) Opened February 29, 1972 for 72 performances.
(Off Off Broadway) Opened February 5, 1976.
(Off Off Broadway) Opened February 3, 1977.
Reviews:
America 10:382, Dec 20, 1958
Catholic World 188:417, Feb 1959
Christian Century 75:1463, Dec 17, 1958
Nation 214:380, Mar 20, 1972
New York Theatre Critics' Reviews 1958:200
                                       1972:334
New York Times II, p. 1, Nov 16, 1958
           p. 26, Nov 21, 1958
           II, p. 1, Nov 30, 1958
           p. 28, Mar 1, 1972
           p. 23, Aug 16, 1972
New Yorker 34:113, Dec 6, 1958
        48:83-4, Mar 11, 1972
Saturday Review 41:37, Dec 6, 1958
Theatre Arts 43:22-3, Feb 1959
Time 99:81, Mar 27, 1972

The Silver Tassie
Productions:
Opened October 24, 1929 for 51 performances.
(Off Broadway) Opened September 1949 in repertory.
Reviews:
Catholic World 130:334-5, Dec 1929
Commonweal 50:631-2, Oct 7, 1949
Fortune 132:851-3, Dec 1929
Literary Digest 98:24-5, Aug 4, 1928
Life (NY) 94:24, Nov 15, 1929

New Republic 61:17-18, Nov 27, 1929
121:21, Sep 19, 1949
New York Times p. 26, Oct 25, 1929
X, p. 1, Nov 10, 1929
p. 16, Jul 22, 1949
II, p. 1, Sep 4, 1949
p. 35, Sep 12, 1969
Theatre Arts 14:6, Jan 1930
15:790-2, Oct 1931

*The Star Turns Red
  Reviews:
    New York Times p. 47, Oct 25, 1962
    Newsweek 13:25, Jun 26, 1939
    Theatre Arts 24:410+, Jun 1940

Time to Go
  Productions:
    (Off Broadway) Season of 1959-1960.
  Reviews:
    New York Times p. 35, May 8, 1952
    p. 33, Mar 23, 1960

Within the Gates
  Productions:
    Opened October 24, 1929 for 141 performances.
    (Off Broadway) Season of 1952-1953.
  Reviews:
    Catholic World 140:338-40, Dec 1934
    Commonweal 21:66, Nov 9, 1934
    Nation 139:546, Nov 7, 1934
    New Republic 80:369, Nov 7, 1934
    New York Times p. 23, Oct 23, 1934
    IX, p. 1, Oct 28, 1934
    Player's Magazine 11:10, Nov-Dec 1934
    Saturday Review 10:519, Mar 3, 1934
    11:256, Nov 3, 1934
    Stage 12:13, Dec 1934
    12:18-19, Dec 1934
    Theatre Arts 18:258-9, Apr 1934
    18:894, Dec 1934
    Time 24:30, Nov 5, 1934
    Vanity Fair 41:42+, Jan 1934
    43:31-2, Jan 1935
    Vogue 84:72, Dec 15, 1934

ORTON, JOE

Crimes of Passion (The Ruffian on the Stair and The Erpingham Camp)

Productions:
(Off Broadway) Opened October 26, 1969 for 9 performances.
Reviews:
New York Times p. 54, Oct 27, 1969
II, p. 3, Nov 9, 1969

Entertaining Mr. Sloane
Productions:
Opened October 12, 1965 for 13 performances.
(Off Off Broadway) Opened June 1975.
(Off Off Broadway) Opened September 1975.
Reviews:
New York Theatre Critics' Reviews 1965:316
New York Times p. 21, Jun 30, 1964
p. 41, Oct 13, 1965
p. 50, Oct 19, 1965
II, p. 1, Oct 24, 1965
II, p. 5, Oct 31, 1965
p. 14, Sep 15, 1975
New Yorker 41:94, Oct 23, 1965
Newsweek 66:102, Oct 25, 1965
Reporter 33:48+, Nov 18, 1965
Saturday Review 48:74, Oct 30, 1965
Time 86:103, Oct 22, 1965
Vogue 144:112, Oct 1, 1964

The Erpingham Camp (see Crimes of Passion)

Funeral Games
Productions:
(Off Off Broadway) Opened January 16, 1973.
No Reviews.

Loot
Productions:
Opened March 18, 1968 for 22 performances.
(Off Off Broadway) Opened May 12, 1973 in repertory.
(Off Off Broadway) Opened April 29, 1976.
Reviews:
Commonweal 88:142+, Apr 19, 1968
Nation 286:484-5, Apr 8, 1968
New York Theatre Critics' Reviews 1968:321
New York Times p. 40, Mar 1968
II, p. 1, Mar 31, 1968
p. 42, Apr 3, 1968
p. 9, May 28, 1973
p. 14, Sep 15, 1975
New Yorker 44:103, Mar 30, 1968
Time 91:91, Mar 29, 1968

The Ruffian on the Stair (see also Crimes of Passion)
    Productions:
        (Off Off Broadway) Opened December 19, 1975.
    No Reviews.

What the Butler Saw
    Productions:
        (Off Broadway) Opened May 4, 1970 for 224 performances.
        (Off Off Broadway) Opened March 1, 1975.
        (Off Off Broadway) Opened February 1976.
        (Off Off Broadway) Opened February 18, 1977.
        (Off Off Broadway) Opened March 1977.
    Reviews:
        Commonweal 93:95, Oct 23, 1970
        New York Theatre Critics' Reviews 1970:232
        New York Times p. 27, Mar 7, 1969
                      p. 56, May 5, 1970
                      II, p. 3, May 17, 1970
                      p. 38, Oct 14, 1970
                      p. 39, Nov 19, 1970
                      II, p. 7, Jun 27, 1971
                      p. 14, Sep 15, 1975
        New Yorker 46:106, May 16, 1970
        Newsweek 75:121, May 18, 1970
        Time 95:72, May 18, 1970

OSBORNE, JOHN

The Blood of the Bambergs (see Two Plays for England)

*The Bond Honored
    Reviews:
        New York Times p. 53, Jun 9, 1966
        Vogue 148:206, Sep 1, 1966

The Entertainer
    Productions:
        Opened February 12, 1958 for 97 performances.
    Reviews:
        America 98:736, Mar 22, 1958
                114:54, Jan 8, 1966
        Catholic World 187:68, Apr 1958
        Life 44:118, Mar 10, 1958
        Nation 186:192-3, Mar 1, 1958
        New York Theatre Critics' Reviews 1958:357
        New York Times p. 22, Feb 13, 1958
                      II, p. 1, Feb 23, 1958
                      p. 52, Nov 22, 1973
        New Yorker 33:153-4, Sep 28, 1957
                34:63, Feb 22, 1958
        Newsweek 51:62, Feb 24, 1958
        Reporter 18:39, Mar 20, 1958

Saturday Review 40:26, May 11, 1957
41:24, Mar 1, 1958
Theatre Arts 42:22-3, Apr 1958
Time 71:52, Feb 24, 1958

Epitaph for George Dillon (with Anthony Creighton)
Productions:
Opened November 4, 1958 for 23 performances.
(Off Broadway) Season of 1960-1961.
Reviews:
America 100:299, Nov 29, 1958
Christian Century 75:1436, Dec 10, 1958
Nation 187:394-5, Nov 22, 1958
New York Theatre Critics' Reviews 1958:219
New York Times p. 33, Feb 12, 1958
p. 44, Nov 5, 1958
II, p. 1, Nov 16, 1958
p. 17, Dec 29, 1960
p. 45, Feb 14, 1961
New Yorker 34:101-3, Nov 15, 1958
36:68+, Jan 14, 1961
Newsweek 52:75, Nov 17, 1958
Saturday Review 41:24-5, Nov 22, 1958
Theatre Arts 43:21-3, Jan 1959
45:68, Mar 1961
Time 72:62, Nov 17, 1958

*Hotel in Amsterdam
Reviews:
Life 65:10, Aug 2, 1968
New York Times II, p. 12, Jul 21, 1968
p. 17, Aug 17, 1968
Vogue 152:268, Sep 1, 1968

Inadmissible Evidence
Productions:
Opened November 30, 1965 for 166 performances.
Reviews:
Christian Century 82:1066, Sep 1, 1965
Commentary 41:75, Mar 1966
Commonweal 83:375, Dec 24, 1965
Harper 232:125, Apr 1966
Life 60:17, Jan 14, 1966
Nation 201:508-9, Dec 20, 1965
National Review 18:325-7, Apr 5, 1966
New Republic 154:34-5, Jan 1, 1966
New York Theatre Critics' Reviews 1965:240
New York Times p. 31, Sep 10, 1964
p. 52, Dec 1, 1965
New Yorker 41:176+, Apr 17, 1965
41:142, Dec 11, 1965
42:47, Oct 8, 1966
Newsweek 66:90, Dec 13, 1965

Reporter 33:38-40+, Nov 4, 1965
Saturday Review 48:31, May 29, 1965
              48:43, Dec 18, 1965
              49:96, Jan 8, 1966
Time 86:76+, Dec 10, 1965
Vogue 146:51-2, Aug 15, 1965
       147:34, Jan 15, 1966

Look Back in Anger
Productions:
Opened October 1, 1957 for 407 performances.
(Off Broadway) Season of 1958-1959.
(Off Off Broadway) Opened January 21, 1977.
(Off Off Broadway) Opened March 2, 1977.
Reviews:
America 98:146, Nov 2, 1957
Catholic World 186:226, Dec 1957
              188:122-8, Nov 1958
Christian Century 74:1262-3, Oct 23, 1957
Commonweal 67:232-3, Nov 29, 1957
Life 43:141-2+, Oct 14, 1957
Nation 185:272, Oct 19, 1957
New Republic 137:16-17, Sep 9, 1957
              137:19-21, Dec 23, 1957
              138:23-4, Jan 20, 1958
              138:22, Feb 10, 1958
New York Theatre Critics' Reviews 1957:243
New York Times VI, p. 28, Aug 25, 1957
              p. 28, Oct 2, 1957
              II, p. 1, Oct 13, 1957
              VI, p. 32, Oct 13, 1957
              p. 38, Nov 1, 1968
New Yorker 33:153-4, Sep 28, 1957
              33:93, Oct 12, 1957
Newsweek 50:114, Oct 14, 1957
Reporter 15:33-5, Oct 18, 1956
              17:38, Nov 14, 1957
Saturday Review 39:30, Oct 13, 1956
              40:30, Oct 12, 1957
Theatre Arts 41:28, May 1957
              41:18, Dec 1957
Time 69:90+, Apr 22, 1957
              70:85+, Oct 14, 1957

Luther
Productions:
Opened September 25, 1963 for 211 performances.
Reviews:
America 107:533, Jul 21, 1962
              109:496-7, Oct 26, 1963
Catholic World 194:99-105, Nov 1961
              198:135-6, Nov 1963
Christian Century 80:1351, Oct 30, 1963

Commonweal 79:103-4, Oct 18, 1963
Nation 193:539-40, Dec 30, 1961
    197:245-6, Oct 19, 1963
National Review 15:446-8+, Nov 19, 1963
New Republic 149:28+, Oct 19, 1963
New York Theatre Critics' Reviews 1963:276
New York Times p. 9, Jul 8, 1961
                p. 10, Jul 28, 1961
                p. 46, Sep 11, 1963
                II, p. 1, Sep 22, 1963
                p. 41, Sep 26, 1963
                II, p. 1, Oct 6, 1963
                p. 30, Feb 15, 1965
New Yorker 37:200-201, Oct 14, 1961
    39:133, Oct 5, 1963
Newsweek 62:96, Oct 7, 1963
Reporter 25:50+, Oct 12, 1961
    29:54+, Oct 24, 1963
Saturday Review 46:30, Oct 12, 1963
Theatre Arts 47:12-13, Dec 1963
Time 77:58-9, Jun 30, 1961
    82:63, Oct 4, 1963
Vogue 143:20, Jan 1, 1964

A Patriot for Me
Productions:
Opened October 5, 1969 for 49 performances.
Reviews:
Christian Century 82:1067, Sep 1, 1965
Commonweal 91:185-6, Nov 7, 1969
Nation 209:451-2, Oct 27, 1969
National Review 21:1334-5, Dec 30, 1969
New Republic 161:22, Nov 1, 1969
New York Theatre Critics' Reviews 1969:244
New York Times II, p. 1, Jul 11, 1965
              II, p. 1, Sep 28, 1969
              p. 58, Oct 6, 1969
              II, p. 1, Oct 12, 1969
New Yorker 41:59-60, Jul 31, 1965
    45:85, Oct 11, 1969
Newsweek 74:129, Oct 20, 1969
Reporter 33:38-40+, Nov 4, 1965
Saturday Review 48:45, Aug 14, 1965
    52:20, Oct 18, 1969
Time 94:71, Oct 17, 1969
Vogue 146:179, Sep 1, 1965
    154:58, Nov 15, 1969

*Sense of Detachment
Reviews:
New Republic 168:25, Jan 6, 1973
Time 100:36, Dec 25, 1972

*Time Present
  Reviews:
      Life 65:10, Aug 2, 1968
      New York Times p. 28, May 25, 1968
                      II, p. 3, Jun 2, 1968
                      p. 20, Jul 5, 1968
      Vogue 152:268, Sep 1, 1968

*Two Plays for England (The Blood of the Bambergs and Under
      Plain Cover)
  Reviews:
      New York Times p. 15, Jul 20, 1962

Under Plain Cover (see Two Plays for England)

*World of Paul Slickey
  Reviews:
      New York Times p. 48, May 6, 1959
                      p. 23, May 8, 1959

PAGNOL, MARCEL

*Marius
  Reviews:
      New York Times p. 27, Feb 6, 1956

Marseilles
  Productions:
      Adapted by Sidney Howard. Opened November 17, 1930
        for 16 performances.
  Reviews:
      Commonweal 13:160, Dec 10, 1930
      New York Times II, p. 3, Nov 9, 1930
                      p. 28, Nov 18, 1930
      Theatre Arts 15:18-19, Jan 1931

Merchants of Glory (with Paul Nivoix)
  Productions:
      Translated by Ralph Roeder. Opened December 14, 1925
        for 42 performances.
  Reviews:
      Dial 80:167-8, Feb 1926
      Drama 16:166, Apr 1926
      Nation 121:765, Dec 30, 1925
      New York Times p. 28, Dec 15, 1925
                     VII, p. 1, Dec 27, 1925

Topaze
  Productions:
      Adapted by Benn W. Levy. Opened February 12, 1930
        for 159 performances.
      Opened August 18, 1930 for 16 performances.

Opened February 16, 1931 for 8 performances.
Opened December 17, 1947 for 1 performance.
Reviews:
Commonweal 11:659, Apr 9, 1930
Life (NY) 95:18, Mar 7, 1930
Nation 130:278, Mar 5, 1930
New York Theatre Critics' Reviews 1947:226
New York Times p. 25, Feb 13, 1930
        IX, p. 1, Mar 2, 1930
        II, p. 3, Dec 21, 1947
        p. 21, Dec 29, 1947
New Outlook 161:49, Mar 1933
        23:45-7, Jan 10, 1948
Outlook 154:353, Feb 26, 1930
Theatre Arts 14:281, Apr 1930
Theatre Magazine 51:44, Apr 1930
        51:32-5, Jun 1930
Vanity Fair 40:43, Apr 1933
        75:132, Apr 12, 1930

PARKER, LOUIS N.

Beauty and the Barge (with W. W. Jacobs)
Productions:
Opened November 13, 1913 for six performances.
Reviews:
Dramatic Mirror 70:6, Nov 19, 1913
New York Times p. 11, Nov 14, 1913

Disraeli
Productions:
Opened September 18, 1911 for 280 performances.
Opened for one matinee on April 25, 1912.
Opened April 9, 1917 for 48 performances.
Reviews:
Blue Book 13:455-8, Jul 1911
Bookman 34:244-5, Nov 1911
Current Literature 51:663-9, Dec 1911
Delineator 79:175, Mar 1912
Dramatic Mirror 66:11, Sep 20, 1911
Dramatist 3:241-2, Apr 1913
Everybody's 25:825-6, Dec 1911
Green Book 6:1208, Dec 1911
Leslie's Weekly 113:383, Oct 5, 1911
Life (NY) 58:524, Sep 28, 1911
Munsey 46:280, Nov 1911
New York Times p. 11, Apr 4, 1917
        VIII, p. 5, Apr 15, 1917
Pearson 26:520-3+, Oct 1911
        26:650-2, Nov 1911
Red Book 18:380-1+, Dec 1911
Theatre Magazine 14:xiii-xiv, Nov 1911

The Highway of Life
  Productions:
    Opened October 26, 1914 for 24 performances.
  Reviews:
    Dramatic Mirror 72:8, Nov 4, 1914
    Green Book 13:121, Jan 1915
    Munsey 53:794-5, Jan 1915
    Nation 99:560-1, Nov 5, 1914
    New York Dramatic News 60:17, Oct 31, 1914
    New York Times p. 11, Oct 27, 1914
                    VIII, p. 8, Nov 1, 1914

Johannes Kreisler (Music by E. H. Von Reznich)
  Productions:
    Adapted from the German of Meinhard and Bernauer.
    Opened December 20, 1922 for 65 performances.
  Reviews:
    Bookman 57:54-5, Mar 1923
    Independent 110:73, Jan 20, 1923
    Life (NY) 81:18, Jan 10, 1923
    New York Clipper 70:20, Jan 3, 1923
    New York Times p. 20, Dec 25, 1922
                    VII, p. 3, Jan 21, 1923
    Scientific American 128:154-5, Mar 1923
    Theatre Magazine 37:15-16, Feb 1923

Joseph and His Brethren
  Productions:
    Opened January 11, 1913 for 121 performances.
  Reviews:
    Blue Book 16:1132-6, Apr 1913
    Bookman 37:63-4, Mar 1913
    Collier's 50:23, Feb 22, 1913
    Current Opinion 54:206-7, Mar 1913
    Dramatic Mirror 69:10, Jan 8, 1913
                    69:7, Jan 22, 1913
                    70:12, Sep 10, 1913
    Dramatist 4:348, Apr 1913
    Everybody's 28:520, Apr 1913
    Green Book 9:566-8+, Apr 1913
    Independent 74:265-6, Jan 30, 1913
    Life (NY) 61:200, Jan 23, 1913
    Munsey 48:1014-15, Mar 1913
            50:473, Dec 1913
    National Magazine 39:417-20, Dec 1913
    New York Dramatic News 57:19, Jan 11, 1913
                    57:22, Jan 18, 1913
    New York Times II, p. 13, Jan 26, 1913
                    VII, p. 6, Jan 26, 1913
    Red Book 20:1073-7, Apr 1913
    Theatre Magazine 17:33-4+, Feb 1913
                    17:94-6+, Mar 1913

The Lady of Coventry
    Productions:
        Opened November 21, 1911 for 16 performances.
    Reviews:
        Dramatic Mirror 66:7-8, Nov 29, 1911
        Green Book 7:286-7, Feb 1912
        Theatre Magazine 15:xi-xii, Jan 1912

The Paper Chase
    Productions:
        Opened November 25, 1912 for 25 performances.
    Reviews:
        Blue Book 16:926-8, Mar 1913
        Dramatic Mirror 68:7, Nov 27, 1912
        Everybody's 28:259, Feb 1913
        Green Book 9:367, Feb 1913
        Theatre Magazine 17:1-3, Jan 1913

Pomander Walk
    Productions:
        Opened December 20, 1910 for 143 performances.
    Reviews:
        American Mercury 71:797-801, Apr 1911
        Blue Book 13:16-18, May 1911
        Book News 30:498-500, Mar 1912
        Bookman 23:606, Feb 1911
        Canadian Magazine 36:475-8, Mar 1911
        Collier's 46:19, Jan 28, 1911
        Dramatic Mirror 64:7+, Dec 28, 1910
        Everybody's 24:559-60, Apr 1911
        Green Book 5:455-7+, Mar 1911
                   6:860-4, Oct 1911
        Harper's Weekly 55:18+, Jan 21, 1911
        Independent 70:151-2, Jan 19, 1911
        Leslie's Weekly 112:11, Jan 5, 1911
        Life (NY) 57:124, Jan 12, 1911
        Metropolitan Magazine 34:126-7, Apr 1911
        Munsey 44:708-9, Feb 1911
        Pearson 25:385-6, Mar 1911
        Red Book 16:945-9, Mar 1911
        Theatre Magazine 13:34-5+, Feb 1911

Rosemary (with Murray Carson)
    Productions:
        Opened January 12, 1915 for 15 performances.
    Reviews:
        Dramatic Mirror 73:8, Jan 20, 1915
        New York Times p. 9, Jan 13, 1915
                    VII, p. 6, Jan 17, 1915

PHILLIPS, STEPHEN

Herod
　Productions:
　　Opened October 26, 1909 for 31 performances.
　Reviews:
　　Collier's 44:9, Nov 13, 1909
　　　　　　44:21, Dec 4, 1909
　　Dramatic Mirror 62:5, Nov 6, 1909
　　Everybody's 22:127-8, Jan 1910
　　Forum 42:578-9, Dec 1909
　　Harper's Weekly 53:24, Nov 13, 1909
　　Independent 67:1124, Nov 18, 1909
　　Leslie's Weekly 109:462, Nov 11, 1909
　　Life (NY) 54:672, Nov 11, 1909
　　Metropolitan Magazine 31:528-9, Jan 1910
　　Munsey 42:595-6, Jan 1910
　　Theatre Magazine 10:169-70, Jan 1910

Paolo and Francesca
　Productions:
　　Opened December 2, 1924 for 8 performances.
　　Opened April 1, 1929 for 16 performances.
　Reviews:
　　Catholic World 129:200-1, May 19, 1929
　　Commonweal 9:684, Apr 17, 1929
　　New York Times p. 24, Dec 3, 1924
　　　　　　　　　VIII, p. 5, Dec 7, 1924
　　　　　　　　　p. 28, Apr 2, 1929
　　Theatre Magazine 6:282, Nov 1906

PINERO, ARTHUR WING

The Amazons
　Productions:
　　Opened April 28, 1913 for 48 performances.
　Reviews:
　　Bookman 37:430, Jun 1913
　　Dramatic Mirror 69:6, Apr 30, 1913
　　Green Book 10:4-6+, Jul 1913
　　New York Dramatic News 57:20, May 3, 1913

Dandy Dick
　Productions:
　　(Off Broadway) Season of 1955-1956.
　Reviews:
　　New York Times p. 37, Jan 11, 1956
　　　　　　　　　p. 23, Aug 13, 1973

The Enchanted Cottage
　Productions:
　　Opened March 31, 1923 for 65 performances.

Reviews:
  Independent 110:302, Apr 28, 1923
  Life (NY) 81:18, Apr 19, 1923
  New York Times p. 22, Apr 2, 1923
                VIII, p. 1, Apr 8, 1923

The Gay Lord Quex
  Productions:
  Opened November 12, 1917 for 40 performances.
  Reviews:
  Bookman 46:475-7, Dec 1917
  Book News 36:219, Feb 1918
  Dramatic Mirror 77:5, Nov 24, 1917
  Dramatist 9:897, Apr 1918
  Life (NY) 70:836, Nov 22, 1917
  New York Times p. 11, Nov 13, 1917

The Magistrate
  Productions:
  (Off Broadway) Opened March 8, 1963 for 9 performances.
  Reviews:
  American Imago 32:200-15, Summer 1975
  New York Times p. 30, May 14, 1959

Mid-Channel
  Productions:
  Opened January 31, 1910 for 96 performances.
  Reviews:
  Dramatic Mirror 63:8, Feb 12, 1910
  Dramatist 3:205-6, Oct 1911
  Everybody's 22:696-8, May 1910
  Green Book 3:764-5, Apr 1910
  Hampton 24:569, Apr 1910
  Harper's Weekly 54:24, Apr 2, 1910
  Life (NY) 55:244, Feb 10, 1910
  Literary Digest 40:350-1, Feb 19, 1910
  Metropolitan Magazine 32:394-5, Jun 1910
  Pearson 23:553-4, Apr 1910
  Theatre Magazine 11:68+, Mar 1910

The Mind-the-Paint Girl
  Productions:
  Opened September 9, 1912 for 13 performances.
  Reviews:
  Blue Book 16:252-6, Dec 1912
  Collier's 50:28, Oct 5, 1912
  Dramatic Mirror 68:6, Sep 11, 1912
  Dramatist 4:335-6, Jan 1913
  Everybody's 27:668-70, Nov 1912
  Green Book 8:772, Nov 1912
            8:988, Dec 1912
  Leslie's Weekly 115:497+, Nov 14, 1912
  Life (NY) 60:1812-13, Sep 19, 1912

Literary Digest 44:534-5, Mar 16, 1912
McClure 40:63-4+, Mar 1913
Metropolitan Magazine 36:33-6, Oct 1912
Munsey 47:985, Sep 1912
    48:349-50, Nov 1912
Red Book 19:945+, Sep 1912

Preserving Mr. Panmure
  Productions:
    Opened February 27, 1912 for 31 performances.
  Reviews:
    American Playwright 1:108-10, Apr 1912
    Blue Book 15:241+, Jun 1912
    Bookman 35:173-4, Apr 1912
    Collier's 48:34-5+, Mar 16, 1912
    Dramatic Mirror 67:6, Mar 6, 1912
    Dramatist 3:256-7, Jul 1912
    Everybody's 26:686-8, May 1912
    Green Book 7:900-2+, May 1912
        7:974-6, May 1912
    Leslie's Weekly 114:293, Mar 14, 1912
    Life (NY) 59:540, Mar 14, 1912
    Munsey 47:130, Apr 1912
    Red Book 19:181-7, May 1912
    Theatre Magazine 15:xiv, Apr 1912

The Second Mrs. Tanqueray
  Productions:
    Opened February 3, 1913 for 16 performances.
    Opened October 27, 1924 for 72 performances.
  Reviews:
    Dramatic Mirror 69:6, Feb 5, 1913
    Dramatist 4:334, Jan 1913
    Fortnightly Review 118:345-8, Aug 1922
    Green Book 6:837-42, Oct 1911
    Independent 113:551, Dec 20, 1924
    Life (NY) 84:18, Nov 13, 1924
    Nation 119:551-2, Nov 19, 1924
    New York Times p. 11, Feb 5, 1913
               p. 27, Oct 28, 1924
               VIII, p. 1, Nov 2, 1924
               VIII, p. 1, Nov 9, 1924
               II, p. 3, Oct 8, 1950
    Theatre Arts 17:xxix, Mar 1913
    Theatre Magazine 40:20, Jan 1925
    Yale Review 5:121-2, Oct 1915

The Thunderbolt
  Productions:
    Opened November 12, 1910 in repertory.
    Opened November 16, 1911 in repertory.
  Reviews:
    Blue Book 12:867-8, Feb 1911

Bookman 23:164-7, Jan 1911
Columbian Magazine 3:701+, Jan 1911
Current Literature 50:184-91, Feb 1911
Dramatic Mirror 66:8, Nov 29, 1911
Dramatist 2:115-18, Jan 1911
Everybody's 24:412+, Mar 1911
Harper's Weekly 54:28-9, Dec 10, 1910
Life (NY) 56:910, Nov 24, 1910
Metropolitan Magazine 33:798, Mar 1911
Munsey 44:562-3, Jan 1911
Nation 91:479, Nov 17, 1910
Pearson 25:117-21, Jan 1911
Theatre 12:163-4+, Dec 1910

Trelawny of the Wells
Productions:
Opened January 1, 1911 for 48 performances.
Opened June 1, 1925 for eight performances.
Opened January 31, 1927 for 56 performances.
(Off Broadway) Opened November 25, 1961 for nine
performances.
(Off Off Broadway) Season of 1969-1970.
(Off Broadway) Opened October 11, 1970 for 48 performances.
Opened October 15, 1975 for 47 performances.
Reviews:
Bookman 65:204, Apr 1927
Commonweal 93:149-50, Nov 6, 1970
Dramatic Mirror 65:11, Jan 4, 1911
Dramatist 18:1336-7, Apr 1927
Life (NY) 57:125, Jan 12, 1911
            89:21, Feb 24, 1927
Munsey 44:710, Feb 1911
Nation 211:444, Nov 2, 1970
        221:475, Nov 8, 1975
New Republic 49:275, Jan 26, 1926
              163:20, Nov 28, 1970
              173:20-1, Nov 8, 1975
New York Theatre Critics' Reviews 1970:138
                                   1975:201
New York Times p. 16, Jun 2, 1925
                p. 24, Feb 1, 1927
                VII, p. 1, Feb 6, 1927
                p. 48, Oct 12, 1970
                II, p. 16, Oct 25, 1970
                p. 45, Oct 16, 1975
                II, p. 5, Oct 26, 1975
New Yorker 46:129-30, Oct 24, 1970
            51:102, Oct 20, 1975
Newsweek 76:86, Oct 26, 1970
          86:52, Oct 27, 1975
Outlook 145:396-7, Mar 30, 1927
Pearson 25:386-7, Mar 1911
Saturday Review 53:59, Nov 14, 1970
Theatre Magazine 13:42+, Feb 1911

PINERO, MIGUEL

The Guntower
    Productions:
        (Off Off Broadway) Opened August 26, 1976.
    No Reviews.

Short Eyes
    Productions:
        (Off Off Broadway) Opened January 3, 1974.
        (Off Broadway) Opened February 28, 1974 for 54 performan-
        ces.
        Opened May 23, 1974 for 102 performances.
    Reviews:
        America 130:457, Jun 8, 1974
        Nation 218:445, Apr 6, 1974
        National Review 26:764-5, Jul 5, 1974
        New Republic 170:20, Apr 20, 1974
        New York Theatre Critics' Reviews 1974:258
        New York Times p. 24, Jan 8, 1974
                      p. 29, Jan 21, 1974
                      p. 45, Mar 14, 1974
                      II, p. 1, Mar 24, 1974
                      p. 45, Mar 27, 1974
                      p. 21, May 24, 1974
                      p. 15, Aug 2, 1974
        New Yorker 50:170, Mar 25, 1974
                   50:68, Jun 3, 1974
        Newsweek 83:81, Apr 8, 1974
        Saturday Review 1:47, Jul 13, 1974

Straight from the Ghetto (with Neil Harris)
    Productions:
        (Off Off Broadway) Opened January 10, 1977.
        (Off Off Broadway) Opened February 1977.
    Reviews:
        New York Times III, p. 3, Jan 14, 1977

The Sun Always Shines for the Cool
    Productions:
        (Off Off Broadway) Opened December 9, 1975.
    No Reviews.

PINTER, HAROLD

Applicant (see The Local Stigmatic)

The Basement
    Productions:
        (Off Broadway) Opened October 15, 1968 for 147 perform-
        ances.
        (Off Off Broadway) Opened November 13, 1975.

Reviews:
Commonweal 89:350-1, Dec 6, 1968
Nation 207:477, Nov 4, 1968
New York Theatre Critics' Reviews 1968:138
New York Times p. 40, Oct 16, 1968
II, p. 7, Nov 3, 1968
New Yorker 44:140-1, Oct 26, 1968
Newsweek 72:135, Oct 28, 1968
Time 92:69, Oct 25, 1968
Vogue 152:170, Dec 1968

The Birthday Party
Productions:
Opened October 3, 1967 for 126 performances.
(Off Broadway) Opened February 5, 1971 for 39 performances.
(Off Off Broadway) Opened September 14, 1974.
(Off Off Broadway) Opened February 1975.
(Off Off Broadway) Opened May 23, 1975.
(Off Off Broadway) Opened August 6, 1976.
Reviews:
America 117:487, Oct 28, 1967
118:10-12, Jan 6, 1968
Christian Century 84:1604, Dec 13, 1967
Commonweal 87:122-3, Oct 27, 1967
Nation 205:412-14, Oct 23, 1967
New Republic 157:36-8, Oct 21, 1967
New York Theatre Critics' Reviews 1967:274, 278
New York Times p. 23, Nov 25, 1963
II, p. 1, Oct 1, 1967
p. 40, Oct 4, 1967
II, p. 1, Oct 15, 1967
p. 39, Jan 17, 1968
p. 22, Feb 6, 1971
New Yorker 43:151, Oct 14, 1967
46:78, Feb 13, 1971
Newsweek 70:104+, Oct 16, 1967
Saturday Review 44:26, Aug 26, 1961
50:50, Oct 21, 1967
50:46-7, Oct 28, 1967
Time 90:71-2, Oct 13, 1967
97:52, Feb 22, 1971
Vogue 150:134, Nov 1, 1967

The Caretaker
Productions:
Opened October 4, 1961 for 165 performances.
(Off Broadway) Opened January 30, 1964 for 94 performances.
(Off Broadway) Opened June 23, 1973 for 36 performances.
(Off Off Broadway) Opened July 18, 1974.
(Off Off Broadway) Opened November 1976.

Reviews:
     America 106:376, Dec 9, 1961
     Christian Century 78:1403-6, Nov 22, 1961
     Commonweal 75:122-3, Oct 27, 1961
              77:366, Dec 28, 1962
     Life 51:195-6, Nov 17, 1961
     Nation 193:276, Oct 21, 1961
     National Review 11:424, Dec 16, 1961
     New Republic 145:29-30, Oct 23, 1961
     New York Theatre Critics' Reviews 1961:247
     New York Times p. 42, Oct 5, 1961
                  II, p. 1, Oct 15, 1961
                     p. 16, Jan 31, 1964
                     p. 24, Jul 5, 1973
     New Yorker 36:60-1, Jul 9, 1960
              37:162, Oct 14, 1961
     Newsweek 58:101, Oct 16, 1961
     Reporter 23:48, Oct 13, 1960
     Saturday Review 44:34, Oct 21, 1961
     Theatre Arts 45:12, Dec 1961
     Time 78:58, Oct 13, 1961

The Collection
     Productions:
          (Off Broadway) Opened November 26, 1962 for 578
              performances.
          (Off Off Broadway) Opened December 19, 1975.
     Reviews:
          Commonweal 77:367, Dec 28, 1962
          Nation 195:430, Dec 15, 1962
          New York Times p. 44, Nov 27, 1962
                       II, p. 5, Dec 9, 1962
          New Yorker 38:148-50, Dec 8, 1962
          Saturday Review 45:30, Dec 15, 1962
          Theatre Arts 47:10-11, Jan 1963
          Time 80:73, Dec 7, 1962

The Dumbwaiter
     Productions:
          (Off Broadway) Opened November 26, 1962 for 578
              performances.
          (Off Off Broadway) Season of 1970-1971.
          (Off Off Broadway) Opened June 1976.
     Reviews:
          Commonweal 77:367, Dec 28, 1962
          Nation 195:429-30, Dec 15, 1962
          New York Times p. 44, Nov 27, 1962
                       II, p. 5, Dec 9, 1962
          New Yorker 38:148-50, Dec 8, 1962
          Saturday Review 45:30, Dec 15, 1962
          Theatre Arts 47:10-11, Jan 1963
          Time 80:72-3, Dec 7, 1962

The Dwarfs
Productions:
(Off Off Broadway) Season of 1974-1975.
Reviews:
America 118:193, Feb 10, 1968
New York Times p. 21, Sep 19, 1963

The Homecoming
Productions:
Opened January 5, 1967 for 324 performances.
(Off Broadway) Opened May 18, 1971 for 32 performances.
(Off Off Broadway) Opened September 7, 1972 in repertory.
(Off Off Broadway) Opened December 11, 1973.
(Off Broadway) Opened November 6, 1975 for 9 performances.
(Off Off Broadway) Opened November 6, 1975.
(Off Broadway) Opened March 6, 1976.
(Off Broadway) Opened October 2, 1976 for 34 performances.
Reviews:
America 116:353, Mar 11, 1967
    125:70-1, Aug 7, 1971
Christian Century 82:1096-7, Sep 8, 1965
    84:276-7, Mar 1, 1967
Commentary 43:73-4, Jun 1967
Commonweal 85:459-60, Jan 27, 1967
Life 62:6, Mar 3, 1967
Nation 204:122-3, Jan 23, 1967
    212:732-3, Jun 7, 1971
    19:316-17, Mar 21, 1967
New Republic 152:29-30, Jun 26, 1965
    156:35-6, Jan 28, 1967
New York Theatre Critics' Reviews 1967:394
    1971:261
New York Times p. 38, Jun 4, 1965
    p. 29, Jan 6, 1967
    II, p. 11, Jan 15, 1967
    II, p. 1, Jan 22, 1967
    II, p. 1, Feb 5, 1967
    p. 47, Oct 5, 1967
    p. 37, May 19, 1971
    II, p. 9, May 30, 1971
    II, p. 1, Jun 6, 1971
    p. 22, Sep 18, 1972
    p. 30, Nov 7, 1975
New Yorker 41:50, Jul 31, 1965
    42:48, Jan 14, 1967
    47:55, May 29, 1971
Newsweek 69:93, Jan 16, 1967
    77:42, May 31, 1972
Reporter 36:46+, Feb 23, 1967
Saturday Review 50:51, Jan 21, 1967
    50:58, Apr 8, 1967
    52:20, Nov 15, 1969
Time 89:43, Jan 13, 1967

Vogue 146:75, Sep 15, 1965
        149:110, Mar 1, 1967
        150:194-5+, Oct 1, 1967

Interview   (see The Local Stigmatic)

Landscape
    Productions:
        (Off Broadway) Opened April 2, 1970 for 53 performances.
        (Off Broadway) Opened February 9, 1971 for 6 performances.
        (Off Off Broadway) Opened December 1974.
        (Off Off Broadway) Opened March 4, 1977.
    Reviews:
        Catholic World 210:124-6, Dec 1969
        New Republic 162:20+, Apr 25, 1970
        New York Theatre Critics' Reviews 1970:245
        New York Times II, p. 8, Jul 13, 1969
                         p. 34, Jul 25, 1969
                         p. 43, Apr 3, 1970
                         II, p. 3, Apr 12, 1970
                         p. 35, Feb 10, 1971
        New Yorker 46:84, Apr 11, 1970
        Saturday Review 53:16, Apr 25, 1970
        Time 94:67, Jul 18, 1969

Last to Go   (see The Local Stigmatic)

The Local Stigmatic (consists of Applicant, Interview, Last to Go,
        Request Stop, That's All, That's Your Trouble, Trouble
        in the Works)
    Productions:
        (Off Broadway) Opened November 3, 1969 for 8 performances.
    Reviews:
        New York Theatre Critics' Reviews 1969:138
        New York Times p. 55, Nov 4, 1969
                       p. 40, Nov 7, 1969
                       II, p. 3, Jul 21, 1974

The Lover
    Productions:
        (Off Broadway) Opened January 4, 1964 for 89 performances.
        (Off Broadway) Opened July 4, 1972 in repertory.
        (Off Off Broadway) Opened August 18, 1976.
    Reviews:
        Commonweal 79:484-5, Jan 24, 1964
        Nation 198:106, Jan 27, 1964
        New Republic 150:28+, Feb 1, 1964
        New York Times p. 35, Jan 6, 1964
                       p. 21, Sep 19, 1963
        New Yorker 39:69-70, Jan 11, 1964
        Saturday Review 47:25, Jan 25, 1964
        Time 83:64, Jan 17, 1964
        Vogue 143:22, Feb 15, 1964

Night
Productions:
    (Off Off Broadway) Opened November 1976.
No Reviews.

No Man's Land
Productions:
    Opened November 9, 1976 for 47 performances.
Reviews:
    America 135:424, Dec 11, 1976
    Atlantic 237:98+, Feb 1976
    Commonweal 104:20-1, Jan 7, 1977
    Nation 221:124, Aug 16, 1975
           223:572-3, Nov 27, 1976
    New Republic 175:24-5, Dec 11, 1976
    New York Theatre Critics' Reviews 1976:112
    New York Times p. 34, Jul 1, 1975
                   III, p. 26, Nov 10, 1976
                   II, p. 3, Nov 21, 1976
    New Yorker 51:117-18, May 2, 1975
               52:109, Nov 22, 1976
    Newsweek 88:74-8+, Nov 29, 1976
    Time 105:80, May 19, 1975
         108:58, Nov 22, 1976

Old Times
Productions:
    Opened November 16, 1971 for 119 performances.
    (Off Off Broadway) Opened October 16, 1974.
    (Off Off Broadway) Season of 1974-1975.
    (Off Off Broadway) Opened January 31, 1975.
    (Off Off Broadway) Opened May 13, 1976.
    (Off Off Broadway) Opened October 8, 1976.
    (Off Off Broadway) Opened January 15, 1977.
Reviews:
    America 125:485, Dec 4, 1971
    Commonweal 95:278-9, Dec 17, 1971
    Look 71:16, Sep 17, 1971
    Nation 212:829-30, Jun 28, 1971
           213:603-4, Dec 6, 1971
    New Republic 165:20+, Dec 18, 1971
    New York Theatre Critics' Reviews 1971:180
    New York Times II, p. 1, Jun 13, 1971
                   p. 14, Aug 28, 1971
                   II, p. 1, Nov 14, 1971
                   p. 41, Nov 17, 1971
                   p. 60, Nov 18, 1971
                   II, p. 1, Nov 28, 1971
                   VI, p. 42, Dec 5, 1971
                   II, p. 1, Jan 2, 1972
                   p. 34, Feb 26, 1972
    New Yorker 47:64-5, Jul 3, 1971
               47:89, Nov 27, 1971

Newsweek 77:70, Jun 14, 1971
        78:110-11, Nov 29, 1971
Saturday Review 54:20, Dec 4, 1971
Time 97:76, Jun 14, 1971
      98:70-1, Nov 29, 1971
Vogue 158:71, Aug 1, 1971

Request Stop (see The Local Stigmatic)

The Room
  Productions:
    (Off Broadway) Opened December 9, 1964 for 343
      performances.
  Reviews:
    Commonweal 82:193, Apr 30, 1965
    Nation 199:523, Dec 28, 1964
    New York Times p. 62, Dec 10, 1964
    New Yorker 40:68+, Dec 19, 1964
    Newsweek 64:75-6, Dec 21, 1964
    Saturday Review 47:33, Dec 26, 1964
    Time 84:86, Dec 18, 1964
    Vogue 145:98, Feb 1, 1965

Silence
  Productions:
    (Off Broadway) Opened February 9, 1971 for 6 performances.
    (Off Off Broadway) Opened March 4, 1977.
  Reviews:
    Catholic World 210:124-6, Dec 1969
    New Republic 162:20, Apr 25, 1970
    New York Theatre Critics' Reviews 1970:245
    New York Times II, p. 8, Jul 13, 1969
               p. 34, Jul 25, 1969
               p. 35, Feb 10, 1971
               p. 43, Apr 3, 1970
               II, p. 3, Apr 12, 1970
    New Yorker 46:84, Apr 11, 1970
    Saturday Review 53:16, Apr 25, 1970
    Time 94:67, Jul 18, 1969

A Slight Ache
  Productions:
    (Off Broadway) Opened December 16, 1962 for 16
      performances.
    (Off Broadway) Opened December 9, 1964 for 343
      performances.
    (Off Off Broadway) Opened November 13, 1975.
  Reviews:
    Commonweal 82:194, Apr 30, 1965
    Nation 199:523, Dec 28, 1964
    New York Times p. 62, Dec 10, 1964
    New Yorker 40:68+, Dec 19, 1964
    Newsweek 64:75-6, Dec 21, 1964

PINTER / 263

Saturday Review 47:33, Dec 26, 1964
Time 84:86, Dec 18, 1964
Vogue 145:98, Feb 1, 1965

Tea Party
Productions:
(Off Broadway) Opened October 15, 1968 for 147 performances.
Reviews:
America 119:447, Nov 9, 1968
Commonweal 89:350-1, Dec 6, 1968
Nation 207:477, Nov 4, 1968
New York Theatre Critics' Reviews 1968:138
New York Times p. 40, Oct 16, 1968
II, p. 7, Nov 3, 1968
New Yorker 44:140-1, Oct 26, 1968
Newsweek 72:135, Oct 28, 1968
Time 92:69, Oct 25, 1968
Vogue 152:170, Dec 1968

That's All (see The Local Stigmatic)

That's Your Trouble (see The Local Stigmatic)

Trouble in the Works (see The Local Stigmatic)

PIRANDELLO, LUIGI

As You Desire Me
Productions:
Adapted by Dmitri Ostrow. Opened January 28, 1931 for
142 performances.
Reviews:
Arts and Decoration 34:84, Apr 1931
Bookman 73:409-10, Jun 1931
Catholic World 132:721, Mar 1931
Commonweal 13:415, Feb 11, 1931
Drama 21:9, Apr 1931
Life (NY) 97:18, Feb 20, 1931
Living Age 338:290-1, May 1, 1930
Nation 132:198, Feb 18, 1931
New Republic 66:19, Feb 18, 1931
66:209, Apr 8, 1931
New York Times p. 21, Jan 29, 1931
Outlook 158:36, May 13, 1931
Sketch Book 8:25, Apr 1931
Theatre Arts 15:277, Apr 1931
Theatre Magazine 53:28-9, Mar 1931
53:26, Apr 1931

Call It Virtue
Productions:
(Off Broadway) Translated by Edward Eager. Opened
March 27, 1963 for 24 performances.

Reviews:
New York Times p. 8, Mar 28, 1963
Newsweek 61:85, Apr 8, 1963

Death as a Life Force
Productions:
(Off Off Broadway) Opened October 1976.
No Reviews.

Each in His Own Way
Productions:
(Off Off Broadway) Opened November 11, 1977.
No Reviews.

Emperor Henry IV   (see Henry IV)

Floriani's Wife
Productions:
Adapted by Ann Sprague MacDonald.   Opened October 13,
1923 for 16 performances.
Reviews:
New Republic 36:207, Oct 17, 1923
New York Times p. 10, Oct 1, 1923
IX, p. 1, Oct 7, 1923

Henry IV
Productions:
Opened January 21, 1924 for 28 performances as The
Living Mask.
(Off Broadway) Opened December 19, 1947 in repertory.
English translation by Stephen Rich.   Opened March 28, 1973
for 37 performances as Emperor Henry IV.
Reviews:
American Mercury 1:371-2, Mar 1924
Arts and Decoration 20:32, Mar 1924
Freeman 8:544-5, Feb 13, 1924
Nation 216:506-8, Apr 16, 1973
New Republic 37:287, Feb 6, 1924
New York Theatre Critics' Reviews 1973:294
New York Times p. 15, Jan 22, 1924
p. 40, Feb 7, 1968
II, p. 1, Mar 25, 1973
p. 42, Mar 29, 1973
II, p. 1, Apr 8, 1973
New Yorker 49:57, Apr 7, 1973
Newsweek 81:119, Apr 9, 1973
Time 91:77, Feb 16, 1968
101:108, Apr 9, 1973

The Jar
Productions:
(Off Broadway) Part of a bill called The Man with the Flower
in His Mouth.   Translated by William Murray.   Opened

April 22, 1969 for 80 performances.
Reviews:
New York Times p. 42, Apr 23, 1969
II, p. 3, May 4, 1969
p. 35, Jul 1, 1969

Lazarus
Productions:
(Off Broadway) Opened April 2, 1963 for six performances.
No Reviews.

The License
Productions:
(Off Broadway) Part of a bill called The Man with the
Flower in His Mouth. Opened April 22, 1969 for
80 performances.
Reviews:
New York Times p. 42, Apr 23, 1969
II, p. 3, May 4, 1969
p. 35, Jul 1, 1969

The Living Mask (see Henry IV)

The Man with the Flower in His Mouth
Productions:
(Off Broadway) Translated by William Murray. Opened
April 22, 1969 for 80 performances.
(Off Off Broadway) Season of 1971-1972.
(Off Off Broadway) Season of 1972-1973.
(Off Off Broadway) Opened October 1976.
Reviews:
New York Times p. 42, Apr 23, 1969
II, p. 3, May 4, 1969
p. 35, Jul 1, 1969
p. 29, Feb 26, 1974
New Yorker 45:107-8, May 3, 1969

*Mountain Giants
Reviews:
New York Times p. 32, Apr 5, 1961

Naked
Productions:
Opened October 20, 1924 in repertory.
Translated by Arthur Livingston. Opened November 8, 1926
for 32 performances.
(Off Broadway) Opened September 1950 in repertory.
(Off Broadway) Season of 1953-1954.
Reviews:
Nation 123:539-40, Nov 24, 1926
New Republic 49:16-17, Nov 24, 1926
New York Times p. 27, Oct 28, 1924
VII, p. 1, Nov 2, 1924

New York Times p. 31, Nov 9, 1926
                p. 39, Sep 7, 1950

Right You Are If You Think You Are
Productions:
Opened March 2, 1927 for 48 performances.
(Off Broadway) Opened July 1950 in repertory.
(Off Broadway) Season of 1956-1957.
(Off Broadway) English version by Eric Bentley.
Opened March 4, 1964 for 53 performances.
English version by Eric Bentley.   Opened November 22, 1966
   for 42 performances in repertory.
(Off Broadway) Opened September 12, 1972 for 64 perform-
   ances.
(Off Off Broadway) Opened February 1975.
Reviews:
American Mercury 11:116-7, May 1927
Life (NY) 89:23, Mar 17, 1927
Nation 124:295, Mar 16, 1927
         203:651, Dec 12, 1966
New Republic 50:141-2, Mar 23, 1927
             156:41-2, Jan 7, 1967
New York Theatre Critics' Reviews 1966:233
New York Times p. 27, Feb 24, 1927
               VII, p. 1, Mar 6, 1927
               p. 37, Jun 29, 1950
               p. 37, Mar 5, 1957
               p. 37, Mar 5, 1964
               p. 34, Nov 23, 1966
               II, p. 3, Dec 11, 1966
               p. 59, Oct 12, 1972
New Yorker 40:109, Mar 14, 1964
Newsweek 68:96+, Dec 5, 1966
Time 88:84, Dec 2, 1966
Vogue 69:86-7, Apr 15, 1927

Rules of the Game
Productions:
(Off Broadway) Season of 1960-1961.
Translated by William Murray. Opened December 12, 1974
   for 12 performances.
Reviews:
Nation 220:26, Jan 11, 1975
New York Theatre Critics' Reviews 1974:142
New York Times p. 44, Dec 20, 1960
               p. 22, Jan 24, 1961
               p. 49, Jun 17, 1971
               p. 63, Dec 13, 1974
New Yorker 36:43-4, Dec 31, 1960
           50:54, Dec 23, 1974
Theatre Arts 45:68, Mar 1961
Time 104:47, Dec 23, 1974

Say It with Flowers
  Productions:
    Translated by Alice Rohe.   Opened December 3, 1926
      for two performances.
  Reviews:
    Dramatist 18:1332-3, Jan 1927
    New York Times p. 29, Dec 6, 1926

Six Characters in Search of an Author
  Productions:
    Opened October 30, 1922 for 136 performances.
    Opened February 6, 1924 for 17 performances.
    Translated by Edward Storer.   Opened April 15, 1931
      for 13 performances.
    Translated by Frank Fauritz.   Adapted by Tyrone Guthrie
      and Michael Wagner.   Opened December 11, 1955 for
      65 performances.
    (Off Broadway) Translated by Paul Aliva Mayer.   Opened
      March 8, 1963 for 529 performances.
    (Off Off Broadway) Opened April 28, 1977.
  Reviews:
    America 94:384, Dec 31, 1955
    Arts and Decoration 35:46, Jun 1931
    Catholic World 116:505-7, Jan 1923
                  182:385-6, Apr 19, 1956
    Commonweal 63:483-4, Feb 10, 1956
              78:105-6, Apr 19, 1963
    Drama 13:130-1, Jan 1923
    Dramatist 14:1177-8, Jul 1923
    Life (NY) 80:18, Nov 23, 1922
    Nation 115:556, Nov 22, 1922
          181:582, Dec 31, 1955
          191:334, Apr 20, 1963
    New Republic 32:335-6, Nov 22, 1922
                33:97, Dec 20, 1922
                148:30, Mar 30, 1963
    New York Clipper 70:20, Nov 8, 1922
    New York Theatre Critics' Reviews 1955:189
    New York Times VIII, p. 1, Nov 5, 1922
                   p. 11, Dec 31, 1922
                   p. 29, Apr 16, 1931
                   II, p. 5, Dec 11, 1955
                   p. 38, Dec 12, 1955
                   II, p. 3, Dec 25, 1955
                   p. 7, Mar 11, 1963
                   p. 39, Nov 26, 1968
    New Yorker 31:46-7, Dec 24, 1955
              39:74-5, Mar 23, 1963
    Newsweek 46:53, Dec 26, 1955
    Saturday Review 38:25, Dec 31, 1955
                   46:28, Mar 23, 1963
    Theatre Arts 15:450-1, Jun 1931
                40:75+, Feb 1956

Theatre Arts 47:13-14, May 1963
Theatre Magazine 37:23, Jan 1923
Time 66:30, Dec 26, 1955

To Clothe the Naked
　Productions:
　　(Off Broadway) Translated by William Murray.　Opened
　　　April 27, 1967 for 30 performances.
　Reviews:
　　New York Times p. 30, Apr 28, 1967
　　　　　　　　　　p. 42, May 17, 1967
　　New Yorker 43:155, May 6, 1967
　　Time 89:58, May 5, 1967

*Tonight We Improvise
　Reviews:
　　New Republic 141:22-3, Dec 7, 1959
　　New York Times p. 27, Nov 7, 1959
　　New Yorker 35:122-4, Nov 14, 1959

PLUNKETT, E. J. M. D.　see　DUNSANY, LORD

PORTO-RICHE, GEORGES DE　see　DE PORTO-RICHE, GEORGES

PRIESTLEY, J. B.

Dangerous Corner
　Productions:
　　Opened October 27, 1932 for 206 performances.
　　Opened July 17, 1933 for 90 performances.
　　(Off Broadway) Opened November 1950 in repertory.
　Reviews:
　　Catholic World 136:334-5, Dec 1932
　　　　　　　　　 137:724, Sep 1933
　　New Outlook 161:47, Dec 1932
　　New York Times p. 20, Jul 18, 1933
　　Stage 10:34, Dec 1932
　　Theatre Arts 16:712-13, Sep 1932
　　　　　　　　　17:22-3, Jan 1933
　　Vanity Fair 39:20-21, Jan 1933

*Desert Highway
　Reviews:
　　New York Times II, p. 1, Jan 2, 1944
　　Theatre Arts 28:340, Jun 1944

Dragon's Mouth
　Productions:
　　(Off Broadway) Season of 1955-1956.

Reviews:
  Catholic World 183:311, Jan 1956
  New York Times II, p. 3, Jun 8, 1952
                    p. 45, Nov 17, 1955

Eden End
  Productions:
    Opened October 21, 1935 for 24 performances.
  Reviews:
    Commonweal 23:48, Nov 8, 1935
    Nation 141:547-8, Nov 6, 1935
    New York Times p. 17, Oct 22, 1935
    New Yorker 50:133-4, Apr 22, 1974
    Theatre Arts 19:894+, Dec 1935

*Ever Since Paradise
  Reviews:
    New York Times p. 18, Jul 12, 1957
    Theatre Arts 31:37, Oct 1947

*The Glass Cage
  Reviews:
    New York Times p. 34, Mar 6, 1957
                    p. 21, Mar 11, 1957

The Good Companions (with Edward Knoblock)
  Productions:
    Opened October 1, 1931 for 68 performances.
  Reviews:
    Catholic World 134:208-9, Nov 1931
    Life (NY) 98:19, Oct 23, 1931
    New York Times p. 31, Oct 2, 1931
                   VIII, p. 1, Oct 11, 1931
                   p. 29, Nov 27, 1931
    Theatre Arts 15:982-3, Dec 1931

*Good Night Children?
  Reviews:
    New York Times VIII, p. 3, Feb 15, 1942

*Home Is Tomorrow
  Reviews:
    New York Times p. 25, Nov 22, 1948
                   II, p. 4, Dec 12, 1948
                   p. 27, Jun 2, 1950

*How They Are at Home
  Reviews:
    New York Times II, p. 1, May 28, 1944

I Have Been Here Before
  Productions:
    Opened October 13, 1938 for 20 performances.

Reviews:
Commonweal 29:21, Oct 28, 1938
New York Times p. 26, Oct 14, 1938
Newsweek 12:34, Oct 24, 1938
Theatre Arts 22:861, Dec 1938
Time 32:56, Oct 24, 1938

An Inspector Calls
Productions:
Opened October 21, 1947 for 95 performances.
Reviews:
Catholic World 166:265, Dec 1947
Commonweal 47:119, Nov 14, 1947
Forum 109:25, Jan 1948
New Republic 117:35, Nov 10, 1947
New York Theatre Critics' Reviews 1947:291
New York Times II, p. 2, Oct 13, 1946
II, p. 1, Oct 10, 1947
p. 38, Oct 22, 1947
II, p. 1, Nov 16, 1947
p. 36, Oct 4, 1951
New Yorker 23:47-8, Nov 1, 1947
Newsweek 30:76+, Nov 3, 1947
School and Society 66:422-3, Nov 29, 1947
Theatre Arts 31:51, Jan 1947
31:61, Dec 1947
32:11, Jan 1948
Time 50:71, Nov 3, 1947

*Jenny Villiers
Reviews:
New York Times II, p. 2, Apr 7, 1946

Laburnum Grove
Productions:
Opened January 14, 1935 for 131 performances.
(Off Off Broadway) Opened July 28, 1974.
Reviews:
Commonweal 21:403, Feb 1, 1935
Catholic World 140:722, Mar 1935
New Republic 81:336, Jan 1935
New York Times p. 23, Jan 15, 1935
X, p. 1, Jan 20, 1935
p. 27, Aug 8, 1974
Newsweek 5:32, Jan 12, 1935
Time 25:62, Jan 24, 1935

The Linden Tree
Productions:
Opened March 2, 1948 for seven performances.
Reviews:
Harper's Bazaar 82:133, Apr 1948
New Republic 118:28, Mar 15, 1948

New York Theatre Critics' Reviews 1948:317
New York Times II, p. 3, Sep 14, 1947
　　　　　p. 28, Mar 3, 1948
　　　　　II, p. 1, Mar 14, 1948
New Yorker 24:48+, Mar 13, 1948
Newsweek 31:78, Mar 15, 1948
Theatre Arts 31:44+, Nov 1947
Time 51:65, Mar 15, 1948
Vogue 111:192, Apr 1, 1948

*Music by Night
　Reviews:
　Theatre Arts 23:866, Dec 1939

The Mystery at Greenfingers
　Productions:
　(Off Broadway) Opened December 8, 1939 for 2 performances
　　in repertory.
　No Reviews.

A Severed Head (with Iris Murdoch)
　Productions:
　Opened October 28, 1964 for 29 performances.
　Reviews:
　Commonweal 81:354, Dec 4, 1964
　New York Theatre Critics' Reviews 1964:177
　New York Times p. 22, Jun 28, 1963
　　　　　p. 40, Oct 29, 1964
　New Yorker 39:96+, Sep 7, 1963
　Saturday Review 47:53, Nov 14, 1964
　Time 84:52, Nov 6, 1964

*Summer Day's Dream
　Reviews:
　New York Times p. 28, Sep 9, 1949
　　　　　II, p. 3, Oct 9, 1949
　New Yorker 25:80, Oct 1, 1949

*They Came to a City
　Reviews:
　American Mercury 57:742-5, Dec 1943
　New York Times II, p. 6, Jun 6, 1943
　Theatre Arts 27:403-4+, Jul 1943

Time and the Conways
　Productions:
　Opened January 3, 1938 for 32 performances.
　Reviews:
　Catholic World 146:598, Feb 1938
　Commonweal 27:358, Jan 21, 1938
　Nation 146:81, Jan 15, 1938
　New Republic 93:310, Jan 19, 1938
　New York Times p. 19, Jan 4, 1938

One Act Play Magazine 1:847-8, Jan 1938
Stage 15:50, Feb 1938
Theatre Arts 21:847, Nov 1937
22:97-8, Feb 1938
Time 31:61, Jan 17, 1938

*Treasure on Pelican
Reviews:
New York Times p. 50, Mar 6, 1955

When We Are Married
Productions:
Opened December 25, 1939 for 156 performances.
Reviews:
Commonweal 31:245, Jan 5, 1940
New York Theatre Critics' Reviews 1940:433
New York Times p. 22, Dec 26, 1939
IX, p. 2, Feb 4, 1940
IX, p. 12, Mar 10, 1940
IX, p. 2, Apr 21, 1940
Theatre Arts 24:168-9, Mar 1940

*The White Countess
Reviews:
New York Times p. 86, Mar 28, 1954

QUINTERO, SERAFIN and JOAQUIN ALVAREZ

*Fortunato
Reviews:
New York Times p. 15, Mar 24, 1956

A Hundred Years Old
Productions:
English translation by Helen and Harley Granville-Barker.
Opened October 1, 1929 for 39 performances.
Reviews:
American Mercury 18:503-4, Dec 1929
Catholic World 130:329-30, Dec 1929
Commonweal 10:616, Oct 16, 1929
Life (NY) 94:22, Oct 25, 1929
Nation 129:474, Oct 23, 1929
New Republic 60:244-5, Oct 16, 1929
New York Times p. 28, Dec 2, 1929
Outlook 135:314, Oct 23, 1929
Review of Reviews 80:158, Dec 1929
Theatre Arts 13:877-8, Dec 1929
Theatre Magazine 50:50, Dec 1929

Malvaloca
Productions:

Translated by Jacob J. Fassett, Jr.   Opened October 2,
1922 for 48 performances.
Reviews:
Forum 68:972-3, Nov 1922
Nation 104:275, Mar 18, 1917
New Republic 32:223-4, Oct 25, 1922
            33:284-6, Feb 7, 1923
New York Clipper 70:20, Oct 11, 1922
New York Times p. 22, Oct 3, 1922
Theatre Magazine 36:373, 376, Dec 1922

A Sunny Morning
   Productions:
Opened December 7, 1935 for 1 performance.
No Reviews.

The Women Have Their Way
   Productions:
Adapted by Harley and Helen Granville-Barker.   Opened
January 27, 1930 for 25 performances.
Opened December 1, 1935 for 1 performance.
Reviews:
Commonweal 11:424, Feb 12, 1930
Nation 130:226, Feb 19, 1930
New York Times p. 28, Jan 28, 1930
Vogue 75:108, Mar 15, 1930

RAPPAPORT, SOLOMON   see   ANSKY, S.

RATTIGAN, TERENCE

*Adventure Story
   Reviews:
New York Times p. 11, Mar 19, 1949
Theatre Arts 33:4-5+, Jun 1949

*A Bequest to the Nation
   Reviews:
Catholic World 212:313, Mar 1971
New York Times p. 36, Sep 25, 1970

The Browning Version
   Productions:
Opened October 12, 1949 for 69 performances.
Reviews:
Catholic World 170:227, Dec 1949
Life 27:93, Oct 31, 1949
New Republic 121:21, Nov 7, 1949
New York Theatre Critics' Reviews 1949:253
New York Times p. 32, Oct 13, 1949
            II, p. 1, Oct 23, 1949

New York Times II, p. 6, Dec 4, 1949
                  p. 17, Mar 7, 1958
New Yorker 25:60, Oct 22, 1949
Newsweek 34:84, Oct 24, 1949
Saturday Review 32:26-7, Nov 5, 1949
School and Society 71:26, Jan 14, 1950
Theatre Arts 33:12, Dec 1949
Time 54:58, Oct 24, 1949

College Sinners (see First Episode)

The Deep Blue Sea
    Productions:
        Opened November 5, 1952 for 132 performances.
    Reviews:
        Catholic World 176:306-7, Jan 1953
        Commonweal 57:197-8, Nov 28, 1952
        Nation 175:472-3, Nov 22, 1952
        New York Theatre Critics' Reviews 1952:207
        New York Times p. 19, Mar 7, 1952
                       II, p. 3, Mar 16, 1952
                       p. 38, Nov 6, 1952
                       II, p. 3, Dec 14, 1952
                       p. 8, Apr 4, 1953
        New Yorker 28:69, Nov 15, 1952
        Newsweek 40:74, Nov 17, 1952
        Saturday Review 35:36-7, Nov 22, 1952
        School and Society 76:402-3, Dec 20, 1952
        Theatre Arts 37:21-2, Jan 1953
        Time 60:102, Nov 17, 1952

First Episode (College Sinners) (with Philip Heinmann)
    Productions:
        Opened September 17, 1934 for 40 performances.
    Reviews:
        New York Times p. 18, Sep 18, 1934

Flare Path
    Productions:
        Opened December 23, 1942 for 14 performances.
    Reviews:
        Commonweal 37:326, Jan 15, 1943
        Current History ns 3:550, Feb 1943
        New York Theatre Critics' Reviews 1942:138+
        New York Times VIII, p. 1, Aug 23, 1942
                       p. 20, Dec 24, 1942
        Theatre Arts 27:77-8, Feb 1943

French without Tears
    Productions:
        Opened September 28, 1937 for 111 performances.
        (Off Broadway) Opened April 1940 in repertory.
        (Off Broadway) Opened March 15, 1974 for 8 performances.

Reviews:
  Catholic World 146:216, Nov 1937
  Commonweal 26:580, Oct 15, 1937
  New Republic 92:270, Oct 13, 1937
  New York Times p. 19, Sep 29, 1937
               p. 28, Mar 19, 1974
  New Yorker 50:52, Apr 1, 1974
  Scribner's Magazine 102:68, Sep 1937
  Theatre Arts 21:828, Nov 1937
  Time 30:55, Oct 11, 1937

Grey Farm (with Hector Bolitho)
  Productions:
  Opened May 3, 1940 for 35 performances.
  Reviews:
  New York Theatre Critics' Reviews 1940:317+

Harlequinade
  Productions:
  Opened October 12, 1949 for 69 performances.
  Reviews:
  Catholic World 170:227, Dec 1949
  Life 27:94-5, Oct 31, 1949
  New Republic 121:21, Nov 7, 1949
  New York Theatre Critics' Reviews 1949:253
  New York Times p. 32, Oct 13, 1949
               p. 15, Feb 14, 1959
  School and Society 71:26, Jan 14, 1950
  Theatre Arts 33:12, Dec 1949
  Time 54:58, Oct 24, 1949

In Praise of Love
  Productions:
  Opened December 10, 1974 for 199 performances.
  Reviews:
  Nation 219:700-701, Dec 28, 1974
  New Republic 172:33-34, Jan 4, 1975
  New York Times Critics' Reviews 1974:150
  New York Times p. 53, Dec 11, 1974
               II, p. 5, Dec 22, 1974
  New Yorker 50:53, Dec 23, 1974
  Newsweek 84:56, Dec 23, 1974
  Time 104:46-7, Dec 23, 1974

Love in Idleness (see O Mistress Mine)

Man and Boy
  Productions:
  Opened November 12, 1963 for 54 performances.
  Reviews:
  New York Theatre Critics' Reviews 1963:199
  New York Times p. 28, Sep 5, 1963
               p. 34, Nov 13, 1963

New York Times II, p. 1, Dec 1, 1963
New Yorker 39:143, Nov 23, 1963
Newsweek 62:71, Nov 25, 1963
Saturday Review 46:24, Nov 30, 1963
Time 82:71, Nov 22, 1963

O Mistress Mine (Love in Idleness)
Productions:
Opened January 23, 1946 for 452 performances.
Reviews:
Catholic World 162:551, Mar 1946
Forum 105:659-60, Mar 1946
Life 20:49-50+, Feb 18, 1946
New Republic 114:158, Feb 4, 1946
New York Theatre Critics' Reviews 1946:474
New York Times p. 13, Dec 22, 1944
　　　　　　　II, p. 2, Jan 7, 1945
　　　　　　　VI, p. 29, Feb 4, 1945
　　　　　　　VI, p. 28, Jan 20, 1946
　　　　　　　p. 25, Jan 24, 1946
　　　　　　　II, p. 1, Feb 3, 1946
　　　　　　　II, p. 1, May 26, 1946
　　　　　　　II, p. 1, Sep 1, 1946
　　　　　　　II, p. 3, Nov 10, 1946
　　　　　　　II, p. 3, Mar 2, 1949
New Yorker 21:34+, Feb 2, 1946
Newsweek 27:80, Feb 4, 1946
Theatre Arts 30:133, Mar 1946
Time 47:61, Feb 4, 1946

Ross
Productions:
Opened December 26, 1961 for 159 performances.
Reviews:
Commonweal 75:435-6, Jan 19, 1962
New Republic 146:20+, Jan 22, 1962
New York Theatre Critics' Reviews 1961:139
New York Times p. 26, May 13, 1960
　　　　　　　II, p. 5, Dec 24, 1961
　　　　　　　p. 20, Dec 27, 1961
　　　　　　　II, p. 1, Jan 7, 1962
New Yorker 36:59-60, Jul 9, 1960
　　　　　　　37:55, Jan 6, 1962
Newsweek 55:78, May 30, 1960
　　　　　　　59:44, Jan 8, 1962
Saturday Review 45:51, Jan 13, 1962
Theatre Arts 45:58-60, Feb 1961
　　　　　　　46:57-8, Mar 1962
Time 75:56, May 23, 1960
　　　　　　　79:52, Jan 5, 1962

Separate Tables (Table by the Window and Table Number Seven)
Productions:

Opened October 25, 1956 for 332 performances.
(Off Broadway) Opened Season of 1958-1959.
(Off Off Broadway) Opened January 1976.
Reviews:
America 96:281+, Dec 1, 1956
Catholic World 184:303, Jan 1957
Christian Century 73:1328-9, Nov 14, 1956
Commonweal 65:234, Nov 30, 1956
Life 41:89-90, Dec 3, 1956
Nation 183:416, Nov 10, 1956
New Republic 135:23, Nov 12, 1956
New York Theatre Critics' Reviews 1956:246
New York Times p. 42, Sep 23, 1954
　　　　　　II, p. 1, May 22, 1955
　　　　　　VI, p. 28, Sep 16, 1956
　　　　　　p. 33, Oct 26, 1956
　　　　　　II, p. 1, Nov 4, 1956
　　　　　　II, p. 1, Sep 15, 1957
New Yorker 32:68+, Nov 3, 1956
Newsweek 48:78, Nov 5, 1956
Reporter 13:43, Oct 20, 1955
Saturday Review 38:33, Sep 17, 1955
　　　　　　　39:29, Nov 3, 1956
Theatre Arts 41:19-20, Jan 1957
Time 68:75, Nov 5, 1956
Vogue 128:72, Oct 15, 1956

The Sleeping Prince
　　Productions:
　　Opened November 1, 1956 for 60 performances.
　　Reviews:
　　America 96:359, Dec 22, 1956
　　Catholic World 184:307, Jan 1957
　　Commonweal 65:235, Nov 30, 1956
　　Nation 183:485, Dec 1, 1956
　　New York Theatre Critics' Reviews 1956:226
　　New York Times p. 25, Sep 29, 1953
　　　　　　　　p. 24, Nov 6, 1953
　　　　　　　　II, p. 4, Dec 20, 1953
　　　　　　　　p. 31, Nov 2, 1956
　　New Yorker 29:163, Dec 12, 1953
　　　　　　　32:112-14, Nov 10, 1956
　　Newsweek 48:54, Nov 12, 1956
　　Saturday Review 39:28, Nov 17, 1956
　　Theatre Arts 41:24, Jan 1957
　　Time 68:71, Nov 12, 1956

Table by the Window　(see Separate Tables)

Table Number Seven　(see Separate Tables)

*Variations on a Theme
_____
Reviews:
New York Times p. 16, May 9, 1958

While the Sun Shines
_____
Productions:
Opened September 19, 1944 for 39 performances.
Reviews:
Catholic World 160:169, Nov 1944
Commonweal 40:589, Oct 6, 1944
Nation 159:389, Sep 30, 1944
New York Theatre Critics' Reviews 1944:130
New York Times p. 21, Sep 20, 1944
II, p. 1, Sep 24, 1944
New Yorker 20:38, Sep 30, 1944
Newsweek 24:99, Oct 2, 1944
Theatre Arts 28:641, Nov 1944
Time 44:59, Oct 2, 1944

*Who Is Sylvia?
_____
Reviews:
Christian Science Monitor Magazine p. 6, Jan 6, 1951
New York Times p. 45, Oct 25, 1950
II, p. 3, Nov 12, 1950

The Winslow Boy
_____
Productions:
Opened October 29, 1947 for 215 performances.
Reviews:
Catholic World 166:264, Dec 1947
Commonweal 47:120, Nov 14, 1947
Forum 109:25, Jan 1948
Life 23:97-8+, Nov 24, 1947
Nation 165:537, Nov 15, 1947
New Republic 117:35, Nov 10, 1947
New York Theatre Critics' Reviews 1947:283
New York Times p. 32, Oct 30, 1947
II, p. 1, Nov 9, 1947
II, p. 1, Nov 16, 1947
p. 10, Apr 17, 1948
New Yorker 23:52, Nov 8, 1947
Newsweek 30:74, Nov 10, 1947
Saturday Review 30:24-9, Nov 29, 1947
School and Society 67:315-16, Apr 24, 1948
Theatre Arts 30:597, Oct 1946
31:43, Jun 1947
32:12, Jan 1948
Time 50:100, Nov 10, 1947

ROBERTSON, THOMAS WILLIAM

Caste
    Productions:
        Opened April 25, 1910 for 48 performances.
    Reviews:
        American Mercury 70:549, Aug 1910
        Bookman 31:420-1, Jun 1910
        Current Literature 49:191-2 Aug 1910
        Dramatic Mirror 63:8, May 7, 1910
        Dramatist 4:381-2, Jul 1913
        Green Book Album 6:640-5, Sep 1911
        Harper's Weekly 54:24-30, Jun 18, 1910
        Leslie's Weekly 110:461, May 12, 1910
        Life (NY) 55:822, May 5, 1910
        Metropolitan Magazine 32:530-1, Jul 1910
        Pearson 24:89-91+, Jul 1910
        Theatre Arts 31:28-9, Mar 1947
        Theatre Magazine 11:174, 181, Jun 1910
        World Today 18:584, Jun 1910

David Garrick
    Productions:
        Opened January 6, 1916 for 20 performances.
    Reviews:
        Dramatic Mirror 75:7, Jan 15, 1916
        Life (NY) 67:118, Jan 20, 1916
        Nation 102:85, Jan 20, 1916
        Theatre Magazine 23:61+, Feb 1916

School
    Productions:
        Opened December 16, 1913 for one special matinee.
    No Reviews.

ROBINSON, LENNOX

Church Street
    Productions:
        Opened November 19, 1934 for one performance.
        (Off Broadway) Season of 1947-1948.
        (Off Broadway) Opened February 9, 1948 for two weeks
            in repertory.
    Reviews:
        New Republic 118:30, Feb 23, 1948
        New York Times p. 27, Feb 10, 1948
        School and Society 67:166, Feb 28, 1948

Crabbed Youth and Age
    Productions:
        Opened May 8, 1924 for one performance.
        Opened October 21, 1932 in repertory.

Reviews:
New York Times p. 25, Nov 4, 1932

Drama at Inish (Is Life Worth Living?)
    Productions:
        Opened November 9, 1933 for 12 performances.
        Opened November 14, 1934 for 3 performances.
        Opened December 13, 1937 for 4 performances.
    Reviews:
        Commonweal 27:272, Dec 31, 1927
        New York Times X, p. 1, Sep 17, 1933
                        p. 24, Nov 15, 1934
                        p. 33, Dec 14, 1937
        Theatre Arts 18:13-14, Jan 1934

The Far-off Hills
    Productions:
        Opened October 18, 1932 for 13 performances.
        Opened November 14, 1934 for one performance.
        Opened October 11, 1937 for 47 performances.
        (Off Broadway) Opened January 1935 in repertory.
        (Off Broadway) Opened Season of 1936-1937.
    Reviews:
        Nation 145:484, Oct 30, 1937
        New York Times p. 22, Oct 19, 1932
                        p. 30, Oct 12, 1937
        Theatre Arts 21:928, Dec 1937

Harvest
    Productions:
        Opened November 20, 1911 in repertory (The Irish Players).
    Reviews:
        Dramatic Mirror 66:7, Dec 20, 1911
        New York Dramatic News 65:6, Feb 16, 1918

Is Life Worth Living? (see Drama at Inish)

The Lost Leader
    Productions:
        Opened November 11, 1919 for 31 performances.
    Reviews:
        Current Opinion 67:166-7, Sep 1919
                        68:47-53, Jan 1920
        Dramatic Mirror 80:1825, Nov 27, 1919
        Living Age 302:399-401, Aug 16, 1919
        New York Times p. 11, Nov 12, 1919
        Theatre Magazine 30:368, Dec 1919
        Weekly Review 1:238-9, Jul 26, 1919

Patriots
    Productions:
        Opened February 4, 1913 in repertory (The Irish Players)

Reviews:
  Collier's 50:25, Mar 15, 1913
  Dramatic Mirror 69:6-7, Feb 19, 1913
  New York Times p. 15, Feb 12, 1913

The White Headed Boy
  Productions:
    Opened September 15, 1921 for 60 performances.
    Opened October 21, 1932 in repertory.
    (Off Broadway) Opened October 31, 1937 in repertory.
    (Off Broadway) Opened November 6, 1938 in repertory.
  Reviews:
    Bookman 54:231-2, Nov 1921
    Dramatic Mirror 84:448, Sep 24, 1921
    Independent 107:36, Oct 8, 1921
    Life (NY) 78:18, Oct 6, 1921
    Nation 113:428, Oct 12, 1921
    New Republic 28:161, Oct 5, 1921
    New York Clipper 69:17, Sep 21, 1921
    New York Times p. 20, Sep 16, 1921
                   p. 27, Aug 11, 1937
    Theatre Magazine 34:386, Dec 1921
                     53:50, Jan 1931
    Weekly Review 3:601-2, Dec 15, 1920

ROMAINS, JULES

Dr. Knock
  Productions:
    Translated by Harley Granville-Barker. Opened February 27,
      1928 for 23 performances.
  Reviews:
    Literary Digest 122:19, Jul 25, 1936
    New York Times p. 15, Feb 24, 1928

Donogoo
  Productions:
    (Off Broadway) Opened Season of 1960-1961.
  Reviews:
    New York Times p. 25, Jan 25, 1961
                   p. 20, Feb 10, 1961
    New Yorker 36:64+, Jan 28, 1961

Volpone (see entry under Zweig, Stefan)

ROSTAND, EDMOND

L'Aiglon (The Eagle)
  Productions:
    Opened December 5, 1910 in repertory.
    Opened June 19, 1911 in repertory.

Opened October 20, 1924 for 48 performances.
Translated by Louis N. Parker. Opened December 26, 1927
    for eight performances.
Adapted by Clemence Dane. Opened November 3, 1934
    for 58 performances.
Reviews:
    Catholic World 140:337-8, Dec 1934
    Commonweal 21:96, Nov 16, 1934
    Dramatic Mirror 64:6-7, Dec 7, 1910
    Dramatist 4:382-3, Jul 1913
    Nation 119:527-8, Nov 12, 1924
            139:601, Nov 21, 1934
    New Republic 81:78, Nov 28, 1934
    New York Times p. 21, Oct 21, 1924
                  p. 24, Dec 27, 1927
                  p. 22, Nov 5, 1934
    Stage 14:87, Aug 1937
    Theatre Arts 19:12, Jan 1935
    Theatre Magazine 47:62, Mar 1928
    Vanity Fair 43:31, Jan 1935
    Vogue 84:72, Dec 15, 1934

Chantecler
    Productions:
        Adapted by Louis N. Parker. Opened January 23, 1911
            for 96 performances.
    Reviews:
        Blue Book 12:1092-5, Apr 1911
        Bookman 31:397-401, Jun 1910
                32:154-6, Oct 1910
        Canadian Magazine 36:482+, Mar 1911
        Collier's 46:19+, Feb 4, 1911
        Colonnade 9:205-15, Jun 1915
        Columbian 4:347-8+, May 1911
        Current Literature 48:319-21, Mar 1910
                           48:544-9, May 1910
                           49:304-16, Sep 1910
                           50:513-15, Mar 1911
        Dramatic Mirror 65:7, Jan 25, 1911
        Everybody's Magazine 24:553-4, Apr 1911
        Fortnightly Review 93:575-90, Mar 1910
        Independent 68:680-5, Apr 27, 1910
                    70:406-7, Feb 23, 1911
        Leslie's Weekly 110:260+, Mar 7, 1910
                        112:153, Feb 9, 1911
        Life (NY) 57:260, Feb 2, 1911
        Literary Digest 40:103, Jan 15, 1910
                        40:349-50, Feb 19, 1910
                        40:441-2, Mar 5, 1910
                        40:1265, Jun 25, 1910
                        42:208-9, Feb 4, 1911
        Living Age 264:696, Mar 12, 1910
                   265:37-43, Apr 2, 1910

Munsey 44:871-2, Mar 1911
Nation 90:491-2, May 12, 1910
    92:264, Mar 16, 1911
New England Magazine ns42:227-31, Apr 1910
Outlook 94:373, Feb 9, 1910
    97:251-2, Feb 4, 1911
Red Book 16:1137-43+, Apr 1911
Theatre Magazine 13:70-1+, Mar 1911

Cyrano de Bergerac
Productions:
Opened November 1, 1923 for 232 performances.
English version by Brian Hooker. Opened February 18, 1926
    for 96 performances.
English version by Brian Hooker. Opened December 25, 1928.
Adapted by Brian Hooker. Opened December 26, 1932
    for 16 performances.
Translated by Brian Hooker. Opened April 27, 1946
    for 40 performances.
English version by Brian Hooker. Opened October 8, 1946
    for 193 performances.
Adapted by Brian Hooker. Opened November 11, 1953
    for 15 performances.
(Off Broadway) Opened January 11, 1964 for eight per-
    formances.
English version by James Forsyth. Opened April 25, 1968
    in repertory for 52 performances.
Reviews:
America 118:739, Jun 1, 1968
American Mercury 64:53-5, Jan 1947
Bookman 48:676-9, Feb 1919
Catholic World 164:168-9, Nov 1946
    178:308-9, Jan 1954
Classic 18:48+, Feb 1924
Commonweal 24:76, May 15, 1936
    45:70, Nov 1, 1946
    88:268, May 17, 1968
Golden Book 16:250-8, Sep 1932
Life (NY) 82:18, Nov 22, 1923
    83:18, Feb 28, 1924
    87:20, Mar 25, 1926
Literary Digest 79:28, Nov 24, 1923
    109:18, Jun 13, 1931
Modern Language Notes 37:47-9, Jan 1922
National Magazine 52:422, Mar 1924
New Republic 37:18, Nov 28, 1923
    115:518, Oct 21, 1946
New York Theatre Critics' Reviews 1946:321
    1953:214
    1968:292
New York Times p. 14, Nov 2, 1923
    VIII, p. 1, Nov 11, 1923
    p. 18, Feb 19, 1926

New York Times p. 14, Dec 26, 1928
p. 11, Dec 27, 1932
p. 16, Dec 29, 1932
p. 1, Apr 17, 1936
II, p. 1, Oct 6, 1946
p. 33, Oct 9, 1946
VI, p. 53, Oct 20, 1946
II, p. 2, Oct 27, 1946
p. 54, Nov 3, 1946
II, p. 1, Nov 3, 1946
II, p. 3, Nov 17, 1946
p. 44, Dec 17, 1946
p. 24, Nov 13, 1953
p. 21, Aug 1, 1962
p. 30, Jun 20, 1963
p. 30, Apr 26, 1968
p. 58, May 20, 1968
p. 31, Sep 20, 1971
VII, p. 6, Dec 26, 1971
p. 32, Jun 29, 1975
New Yorker 22:57-8, Oct 19, 1946
29:88, Nov 21, 1953
44:129-30, May 4, 1968
Newsweek 7:44, May 9, 1936
28:93, Oct 21, 1953
42:64, Nov 23, 1953
71:94, May 6, 1968
Outlook 151:299, Feb 20, 1929
Saturday Review 29:28-30, Nov 2, 1946
48:18, Sep 1, 1962
54:18, Aug 21, 1971
Theatre Arts 30:690+, Dec 1946
31:50, Jan 1947
38:25, Jan 1954
47:69, Aug 1963
Theatre Magazine 39:23, Jan 1924
Time 48:78, Oct 1, 1946
49:48, Mar 3, 1947

The Eagle (see L'Aiglon)

The Lady of Dreams
Productions:
Adapted by Louis N. Parker from Rostand's La Princesse
Lointaine. Opened February 28, 1912 for 21 performances.
Reviews:
American Playwright 1:114-16, Apr 1912
Dramatic Mirror 67:6-7, Mar 6, 1912
Everybody's Magazine 26:688-9, May 1912
Green Book 7:810-12+, May 1912
7:973-4, May 1912
Life (NY) 59:540-1, May 14, 1912

Munsey 47:130, Apr 1912
Theatre Magazine 15:107-8+, Apr 1912

Last Night of Don Juan
  Productions:
    Translated by Sidney Howard. Opened November 9, 1925
      for 16 performances.
  Reviews:
    Drama 16:133, Jan 1926
    Life (NY) 86:22, Nov 26, 1925
    Nation 121:603-4, Nov 25, 1925
    New Republic 45:86-7, Dec 9, 1925
    New York Times p. 23, Nov 10, 1925
    Theatre Arts 10:5-7, Jan 1926
    Vanity Fair 25:40, Jan 1926

La Samaritaine
  Productions:
    Opened December 5, 1910 in repertory.
  Reviews:
    Bookman 23:602-4, Feb 1911
    Current Literature 50:193-6, Feb 1911
    Literary Digest 41:1203, Dec 24, 1910

RUDKIN, DAVID

*Afore Night Come
  Reviews:
    New York Times p. 34, Jun 26, 1964

Ashes
  Productions:
    (Off Off Broadway) Opened October 20, 1976.
    (Off Broadway) Opened January 25, 1977 for (145)
      performances.
  Reviews:
    America 136:149, Feb 19, 1977
    Commonweal 104:370-71, Jun 10, 1977
    Nation 224:29, Jan 1, 1977
    New Republic 176:20-1, Feb 19, 1977
    New York Times Critics' Reviews 1977:314
    New York Times II, p. 7, May 16, 1976
                III, p. 22, Dec 15, 1976
                II, p. 5, Jan 23, 1977
                III, p. 17, Feb 9, 1977
                III, p. 3, Feb 18, 1977
                II, p. 3, Feb 20, 1977
                II, p. 22, Mar 6, 1977
                II, p. 1, Apr 24, 1977
    New Yorker 52:52-3, Dec 27, 1976
    Newsweek 88:39, Dec 27, 1976
    Saturday Review 4:46-7, Mar 19, 1977
    Time 109:65, Jan 3, 1977

SAKI see MUNRO, H. H.

SALACROU, ARMAND

*L'archipel Lenoir
  Reviews:
    Theatre Arts 32:29, Feb 1948

Nights of Fury (see Les Nuits de la Colère)

Nights of Wrath (see Les Nuits de la Colère)

Les Nuits de la Colère
  Productions:
    Opened January 30, 1957 in repertory.
  Reviews:
    Catholic World 185:67, Apr 1957
    Commonweal 47:494-5, Feb 27, 1948
    New York Theatre Critics' Reviews 1957:351
    New York Times p. 31, Feb 12, 1957
    Theatre Arts 31:46, May 1947
              41:82, Apr 1957

SARDOU, VICTORIEN

Diplomacy
  Productions:
    Opened September 13, 1910 for 33 performances.
    Opened October 20, 1914 for 63 performances.
    Opened May 28, 1928 for 40 performances.
  Reviews:
    American Mercury 79:88-9, Feb 1915
    Book News 33:190, Dec 1914
    Dramatic Mirror 72:8, Oct 28, 1914
                    72:2, Nov 11, 1914
    Harper's Weekly 54:24, Nov 12, 1910
    Life (NY) 56:518, Sep 29, 1910
    Nation 99:560, Nov 5, 1914
           126:727, Jun 27, 1928
    New Republic 55:95-6, Jun 13, 1928
    New York Times p. 3, Feb 3, 1914
                   p. 11, Oct 21, 1914
                   VII, p. 9, Nov 8, 1914
                   VIII, p. 1, Feb 19, 1928
                   p. 16, May 29, 1928
                   VIII, p. 1, Jun 3, 1928
                   VIII, p. 2, Jun 17, 1928
    Theatre Magazine 12:xi-xiii, Nov 1910
                     20:214-16+, Nov 1914
                     20:262+, Dec 1914
    Vogue 72:84, Aug 1, 1928

Divorcons (with Emile de Nejac)
Productions:
Adapted from the French by Margaret Mayo.   Opened
April 1, 1913 for 55 performances.
Reviews:
Bookman 37:312-13, May 1913
Dramatic Mirror 69:6, Apr 9, 1913
69:2, Apr 16, 1913
Green Book 9:927-8+, Jun 1913
Harper's Weekly 57:20, Apr 19, 1913
Life (NY) 61:784, Apr 17, 1913
New York Times p. 11, Apr 2, 1913
p. 11, Dec 29, 1914
p. 9, Feb 9, 1916
Theatre Magazine 17:130-1, May 1913

Fedora
Productions:
Opened February 10, 1922 for 12 performances.
Reviews:
New York Clipper 70:20, Feb 22, 1922
New York Times p. 18, Feb 11, 1922

Madame Sans-Gêne
Productions:
Opened October 20, 1924 in repertory.
Reviews:
New York Times p. 30, Nov 4, 1924
Theatre Arts 21:196, Mar 1937

A Scrap of Paper
Productions:
Opened May 11, 1914 for 32 performances.
Reviews:
American Playwright 3:201-6, Jun 1914
Dramatic Mirror 71:5, May 20, 1914
71:16, May 13, 1914
Dramatist 5:476-7, Jul 1914
Green Book 12:98-9, Jul 1914
Life (NY) 63:928, May 21, 1914
New York Drama News 59:19, May 16, 1914
New York Times VIII, p. 5, May 10, 1914
p. 11, May 12, 1914
III, p. 3, Jun 28, 1914
Theatre Magazine 19:281+, Jun 1914

The Sorceress
Productions:
Opened December 5, 1910 in repertory.
No Reviews.

SARTRE, JEAN-PAUL

The Condemned of Altona (Les Sequestres d'Altona)
  Productions:
    Adapted by Justin O'Brien. Opened February 3, 1966
      for 46 performances.
  Reviews:
    America 114:272-3, Feb 19, 1966
    Nation 189:492-3, Dec 26, 1959
           202:222-4, Feb 21, 1966
    New Republic 154:42-3, Feb 26, 1966
    New York Theatre Critics' Reviews 1966:372
    New York Times p. 21, Feb 4, 1966
              II, p. 1, Feb 13, 1966
    New York Times Magazine p. 84, Nov 29, 1959
    New Yorker 41:206+, Oct 2, 1965
               41:110+, Feb 12, 1966
    Newsweek 67:88, Feb 14, 1966
    Saturday Review 49:52, Feb 19, 1966
    Time 87:67, Feb 18, 1966
    Vogue 147:58, Mar 15, 1966

*Crime Passionel
  Reviews:
    New York Times p. 19, Jun 18, 1948
    New York Times Magazine p. 20, Jul 11, 1948

Deferential Prostitute (see The Respectful Prostitute)

*The Devil and the Good Lord
  Reviews:
    New Republic 125:22, Jul 23, 1951
                 125:21-2, Aug 6, 1951
                 125:9, Sep 10, 1951
    New York Times p. 32, Jun 8, 1951
              II, p. 1, Jun 24, 1951
              II, p. 1, Aug 19, 1951
    New Yorker 27:46, Jun 30, 1951
    20th Century 150:221-30, Sep 1951

Le Diable et le bon Dieu (see The Devil and the Good Lord)

Dutiful Prostitute (see The Respectful Prostitute)

The Flies
  Productions:
    (Off Broadway) Opened April 17, 1947.
    (Off Off Broadway) Season of 1973-1974.
  Reviews:
    Commonweal 46:93-4, May 9, 1947
    Forum 107:541-5, Jun 1947
    New York Times p. 26, Apr 18, 1947

New York Times II, p. 2, Feb 29, 1948
           p. 18, Sep 10, 1954
New Yorker 23:52, May 24, 1947

God and the Devil   (see The Devil and the Good Lord)

Huis Clos   (see No Exit)

*Kean
   Reviews:
   New York Times p. 23, Jan 30, 1971
                  p. 45, Sep 1, 1971

Lizzie McKay   (see The Respectful Prostitute)

Les Mains Sales   (see Soiled Hands)

Morts sans Sepulture   (see Unburied Dead)

*Nekrassov
   Reviews:
   New York Times p. 22, Aug 20, 1957
   New Yorker 31:66, Jul 2, 1955

No Exit
   Productions:
   Adapted by Paul Bowles.   Opened November 26, 1946
      for 31 performances.
   (Off Broadway) Opened June 9, 1947 in repertory.
   (Off Broadway) Season of 1952-1953.
   (Off Broadway) Season of 1956-1957.
   (Off Broadway) Adapted by Paul Bowles.   Opened October 30,
      1967 for 8 performances.
   (Off Off Broadway) Opened February 15, 1974.
   (Off Off Broadway) Season of 1974-1975.
   (Off Off Broadway) Opened April 1975.
   (Off Off Broadway) Opened May 21, 1976.
   Reviews:
   Catholic World 164:358, Jan 1947
   Commonweal 45:229, Dec 13, 1946
   Harper's Bazaar 80:220, Dec 1946
   Nation 163:708, Dec 14, 1946
   New Republic 115:764, Dec 9, 1946
   New York Theatre Critics' Reviews 1946:241
   New York Times p. 21, Nov 27, 1946
               II, p. 3, Dec 22, 1946
                  p. 23, Aug 15, 1956
                  p. 30, Jan 16, 1962
                  p. 38, Oct 31, 1967
   New Yorker 22:69, Dec 7, 1946
   Newsweek 28:92, Dec 9, 1946
   Saturday Review 29:26-8, Dec 28, 1946

        Theatre Arts 30:641+, Nov 1946
                   31:16+, Jan 1947
                   31:70, Dec 1947
        Time 48:83, Dec 9, 1946
        Vogue 108:200, Dec 1, 1946

Putain Respectueuse   (see The Respectful Prostitute)

Red Gloves
    Productions:
        Adapted by Daniel Teradash.   Opened December 4, 1948
            for 113 performances.
    Reviews:
        Catholic World 168:322-3, Jan 1949
        Forum 111:162, Mar 1949
        Harper's Bazaar 82:92, Dec 1948
        Life 26:49+, Jan 3, 1949
        Nation 167:731-2, Dec 25, 1948
               168:19, Jan 1, 1949
        New Republic 119:28-9, Dec 20, 1948
        New York Theatre Critics' Reviews 1948:132
        New York Times p. 28, Dec 6, 1948
                       II, p. 3, Dec 12, 1948
        New York Times Magazine p. 20, Jul 1948
        New Yorker 24:57-8, Dec 11, 1948
        Newsweek 32:84, Dec 13, 1948
        Saturday Review 32:24-7, Jan 1, 1949
        School and Society 69:84-6, Jan 29, 1949
        Theatre Arts 33:18+, Jan 1949
        Time 52:69, Dec 13, 1948

    The Respectful Prostitute
        Productions:
            (Off Broadway) Opened February 9, 1948 for two weeks in
                repertory.
            Adapted by Eva Wolas.   Opened March 16, 1948 for 348
                performances.
            (Off Broadway) Opened December 1948.
            (Off Off Broadway) Opened November 5, 1975.
        Reviews:
            Catholic World 167:71, Apr 1948
            Commonweal 47:566, Mar 19, 1948
            Life 24:83-4, Mar 29, 1948
            Nation 166:257, Feb 28, 1948
            New Republic 118:29, Feb 23, 1948
            New York Times p. 12, Nov 9, 1946
                           p. 40, Nov 20, 1946
                           II, p. 4, Dec 22, 1946
                           VI, p. 21, Feb 2, 1947
                           p. 27, Feb 10, 1948
                           II, p. 1, Feb 15, 1948
                           II, p. 3, Mar 21, 1948
                           p. 21, Jan 3, 1950

New York Times p. 44, Nov 17, 1951
New Yorker 24:50+, Mar 27, 1948
Saturday Review 31:26-7, Mar 13, 1948
School and Society 67:166, Feb 28, 1948
Theatre Arts 31:45, Feb 1947
32:21, Oct 1948
32:31-2, Apr 1948
Time 51:46, Apr 5, 1948
U. N. World 1:60, Feb 1947
Vogue 111:150-51, Apr 1, 1948

Les Sequestres d'Altona   (see The Condemned of Altona)

*Soiled Hands (Les Mains Sales)
Reviews:
New York Times II, p. 1, Apr 18, 1948

Tombless Dead   (see Unburied Dead)

*Unburied Dead
Reviews:
New York Times p. 12, Nov 9, 1946
II, p. 4, Dec 22, 1946
VI, p. 21, Feb 2, 1947
Theatre Arts 31:44, Feb 1947
United Nations World 1:60-1, Feb 1947

Vicious Circle   (see No Exit)

The Victors
Productions:
(Off Broadway) Adapted by Thornton Wilder.   Opened
December 1948 in repertory.
Reviews:
Commonweal 49:352, Jan 14, 1949
Forum 111:162-3, Mar 1949
New Republic 120:19, Jan 10, 1949
New York Times p. 17, Dec 27, 1948
II, p. 1, Jan 2, 1949
II, p. 2, Jan 9, 1949
School and Society 69:85, Jan 29, 1949
Theatre Arts 31:44, Feb 1947
33:17, Mar 1949
Time 53:49, Jan 3, 1949
U. N. World 1:60-1, Feb 1947

SAUNDERS, JAMES

After Liverpool   (see Games/After Liverpool)

Games/After Liverpool
  Productions:
    (Off Off Broadway) Season of 1972-1973.
  Reviews:
    New York Times p. 33, Jan 24, 1973

Neighbors
  Productions:
    (Off Off Broadway) Opened January 13, 1969 for 2
      performances.
  Reviews:
    New York Times p. 38, Jan 15, 1969

Next Time I'll Sing to You
  Productions:
    (Off Broadway) Opened November 27, 1963 for 23 perform-
      ances.
    (Off Off Broadway) Opened March 1, 1968 for 9 performances.
    (Off Broadway) Opened October 25, 1972 for 2 performances
      in repertory.
    Opened January 2, 1974 for 2 performances.
  Reviews:
    Commonweal 79:404, Dec 27, 1963
    New York Times p. 69, Nov 28, 1963
               p. 39, Oct 26, 1972
               p. 43, Jan 3, 1974
    New Yorker 39:148+, May 25, 1963
               39:131-2, Dec 7, 1963
    Saturday Review 46:25, Dec 14, 1963

A Scent of Flowers
  Productions:
    (Off Broadway) Opened October 20, 1969 for 72 performances.
  Reviews:
    Nation 209:547+, Nov 17, 1969
    New York Theatre Critics' Reviews 1969:140
    New York Times p. 42, Oct 21, 1969
               II, p. 3, Nov 3, 1969
    New Yorker 45:128-30, Nov 1, 1969
    Newsweek 74:93, Nov 3, 1969
    Saturday Review 52:28, Nov 8, 1969

*The Travails of Sancho Panza
  Reviews:
    New York Times p. 35, Dec 20, 1969

SAVOIR, ALFRED

Banco
  Productions:
    Adapted by Clare Kummer. Opened September 20, 1922
      for 69 performances.

Reviews:
Life 80:10, Oct 12, 1922
New York Clipper 70:39, Oct 4, 1922
New York Times p. 18, Sep 21, 1922
Theatre Magazine 36:297, Nov 1922

Bluebeard's Eighth Wife
Productions:
Adapted by Charlton Andrews. Opened September 19, 1921
for 155 performances.
(Off Broadway) Opened January 26, 1936.
Reviews:
Dramatic Mirror 84:448, Sep 24, 1921
Independent 107:63, Oct 15, 1921
Life (NY) 78:18, Oct 6, 1921
Nation 112:427-8, Oct 12, 1921
New York Clipper 69:28, Sep 28, 1921
New York Times p. 12, Sep 20, 1921
Theatre Magazine 34:386-7, Dec 1921

The Grand Duchess and the Waiter
Productions:
Opened October 13, 1925 for 31 performances.
Reviews:
Bookman 62:479, Dec 1925
Life (NY) 86:22, Nov 5, 1925
New York Times p. 31, Oct 14, 1925

He
Productions:
Adapted by Chester Erskin. Opened September 21, 1931
for 40 performances.
Reviews:
Bookman 74:299, Nov 1931
Catholic World 134:209, Nov 1931
Commonweal 14:555, Oct 7, 1931
Nation 133:373-4, Oct 7, 1931
New Republic 68:207-9, Oct 7, 1931
New York Times p. 33, Sep 22, 1931
Vanity Fair 37:36, 80, Nov 1931

The Lion Tamer
Productions:
Translated by Winifred Katzin. Opened October 7, 1926
for 29 performances.
Reviews:
Life (NY) 88:19, Oct 28, 1926
Nation 123:408-9, Oct 20, 1926
New Republic 48:323-4, Nov 10, 1926
New York Times p. 26, Oct 8, 1926
VIII, p. 1, Oct 17, 1926
Theatre Arts 10:812-13, Dec 1926

SCHNITZLER, ARTHUR

<u>The Affairs of Anatol</u> (see also <u>Anatol</u>)
<u>Productions:</u>
  Opened October 14, 1912 for 72 performances.
Reviews:
  American Playwright 1:367-8, Nov 1912
  Blue Book 16:458-62, Jan 1913
  Collier's 50:18+, Nov 2, 1912
  Dramatic Mirror 68:6, Oct 16, 1912
  Everybody's 28:111, Jan 1913
  Green Book 8:818-24, Nov 1912
            9:64+, Jan 1913
  Life (NY) 60:2050, Oct 24, 1913
  Munsey 48:527, Dec 1912
  New York Dramatic News 56:19, Oct 19, 1912
  Red Book 20:497-500, Jan 1913
  Theatre Magazine 16:106+, Oct 1912
                   16:131, Nov 1912

<u>Anatol</u> (see also <u>The Affairs of Anatol</u>)
<u>Productions:</u>
  Adapted by Harley Granville-Barker. Opened January 16,
    1931 for 45 performances.
Reviews:
  Bookman 73:71, Mar 1931
  Catholic World 132:720-1, Mar 1931
  Commonweal 13:385, Feb 4, 1931
  Life (NY) 97:18, Feb 6, 1931
  Nation 132:134-5, Feb 4, 1931
  New Republic 65:323, Feb 4, 1931
  New York Times p. 23, Jan 17, 1931
  Outlook 157:190, Feb 4, 1931
  Theatre Magazine 53:25-6, Mar 1931

<u>The Big Scene</u>
<u>Productions:</u>
  Translated by Charles Henry Meltzer. Opened April 15,
    1918 in repertory (The Greenwich Village Players).
Reviews:
  New York Times p. 13, Apr 19, 1918

<u>The Call of Life</u>
<u>Productions:</u>
  English version by Dorothy Donnelly. Opened October 9,
    1925 for 19 performances.
Reviews:
  Bookman 62:478, Dec 1925
  Nation 121:494-5, Oct 28, 1925
  New Republic 44:255-6, Oct 28, 1925
  New York Times p. 10, Oct 10, 1925

The Green Cockatoo   (see also Der Grüne Kakadu)
  Productions:
    Translated by Philip Littel and George Rublee.   Opened
      April 11, 1910 for 16 performances.
    Opened October 6, 1930 in repertory.
  Reviews:
    Bookman 31:418, Jun 1910
    Dramatic Mirror 63:7, Apr 23, 1910
    New York Times p. 20, Oct 10, 1910
    Theatre Magazine 11:xxix, Jun 1910

Der Grüne Kakadu   (see also The Green Cockatoo)
  Productions:
    (Off Off Broadway) Translated and adapted by S. J. Vogel.
      Season of 1967-1968.
  No Reviews.

Literature
  Productions:
    Opened October 4, 1915 in repertory (Washington Square
      Players).
    Translated by Andre Tridon.   Opened August 30, 1916 in
      repertory (Washington Square Players).
  Reviews:
    Bookman 42:646+, Feb 1916
    Dramatic Mirror 74:8, Nov 13, 1915
    New York Times p. 13, Nov 10, 1915

Professor Bernhardi
  Productions:
    Opened March 19, 1968 in repertory for 6 performances.
  Reviews:
    Commonweal 88:144-5, Apr 19, 1968
    Nation 206:485, Apr 8, 1968
    New York Times p. 38, Mar 20, 1968

*Reigen
  Reviews:
    New Republic 130:21, Apr 5, 1954

La Ronde
  Productions:
    (Off Broadway) Season of 1959-1960.
    (Off Off Broadway) Opened January 1976.
  Reviews:
    New York Times p. 24, Jun 28, 1955
                   p. 44, May 10, 1960
                   p. 42, Dec 16, 1960
                   p. 10, Dec 31, 1960
    New Yorker 36:117, May 21, 1960
    Theatre Arts 39:80, Oct 1955
                 40:77-8+, Feb 1956

SHAFFER, ANTHONY

Sleuth
    Productions:
        Opened November 12, 1970 for 1,222 performances.
    Reviews:
        America 124:47, Jan 16, 1971
        Nation 211:572, Nov 30, 1970
        National Review 23:324, Mar 23, 1971
        New York Theatre Critics' Reviews 1970:157
        New York Times p. 25, Nov 13, 1970
                       p. 38, Nov 18, 1970
                       II, p. 18, Nov 22, 1970
                       II, p. 15, Mar 14, 1971
                       p. 23, Oct 16, 1971
                       p. 43, Sep 26, 1972
                       p. 55, Apr 5, 1973
                       p. 37, Sep 25, 1973
        New Yorker 46:103, Nov 21, 1970
        Newsweek 76:138, Nov 23, 1970
        Saturday Review 53:6+, Nov 28, 1970
        Time 95:77, Mar 30, 1970
             96:100, Nov 23, 1970

SHAFFER, PETER

*Battle of Shrivings
    Reviews:
        New York Times p. 23, Feb 7, 1970
        Time 95:77, Mar 30, 1970

Black Comedy
    Productions:
        Opened February 12, 1967 for 337 performances.
        (Off Off Broadway) Opened November 12, 1976.
    Reviews:
        Commentary 43:74-5, Jun 1967
        Life 62:70A-70B+, Mar 10, 1967
        Nation 204:285-6, Feb 27, 1967
        New York Theatre Critics' Reviews 1967:371
        New York Times p. 19, Jul 29, 1965
                       p. 42, Feb 13, 1967
                       II, p. 1, Feb 26, 1967
                       p. 58, Oct 19, 1967
        New Yorker 43:91, Feb 25, 1967
        Newsweek 69:102-3, Feb 20, 1967
        Reporter 36:50+, Mar 9, 1967
        Saturday Review 50:59, Feb 25, 1967
        Time 89:70, Feb 17, 1967
        Vogue 149:54, Mar 15, 1967

Equus
  Productions:
    Opened October 24, 1974 for (1,068) performances.
  Reviews:
    America 129:443-4, Dec 8, 1973
            131:349, Nov 30, 1974
            133:419-22, Dec 13, 1975
    Christian Century 92:1162+, Dec 17, 1975
                      94:472-6, May 18, 1977
    Commentary 59:77-8, Feb 1975
    Commonweal 102:78-9, Apr 25, 1975
    Dance Magazine 49:48-50, May 1975
    Harper's Bazaar 107:133, Oct 1974
    Nation 219:506-7, Nov 16, 1974
    National Review 27:114-5, Jan 31, 1975
    New Republic 171:18+, Dec 7, 1974
                 177:24-6, Nov 5, 1977
    New York Theatre Critics' Reviews 1974:201
    New York Times p. 11, Aug 17, 1973
                   II, p. 1, Sep 2, 1973
                   p. 50, Oct 24, 1974
                   p. 26, Oct 25, 1974
                   II, p. 1, Oct 27, 1974
                   II, p. 1, Nov 3, 1974
                   II, p. 1, Dec 18, 1974
                   VI, p. 20, Apr 13, 1975
                   p. 19, Jul 17, 1975
                   II, p. 1, Oct 5, 1975
                   p. 16, Feb 27, 1976
                   II, p. 1, Mar 7, 1976
                   II, p. 7, Mar 21, 1976
                   II, p. 5, Apr 4, 1976
                   III, p. 6, Apr 30, 1976
                   p. 23, Feb 28, 1977
    New Yorker 49:184, Nov 12, 1973
               50:123, Nov 4, 1974
    Newsweek 84:121, Nov 11, 1974
             84:60, Nov 4, 1974
             87:70, Mar 8, 1976
    Psychology Today 11:21-2, Oct 1977
    Saturday Review 2:54, Jan 25, 1975
    Sports Illustrated 42:9, Mar 3, 1975
    Time 104:119, Nov 4, 1974
         104:117+, Nov 11, 1974
    Vogue 165:136-7+, Feb 1975

Five-Finger Exercise
  Productions:
    Opened December 2, 1959 for 337 performances.
    (Off Off Broadway) Opened January 10, 1969 for 9
      performances.
  Reviews:
    America 102:428, Jan 9, 1960

Christian Century 77:16, Jan 6, 1960
Commonweal 71:395, Jan 1, 1960
Life 48:93-4+, Mar 21, 1960
New York Theatre Critics' Reviews 1959:207
New York Times II, p. 1, Aug 17, 1958
             II, p. 1, Nov 29, 1959
                p. 45, Dec 3, 1959
             II, p. 3, Dec 13, 1959
New Yorker 31:121, Sep 6, 1958
             35:100-2, Dec 12, 1959
Reporter 22:36-7, Jan 7, 1960
Saturday Review 42:24, Dec 19, 1959
Theatre Arts 44:14, Feb 1960
Time 74:77, Dec 14, 1959

The Private Ear
    Productions:
        Opened October 9, 1963 for 163 performances.
    Reviews:
        America 109:752, Dec 7, 1963
        Nation 197:306, Nov 9, 1963
        New York Theatre Critics' Reviews 1963:248
        New York Times p. 51, Oct 10, 1963
                    II, p. 1, Oct 20, 1963
                    VI, p. 108, Oct 20, 1963
        Newsweek 62:104, Oct 21, 1963
        Theatre Arts 48:65, Jan 1964
        Time 82:76+, Oct 18, 1963

The Public Eye
    Productions:
        Opened October 9, 1963 for 163 performances.
    Reviews:
        America 109:752, Dec 7, 1963
        New York Theatre Critics' Reviews 1963:248
        New York Times p. 51, Oct 10, 1963
                    II, p. 1, Oct 20, 1963
                    VI, p. 108, Oct 20, 1963
        Newsweek 62:104, Oct 21, 1963
        Saturday Review 46:32, Oct 26, 1963
        Theatre Arts 48:65, Jan 1964
        Time 82:76+, Oct 18, 1963

Royal Hunt of the Sun
    Productions:
        Opened October 26, 1965 for 261 performances.
    Reviews:
        America 113:648-9, Nov 20, 1965
        Commonweal 83:215, Nov 19, 1965
        Dance Magazine 39:138-9, Dec 1965
        Life 59:134-5+, Dec 10, 1965
        Nation 201:397, Nov 22, 1965
        National Review 18:37, Jan 11, 1966

New Republic 153:45-6, Nov 27, 1965
New York Theatre Critics' Reviews 1965:293
New York Times p. 40, Jul 8, 1964
                  II, p. 3, Oct 24, 1965
                  p. 36, Oct 27, 1965
                  II, p. 1, Nov 14, 1965
                  p. 50, Jun 6, 1966
                  p. 53, Jun 7, 1966
New Yorker 41:115, Nov 6, 1965
Newsweek 66:96, Nov 8, 1965
Saturday Review 48:31, May 29, 1965
                 48:71, Nov 13, 1965
                 49:72, Nov 19, 1966
Time 86:77, Nov 5, 1965
Vogue 144:112, Oct 1, 1964

The White Liars
    Productions:
    (Off Off Broadway) Opened May 15, 1976.
    No Reviews.

White Lies
    Productions:
    Opened February 12, 1967 for 337 performances.
    Reviews:
    Nation 204:286, Feb 27, 1967
    New York Theatre Critics' Reviews 1967:371
    New York Times p. 42, Feb 13, 1967
                     II, p. 1, Feb 26, 1967
                     p. 58, Oct 19, 1967
    New Yorker 43:91, Feb 25, 1967
    Reporter 36:50+, Mar 9, 1967
    Saturday Review 50:59, Feb 25, 1967

SHAIRP, MORDAUNT

The Green Bay Tree
    Productions:
    Opened October 20, 1933 for 166 performances.
    Opened February 1, 1951 for 20 performances.
    (Off Off Broadway) Season of 1975-1976.
    Reviews:
    Catholic World 138:339-40, Dec 1933
    Commonweal 53:494, Feb 23, 1951
    Literary Digest 116:19, Nov 4, 1933
    Nation 137:548+, Nov 4, 1933
    New Outlook 162:46, Dec 1933
    New Republic 77:17-19, Nov 15, 1933
    New York Theatre Critics' Reviews 1951:368
    New York Times IX, p. 3, Nov 12, 1933
                     p. 21, Mar 12, 1934

New York Times IV, p. 7, Aug 5, 1934
           p. 18, Feb 2, 1951
New Yorker 26:60, Feb 10, 1951
Newsweek 37:72, Feb 12, 1951
Player's Magazine 10:13+, Nov-Dec 1933
Review of Reviews 89:39, Feb 1934
Saturday Review 34:24-6, Feb 24, 1951
Stage 11:20-21, Dec 1933
Theatre Arts 17:335+, May 1933
         17:912+, Dec 1933
Time 22:30, Oct 30, 1933
     57:55, Feb 12, 1951
Vanity Fair 41:41, Jan 1934

The Offense
Productions:
    Opened November 16, 1925 for four performances.
Reviews:
    New York Times p. 25, Nov 16, 1925

SHAW, GEORGE BERNARD

Admirable Bashville
Productions:
    (Off Broadway) 1955-1956.
Reviews:
    Catholic World 183:150, May 1956
    New York Times p. 38, Feb 21, 1956
    Saturday Review 39:26, Mar 17, 1956

Androcles and the Lion
Productions:
    Opened January 27, 1915 in repertory.
    Opened November 23, 1925 for 68 performances.
    Opened December 16, 1938 for 104 performances.
    Opened December 19, 1946 for 40 performances.
    (Off Broadway) Opened November 21, 1961 for 48
       performances.
Reviews:
    American Playwright 4:49-52, Feb 1915
    Book News 33:353-4, Mar 1915
    Catholic World 100:577-9, Feb 1915
              148:601, Feb 1939
              164:456, Feb 1947
    Collier's 52:14, Oct 4, 1913
    Commonweal 45:325, Jan 10, 1947
    Current Opinion 55:330-1, Nov 1913
              57:244-8, Oct 1914
    Dramatic Mirror 73:8, Feb 3, 1915
    Green Book 13:767-8, Apr 1915
           13:695-6, Apr 1915
    Independent 116:48, Jan 9, 1946

Life (NY) 65:240, Feb 11, 1915
Life 21:109, Dec 23, 1946
Nation 100:150, Feb 4, 1915
      121:688-9, Dec 9, 1925
      164:25, Jan 4, 1947
New Republic 1:25, Jan 30, 1915
      116:42, Jan 6, 1947
New York Theatre Critics' Reviews 1946:217
New York Times p. 9, Jan 8, 1915
      p. 28, Nov 24, 1925
      II, p. 1, Nov 29, 1925
      p. 10, Dec 17, 1938
      p. 29, Dec 20, 1946
      II, p. 1, Dec 29, 1946
      p. 8, Feb 22, 1958
      p. 24, Nov 22, 1961
      p. 47, Jun 27, 1968
New Yorker 22:36+, Dec 28, 1946
      37:119, Dec 2, 1961
Newsweek 28:71, Dec 30, 1946
North American Review 201:439-42, Mar 1915
Saturday Review 30:24-7, Jan 11, 1947
School and Society 65:251, Apr 5, 1947
Theatre Arts 10:8-10, Jan 1926
      31:17-18, Feb 1947
Theatre Magazine 21:110-111, Mar 1915
      43:16-17, Feb 1926
Time 32:25, Dec 26, 1938
      48:34, Dec 30, 1946
Vogue 67:130, Jan 15, 1926

Annajanska, the Bolshevik Empress
  Productions:
    (Off Off Broadway) Season of 1967-1968.
    (Off Off Broadway) Opened February 1975.
    (Off Off Broadway) Opened February 1977.
  No Reviews.

The Apple Cart
  Productions:
    Opened February 24, 1930 for 88 performances.
    Opened October 18, 1956 for 124 performances.
    (Off Off Broadway) Opened February 8, 1977.
  Reviews:
    America 96:359, Dec 22, 1956
    Catholic World 131:78-9, Apr 1930
        184:225, Dec 1956
    Christian Century 73:1328, Nov 14, 1956
    Commonweal 10:497-8, Sep 18, 1929
        11:535, Mar 12, 1930
    Drama 20:6-8, Oct 1929
    English Journal 61:670-2+, May 1972
    Life (NY) 95:18, Mar 14, 1930

Literary Digest 101:25, Jun 8, 1929
102:19-20, Jul 20, 1929
104:23-4, Mar 15, 1930
Nation 130:338, Mar 19, 1930
183:374, Nov 3, 1956
New Republic 62:99, Mar 12, 1930
135:21-2, Dec 3, 1956
New York Theatre Critics' Reviews 1956:258
New York Times p. 30, Feb 25, 1930
p. 29, May 8, 1953
VI, p. 28, Sep 16, 1956
VI, p. 32, Oct 7, 1956
p. 23, Oct 19, 1956
II, p. 1, Oct 28, 1956
New Yorker 29:66+, Jul 18, 1953
32:117-18, Oct 27, 1956
Newsweek 48:76, Oct 29, 1956
Outlook 154:429, Mar 12, 1930
Review of Reviews 81:144-5, Apr 1930
Saturday Review 36:24, Aug 1, 1953
39:24, Nov 10, 1956
Theatre Arts 13:729-33, Oct 1929
14:370, May 1930
Time 68:98+, Oct 29, 1956
Vogue 75:132, Apr 12, 1930
Yale Review 20:815-16, Summer 1931

Arms and the Man
Productions:
Opened May 3, 1915 in repertory.
Opened September 14, 1925 for 180 performances.
Opened October 19, 1950 for 110 performances.
(Off Broadway) Season of 1956-1957.
(Off Broadway) Opened April 27, 1964 for 23 performances.
(Off Broadway) Opened January 14, 1966 for 10 matinees
(ANTA).
(Off Broadway) Opened June 22, 1967 for 189 performances.
(Off Off Broadway) Opened October 17, 1974.
(Off Off Broadway) Opened October 31, 1975.
(Off Off Broadway) Opened October 27, 1976.
Reviews:
America 117:63, Jul 15, 1967
Bookman 62:321, Nov 1925
Catholic World 172:227, Dec 1950
Christian Science Monitor Magazine p. 8, Oct 28, 1950
Commonweal 53:121, Nov 10, 1950
Dramatic Mirror 73:8, May 5, 1915
Dramatist 17:1291-2, Jan 1926
Nation 100:545, May 13, 1915
121:364, Sep 30, 1925
New Republic 3:18, May 8, 1915
123:20, Nov 13, 1950
New York Theatre Critics' Reviews 1950:235

New York Times p. 15, May 4, 1915
              IX, p. 1, Oct 4, 1925
              II, p. 1, Oct 1, 1944
              p. 34, Oct 20, 1950
              p. 39, Oct 2, 1956
              p. 41, Apr 28, 1964
              p. 32, Jun 24, 1965
              p. 44, Jun 23, 1967
              p. 18, Jul 10, 1970
              p. 36, Aug 26, 1970
              p. 19, Aug 20, 1973
Newsweek 36:78, Oct 30, 1950
Theatre Magazine 21:280-1, Jun 1915

Augustus Does His Bit
Productions:
  Opened March 12, 1919 for five performances.
Reviews:
  Current Opinion 62:405, Jun 1917
  Life (NY) 73:504, Mar 27, 1919
  New York Times p. 9, Nov 13, 1919
              p. 8, Feb 22, 1958

Back to Methuselah
Productions:
  Opened February 27, 1922 for 25 performances.
  Two act version by Arnold Moss. Opened March 26, 1958
    for 29 performances.
  (Off Broadway) Season of 1959-1960 as A Glimpse of the
    Domesticity of Franklin Barnabas.
  (Off Off Broadway) Opened March 19, 1977.
Reviews:
  Arts and Decoration 16:426-7, Apr 1922
  Bookman 53:550, Aug 1921
          55:279, Aug 1922
  Catholic World 187:226-7, Jan 1958
  Century 102:631-5, Aug 1921
  Dial 72:444, Apr 1922
  Everybody's 46:141-8, Jun 1922
  Fortune 120:827-34, Nov 1923
  Independent 108:310, Mar 25, 1922
  Life (NY) 79:18, Mar 16, 1922
  Nation 114:323, Mar 15, 1922
       186:349, Apr 19, 1958
  New Republic 30:80-1, Mar 15, 1922
            38:21, Apr 1958
  New York Clipper 70:20, Mar 22, 1922
  New York Theatre Critics' Reviews 1958:322
  New York Times p. 8, Jan 23, 1922
              IV, p. 1, Feb 5, 1922
              p. 11, Mar 7, 1922
              p. 11, Mar 14, 1922
              II, p. 1, Mar 23, 1958

New York Times p. 41, Mar 27, 1958
II, p. 1, Apr 6, 1958
p. 24, Mar 7, 1960
p. 46, Aug 31, 1969
Theatre Arts 31:35-6, May 1947
38:24-5, Jun 1954
Theatre Magazine 35:290+, May 1922
Time 94:52, Aug 15, 1969
Yale Review 11:429, Jan 1922

The Bolshevik Empress (see also Annajanska, the Bolshevik
Empress)
Productions:
(Off Off Broadway) Opened February 1975.
No Reviews.

Buoyant Billions
Productions:
(Off Broadway) Season of 1959-1960.
Reviews:
America 101:438, Jun 13, 1959
New York Times p. 58, Aug 14, 1949
p. 6, Aug 13, 1955
p. 32, May 27, 1959
p. 30, Jun 3, 1959
II, p. 1, Jun 7, 1959
New Yorker 35:120+, Jun 6, 1959

Caesar and Cleopatra
Productions:
Opened in the fall of 1913 in repertory (Forbes-Robertson).
Opened April 13, 1925 for 48 performances.
Opened December 21, 1949 for 149 performances.
Opened December 19, 1951 for 67 performances.
Opened February 24, 1977 for 12 performances.
Reviews:
American Mercury 5:244, Jan 1925
Catholic World 170:384, Feb 1950
174:389-90, Feb 1952
Christian Science Monitor Magazine p. 5, Mar 4, 1950
Collier's 128:21+, Dec 22, 1951
Commonweal 51:390, Jan 13, 1950
55:349, Jan 11, 1952
Dial 78:525, Jun 1925
Dramatic Mirror 70:7, Oct 22, 1913
Life 28:46-8, Jan 30, 1950
31:82-4, Dec 17, 1951
Life (NY) 62:791, Nov 6, 1913
85:20, Apr 30, 1925
Nation 120:500, Apr 29, 1925
169:650-1, Dec 31, 1949
174:17-18, Jan 5, 1952
New Republic 42:262-3, Apr 29, 1925

New Republic 122:21, Jan 2, 1950
    126:22, Jan 21, 1952
New York Theatre Critics' Reviews 1949:193
    1951:132
    1977:332
New York Times p. 27, Apr 14, 1925
    II, p. 3, Dec 18, 1949
    p. 28, Dec 22, 1949
    II, p. 1, Jan 8, 1950
    p. 21, Feb 21, 1950
    p. 32, May 11, 1951
    II, p. 1, Dec 30, 1951
    II, p. 1, Jan 6, 1952
    p. 18, Aug 1, 1963
    p. 12, Jul 17, 1971
    II, p. 1, Jan 2, 1977
    III, p. 4, Feb 25, 1977
    III, p. 23, May 5, 1977
New York Times Magazine p. 16, Dec 18, 1949
New Yorker 25:38+, Dec 31, 1949
    27:50, Dec 29, 1957
    53:65, Mar 14, 1977
Newsweek 35:48, Jan 2, 1950
    38:53, Dec 31, 1957
Saturday Review 33:26-8, Jan 14, 1950
    35:24-7, Jan 12, 1952
    4:46-7, Mar 5, 1977
School and Society 71:215-17, Apr 8, 1950
    75:104-6, Feb 16, 1952
Theatre Arts 34:8, Mar 1950
    35:10-11, Dec 1957
Time 55:52, Jan 2, 1950
    58:44-7, Dec 31, 1951
    109:71, Mar 7, 1977

Candida
Productions:
Opened May 18, 1915 in repertory.
Opened March 22, 1922 for 43 performances.
Opened December 12, 1924 for 143 performances.
Opened November 9, 1925 for 24 performances.
Opened March 10, 1937 for 50 performances.
(Off Broadway) Opened January 16, 1938 in repertory.
Opened April 27, 1942 for 27 performances.
Opened April 3, 1946 for 24 performances.
(Off Broadway) Opened October 1951.
Opened April 22, 1952 for 31 performances.
(Off Broadway) Season of 1955-56.
(Off Broadway) Opened December 7, 1963 for eight
    performances.
(Off Off Broadway) Season of 1968-1969.
Opened April 6, 1970 for 6 performances.
(Off Off Broadway) Opened May 29, 1976.

(Off Off Broadway) Opened March 23, 1977.
Reviews:
American Mercury 4:244, Feb 1925
Bookman 55:388, Jun 1922
Canadian Magazine 64:74-5, Apr 1925
Catholic World 145:211-13, May 1937
            155:338-40, Jun 1942
            163:167, May 1946
Commonweal 25:612, Mar 26, 1937
          36:135-6, May 29, 1942
          56:140, May 16, 1952
Delineator 111:38, Oct 1927
Dramatic Mirror 73:8, May 26, 1915
Dramatist 2:164, Apr 1911
Fortnightly Review 177:122-7, Feb 1952
Life 19:65-6, Aug 20, 1945
Literary Digest 84:28-9, Feb 7, 1925
         123:28, Mar 20, 1937
Living Age 274:781, Sep 28, 1912
McCalls 90:28, Mar 1963
Nation 144:361-2, Mar 27, 1937
     162:487, Apr 20, 1945
New Republic 90:322, Apr 21, 1937
New York Clipper 70:20, Mar 29, 1922
New York Theatre Critics' Reviews 1942:301
                                  1946:412
                                  1952:307
                                  1970:307
New York Times p. 13, May 21, 1915
              p. 11, Nov 23, 1922
              p. 12, Dec 13, 1924
              VIII, p. 1, Dec 21, 1924
              p. 9, Dec 31, 1924
              p. 16, Jul 24, 1925
              p. 23, Nov 10, 1925
              p. 20, Nov 11, 1937
              XI, p. 1, Nov 21, 1937
              p. 13, Aug 31, 1938
              p. 24, Apr 28, 1942
              p. 16, Aug 2, 1945
              p. 25, Aug 7, 1945
              p. 33, Apr 4, 1946
              II, p. 1, Apr 14, 1946
              p. 44, Dec 4, 1946
              p. 39, Apr 2, 1952
              p. 23, Apr 23, 1952
              p. 14, Feb 9, 1957
              p. 39, Feb 3, 1969
              p. 41, Apr 7, 1970
              XXII, p. 14, May 29, 1977
New Yorker 21:36, Aug 18, 1945
          28:68, May 3, 1952
          46:79, Apr 18, 1970

Newsweek 9:22, Mar 20, 1937
        19:42+, May 25, 1942
        26:89, Aug 20, 1945
        27:84, Apr 15, 1946
        39:94, May 5, 1952
Saturday Review 29:28-30, May 4, 1946
Stage 14:78, Apr 1937
Theatre Arts 21:344, May 1937
        26:421-2, Jul 1942
Theatre Magazine 35:374, 379, Jun 1922
        40:64, Feb 1925
Time 39:40, May 11, 1942
        47:91, Apr 15, 1946
        59:54, May 5, 1952

Captain Brassbound's Conversion

Productions:
    Opened March 29, 1916 in repertory.
    Opened December 27, 1950 for 15 performances.
    Opened April 17, 1972 for 16 performances.
Reviews:
    Catholic World 172:388, Feb 1951
    Christian Science Monitor Magazine p. 6, Jan 6, 1951
    Commonweal 53:374, Jan 19, 1951
    Dramatic Mirror 75:8, Apr 8, 1916
    Green Book 15:978, 982, Jun 1916
    Harper's Weekly 62:398, Apr 15, 1916
    Nation 102:392, Apr 6, 1916
        172:18, Jan 6, 1951
    New Republic 6:269, Apr 8, 1916
        118:32, Jan 5, 1948
    New York Theatre Critics' Reviews 1950:157
                            1972:311
    New York Times p. 11, Mar 30, 1916
        II, p. 1, Apr 2, 1916
        p. 21, Dec 28, 1950
        p. 13, Feb 20, 1971
        p. 35, Mar 20, 1971
        p. 67, Mar 19, 1972
        p. 55, Apr 18, 1972
        II, p. 1, Apr 23, 1972
    New Yorker 48:103, Apr 29, 1972
    Newsweek 31:68, Jan 5, 1948
        37:67, Jan 8, 1951
    School and Society 73:101-2, Feb 17, 1951
    Theatre Arts 35:14, Mar 1951
    Theatre Magazine 23:273, May 1916
        51:71, Jan 5, 1948
        57:30, Jan 8, 1951
    Time 99:53, May 1, 1972

The Dark Lady of the Sonnets

Productions:

(Off Broadway) Season of 1959-1960.
(Off Off Broadway) Opened February 1975.
Reviews:
    Catholic World 183:151, May 1956
    New York Times p. 38, Feb 21, 1956
                II, p. 1, Mar 4, 1956
                p. 13, Aug 21, 1959
                p. 48, Dec 15, 1961
    Saturday Review 39:26, Mar 17, 1956

The Devil's Disciple
    Productions:
        Opened April 23, 1923 for 64 performances.
        Opened January 25, 1950 for 127 performances.
        (Off Broadway) Opened January 4, 1963 for nine performances.
        (Off Off Broadway) Opened September 11, 1975.
        (Off Off Broadway) Opened November 6, 1975.
    Reviews:
        America 116:880, Jun 24, 1967
               123:104, Aug 22, 1970
        Catholic World 170:468, Mar 1950
        Christian Science Monitor Magazine p. 5+, Mar 4, 1950
        Commonweal 51:535-6, Feb 24, 1950
        Dial 75:100, Jul 1923
        Life 28:53-4+, Mar 6, 1950
        Literary Digest 106:16, Sep 27, 1930
        Nation 170:114, Feb 4, 1950
              116:578, May 16, 1923
        New Republic 34:299-300, May 9, 1923
               122:20, Feb 27, 1950
        New York Clipper 71:14, Apr 25, 1923
        New York Theatre Critics' Reviews 1950:344
        New York Times p. 24, Apr 24, 1923
                p. 20, Sep 11, 1941
                p. 23, Jan 26, 1950
                II, p. 1, Feb 5, 1950
                p. 34, Oct 22, 1953
                p. 48, Jun 30, 1970
                p. 32, Jul 7, 1971
                II, p. 1, Aug 18, 1974
                II, p. 5, Oct 19, 1975
        School and Society 71:215-17, Apr 8, 1950
        Theatre Arts 34:13, Apr 1950
        Theatre Magazine 38:17, 20, Jul 1923
        Time 55:66, Feb 6, 1950

The Doctor's Dilemma
    Productions:
        Opened March 26, 1915 in repertory.
        Opened November 21, 1927 for 115 performances.
        Opened March 11, 1941 for 121 performances.
        (Off Broadway) Season of 1954-1955.
        Opened January 11, 1955 for 48 performances.

(Off Off Broadway) Opened September 16, 1976.
Reviews:
Bookman 41:279, May 1915
Book News 33:453, May 1915
Catholic World 153:216, May 1941
                180:468-9, Mar 1955
Commonweal 61:524-5, Feb 18, 1955
Current Literature 50:419, Apr 1911
Dramatic Mirror 73:8, Mar 31, 1915
Green Book 13:1045-8, Jun 1915
Harpers' Bazaar 75:54, Mar 15, 1941
Life (NY) 65:624, Apr 8, 1915
         90:21, Dec 15, 1927
Life 10:82-4, May 5, 1941
Nation 92:325, Mar 30, 1911
      100:364, Apr 1, 1915
      125:690, Dec 14, 1927
      152:331, Mar 22, 1941
      180:107, Jan 29, 1957
      203:427-8, Oct 24, 1966
New Republic 2:264, Apr 10, 1915
        53:96-7, Dec 14, 1927
        104:404, Mar 24, 1941
        132:22, Feb 7, 1955
New York Theatre Critics' Reviews 1941:364
                             1955:397
New York Times p. 11, Mar 27, 1915
           p. 33, Nov 22, 1927
           X, p. 1, Dec 4, 1927
           p. 26, Feb 18, 1941
           p. 18, Mar 12, 1941
           IX, p. 1, Mar 30, 1941
           IX, p. 5, Dec 14, 1941
           VIII, p. 1, Mar 15, 1942
           p. 22, Jan 12, 1955
           II, p. 1, Jan 23, 1955
           p. 37, Jun 24, 1969
New Yorker 17:36, Mar 22, 1941
Newsweek 17:70, Mar 24, 1941
Outlook 147:532, Dec 28, 1927
Saturday Review 4:372, Dec 3, 1927
          38:24, Jan 29, 1955
Theatre Arts 12:94-6, Feb 1928
        25:327-9, May 1941
        39:92, Mar 1955
Theatre Magazine 21:228, May 1915
            47:38, 40, Feb 1928
Time 37:43, Mar 24, 1941
Vogue 71:120, Jan 15, 1928

Don Juan in Hell (Act III of Man and Superman)
Productions:
Opened April 6, 1952 for 105 performances.

(Off Broadway) Season of 1960-1961.
(Off Broadway) Opened June 19, 1962 for 17 performances.
Opened January 15, 1973 for 24 performances.
(Off Off Broadway) Opened June 5, 1974.
(Off Off Broadway) Opened September 1974.
(Off Off Broadway) Opened September 18, 1975.
(Off Off Broadway) Opened May 1976.
Reviews:
Nation 216:186, Feb 5, 1973
New York Theatre Critics' Reviews 1952:193
1973:385
New York Times p. 29, Oct 11, 1946
p. 37, Jun 8, 1950
II, p. 3, Oct 21, 1951
p. 34, Oct 23, 1951
II, p. 1, Nov 4, 1951
II, p. 3, Jan 6, 1952
II, p. 1, Jun 1, 1952
p. 47, Oct 4, 1960
p. 33, Jan 16, 1973
New York Times Magazine p. 21, Nov 4, 1951
Theatre Arts 36:50-66, Apr 1952
Time 58:63-4+, Nov 5, 1951
101:61, Jan 29, 1973

*Evening with Shaw (Consists of Far-Fetched Fables, Getting
Married, Man and Superman, and Buoyant Billions)
Reviews:
New York Times p. 6, Aug 13, 1955

Fanny's First Play
Productions:
Opened September 16, 1912 for 256 performances.
Reviews:
American Playwright 1:321-4, Oct 1912
Blue Book 16:478-80, Jan 1913
Book News 32:178-9, Nov 1913
Collier's 50:24+, Oct 5, 1912
Dramatic Mirror 68:7, Sep 18, 1912
Dramatist 4:245-6, Apr 1913
Everybody's 27:808-12, Dec 1912
Green Book 8:932-4, 987, Dec 1912
Independent 73:1095-6, Nov 7, 1912
Leslie's Weekly 115:497, Nov 14, 1912
Life (NY) 60:1859, Sep 26, 1912
McClure's 40:64-6, Mar 1913
Munsey 48:352-3, Nov 1912
National Magazine 40:186-90, May 1914
New York Dramatic News 56:11-12, Sep 27, 1912
New York Times p. 22, Sep 5, 1956
II, p. 3, Aug 19, 1973
North American Review 200:147-52, Jul 1914
Red Book 19:958, Sep 1912
Theatre Magazine 16:15, Oct 1912

*Far-Fetched Fables   (see also Evening with Shaw)
    Reviews:
        Christian Science Monitor Magazine p. 7, Sep 16, 1950
        New York Times p. 15, Aug 11, 1950
                        p. 39, Sep 7, 1950
        New Yorker 26:58, Sep 30, 1950

Geneva
    Productions:
        Opened January 30, 1940 for 15 performances.
    Reviews:
        Canadian Forum 19:288, Dec 1939
        Catholic World 150:729, Mar 1940
        Commonweal 31:367, Feb 16, 1940
        New York Theatre Critics' Reviews 1940:403
        New York Times IX, p. 1, Jan 25, 1940
                        p. 14, Jan 30, 1940
                        p. 15, Jan 31, 1940
        Newsweek 15:38, Feb 12, 1940
        Nineteenth Century 125:88-90, Feb 1939
                        126:449-57, Oct 1939
        Theatre Arts 23:100, Feb 1939
                    24:238, Apr 1940
        Time 34:59-60, Nov 13, 1939

Getting Married
    Productions:
        Opened November 6, 1916 for 112 performances.
        Opened March 30, 1931 for 48 performances.
        Opened May 7, 1951 for 16 performances.
        (Off Broadway) Season of 1952-1953.
        (Off Broadway) Season of 1959-1960.
        (Off Off Broadway) Opened January 15, 1970 for 12 perform-
            ances.
    Reviews:
        Bookman 73:411, Jun 1931
        Book News 35:206, Jan 1917
        Catholic World 133:207, May 1931
        Commonweal 13:666, Apr 15, 1931
                    54:189, Jun 1, 1951
        Drama 21:9, May 1931
        Dramatic Mirror 76:4, 7, Nov 18, 1916
        Hearst 32:38, 79, Jul 1917
        Green Book 17:5, Jan 1917
        Life (NY) 68:904-5, Nov 23, 1916
                97:20, Apr 17, 1931
        Nation 92:325, Mar 30, 1911
                103:470, Nov 16, 1916
                132:430, Apr 15, 1931
        New Republic 10:77, Feb 17, 1917
                    66:236, Apr 15, 1931
        New York Dramatic News 63:11, Nov 11, 1916
        New York Theatre Critics' Reviews 1951:268

New York Times p. 9, Nov 7, 1916
          II, p. 6, Nov 12, 1916
          p. 25, Mar 31, 1931
          p. 41, Jun 14, 1950
          p. 28, May 14, 1951
          p. 6, Aug 13, 1955
          p. 18, Jun 5, 1959
          II, p. 1, Jun 7, 1959
          p. 46, Jan 20, 1970
New Yorker 35:84, Jun 13, 1959
North American Review 203:925, Dec 1916
          204:925-7, Dec 1917
Outlook 157:538, Apr 1915
Theatre Magazine 24:358, Jan 1916
          25:32, 56, Jan 1917
Vogue 77:100, 102, Jun 15, 1931

A Glimpse of the Domesticity of Franklin Barnabas (see Back to Methuselah)

The Great Catherine
Productions:
   Opened December 18, 1916 in repertory (Gertrude Kingston).
   Opened May 13, 1936 for three performances.
Reviews:
   Collier's 58:38, Jan 27, 1917
   Dramatic Mirror 76:7, Nov 25, 1916
   Everybody's 32:193-212, Feb 1915
   New York Times p. 9, Nov 15, 1916
              p. 28, May 14, 1936

Heartbreak House
Productions:
   Opened November 10, 1920 for 125 performances.
   Opened April 29, 1938 for 48 performances.
   (Off Broadway) Opened March 1950 in repertory.
   (Off Broadway) Season of 1955-1956.
   Opened October 18, 1959 for 112 performances.
   (Off Off Broadway) Opened July 13, 1972.
   (Off Off Broadway) Opened January 9, 1975.
   (Off Off Broadway) Opened March 6, 1976.
   (Off Broadway) Opened October 1, 1976 for 23 performances.
   (Off Off Broadway) Opened November 11, 1976.
Reviews:
   America 102:218, Nov 14, 1959
   Arts and Decoration 14:213, Jan 1921
   Bookman 52:565-6, Feb 1921
   Catholic World 147:344-5, Jun 1938
              171:148, May 1950
   Christian Century 76:1345, Nov 18, 1959
   Commonweal 28:77, May 14, 1938
   Current Opinion 67:228-32, Oct 1919
              70:207-9, Feb 1921

Dramatic Mirror 181:947, Nov 20, 1920
Dramatist 12:1041-2, Jan 1921
Independent 104:289, Nov 27, 1920
Hearst 39:41-3+, Feb 1921
Life (NY) 76:1100, Dec 9, 1920
Living Age 334:733-5, Apr 15, 1928
Nation 111:623, Dec 1920
    146:556-7, May 14, 1938
    177:152, Aug 22, 1953
    189:338, Nov 2, 1959
New Republic 95:130, Jun 8, 1938
    141:20-1, Nov 2, 1959
New York Clipper 68:32, Nov 17, 1920
New York Theatre Critics' Reviews 1959:258
New York Times p. 11, Nov 11, 1920
    VI, p. 1, Nov 21, 1920
    p. 18, Apr 30, 1938
    X, p. 1, May 8, 1938
    p. 33, Mar 22, 1950
    VI, p. 86, Sep 20, 1959
    p. 37, Oct 19, 1959
    II, p. 1, Oct 25, 1959
    p. 14, Jun 8, 1963
    p. 24, Jun 28, 1963
    II, p. 1, Aug 27, 1967
    p. 9, Jul 6, 1968
    p. 34, Jul 1, 1975
    p. 23, Mar 2, 1976
    p. 13, Nov 13, 1976
New Yorker 35:131, Oct 31, 1959
Newsweek 54:97-8, Nov 2, 1959
Outlook 127:131, Jan 26, 1921
Reporter 21:33-5, Nov 26, 1959
Saturday Review 42:26, Oct 31, 1959
Theatre Arts 43:85+, Dec 1959
Theatre Magazine 33:31-2, Jan 1921
Time 74:32, Nov 2, 1959
Weekly Review 3:540-41, Dec 1, 1920

How He Lied to Her Husband
  Productions:
    Opened December 18, 1916 in repertory (Gertrude Kingston).
    (Off Off Broadway) Season of 1970-1971.
    (Off Broadway) Opened August 1, 1972 in repertory.
    (Off Off Broadway) Opened October 18, 1973.
    (Off Off Broadway) Opened February 1975.
    (Off Off Broadway) Opened May 15, 1976.
    (Off Off Broadway) Opened February 1977.
    (Off Off Broadway) Opened May 6, 1977.
  Reviews:
    New York Times p. 27, May 23, 1956

In Good King Charles' Golden Days
   Productions:
     (Off Broadway) Season of 1956-1957.
   Reviews:
     Catholic World 185:387, Aug 1957
     Nation 185:99, Aug 31, 1957
     New York Times IX, p. 1, May 19, 1940
                p. 46, Dec 11, 1952
                p. 16, Jan 25, 1957
                II, p. 1, Feb 3, 1957
     Newsweek 49:78, Feb 4, 1957
     Saturday Review 40:25, Feb 9, 1957

John Bull's Other Island
   Productions:
     Opened February 10, 1948 for eight performances.
   Reviews:
     Catholic World 167:71, Apr 1948
     Commonweal 47:494, Feb 27, 1948
     Nation 166:219-21, Feb 21, 1948
     New Republic 118:24, Mar 1, 1948
     New York Theatre Critics' Reviews 1948:351
     New York Times p. 33, Feb 11, 1948
                 p. 73, May 16, 1971
                 p. 31, May 22, 1971
     New Yorker 23:53, Feb 21, 1948
     Newsweek 31:80, Feb 23, 1948
     Time 51:56, Feb 23, 1948

Major Barbara
   Productions:
     Opened December 9, 1915 in repertory.
     Opened November 19, 1928 for 84 performances.
     (Off Broadway) Opened February 1951 in repertory.
     (Off Broadway) Season of 1954-1955.
     Opened October 30, 1956 for 232 performances.
     (Off Off Broadway) Opened June 1976.
   Reviews:
     America 96:358, Dec 22, 1956
     Bookman 42:648-50, Feb 1916
            63:32-6, Mar 1916
     Catholic World 184:305, Jan 1957
     Christian Century 74:658, May 22, 1957
     Collier's 57:23, May 13, 1916
     Commonweal 60:558, Sep 10, 1954
            65:228-9, Dec 14, 1956
     Current Opinion 60:172-5, Mar 1916
     Dial 86:169-70, Feb 1929
     Dramatic Mirror 74:8, Dec 18, 1915
     Green Book 15:311-13, Sep 1916
     Harper's Bazaar 75:55, Mar 15, 1941
     Harper's Weekly 61:611, Dec 25, 1915
     International 10:28-9, Jan 1916

Life (NY) 66:1242-3, Dec 23, 1915
92:13, Dec 24, 1928
Life 41:123-4, Dec 10, 1956
Literary Digest 52:438-9, Feb 19, 1916
Nation 101:725-6, Dec 16, 1915
127:666-7, Dec 12, 1928
183:439, Nov 27, 1956
New Republic 5:175, Dec 18, 1915
135:22-3, Dec 3, 1956
136:23, May 20, 1957
New York Dramatic News 62:17, Dec 18, 1915
New York Theatre Critics' Reviews 1956:233
New York Times p. 13, Jan 7, 1915
VII, p. 6, Jan 10, 1915
X, p. 1, Dec 2, 1928
p. 10, Feb 24, 1951
p. 23, Jun 30, 1954
p. 27, Oct 31, 1956
p. 35, Jun 29, 1972
II, p. 1, Jul 9, 1972
p. 52, Nov 11, 1976
New Yorker 32:114+, Nov 10, 1957
Newsweek 48:54-5, Nov 12, 1956
North American Review 203:136-8, Jan 1916
Review of Reviews 79:152-4, Jan 1929
Saturday Review 39:28, Nov 17, 1956
Theatre Arts 41:21-2, Jan 1957
Theatre Magazine 23:5+, Jan 1916
Time 68:72, Nov 12, 1956
100:54, Jul 24, 1972
Vogue 128:118, Sep 15, 1956

Man and Superman
  Productions:
    Opened September 30, 1912 for 32 performances.
    Opened October 8, 1947 for 295 performances.
    Opened May 16, 1949 for 16 performances.
    Opened April 6, 1952 (see Don Juan in Hell).
    (Off Broadway) Season of 1952-1953.
    (Off Broadway) Season of 1960-1961.
    (Off Broadway) Opened December 6, 1964 for 100 perform-
      ances.
    (Off Off Broadway) Season of 1967-1968.
    (Off Off Broadway) Season of 1969-1970.
    (Off Off Broadway) Season of 1970-1971.
    (Off Off Broadway) Opened February 18, 1977.
  Reviews:
    Catholic World 166:169, Nov 1947
    Commonweal 47:41, Oct 24, 1947
    Everybody's 27:812-13, Dec 1912
    Life 23:107-8+, Oct 27, 1947
      58:10, Jan 15, 1965
    Munsey 48:528, Dec 1912

Nation 165:454, Oct 25, 1947
    177:158, Aug 22, 1953
    199:522-3, Dec 28, 1964
New Republic 117:38, Oct 20, 1947
    152:33, Jan 30, 1965
New York Theatre Critics' Reviews 1947:308
New York Times II, p. 1, Oct 5, 1947
    II, p. 3, Oct 5, 1947
    p. 31, Oct 9, 1947
    II, p. 1, Oct 19, 1947
    II, p. 3, May 8, 1949
    p. 28, May 17, 1949
    VI, p. 21, Mar 23, 1952
    II, p. 1, Jun 1, 1952
    p. 11, Feb 21, 1953
    p. 6, Aug 13, 1955
    p. 35, Aug 17, 1960
    p. 46, Nov 7, 1960
    p. 45, Dec 7, 1964
    p. 48, Feb 24, 1970
New York Times Magazine pp. 36-7, Oct 5, 1947
New Yorker 23:58-9, Oct 18, 1947
    40:66+, Dec 19, 1964
Newsweek 30:88+, Oct 20, 1947
Saturday Review 30:28-32, Nov 1, 1947
    47:33, Dec 26, 1964
School and Society 67:314-15, Apr 24, 1948
Theatre Arts 31:18, Nov 1947
    31:12, Dec 1947
Time 50:73, Oct 20, 1947
    110:46, Aug 8, 1977
Vogue 110:181, Sep 1, 1947
    110:112, Nov 15, 1947

The Man of Destiny
Productions:
Opened November 23, 1925 for 68 performances.
(Off Broadway) Season of 1936-1937.
(Off Broadway) Season of 1942-1943 in repertory.
(Off Broadway) Season of 1955-1956.
(Off Broadway) Opened August 15, 1972 in repertory.
(Off Off Broadway) Opened December 1976.
Reviews:
New York Times p. 28, Nov 24, 1925
    p. 38, Apr 26, 1956
    p. 21, Apr 1, 1957
Vogue 67:87+, Jan 15, 1926

The Millionairess
Productions:
Opened October 17, 1952 for 83 performances.
(Off Broadway) Opened March 2, 1969 for 16 performances.

Reviews:
    Catholic World 176:227, Dec 1952
    Commonweal 57:198-9, Nov 28, 1952
    Life 33:163-5, Oct 13, 1952
    Nation 175:413, Nov 1, 1952
    New Republic 127:22-3, Nov 3, 1952
    New York Theatre Critics' Reviews 1952:228
    New York Times p. 38, Apr 7, 1949
                 p. 12, Jun 28, 1952
                 II, p. 1, Jul 6, 1952
                 p. 17, Oct 18, 1952
                 II, p. 1, Oct 26, 1952
                 p. 28, Mar 3, 1969
    New York Times Magazine p. 17, Jul 13, 1952
    New Yorker 28:65, Jul 19, 1953
               28:74+, Oct 25, 1952
               45:133-4, Mar 15, 1969
    Newsweek 40:76, Oct 27, 1952
    Saturday Review 14:10, Jun 13, 1936
    Theatre Arts 36:18-20, Nov 1952
    Time 60:75, Oct 27, 1952

Misalliance
  Productions:
    Opened September 27, 1917 for 52 performances.
    (Off Broadway) Opened October 1950 in repertory.
    Opened February 18, 1953 for 146 performances.
    (Off Broadway) Opened September 25, 1961 for 156
      performances.
    (Off Broadway) Opened March 28, 1972 for 46 performances.
    (Off Off Broadway) Opened January 8, 1976.
  Reviews:
    America 88:632, Mar 7, 1953
    Catholic World 177:68-9, Apr 1953
    Commonweal 57:648-9, Apr 3, 1953
               75:38-9, Jan 5, 1962
    Current Opinion 63:315-16, Nov 1917
    Dramatic Mirror 77:5, Oct 6, 1917
    Green Book 18:965-8, Dec 1917
    Life (NY) 70:590, Oct 11, 1917
    Life 34:155-6, Apr 8, 1953
    Nation 176:212, Mar 7, 1953
    New Republic 12:276, Oct 6, 1917
    New York Theatre Critics' Reviews 1953:354
    New York Times p. 9, Sep 28, 1917
                 p. 20, Feb 19, 1953
                 II, p. 1, Mar 22, 1953
                 II, p. 3, May 17, 1953
                 p. 10, Feb 12, 1955
                 p. 32, Sep 26, 1961
                 p. 36, Sep 24, 1971
                 p. 36, Mar 29, 1972

New York Times II, p. 3, Apr 9, 1972
            III, p. 16, Jul 7, 1977
New Yorker 29:60, Mar 7, 1953
            37:132-3, Oct 21, 1961
Newsweek 41:84, Mar 2, 1953
Saturday Review 36:34, Mar 7, 1953
Theatre Arts 37:16+, May 1953
            37:63-4+, Jul 1953
            45:71, Dec 1961
Theatre Magazine 26:280, 291, Nov 1917
Time 61:74+, Mar 2, 1953
            78:88, Oct 6, 1961

Mrs. Warren's Profession

Productions:
    Opened March 11, 1918 in repertory (The Washington
      Square Players).
    Opened February 22, 1922 for 25 performances.
    (Off Broadway) Opened November 1950.
    (Off Broadway) Opened April 24, 1963 for 15 performances.
    (Off Off Broadway) Opened March 1975.
    Opened February 18, 1976 for 55 performances.

Reviews:
    America 134:208, Mar 13, 1976
    Catholic World 172:226-7, Dec 1950
    Christian Science Monitor Magazine p. 6, Nov 4, 1950
    Dramatic Mirror 78:7, Mar 23, 1918
    Life (NY) 71:518, Mar 28, 1918
    Nation 171:418, Nov 4, 1950
        222:283-4, Mar 6, 1976
    New Republic 123:21, Nov 13, 1950
        174:18, Mar 20, 1976
    New York Theatre Critics' Reviews 1976:364
    New York Times p. 11, Mar 12, 1918
        II, p. 1, Oct 22, 1950
        p. 39, Oct 26, 1950
        p. 35, Jun 7, 1956
        p. 22, Jun 26, 1958
        p. 34, Apr 10, 1963
        p. 39, Apr 25, 1963
        p. 17, Jan 1, 1971
        p. 45, Feb 19, 1976
        II, p. 7, Mar 21, 1976
    New Yorker 39:93, May 4, 1963
        52:76, Mar 1, 1976
    Newsweek 36:89, Nov 6, 1950
    Theatre Magazine 27:218, Apr 1918
    Time 56:58, Nov 6, 1950
        107:51, Mar 1, 1976

The Music Cure

Productions:
    (Off Off Broadway) Opened October 19, 1972 in repertory.
No Reviews.

O'Flaherty, V. C.
　Productions:
　　Opened June 1920.
　　(Off Broadway) Season of 1936-1937.
　Reviews:
　　Current Opinion 61:103, Aug 1916
　　　　　　　　　63:167-70, Sep 1917
　　Dial 59:551, Dec 9, 1915
　　Dramatic Mirror 76:3, Jul 22, 1916
　　Hearst 32:88-91, 158-9, Aug 1917
　　　　　　38:41-3, Sep 1920
　　Literary Digest 53:69-70, Jul 8, 1916
　　New York Times p. 9, Jun 22, 1920
　　　　　　　　p. 35, Feb 19, 1957
　　Weekly Review 3:114-16, Aug 4, 1920

On the Rocks
　Productions:
　　Opened June 15, 1938 for 66 performances (Federal
　　　Theatre Project).
　Reviews:
　　Commonweal 28:273, Jul 1, 1938
　　Literary Digest 118:24, Aug 18, 1934
　　New Republic 95:251, Jul 6, 1938
　　New York Times p. 20, Jun 16, 1938
　　Theatre Arts 18:98-9, Feb 1934
　　Time 31:33, Jun 27, 1938

Overruled
　Productions:
　　Opened December 18, 1916 in repertory (Gertrude Kingston).
　　(Off Broadway) Season of 1959-1960.
　　(Off Off Broadway) Opened October 27, 1975.
　　(Off Off Broadway) Opened November 1975.
　　(Off Off Broadway) Opened May 6, 1977.
　Reviews:
　　New York Times p. 11, Feb 3, 1917
　　　　　　　　p. 32, May 27, 1959
　　　　　　　　II, p. 1, Jun 7, 1959
　　　　　　　　p. 13, Aug 21, 1959

Passion, Poison, and Putrefaction
　Productions:
　　(Off Broadway) Season of 1959-1960.
　Reviews:
　　New York Times p. 13, Aug 21, 1959

The Philanderer
　Productions:
　　Opened December 30, 1913 for 103 performances.
　　(Off Broadway) Season of 1955-1956.
　　(Off Broadway) Opened September 9, 1976 for 50 perform-
　　　ances.

Reviews:
American Mercury 77:104, Jun 1914
American Playwright 3:42-7, Feb 1914
Bookman 38:610-11, Feb 1914
Collier's 52:24, Feb 21, 1914
Dramatic Mirror 70:6, Dec 31, 1913
Green Book 11:413-14, Mar 1914
Harper's Weekly 58:22, Jan 17, 1914
Independent 77:59, Jan 12, 1914
International 8:68, Feb 1914
Nation 223:377-8, Oct 16, 1976
New York Times p. 7, Dec 29, 1913
          p. 26, May 13, 1958
          II, p. 5, Jul 4, 1971
          p. 36, Sep 30, 1976
          p. 53, Oct 19, 1976
New Yorker 52:81, Oct 11, 1976
Outlook 106:391, Feb 21, 1914
Theatre Magazine 19:58+, Feb 1914
Time 108:102, Oct 11, 1976

Press Cuttings
Productions:
(Off Off Broadway) Opened October 19, 1972 in repertory.
Reviews:
New York Times p. 35, Feb 19, 1957

Pygmalion
Productions:
Opened October 12, 1914 for 72 performances.
Opened November 15, 1926 for 143 performances.
Opened January 25, 1938 for two performances (WPA New
    York State Federal Theatre Project).
Opened December 26, 1945 for 179 performances.
(Off Broadway) Opened February 1952.
(Off Off Broadway) Opened October 30, 1972.
Reviews:
American Mercury 79:42, Feb 1915
Bookman 40:413-14, Dec 1914
        64:731, Feb 1927
Collier's 54:9, Jan 2, 1915
Commonweal 27:496, Feb 25, 1938
Current Opinion 56:30-1, Jan 1914
        56:358-9, May 1914
Forum 100:921-32, May 1914
        105:562-4, Feb 1946
Dramatic Mirror 71:12, Apr 1, 1914
        72:8-9, Oct 21, 1914
Dramatist 6:538-40, Jan 1915
        6:602-4, Jul 1915
        17:1319, Oct 1926
English Journal 59:1234-8, Dec 1970

Green Book 12:1057-8, Dec 1914
    13:118, Jan 1915
Harper's Weekly 58:14-15, Apr 11, 1914
    59:483, Nov 21, 1914
International 8:132, Apr 1914
Life 20:67-8, Jan 14, 1946
Life (NY) 64:120, Oct 22, 1914
Literary Digest 48:1180-1, May 16, 1914
Mademoiselle 44:104-6, Dec 1956
Munsey 53:555-6, Dec 1914
Nation 99:504-5, Oct 22, 1914
    100:150, Dec 4, 1915
    123:566-7, Dec 1, 1926
    162:176, Feb 9, 1946
New Republic 1:25, Nov 7, 1914
    49:41-2, Dec 1, 1926
    114:91, Jan 21, 1946
New York Dramatic News 60:18-19, Oct 17, 1914
New York Theatre Critics' Reviews 1945:57
New York Times p. 11, Mar 25, 1914
    p. 11, Oct 13, 1914
    p. 24, Nov 16, 1926
    VIII, p. 1, Nov 21, 1926
    p. 16, Jan 27, 1938
    p. 37, Dec 16, 1945
    II, p. 1, Jan 6, 1946
    p. 29, Feb 26, 1947
    p. 11, Feb 9, 1952
    p. 38, Oct 30, 1972
    p. 16, Aug 17, 1974
    p. 48, Jun 10, 1975
New Yorker 21:40, Jan 5, 1946
Newsweek 27:82, Jan 7, 1946
    76:90A, Oct 26, 1970
North American Review 200:933-4, Dec 1914
Saturday Review 29:24-6, Jan 12, 1946
Stage 14:76, Aug 1937
Theatre Arts 30:69-71, Feb 1946
    30:134+, Mar 1946
    40:29-31, Dec 1956
Theatre Magazine 20:262, Dec 1914
    45:15+, Jan 1927
Time 47:88, Jan 7, 1946
Vogue 69:82-3, Jan 15, 1927
    144:152-5+, Nov 1, 1964

Saint Joan
  Productions:
    Opened December 28, 1923 for 195 performances.
    Opened March 9, 1936 for 89 performances.
    (Off Broadway) Season of 1943-1944 in repertory.
    (Off Broadway) Season of 1949-1950 for 4 performances in
    repertory.

(Off Broadway) Opened March 1950.
Opened October 4, 1951 for 142 performances.
Opened September 11, 1956 for 77 performances.
Opened February 20, 1962 in repertory (Old Vic Company).
Opened January 4, 1968 for 44 performances in repertory.
Reviews:
America 95:630-2, Sep 29, 1956
        118:131, Jan 27, 1968
American Mercury 1:241-3, Feb 1924
Arts and Decoration 20:17, Feb 1924
Bookman 59:60-1, Mar 1921
Catholic World 119:196-205, May 1924
        143:85-6, Apr 1936
        174:147-8, Nov 1951
        184:146-7, Nov 1956
Christian Century 73:1138, Oct 3, 1956
Commonweal 23:609, Mar 27, 1936
        55:38, Oct 19, 1951
        65:46-7, Oct 12, 1956
        75:666-7, Mar 23, 1962
        87:538-9, Feb 2, 1968
Current Opinion 76:316-29, Mar 1924
Dial 76:206, Feb 1924
Drama 14:178-9, Feb 1924
Freeman 8:447-9, Jan 16, 1924
Independent 112:55, Jan 19, 1924
Independent Woman 25:101-2, Apr 1946
Life (NY) 83:18, Jan 24, 1924
Life 31:141-2, Oct 22, 1951
    41:59-60, Sep 10, 1956
    41:90-7, Oct 15, 1956
Literary Digest 80:267, Jan 19, 1924
        121:19, Mar 21, 1936
Living Age 322:175-8, Jul 26, 1924
Metropolitan Magazine 59:42, May 1924
Nation 118:96-7, Jan 23, 1924
     142:392, Mar 25, 1936
     173:360-1, Oct 27, 1951
     183:274-5, Sep 27, 1962
     194:221, Mar 10, 1962
     199:60, Aug 10, 1964
     206:125-6, Jan 22, 1968
New Republic 37:205-6, Jan 16, 1924
       40:380-1, Aug 27, 1924
       86:198, Mar 25, 1936
       88:173, Sep 23, 1936
       125:29-30, Oct 29, 1951
       146:37-8, Mar 5, 1962
New York Theatre Critics' Reviews 1952:220
              1956:233
              1962:344
              1968:397

New York Times p. 27, Mar 10, 1936
                X, p. 1, Mar 15, 1936
                p. 10, Mar 11, 1940
                II, p. 3, Jan 11, 1948
                p. 10, Mar 4, 1950
                II, p. 1, Mar 5, 1950
                II, p. 1, Sep 30, 1951
                p. 23, Oct 5, 1951
                II, p. 1 and VI, p. 17, Oct 14, 1951
                II, p. 3, Nov 4, 1951
                p. 27, Jan 11, 1955
                II, p. 3, Feb 13, 1955
                II, p. 1, May 29, 1955
                VI, p. 62, Sep 2, 1956
                p. 42, Sep 12, 1956
                II, p. 1, Sep 16, 1956
                p. 20, Dec 15, 1956
                p. 57, Feb 21, 1962
                p. 23, Jan 25, 1963
                p. 41, May 14, 1964
                p. 34, Aug 14, 1967
                II, p. 1 and X, p. 1, Dec 31, 1967
                p. 42, Jan 5, 1968
                II, p. 1, Jan 14, 1968
                p. 50, Jun 11, 1975
                p. 31, Mar 7, 1977
New Yorker 27:83, Oct 13, 1951
            32:96, Sep 22, 1956
            38:93, Mar 3, 1962
            43:57, Jan 13, 1968
Newsweek 7:22, Mar 21, 1936
          38:84, Oct 15, 1951
          48:102, Sep 24, 1956
          71:78-9, Jan 15, 1968
Outlook 136:338, Feb 27, 1924
Pictorial Review 37:55, Jun 1936
Saturday Review 37:32, Oct 23, 1954
                39:70-1, Sep 1955
                51:18, Jan 20, 1968
School and Society 74:405-6, Dec 22, 1951
Stage 13:30-33, Apr 1936
Survey 87:525-6, Dec 1951
Theatre Arts 20:329-38, May 1936
              20:463-4, Jun 1936
              35:3, Dec 1951
              36:34-5, Jun 1952
              39:70-1, Dec 1955
              40:80-1, Nov 1956
              41:30+, Mar 1957
Theatre Magazine 39:14-16, Mar 1924
Time 27:55, Mar 23, 1936
      58:73, Oct 15, 1951
      68:78+, Sep 24, 1956

  Time 79:64, Mar 2, 1962
   91:40, Jan 12, 1968
   105:66+, Jun 30, 1975
  Vogue 151:42, Feb 15, 1968
  Woman Citizen 8:13, Feb 9, 1924

The Shewing-up of Blanco Posnet
 Productions:
  Opened November 20, 1911 in repertory.
  Opened February 4, 1913 in repertory (The Irish Players).
  Opened October 16, 1923 for 49 performances.
  (Off Broadway) Season of 1959-1960.
 Reviews:
  American Playwright 3:79-84, Mar 1914
  Collier's 50:25, Mar 13, 1915
  Dramatic Mirror 66:8-9, Nov 29, 1911
  Everybody's 28:680, May 1913
  Munsey 46:589-90, Jan 1912
  Nation 92:325-6, Mar 30, 1911
  New Republic 36:257, Oct 31, 1923
  New York Times p. 14, Oct 17, 1923
       p. 26, Sep 19, 1959
       II, p. 1, Oct 4, 1959
  Newsweek 35:95-6, Sep 26, 1959

The Simpleton of Unexpected Isles
 Productions:
  Opened February 18, 1935 for 40 performances.
  (Off Broadway) Season of 1953-1954.
 Reviews:
  Catholic World 141:87-8, Apr 1935
  Commonweal 21:542, Mar 8, 1935
  Literary Digest 119:23, Mar 2, 1935
  Nation 140:286-7, Mar 6, 1935
  New Republic 82:105, Mar 6, 1935
  New York Times p. 27, Feb 19, 1935
       VIII, p. 1, Feb 24, 1935
       p. 7, Jul 30, 1935
       X, p. 1, Aug 25, 1935
       p. 19, Jan 12, 1954
  Saturday Review 14:10, Jun 13, 1936
  Stage 12:12-13, Aug 1935
  Theatre Arts 19:244, 247, 283-4, Apr 1935
  Time 25:39, Mar 4, 1935

*Six of Calais
 Reviews:
  Saturday Review 14:10, Jun 13, 1936

Too True to Be Good
 Productions:
  Opened April 4, 1932 for 57 performances.
  Opened March 12, 1963 for 94 performances.

Reviews:
America 108:591, Apr 20, 1963
Bookman 75:75-6, Apr 1932
Catholic World 135:206-7, May 1932
Commonweal 15:691, Apr 20, 1932
Literary Digest 113:14, Apr 30, 1932
114:15, Nov 12, 1932
Nation 134:477-8, Apr 20, 1932
177:157, Aug 22, 1953
196:275, Mar 30, 1963
New Republic 70:271-3, Apr 20, 1932
148:29, Mar 30, 1963
New York Theatre Critics' Reviews 1963:315
New York Times p. 1, Mar 6, 1932
p. 8, Mar 14, 1963
p. 5, Mar 23, 1963
p. 28, Apr 9, 1963
New Yorker 39:73, Mar 23, 1963
Newsweek 61:97, Mar 25, 1963
Stage 9:5-7, May 1932
Theatre Arts 16:437-9, Jun 1932
16:877-8, Nov 1932
47:69, May 1963
Theatre Guild Magazine 9:14-17, Apr 1932
Time 81:74, Mar 22, 1963
Vogue 79:76, Jun 1, 1932

Village Wooing
Productions:
(Off Broadway) May 1943.
(Off Off Broadway) Opened January 10, 1974.
Reviews:
Catholic World 181:63, Oct 1955
New York Times p. 6, Aug 13, 1955
p. 22, Sep 5, 1956
Newsweek 3:39, Apr 28, 1934
Saturday Review 38:37, Nov 19, 1955
Time 23:26, Apr 30, 1934

*What's in It for Me?
Reviews:
New York Times p. 19, Aug 20, 1973

*Why She Would Not
Reviews:
Theatre Arts 40:20-1+, Aug 1956
40:16, Dec 1956

Widower's Houses
Productions:
(Off Broadway) Opened February 1939 for one performance
(Irish Repertory Players).
(Off Broadway) Season of 1952-1953.

Reviews:
New York Times II, p. 1, Sep 21, 1952
p. 39, Mar 3, 1959
New Yorker 35:102-3, Mar 21, 1959

You Never Can Tell
Productions:
Opened April 5, 1915 in repertory.
Opened May 16, 1948 for 39 performances.
(Off Broadway) Season of 1952-1953.
(Off Broadway) Opened October 21, 1966 for 9 performances.
Reviews:
Canadian Magazine 42:634-7, Apr 1914
Catholic World 167:169, May 1948
Commonweal 48:635, Apr 16, 1948
Dramatic Mirror 73:9, Apr 14, 1915
Nation 100:424-5, Apr 15, 1915
166:361, Mar 27, 1948
New Republic 118:30, Mar 29, 1948
New York Theatre Critics' Reviews 1948:307
New York Times VII, p. 6, Apr 11, 1915
p. 31, Mar 17, 1948
p. 25, Jun 17, 1958
p. 18, Jun 22, 1973
II, p. 3, Aug 19, 1973
New Yorker 24:49, Mar 27, 1948
Newsweek 31:82, Mar 29, 1948
Saturday Review 31:32-4, Apr 24, 1948
Theatre Arts 32:47, Jan 1948
Time 51:56, Mar 29, 1948

SHAW, ROBERT

The Man in the Glass Booth
Productions:
Opened September 26, 1968 for 268 performances.
Reviews:
America 119:336, Oct 12, 1968
Christian Century 85:1438, Nov 13, 1968
Commentary 47:25-6, Feb 1969
Commonweal 89:253, Nov 15, 1968
Life 65:20, Oct 25, 1968
Nation 207:411-12, Oct 21, 1968
National Review 20:1282-3, Dec 17, 1968
New Republic 159:37, Oct 19, 1968
New York Theatre Critics' Reviews 1968:236
New York Times p. 12, Jul 29, 1967
II, p. 1, Aug 27, 1967
p. 41, Sep 27, 1968
II, p. 5, Oct 6, 1968
p. 58, Apr 17, 1969
p. 37, Apr 18, 1969

New York Times p. 58, Apr 21, 1969
New Yorker 44:95, Oct 5, 1968
Newsweek 72:116, Oct 7, 1968
Saturday Review 51:52-3, Oct 12, 1968
Time 90:44+, Aug 11, 1967
    92:65-6, Oct 4, 1968
Vogue 150:70, Oct 15, 1967
    152:124, Nov 1, 1968

SHERRIFF, R. C.

*Home at Seven
   Reviews:
      Christian Science Monitor Magazine p. 4, Apr 1, 1950
      New York Times p. 34, Mar 8, 1950

Journey's End
   Productions:
      Opened March 22, 1929 for 485 performances.
      Opened September 18, 1939 for 16 performances.
      (Off Off Broadway) Season of 1968-1969.
   Reviews:
      American Mercury 17:245-7, Jun 1929
                 17:376-7, Jul 1929
      Bookman 69:173-6, Apr 1929
      Catholic World 129:201-2, May 1929
                130:326-7, Dec 1929
                150:214-15, Nov 1939
      Christian Century 46:1332, Oct 30, 1929
      Collier's 83:7, Jun 8, 1929
      Commonweal 9:656-7, Apr 10, 1929
              30:519, Sep 29, 1939
      Life (NY) 93:28, Apr 19, 1929
             95:20, May 2, 1930
      Literary Digest 100:22-3, Mar 30, 1929
                105:18-19, May 3, 1930
      Nation 128:434, Apr 10, 1929
           130:141, Feb 5, 1930
           130:524-5, Apr 30, 1930
           149:355-7, Sep 30, 1939
      New Republic 58:225-6, Apr 10, 1929
      New York Times p. 23, Mar 23, 1929
                 VIII, p. 1, Mar 31, 1929
                 IX, p. 2, May 5, 1929
                 p. 20, Jan 17, 1930
                 p. 29, Sep 19, 1939
                 IX, p. 1, Sep 24, 1939
                 p. 55, Oct 28, 1969
                 p. 52, Jun 13, 1972
                 p. 21, Jul 21, 1972
      Newsweek 14:35, Oct 2, 1939
             14:44, Oct 16, 1939

Nineteenth Century 105:844-8, Jun 1929
Outlook 151:590, Apr 10, 1929
    154:670, Apr 23, 1930
Saturday Review 5:1021, May 18, 1929
Theatre Arts 13:325-30, May 1929
    13:493-7, Jul 1929
    14:738, Sep 1930
    23:777-9, Nov 1939
Theatre Magazine 49:43-5, Jun 1929
    50:25-6+, Sep 1929
    52:44, Jul 1930
Time 34:38, Oct 2, 1939
Vanity Fair 32:52-3+, Jun 1929
Vogue 73:186, May 11, 1929
    73:74-5, Jun 8, 1929

*Miss Mabel
  Reviews:
    New York Times II, p. 4, Dec 12, 1948

Saint Helena (with Jeanne de Casalis)
  Productions:
    Opened October 6, 1936 for 63 performances.
  Reviews:
    Catholic World 144:212-13, Nov 1936
    Commonweal 24:617, Oct 23, 1936
    Nation 143:457, Oct 17, 1936
    New Republic 88:314, Oct 21, 1936
    New York Times p. 32, Oct 7, 1936
        X, p. 1, Oct 11, 1936
    Newsweek 8:28-9, Oct 17, 1938
    Saturday Review 15:17, Oct 31, 1936
    Theatre Arts 20:840+, Nov 1936
    Time 28:44, Oct 19, 1936

SHIELS, GEORGE

The New Gossoon
  Productions:
    Opened October 21, 1932 for 14 performances.
    Opened November 13, 1934 for 2 performances.
    Opened November 29, 1937 for 8 performances (Abbey
      Theatre Players).
  Reviews:
    Literary Digest 114:17, Nov 19, 1932
    Nation 139:629, Nov 28, 1934
    New York Times p. 18, Oct 22, 1932
            p. 26, Nov 30, 1937

SIERRA, GREGORIO MARTINEZ see MARTINEZ-SIERRA,
    GREGORIO

SIGURJONSSON, JOHANN

Eyvind of the Hills
    Productions:
        Opened February 1921 for 24 performances.
    Reviews:
        Dramatic Mirror 83:288, Feb 12, 1921
        New York Clipper 69:19, Feb 9, 1921
        New York Times p. 14, Feb 2, 1921
        Theatre Magazine 33:261, Apr 1921
        Weekly Review 4:255, Mar 16, 1921

SIMONOV, KONSTANTIN

Alien Shadow   (see Strange Shadow)

The Russian People (The Russians)
    Productions:
        American acting version by Clifford Odets.   Opened
            December 29, 1942 for 39 performances.
    Reviews:
        Catholic World 156:599, Feb 1943
        Commonweal 37:349, Jan 22, 1943
        Current History ns3:549, Feb 1943
        Nation 156:103, Jan 16, 1943
        New York Theatre Critics' Reviews 1942:127+
        New York Times p. 17, Dec 30, 1942
        Newsweek 21:66, Jan 11, 1943
        Theatre Arts 27:70-1, Feb 1943
                      27:141-2+, Mar 1943

*Russian Question
    Reviews:
        Life 22:51-2+, May 26, 1947
        New York Times p. 18, Dec 14, 1946
                      II, p. 3, Feb 16, 1947
                      p. 54, May 4, 1947
                      p. 24, Jun 17, 1947
        Newsweek 29:80, Jun 2, 1947
        Time 49:34, Apr 14, 1947

*Strange Shadow (Alien Shadow)
    Reviews:
        Collier's 124:78, Sep 17, 1949
        New York Times p. 30, Jul 20, 1949
                      p. 16, Jul 22, 1949

The Whole World Over
    Productions:
        Adapted by Thelma Schnee.   Opened March 27, 1947
            for 100 performances.
    Reviews:

Catholic World 165:168-9, May 1947
Commonweal 46:15, Apr 18, 1947
Nation 164:459, Apr 19, 1947
New York Theatre Critics' Reviews 1947:411
New York Times II, p. 1, Mar 23, 1947
                p. 28, Mar 28, 1947
                II, p. 1, Apr 6, 1947
                II, p. 3, May 4, 1947
New Yorker 23:50+, Apr 5, 1947
Newsweek 29:80, Apr 7, 1947
School and Society 65:403-4, May 31, 1947
Time 49:78, Apr 7, 1947

SIMPSON, N. F.

The Hole
    Productions:
        (Off Broadway) Season of 1960-1961.
    Reviews:
        New York Times p. 42, Apr 4, 1961
        New Yorker 37:76+, Apr 15, 1961

One Way Pendulum
    Productions:
        (Off Broadway) Opened September 18, 1961 for 40
            performances.
    Reviews:
        America 106:29, Oct 7, 1961
        Commonweal 75:94, Oct 20, 1961
        New York Times p. 38, Sep 19, 1961
        New Yorker 36:104, May 28, 1960
                   37:118-20, Sep 30, 1961
        Saturday Review 44:38, Oct 7, 1961
        Theatre Arts 45:58-9, Nov 1961

The Only Sense Is Nonsense (see The Hole/The Resounding Tinkle)

Resounding Tinkle
    Productions:
        (Off Broadway) Season of 1960-1961.
    Reviews:
        New York Times p. 42, Apr 4, 1961
        New Yorker 37:76+, Apr 15, 1961

*Was He Anyone?
    Reviews:
        New York Times p. 16, Aug 26, 1972

SLADE, BERNARD

Same Time, Next Year

Productions:
Opened March 13, 1975 for (927) performances.
Reviews:
Nation 220:413-14, Apr 5, 1975
New Republic 172:20+, Apr 12, 1975
New York Theatre Critics' Reviews 1975:300
New York Times p. 24, Mar 14, 1975
II, p. 1, Mar 23, 1975
p. 38, Mar 31, 1975
II, p. 5, Apr 13, 1975
p. 15, Feb 21, 1976
II, p. 1, Sep 10, 1976
New Yorker 51:61, Mar 24, 1975
Newsweek 85:69, Mar 24, 1975
Saturday Review 2:52, May 17, 1975
Time 105:85, Mar 24, 1975

SMITH, DODIE

Autumn Crocus (written under the pseud. C. L. Anthony)
Productions:
Opened November 19, 1932 for 210 performances.
Reviews:
Catholic World 136:465-6, Jan 1933
Commonweal 17:469, Feb 22, 1933
17:525, Mar 8, 1933
Nation 135:577, Dec 7, 1932
New Republic 73:99-100, Dec 7, 1932
New York Times p. 20, Nov 21, 1932
p. 24, Jun 22, 1954
p. 23, Jul 7, 1954
Stage 10:9-10, Jan 1933
Theatre Arts 15:461-2, Jun 1931
17:109-10, Feb 1933
Town and Country 87:38, Dec 15, 1932
Vogue 81:39+, Jan 15, 1933

Call It a Day
Productions:
Opened January 28, 1936 for 194 performances.
Reviews:
Catholic World 142:724, Mar 1936
Commonweal 23:440, Feb 14, 1936
Literary Digest 121:20, Feb 8, 1936
Nation 142:201-2, Feb 12, 1936
New Republic 86:78, Feb 26, 1936
New York Times p. 26, Jan 21, 1936
p. 15, Jan 29, 1936
X, p. 1, Feb 9, 1936
Newsweek 7:25-6, Feb 8, 1936
Theatre Arts 20:183, Mar 1936

Time 27:47-8, Feb 10, 1936

Dear Octopus
  Productions:
    Opened January 11, 1939 for 53 performances.
  Reviews:
    Catholic World 148:731, Mar 1939
    Commonweal 29:413, Feb 3, 1939
    Nation 148:128, Jan 28, 1939
    New Republic 97:343, Jan 25, 1939
    New York Times p. 22, Jan 12, 1939
    Theatre Arts 23:171-2, Mar 1939
    Time 33:21, Jan 23, 1939

*Letter from Paris
  Reviews:
    New York Times p. 17, Oct 11, 1952

Lovers and Friends
  Productions:
    Opened November 29, 1943 for 168 performances.
  Reviews:
    Catholic World 158:393, Jan 1944
    Commonweal 39:231, Dec 17, 1943
    Nation 157:740, Dec 18, 1943
    New York Theatre Critics' Reviews 1943:210
    New York Times p. 23, Nov 30, 1943
                  II, p. 5, Dec 5, 1943
    New York Times Magazine p. 16, Nov 21, 1943
    Newsweek 22:90, Dec 13, 1943
    Theatre Arts 28:74+, Feb 1944
    Time 42:44, Dec 13, 1943

STERNHEIM, CARL

Bloomers (see also Underpants)
  Productions:
    (Off Off Broadway) Translated by M. A. McHaffie. Opened
      April 18, 1974.
  Reviews:
    New York Times p. 34, Apr 23, 1974.

Bürger Schippel
  Productions:
    (Off Broadway) Opened December 11, 1966 in repertory
      for 2 performances.
  Reviews:
    National Magazine 19:316, Mar 21, 1967

The Snob
  Productions:
    (Off Off Broadway) Opened September 8, 1976.
  No Reviews.

The Underpants   (see also Bloomers)
   Productions:
      (Off Off Broadway) Season of 1968-1969.
      (Off Off Broadway) Translated by Eric Bentley.   Opened
         March 10, 1977.
   No Reviews.

STOPPARD, TOM

After Magritte
   Productions:
      (Off Broadway) Opened April 23, 1972 for 465 performances.
   Reviews:
      Nation 214:637, May 15, 1972
      New York Theatre Critics' Reviews 1972:263
      New York Times p. 41, Apr 24, 1972
               p. 46, Oct 16, 1972
      New Yorker 48:61-2, May 6, 1972
      Saturday Review 55:66, Aug 26, 1972
      Time 99:75, May 8, 1972

Dirty Linen and New-Found-Land
   Productions:
      Opened January 11, 1977 for 159 performances.
   Reviews:
      America 136:149, Feb 19, 1977
      Commonweal 104:180-1, Mar 18, 1977
      Nation 224:125, Jan 29, 1977
      New York Theatre Critics' Reviews 1977:388
      New York Times p. 45, Jun 21, 1976
                II, p. 5, Jun 27, 1976
                II, p. 1, Jan 9, 1977
                III, p. 18, Jan 13, 1977
                II, p. 3, Jan 23, 1977
      New Yorker 52:63, Jan 24, 1977
      Newsweek 88:103, Oct 18, 1976
      Time 109:55, Jan 24, 1977

Enter a Free Man
   Productions:
      (Off Off Broadway) Opened December 17, 1974.
   Reviews:
      New York Times II, p. 8, Apr 7, 1968
                p. 51, Dec 18, 1974
      New Yorker 50:50, Jan 6, 1975
      Newsweek 76:77, Aug 31, 1970
           85:64, Jan 6, 1975

Jumpers
   Productions:
      Opened April 22, 1974 for 48 performances.
   Reviews:

America 126:376-7, Apr 8, 1972
      130:395, May 18, 1974
Commentary 57:79-80, Jun 1974
Nation 217:123-4, Aug 13, 1973
      218:604, May 11, 1974
      218:637-8, May 18, 1974
National Review 26:377-8, May 29, 1974
New Republic 170:18+, May 18, 1974
New York Theatre Critics' Reviews 1974:298
New York Times p. 24, Aug 9, 1972
              p. 28, Feb 20, 1974
              II, p. 1, Mar 3, 1974
              p. 36, Apr 23, 1974
              II, p. 3, May 5, 1974
New Yorker 50:75, May 6, 1974
Newsweek 83:87, Mar 4, 1974
Time 100:75, Sep 18, 1972
     103:103, Mar 11, 1974
     103:85, May 6, 1974

New Found-Land (see Dirty Linen and New-Found-Land)

The Real Inspector Hound
  Productions:
    (Off Broadway) Opened April 23, 1972 for 465 performances.
    (Off Off Broadway) Opened May 1975.
    (Off Off Broadway) Opened June 4, 1976.
  Reviews:
    America 126:515, May 13, 1972
    Nation 214:637, May 15, 1972
    New York Theatre Critics' Reviews 1972:263
    New York Times p. 38, Jun 19, 1968
                  p. 45, Jul 8, 1968
                  II, p. 4, Jul 14, 1968
                  p. 41, Apr 24, 1972
                  p. 54, Apr 26, 1972
                  II, p. 3, May 7, 1972
                  p. 46, Oct 16, 1972
    New Yorker 48:61-2, May 6, 1972
    Saturday Review 55:66, Aug 26, 1972
    Time 99:75, May 8, 1972

Rosencrantz and Guildenstern Are Dead
  Productions:
    Opened October 16, 1967 for 420 performances.
    (Off Off Broadway) Season of 1970-1971.
    (Off Off Broadway) Opened September 14, 1972 in repertory.
    (Off Off Broadway) Opened January 22, 1974.
  Reviews:
    Commentary 44:82-4, Dec 1967
    Commonweal 87:171-2, Nov 10, 1967
    Life 64:72-3+, Feb 9, 1968
    Look 31:92-6, Dec 26, 1967

Nation 205:476, Nov 6, 1967
National Review 19:1393-5, Dec 12, 1967
New Republic 157:25-6, Nov 4, 1967
New York Theatre Critics' Reviews 1967:250, 254
New York Times p. 27, Aug 29, 1967
            p. 53, Oct 17, 1967
            p. 55, Oct 23, 1967
            II, p. 1, Oct 29, 1967
            p. 39, Oct 15, 1968
            p. 39, Nov 19, 1970
            p. 15, Feb 1, 1974
            p. 15, Sep 13, 1975
New Yorker 43:179-80, May 6, 1967
            43:105, Oct 28, 1967
            43:52, Nov 4, 1967
            50:70, Mar 4, 1974
Newsweek 70:90+, Oct 30, 1967
Reporter 37:39-40, Nov 16, 1967
Saturday Review 50:28, Nov 4, 1967
            52:20, Jul 5, 1969
Time 90:84, Oct 27, 1967
Travel 128:22, Dec 1967
Vogue 150:72, Nov 15, 1967

Travesties
   Productions:
     Opened October 30, 1975 for 155 performances.
   Reviews:
     America 133:408, Dec 6, 1975
     Commentary 61:71-4, Jan 1976
     Commonweal 103:114, Feb 13, 1976
     Nation 221:540, Nov 22, 1975
     New Republic 173:18-19, Nov 22, 1975
     New York Theatre Critics' Reviews 1975:166
     New York Times p. 31, Jun 17, 1974
                 p. 24, Aug 9, 1974
                 p. 21, Oct 31, 1975
                 II, p. 1, Nov 9, 1975
                 p. 25, Nov 14, 1975
                 p. 25, Feb 5, 1976
     New Yorker 51:135, Nov 10, 1975
     Newsweek 83:77, Jun 24, 1974
            86:66, Nov 10, 1975
     Saturday Review 3:36-7, Nov 15, 1975
     Time 106:75, Nov 10, 1975

STOREY, DAVID

The Changing Room
   Productions:
     Opened March 6, 1973 for 192 performances.
   Reviews:

America 126:379, Apr 8, 1972
                128:290, Mar 31, 1972
Commonweal 98:114, Apr 6, 1973
Nation 216:410-11, Mar 26, 1973
New Republic 168:22+, Apr 14, 1973
New York Theatre Critics' Reviews 1973:336
New York Times p. 79, Nov 19, 1972
                        II, p. 13, Dec 3, 1972
                        p. 37, Mar 7, 1973
                        II, p. 1, Mar 18, 1973
                        p. 14, Apr 20, 1973
                        II, p. 1, Jun 10, 1973
New Yorker 49:92, Mar 17, 1973
Newsweek 80:71, Dec 11, 1972
                81:86, Mar 19, 1973
Saturday Review 1:77, Apr 1973
Sports Illustrated 38:66-9, Mar 5, 1973
Time 100:84-5, Dec 18, 1972

The Contractor
    Productions:
        (Off Broadway) Opened October 17, 1973 for 72 performances.
    Reviews:
        America 129:334, Nov 3, 1973
        Nation 217:478, Nov 5, 1973
        New York Theatre Critics' Reviews 1973:175
        New York Times p. 32, Aug 17, 1970
                        p. 63, Dec 9, 1971
                        p. 66, Oct 18, 1973
                        II, p. 3, Oct 28, 1973
        New Yorker 49:107-9, Oct 29, 1973
        Saturday Review 1:47, Dec 18, 1973
        Time 102:84, Nov 5, 1973

*Cromwell
    Reviews:
        New York Times II, p. 1, Sep 9, 1973
                        p. 55, Sep 11, 1973

The Farm
    Productions:
        (Off Broadway) Opened October 10, 1976 for 42 performances.
    Reviews:
        America 135:304, Nov 6, 1976
        Nation 223:443-4, Oct 30, 1976
        New York Theatre Critics' Reviews 1976:126
        New York Times II, p. 5, Oct 3, 1976
                        p. 45, Oct 12, 1976
                        II, p. 9, Oct 24, 1976
                        III, p. 3, Nov 12, 1976
        New Yorker 52:61-2, Oct 25, 1976
        Time 108:87, Oct 25, 1976

Home
Productions:
Opened November 17, 1970 for 110 performances.
Reviews:
America 124:46-7, Jan 16, 1971
Commonweal 93:373-4, Jan 15, 1971
Nation 211:252-3, Sep 21, 1970
211:605, Dec 7, 1970
New Republic 163:20+, Dec 12, 1970
New York Theatre Critics' Reviews 1970:146
New York Times p. 23, Jun 20, 1970
II, p. 1, Nov 15, 1970
p. 41, Nov 18, 1970
II, p. 1, Nov 29, 1970
II, p. 6, Jan 24, 1971
II, p. 18, Feb 7, 1971
New Yorker 46:141, Nov 28, 1970
Newsweek 76:98, Nov 30, 1970
Saturday Review 53:16+, Dec 12, 1970
Time 96:48, Nov 30, 1970

*In Celebration
Reviews:
Time 103:106, Jun 10, 1974

Life Class
Productions:
(Off Off Broadway) Opened December 1975.
Reviews:
Nation 222:27, Jan 3, 1976
New York Times p. 43, Dec 15, 1975
New Yorker 51:43, Dec 29, 1975
Time 107:77, Jan 5, 1976

*This Sporting Life
Reviews:
Commonweal 93:373, Jan 15, 1971

STRINDBERG, AUGUST

The Bond
Productions:
(Off Off Broadway) Season of 1967-1968.
No Reviews.

The Bridal Crown
Productions:
Opened February 5, 1938 for one performance.
Reviews:
New York Times p. 11, Feb 7, 1938
Newsweek 11:28, Feb 21, 1938
Time 31:36, Feb 14, 1938

*Comrades
  Reviews:
    New York Times p. 38, Jun 6, 1956

Countess Julia (see Miss Julie)
  Productions:
    Opened May 2, 1913 for three performances.
  Reviews:
    New York Times p. 9, Apr 29, 1913

The Creditors
  Productions:
    Season of 1921-1922.
    (Off Broadway) Adapted by Paul Shyer. Opened January 25,
      1962 for 46 performances.
    (Off Off Broadway) Season of 1970-1971.
    (Off Broadway) Opened July 4, 1972 in repertory.
    (Off Off Broadway) Translated by Palaemona Morner and
      R. Spacek. Opened January 12, 1977.
    (Off Off Broadway) Adapted by Linda Mussman. Opened
      February 16, 1977.
    (Off Broadway) New translation by Palaemona Morner and
      R. Spacek. Opened April 15, 1977 for 56 performances.
  Reviews:
    Commonweal 51:267-8, Dec 9, 1949
                75:543, Feb 16, 1962
    Forum 113:26-7, Jan 1950
    Nation 194:126, Feb 10, 1962
    New Republic 122:22, Jan 2, 1950
                 146:20-1, Feb 19, 1962
    New York Clipper 70:20, May 10, 1922
    New York Theatre Critics' Reviews 1977:217
    New York Times p. 27, May 3, 1922
                   p. 36, Nov 2, 1949
                   II, p. 1, Nov 27, 1949
                   p. 19, Jan 26, 1962
                   p. 18, Nov 10, 1973
                   II, p. 19, May 18, 1977
    New Yorker 37:72, Feb 3, 1962
    Theatre Arts 46:63+, Apr 1962
    Time 109:76, May 30, 1977

Crime and Crime
  Productions:
    (Off Broadway) Translated by Elizabeth Sprigge. Opened
      December 16, 1963 for one performance.
  Reviews:
    New York Times p. 51, Dec 17, 1963
                   p. 35, Jan 19, 1970
    Newsweek 75:74, Jan 26, 1970

The Dance of Death (see also The Last Dance)
  Productions:

Season of 1919-1920.
(Off Broadway) Adapted by John Bowman.   Opened September
    13, 1960 for 32 performances.
Adapted by Paul Avila Mayer.   Opened April 28, 1971 for
    5 performances.
Adapted by A. J. Antoon from the Elizabeth Sprigge
    translation.   Opened April 4, 1974 for 37 performances.
(Off Off Broadway) Opened February 1975.
Reviews:
    America 130:343, May 4, 1974
    Dramatic Mirror 86:1146, May 22, 1920
    Independent 102:273, May 29, 1920
    Nation 110:774-5, Jan 5, 1920
        118:16-17, Jan 1924
        218:507-9, Apr 20, 1974
    New York Clipper 68:19, May 19, 1920
    New York Theatre Critics' Reviews 1971:292
                                        1974:322
    New York Times p. 51, Sep 14, 1960
                   p. 31, Jun 3, 1966
                   p. 52, Jun 16, 1966
                   p. 50, Oct 20, 1967
                   II, p. 5, Oct 29, 1967
                   p. 53, May 26, 1969
                   p. 47, Apr 29, 1971
                   II, p. 1, and p. 3, May 9, 1971
                   II, p. 13, May 9, 1971
                   II, p. 1, Mar 31, 1974
                   p. 24, Apr 5, 1974
                   II, p. 1, Apr 14, 1974
                   p. 46, Apr 26, 1977
    New Yorker 50:36, Jul 1, 1967
              63:12, May 16, 1970
    Theatre Arts 44:9, Nov 1960
    Theatre Magazine 15:xv, Jun 1912
                    32:30, Jul-Aug 1920
    Time 109:50, May 9, 1970

    (see also Friedrich Duerrenmatt's Play Strindberg)

The Dream Play
    Productions:
        Translated by Edwin Bjorkman.   Opened January 30,
            1926 for 27 performances.
        (Off Broadway) Season of 1960-1961.
    Reviews:
        Nation 122:122-3, Feb 3, 1926
        New York Times p. 18, Jan 21, 1926
                       p. 22, Nov 23, 1960
                       p. 45, Apr 17, 1970
                       II, p. 3, Jun 5, 1977
        New Yorker 36:103, Dec 3, 1960
        Theatre Magazine 15:xv, Jun 1912

Easter One Day More (Easter)
 Productions:
  Opened March 18, 1926 for 28 performances.
 Reviews:
  America 96:511, Feb 2, 1957
  Dramatic Mirror 78:29, Apr 6, 1918
  Life (NY) 87:27, Apr 8, 1926
  New York Times p. 24, Mar 19, 1962
               II, p. 3, Jan 13, 1957
                  p. 35, Jan 17, 1957
               II, p. 1, Feb 3, 1957

The Father
 Productions:
  Opened April 9, 1912 for 31 performances.
  English version by Robert Whittier. Opened May 11, 1928
   for eight performances.
  Opened October 8, 1931 for 20 performances.
  (Off Broadway) August to October 15, 1949 in repertory.
  English version by Robert L. Joseph. Opened November 16,
   1949 for 69 performances.
  Opened May 14, 1962 for three performances.
  (Off Broadway) Opened November 10, 1965 for 11
   performances.
  (Off Broadway) Adapted by Gene Feist. Opened September
   11, 1973 for 97 performances.
  (Off Off Broadway) Opened March 19, 1976.
  (Off Off Broadway) Opened May 13, 1976.
 Reviews:
  American Playwright 1:146, May 1912
  Arts and Decoration 36:55, Dec 1931
  Blue Book 15:694-6, Aug 1912
  Catholic World 170:307-8, Jan 1950
  Commonweal 51:267-8, Dec 9, 1949
  Dramatic Mirror 67:6, Apr 17, 1912
  Forum 113:26, Jan 1950
  Green Book 7:1204, Jun 1912
            8:9-11+, Jul 1912
  Life (NY) 59:869-72, Apr 25, 1912
  Munsey 47:467, Jun 1912
  Nation 95:153, Aug 15, 1912
         169:525, Nov 26, 1949
  New Republic 68:301, Oct 28, 1931
              121:22, Sep 19, 1949
              121:21, Dec 19, 1949
  New York Dramatic News 55:17, Apr 13, 1912
                         55:18, Apr 20, 1912
  New York Theatre Critics' Reviews 1949:223
  New York Times p. 9, May 12, 1928
                p. 21, Oct 9, 1931
                II, p. 1, Aug 21, 1949
                p. 36, Nov 17, 1949
                II, p. 1, Nov 27, 1949

New York Times p. 49, May 15, 1962
      p. 53, Oct 17, 1973
      II, p. 3, Oct 21, 1973
      p. 40, Mar 4, 1975
      II, p. 1, Mar 16, 1975
New Yorker 25:52, Nov 26, 1949
     49:109, Oct 29, 1973
Newsweek 34:67, Nov 28, 1949
Outlook 159:280, Oct 28, 1931
Red Book 19:564, Jul 1912
Theatre Arts 15:981, Dec 1931
      34:15, Jan 1950
Theatre Magazine 15:176, Jun 1912
Time 54:61, Nov 28, 1949

The Ghost Sonata (see also Spook Sonata)
  Productions:
   (Off Off Broadway) Season of 1970-1971.
   (Off Off Broadway) Opened February 20, 1972 in repertory.
  No Reviews.

The Last Dance (see also Dance of Death)
  Productions:
   Adapted by Peter Goldbaum and Robin Short. Opened
    January 27, 1948 for seven performances.
  Reviews:
   Forum 109:158, Mar 1948
   New Republic 118:34, Feb 9, 1948
   New York Times p. 27, Jan 28, 1948
   New Yorker 23:42, Feb 7, 1948
   Newsweek 31:70, Feb 9, 1948

Miss Julie (Miss Julia) (see also Countess Julia)
  Productions:
   (Off Broadway) Season of 1953-1954.
   Adapted by George Tabori. Opened February 21, 1956
    for 33 performances.
   Opened May 16, 1962 in repertory (Royal Dramatic
    Theatre of Sweden).
   (Off Broadway) Opened November 10, 1965 for 11
    performances.
   (Off Off Broadway) Adapted by Julianne Boyd. Opened
    November 20, 1973.
   (Off Off Broadway) Opened September 1974.
   (Off Off Broadway) Opened October 3, 1975.
   (Off Off Broadway) Translated by Palaemona Morner and
    R. Spacek. Opened January 12, 1977.
  Reviews:
   Book News 32:72-3, Sep 1913
   Catholic World 183:66, Apr 1956
   Dramatic Mirror 69:6, Apr 30, 1913
   Life (NY) 61:930, May 8, 1913
   Nation 182:205, Mar 10, 1956

New York Theatre Critics' Reviews 1956:353
New York Times p. 24, Mar 29, 1954
              p. 23, Feb 22, 1956
              II, p. 1, Mar 4, 1956
              p. 31, May 17, 1962
              p. 19, Jul 29, 1965
              p. 59, Nov 11, 1965
              p. 23, Aug 10, 1973
              p. 52, Nov 22, 1973
              III, p. 3, Jun 10, 1977
Newsweek 32:62+, Mar 3, 1956
Saturday Review 39:25, Mar 10, 1956
Time 67:47, Mar 5, 1956

Motherlove
    Productions:
        Opened January 1977.
    No Reviews.

Pariah
    Productions:
        Translated by Edwin Bjorkman. Opened March 18, 1913
            for one performance.
        Opened 1917 in repertory (Washington Square Players).
    Reviews:
        Dramatic Mirror 69:6, Apr 2, 1913
                        77:7, Jun 9, 1917
        New York Times p. 13, May 29, 1917
        Theatre Magazine 26:15+, Jul 1917

Playing with Fire
    Productions:
        (Off Off Broadway) Opened January 24, 1977.
        (Off Off Broadway) Opened January 28, 1977.
    Reviews:
        New York Times p. 18, Nov 10, 1973

The Spook Sonata   (see also Ghost Sonata)
    Productions:
        Opened January 5, 1924 for 24 performances.
    Reviews:
        Dial 76:205, Feb 1924
        Freeman 8:472, Jan 23, 1924
        Life (NY) 83:18, Jan 24, 1924
        Nation 118:147-8, Feb 6, 1924
        New Republic 37:231-2, Jan 23, 1924
        New York Times p. 23, Jan 7, 1924
                        VII, p. 1, Jan 13, 1924

The Stronger
    Productions:
        Translated by Edith and Warner Oland. Opened March 18,
            1913 for one performance.

Adapted by George Tabori.   Opened February 21, 1956
    for 33 performances.
(Off Off Broadway) Season of 1971-1972.
(Off Off Broadway) Season of 1972-1973.
(Off Off Broadway) Opened October 3, 1975.
(Off Off Broadway) Translated by Palaemona Morner and
    R. Spacek.   Opened January 12, 1977.
(Off Broadway) Opened April 5, 1977 for 56 performances.
Reviews:
    Dramatic Mirror 69:6, Apr 2, 1913
    New York Theatre Critics' Reviews 1956:353
                                      1977:217
    New York Times p. 23, Feb 22, 1956
                   p. 59, Nov 11, 1965
                   p. 27, Aug 11, 1970
                   p. 29, Feb 26, 1974
                   III, p. 3, Jan 28, 1977
                   II, p. 19, May 18, 1977
    Saturday Review 39:25, Mar 10, 1956

To Damascus
    Productions:
    (Off Broadway) Translated by S. E. Davidson and adapted
        by M. Winston.   Season of 1960-1961.
    Reviews:
    New York Times p. 40, Feb 15, 1961
    New Yorker 37:77, Feb 25, 1961

SUDERMANN, HERMANN

Magda
    Productions:
    Translated by Charles Edward Amory Winslow.   Opened
        January 26, 1926 for 24 performances.
    Reviews:
    American Playwright 1:192-7, Jun 1913
    New York Times p. 16, Jan 27, 1926

Song of Songs
    Productions:
    Opened December 22, 1914 for 191 performances.
    Reviews:
    Bookman 40:637-8, Feb 1915
    Current Opinion 58:97-8, Feb 1915
    Dramatic Mirror 72:8, Dec 30, 1914
    Green Book 13:478-9, Mar 1915
              13:570-1, Mar 1915
    Hearst 27:299-301; 316-17, Mar 1915
    Nation 100:87, Jan 21, 1915
    New Republic 1:25, Jan 2, 1915
    New York Times p. 13, Dec 5, 1914
                   VIII, p. 8, Dec 13, 1914

Smart Set 45:453-4, Jan 1915
Theatre Magazine 21:58, Feb 1915

SYNGE, JOHN MILLINGTON

Deirdre of the Sorrows
    Productions:
        Season of 1920-1921.
        (Off Broadway) Opened December 1948.
    Reviews:
        America 102:217, Nov 14, 1959
        Forum 113:27, Jan 1950
        New York Clipper 68:19, Sep 29, 1920
        New York Times VI, p. 1, Sep 26, 1920
                        p. 51, Dec 15, 1949
                        p. 46, Oct 15, 1959
        New Yorker 35:95, Oct 24, 1959
        Weekly Review 3:297, Oct 1920

God and Kate Murphy (with Kiernan Tunney)
    Productions:
        Opened February 26, 1959 for 12 performances.
    Reviews:
        Nation 188:234-5, Mar 14, 1959
        New York Times p. 21, Feb 27, 1959
        New Yorker 35:80+, Mar 7, 1959
        Theatre Arts 43:66-7, May 1959

In the Shadow of the Glen
    Productions:
        Opened November 20, 1911 in repertory (The Irish Players).
        Opened October 21, 1932 in repertory (Irish Repertory
            Company).
        Opened November 17, 1934 for one performance.
        (Off Broadway) Season of 1956-1957.
        (Off Off Broadway) Opened March 1976.
    Reviews:
        Catholic World 185:148, May 1957
        Dramatic Mirror 66:6-7, Dec 20, 1911
        New York Times p. 25, Nov 4, 1932
                        p. 27, Dec 27, 1954
                        p. 24, Mar 7, 1957
                        II, p. 1, Mar 17, 1957

Playboy of the Western World
    Productions:
        Opened November 20, 1911 in repertory (Irish Repertory
            Company).
        Opened February 4, 1913 in repertory (Irish Repertory
            Company).
        Opened April 16, 1921 in repertory (Irish Repertory Company).
        Opened June 2, 1930 in repertory (Irish Repertory Company).

Opened October 21, 1932 in repertory (Irish Repertory
  Company).
Opened November 17, 1934 for 7 performances.
Opened November 20, 1937 for 9 performances.
(Off Broadway) Opened July 22, 1945 in repertory.
Opened October 26, 1946 for 81 performances.
(Off Broadway) Opened June 23, 1947.
(Off Broadway) Season of 1957-1958.
Opened January 7, 1971 in repertory for 52 performances.
(Off Off Broadway) Opened May 3, 1974.
(Off Off Broadway) Opened November 1974.
Reviews:
  American Playwright 1:24-5, Jan 1912
  Bookman 32:145-6, Oct 1910
  Catholic World 164:262-3, Dec 1946
            187:312-13, Jul 1958
  Collier's 48:33-4, Feb 10, 1912
  Commonweal 45:95, Nov 8, 1946
            68:303-4, Jan 20, 1958
  Dramatic Mirror 66:7+, Nov 29, 1911
            66:6, Dec 6, 1911
  Dramatist 3:224-5, Jan 1912
  Everybody's Magazine 26:233+, Feb 1912
  Forum 47:380-1, Mar 1912
  Green Book 7:237-8+, Feb 1912
  Harper's Bazaar 80:220, Dec 1946
  Life (NY) 58:1090, Dec 14, 1911
  Life 24:85-6+, May 24, 1948
  Munsey 46:588-9, Jan 1912
  Nation 93:529, Nov 30, 1911
          163:536, Nov 9, 1946
          166:557, May 15, 1948
          212:124-5, Jan 25, 1971
  New Republic 27:117, Jun 22, 1921
              115:628, Nov 11, 1946
              118:34, May 19, 1948
              164:24+, Jan 30, 1971
  New York Clipper 69:23, Apr 20, 1921
  New York Theatre Critics' Reviews 1946:287
                                    1971:396
  New York Times p. 20, Jan 30, 1930
                p. 25, Oct 21, 1932
                p. 14, Nov 22, 1937
                II, p. 1 and p. 3, Oct 20, 1946
                p. 18, Oct 28, 1946
                II, p. 1, Nov 10, 1946
                II, p. 1, Nov 24, 1946
                VI, p. 8, Dec 22, 1946
                p. 19, May 9, 1958
                p. 40, Sep 4, 1968
                p. 18, Jan 8, 1971
                II, p. 1, Jan 17, 1971
                II, p. 22, Feb 7, 1971

New York Times p. 53, Jun 13, 1974
New Yorker 22:57, Nov 2, 1946
      46:75, Jan 16, 1971
Newsweek 28:85, Nov 4, 1946
      31:77, May 10, 1948
      77:79, Jan 18, 1971
Red Book 18:753-62, Feb 1912
Saturday Review 31:20-1, May 29, 1948
      54:75-6, Jan 23, 1971
Theatre Arts 16:228-36, Mar 1932
      31:21-2, Jan 1947
      32:13+, Summer 1948
Theatre Magazine 15:ii+, Jan 1912
      34:14+, Jul 1921
Time 48:55, Nov 4, 1946
      51:81, May 10, 1948
      97:37, Jan 18, 1971
Weekly Review 4:496-7, May 21, 1921

Riders to the Sea
Productions:
    Opened November 20, 1911 in repertory.
    Opened February 4, 1913 in repertory (The Irish Players).
    Opened in the Fall of 1934 in repertory for two
        performances (Abbey Theatre Players).
    (Off Broadway) Season of 1936-1937.
    (Off Broadway) Season of 1937-1938 in repertory.
    (Off Broadway) Opened February 1949 in repertory.
    (Off Broadway) Season of 1956-1957.
    (Off Off Broadway) Opened March 1976.
Reviews:
    Catholic World 185:148, May 1957
    Drama 15:106, Feb 1925
    Dramatic Mirror 66:7, Dec 13, 1911
    Green Book 7:239+, Feb 1912
    New York Times p. 13, Feb 15, 1937
                    p. 30, Feb 4, 1949
                    p. 24, Mar 7, 1957
                    II, p. 1, Mar 17, 1957
    Weekly Review 3:155-6, Aug 18, 1920

Tinker's Wedding
Productions:
    (Off Broadway) Season of 1956-1957.
    (Off Off Broadway) Season of 1967-1968.
    (Off Off Broadway) Opened March 1976.
Reviews:
    Catholic World 185:148, May 1957
    New York Times p. 24, Mar 7, 1957
                    II, p. 1, Mar 17, 1957

The Well of the Saints
Productions:

Opened November 20, 1911 in repertory (The Irish Players).
Opened January 21, 1932 for five performances.
Opened November 21, 1934 for one performance.
(Off Broadway) Opened June 1938 in repertory.
(Off Broadway) Season of 1938-1939 in repertory.
Reviews:
  Arts and Decoration 36:42+, Mar 1932
  Catholic World 189:243, Jun 1959
  Dramatic Mirror 66:9, Nov 29, 1911
  New York Times p. 15, Jan 22, 1932
               p. 26, Nov 22, 1934
               p. 15, Apr 11, 1959
               p. 34, Aug 10, 1970
  New Yorker 35:82-3, Apr 18, 1959

TABORI, GEORGE

Brecht on Brecht (stage reading)
  Productions:
    (Off Broadway) Arranged and translated by George Tabori.
      Opened January 3, 1962 for 424 performances.
    (Off Broadway) Arranged and translated by George Tabori.
      Opened July 9, 1963 for 47 performances.
    (Off Off Broadway) Opened September 21, 1975.
  Reviews:
    New Republic 146:23, Jan 22, 1962
    New York Times p. 26, Jan 4, 1962
                 II, p. 1, Jan 14, 1962
    Theatre Arts 46:60-1, Mar 1962

Brouhaha
  Productions:
    (Off Broadway) Season of 1959-1960.
  Reviews:
    New York Times p. 18, Aug 28, 1958
                 p. 31, Apr 27, 1960
                 p. 25, Apr 29, 1960

The Cannibals
  Productions:
    (Off Broadway) Opened October 7, 1968 for 40 performances.
  Reviews:
    Nation 207:603, Dec 2, 1968
    New York Times p. 60, Nov 4, 1968
                 II, p. 5, Nov 10, 1968
    New Yorker 44:118+, Nov 9, 1968

The Demonstration (see The Niggerlovers)

The Emperor's Clothes
  Productions:
    Opened February 9, 1953 for 16 performances.

Reviews:
    Commonweal 57:551, Mar 6, 1953
    Nation 176:174, Feb 21, 1953
    New Republic 128:22-3, Feb 23, 1953
    New York Theatre Critics' Reviews 1953:368
    New York Times p. 24, Feb 20, 1953
                II, p. 3, Feb 22, 1953
                II, p. 3, Mar 1, 1953
    New Yorker 29:62, Feb 21, 1953
    Saturday Review 36:37, Feb 28, 1953
             36:33, Nov 7, 1953
    Theatre Arts 37:28, Apr 1953
    Time 61:86, Feb 23, 1953

Flight into Egypt
    Productions:
    Opened March 18, 1952 for 46 performances.
    Reviews:
    Catholic World 175:147, May 1952
    Commonweal 55:638, Apr 4, 1952
    Nation 174:306, Mar 29, 1952
          174:328, Apr 5, 1952
    New York Theatre Critics' Reviews 1952:341
    New York Times p. 33, Mar 19, 1952
                II, p. 1, Mar 30, 1952
                II, p. 3, Mar 30, 1952
    New Yorker 28:60+, Mar 29, 1952
    Newsweek 39:84, Mar 31, 1952
    Saturday Review 35:28-9, Mar 22, 1952
             35:27, May 3, 1952
    Theatre Arts 36:90, May 1952
    Time 59:68, Mar 31, 1952

Man and Dog (see The Niggerlovers)

The Niggerlovers (The Demonstration and Man and Dog)
    Productions:
    (Off Broadway) Opened October 1, 1967 for 25 performances.
    Reviews:
    New York Times p. 54, Oct 2, 1967
                II, p. 3, Oct 15, 1967
                p. 57, Oct 20, 1967
    New Yorker 43:152-3, Oct 14, 1967
    Newsweek 70:109, Oct 16, 1967

Pinkville
    Productions:
    (Off Broadway) Opened February 22, 1971 for 42 perform-
        ances.
    Reviews:
    New York Times p. 45, Mar 18, 1971
                II, p. 3, Mar 21, 1971
    Newsweek 77:109, Mar 29, 1971

The Resistible Rise of Arturo Ui   (see entry under Brecht,
          Bertoldt)

TAGGER, THEODOR   see   BRUCKNER, FERDINAND

TAYLOR, TOM

Our American Cousin
    Productions:
        Opened November 29, 1915 for 40 performances.
    Reviews:
        Green Book 7:121-8, Jan 1912
        Green Book Album 2:93-7, Jul 1909
        Literary Digest 51:1428-9, Dec 18, 1915
        Theatre Magazine 8:61-2, Mar 1908

Ticket of Leave Man, or Hawkshaw the Detective
    Productions:
        (Off Broadway) Opened June 24, 1934.
        (Off Broadway) Opened December 22, 1961 for 31 perform-
          ances.
    Reviews:
        New York Times p. 18, Jun 25, 1934
                        p. 15, Dec 23, 1961

THOMAS, BRANDON

Charley's Aunt
    Productions:
        Opened June 1, 1925 for 8 performances.
        Opened October 17, 1940 for 233 performances.
        Opened December 22, 1933 for 15 performances.
        (Off Broadway) Opened April 7, 1962 for 9 performances.
        Opened July 4, 1970 for 9 performances.
    Reviews:
        Catholic World 152:334, Dec 1940
                       178:387, Feb 1954
        Commonweal 33:80, Nov 8, 1940
        Life 6:72-3, May 29, 1939
             9:47-50, Nov 18, 1940
        Nation 151:431, Nov 2, 1940
        New Republic 103:629, Nov 4, 1940
        New York Theatre Critics' Reviews 1940:24
                                          1953:179
                                          1970:222
        New York Times p. 16, Jun 2, 1925
                       p. 24, Oct 18, 1940
                       X, p. 7, Dec 8, 1940
                       p. 12, Jul 31, 1941
                       p. 22, Dec 23, 1953

New York Times II, p. 5, Feb 7, 1965
            p. 38, Jul 6, 1970
            p. 36, Jul 13, 1970
New Yorker 46:48, Jul 11, 1970
Theatre Arts 24:848, Dec 1940
            38:18, Mar 1954
Time 36:51, Nov 4, 1940
Vogue 97:34, Jan 1, 1941

Under Orders
  Productions:
    Opened August 20, 1918 for 167 performances.
  Reviews:
    Current Opinion 65:299-302, Nov 1918
    Dramatic Mirror 79:301, Aug 31, 1918
    Dramatist 11:1016-17, Jul 1920
    Green Book 20:772+, Nov 1918
    Life (NY) 72:344, Sep 5, 1918
    New York Times p. 7, Aug 21, 1918
                III, p. 4, Aug 25, 1918
    Theatre Magazine 28:218-20, Oct 1918

THOMAS, DYLAN

A Boy Growing Up   (see entry under Williams, Emyln)

*The Doctor and the Devil
  Reviews:
    New York Times p. 28, Aug 22, 1962

Dylan Thomas Growing Up   (see entry under Williams, Emyln)

Songs from Milk Wood
  Productions:
    Adapted from Under Milk Wood by Bernard Bragg with
      Dorothy Miles.   Opened January 12, 1970 for
      8 performances.
  Reviews:
    New York Times p. 41, Jan 13, 1970

Under Milk Wood
  Productions:
    Opened October 15, 1957 for 39 performances.
    (Off Broadway) Season of 1960-1961 for 7 performances.
    (Off Broadway) Opened March 29, 1961 for 202
      performances.
    (Off Broadway) Opened November 16, 1962 for 54
      performances.
    (Off Off Broadway) Opened September 25, 1976.
  Reviews:
    Christian Century 74:1324, Nov 6, 1957
                78:535-7, Apr 26, 1961

Commonweal 58:297, Jun 26, 1953
   67:151, Nov 8, 1967
Nation 185:309, Nov 2, 1957
New York Theatre Critics' Reviews 1957:223
New York Times p. 17, May 29, 1953
    II, p. 1, May 16, 1954
    p. 25, Aug 22, 1956
    VI, p. 29, Aug 25, 1957
    p. 42, Oct 16, 1957
    II, p. 1, Nov 10, 1957
    p. 25, Mar 30, 1961
    II, p. 1, Apr 9, 1961
    p. 48, Oct 18, 1961
    p. 13, Oct 6, 1962
New Yorker 33:95, Oct 26, 1957
   37:132+, Apr 8, 1961
   38:132, Dec 15, 1962
Reporter 17:39, Nov 14, 1962
Saturday Review 36:24-5, Jun 6, 1953
   39:39, Oct 6, 1956
   43:30, Jun 4, 1960
Theatre Arts 41:92-3, May 1957
   41:22-3, Dec 1957
Time 70:93, Oct 28, 1957
Vogue 130:212-13, Sep 1, 1957

TOLLER, ERNST

Bloody Laughter
 Productions:
  Adapted by Forrest Wilson and William Schack.
  Opened December 4, 1931 for 35 performances.
 Reviews:
  Commonweal 15:214, Dec 23, 1931
  New York Times p. 20, Dec 5, 1931
  Theatre Arts 16:95-6, Feb 1932

Man and the Masses
 Productions:
  Translated by Louis H. Untermeyer. Opened April 14,
   1924 for 32 performances.
 Reviews:
  American Mercury 2:244, Jun 1924
  Life (NY) 83:20, May 8, 1924
  Living Age 322:175-8, Jul 26, 1924
  Nation 118:512-13, Apr 10, 1924
  New Republic 38:262, Apr 30, 1924
  New York Times p. 25, Apr 15, 1924
  Theatre Magazine 39:54, Jun 1924

No More Peace
 Productions:

Translated by Edward Crankshaw. Opened January 25, 1938 for 4 performances (Federal Theatre Project).
Reviews:
New York Times p. 13, Jan 29, 1938
One Act Play Magazine 1:950, Feb 1938

TOLSTOY, LEO

The Cause of It All
Productions:
(Off Broadway) Season of 1942-1943 in repertory.
No Reviews.

*Ivan the Terrible
Reviews:
New York Times II, p. 1, Nov 12, 1944

The Kreutzer Sonata
Productions:
(Off Broadway) Adapted by Hannah Watt and Roderick Lovell. Season of 1960-1961.
Reviews:
New York Times p. 24, Feb 16, 1961
p. 38, Feb 28, 1961
New Yorker 37:77-8, Feb 25, 1961

The Living Corpse (see Redemption)

*Patriotic War of 1812
Reviews:
New York Times p. 2, Feb 25, 1942

The Power of Darkness
Productions:
Opened January 15, 1920 for 40 performances.
(Off Broadway) Season of 1959-1960.
Reviews:
Nation 110:178, Feb 7, 1920
New Republic 21:296, Feb 4, 1920
New York Times p. 22, Jan 22, 1920
VIII, p. 2, Jan 25, 1920
p. 28, Oct 11, 1948
p. 33, Sep 30, 1959
p. 15, Oct 31, 1959
p. 26, Jun 21, 1962
New Yorker 35:129-30, Oct 10, 1959
Review 2:137-8, Feb 7, 1920

Redemption (Living Corpse)
Productions:
Opened October 3, 1918 for 204 performances.
Opened November 19, 1928 for 20 performances.

Adapted by August Scholz.
Opened December 6, 1929.
Reviews:
Arts and Decoration 32:96, Feb 1930
Commonweal 11:299, Dec 25, 1929
Current Opinion 65:305, Nov 1918
Dramatic Mirror 79:580, Oct 19, 1918
Forum 60:621-2, Nov 1918
Green Book 20:958-9, Dec 1918
Nation 107:459, Oct 19, 1918
        127:640-1, Dec 5, 1928
        129:785-6, Dec 25, 1929
New Republic 17:46, Nov 9, 1918
              16:349, Oct 19, 1918
Theatre Arts 14:107-8, Feb 1930
Theatre Magazine 28:277, Nov 1918
                  28:358-9, Dec 1918

Tsar Fyodor Ivanovitch
Productions:
Opened January 1923 in repertory.
Opened November 1923 in repertory.
Reviews:
Hearst 43:93-5, Feb 1923
Independent 110:98, Feb 3, 1923
New York Clipper 70:14, Jan 17, 1923
New York Times p. 14, May 22, 1923

TURGENEV, IVAN

*The Country Woman
Reviews:
New York Times p. 61, Mar 26, 1972

Lady from the Provinces
Productions:
Opened February 1923 for 8 performances in repertory.
No Reviews.

A Month in the Country
Productions:
Opened March 17, 1930 for 71 performances.
Adapted by Emlyn Williams. Opened April 3, 1956 for 48
    performances.
(Off Broadway) Adapted by Carmel Ross from Constance
    Garnett's translation. Opened May 28, 1963 for 48
    performances.
(Off Off Broadway) Opened May 23, 1975.
(Off Off Broadway) Adapted by David Morgan. Opened
    December 4, 1975.
(Off Broadway) Opened June 9, 1976 for 12 performances.
(Off Off Broadway) Adapted by David Morgan.

Opened August 1976.
Reviews:
America 95:91, Apr 21, 1956
Arts and Decoration 33:62, May 1930
Catholic World 183:228, Jun 1956
Commonweal 11:622, Apr 2, 1930
      64:150, May 11, 1956
      78:354, Jun 21, 1963
Life (NY) 95:16, Apr 4, 1930
Nation 130:430+, Apr 9, 1930
    182:348, Apr 21, 1956
New Republic 62:246-7, Apr 16, 1930
    134:21-2, Apr 23, 1956
New York Times p. 30, Mar 18, 1930
    II, p. 3, Apr 1, 1956
    p. 23, Apr 4, 1956
    II, p. 1, Apr 15, 1956
    p. 32, Mar 2, 1959
    p. 39, May 29, 1963
    p. 37, Sep 10, 1974
New Yorker 32:72+, Apr 14, 1956
    39:126, Jun 8, 1963
Newsweek 47:106, Apr 16, 1956
Outlook 154:550, Apr 2, 1930
Saturday Review 39:24, Apr 21, 1956
Theatre Arts 14:368+, May 1930
    40:82, Jun 1956
    47:10-11, Aug 1963
Theatre Magazine 51:42+, May 1930
Time 67:63, Apr 16, 1956

USTINOV, PETER

*Blow Your Own Trumpet
Reviews:
New York Times II, p. 1, Sep 19, 1943
Theatre Arts 27:719-20, Dec 1943

*Frenzy
Reviews:
New York Times p. 35, Apr 22, 1948

Halfway up the Tree
Productions:
Opened November 7, 1967 for 64 performances.
Reviews:
America 117:724, Dec 9, 1967
Nation 205:572-3, Nov 27, 1967
New York Theatre Critics' Reviews 1967:220, 222
New York Times p. 54, Sep 12, 1967
    p. 52, Nov 8, 1967
    II, p. 5, Nov 19, 1967

New York Times p. 60, Nov 24, 1967
             II, p. 3, Dec 31, 1967
             X, p. 3, Dec 31, 1967
New Yorker 43:131, Nov 18, 1967
Saturday Review 50:70, Nov 25, 1967
Time 90:50, Nov 17, 1967

*House of Regrets
  Reviews:
    New York Times II, p. 2, Mar 14, 1948
    Theatre Arts 27:51-2, Jan 1943

*Indifferent Shepherd
  Reviews:
    New York Times II, p. 2, Mar 14, 1948

The Love of Four Colonels
  Productions:
    Opened January 15, 1953 for 141 performances.
  Reviews:
    Catholic World 176:466-7, Mar 1953
    Commonweal 57:450, Feb 6, 1953
    Harper 203:110, Nov 1951
    Life 34:95-6+, Feb 2, 1953
    Look 17:17, Feb 24, 1953
    Nation 176:132, Feb 7, 1953
    New Republic 128:22-3, Feb 2, 1953
    New York Theatre Critics' Reviews 1953:394
    New York Times VI, p. 38, Jan 4, 1953
                II, p. 1, Jan 11, 1953
                 p. 17, Jan 16, 1953
    New Yorker 28:54+, Jan 24, 1953
    Newsweek 41:95, Jan 26, 1953
    Saturday Review 36:26, Jan 31, 1953
    Theatre Arts 37:66-8, Mar 1953
    Time 61:52, Jan 26, 1953

*Man in the Raincoat
  Reviews:
    New York Times II, p. 2, Sep 11, 1949

*Moment of Truth
  Reviews:
    New York Times II, p. 7, Dec 9, 1951

*No Sign of the Dove
  Reviews:
    New York Times p. 23, Dec 12, 1953
              II, p. 4, Dec 20, 1953

Photo Finish
  Productions:
    Opened February 12, 1963 for 159 performances.

Reviews:
    Nation 196:214, Nov 9, 1963
    New York Theatre Critics' Reviews 1963:377
    New York Times p. 35, Mar 28, 1962
                  p. 23, Apr 26, 1962
                  p. 5, Jan 23, 1963
                  p. 5, Feb 14, 1963
    New Yorker 39:112, Feb 23, 1963
    Newsweek 61:60, Feb 25, 1963
    Saturday Review 46:30, Mar 2, 1963
    Theatre Arts 47:10-11, Apr 1963
    Time 81:75, Feb 22, 1963

Romanoff and Juliet

Productions:
    Opened October 10, 1957 for 389 performances.
Reviews:
    America 98:355, Dec 14, 1957
    Catholic World 186:225, Dec 1957
    Christian Century 74:1424, Nov 27, 1957
    Commonweal 67:175, Nov 15, 1957
    Life 43:111-12, Nov 25, 1957
    Nation 185:291, Oct 26, 1957
    New Republic 137:20, Oct 28, 1957
    New York Theatre Critics' Reviews 1957:228
    New York Times p. 12, May 19, 1956
                  II, p. 1, Jul 1, 1956
                  VI, p. 28, Aug 25, 1957
                  p. 24, Oct 11, 1957
                  p. 23, Aug 13, 1973
    New Yorker 33:81, Oct 19, 1957
    Newsweek 50:99, Oct 21, 1957
    Reporter 15:38, Nov 1, 1956
             17:39, Nov 14, 1957
    Saturday Review, 39:30, Oct 13, 1956
                 40:27, Oct 26, 1957
    Theatre Arts 41:92, May 1957
              41:19-20, Dec 1957
    Time 70:57, Oct 21, 1957

The Unknown Soldier and His Wife

Productions:
    Opened July 6, 1967 for 148 performances.
Reviews:
    America 117:139, Aug 5, 1967
    Christian Century 84:1131, Sep 6, 1967
    Commonweal 86:472-3, Jul 28, 1967
    Life 63:12, Aug 25, 1967
    New York Times Critics' Reviews 1967:293
    New York Times p. 17, Jan 13, 1967
                  p. 41, Jun 19, 1967
                  II, p. 1, Jul 2, 1967
                  p. 22, Jul 7, 1967

New York Times p. 35, Jul 17, 1967
               p. 26, Nov 11, 1967
New Yorker 43:23-5, Jul 15, 1967
           43:94, Jul 15, 1967
Newsweek 70:67, Jul 17, 1967
Saturday Review 50:48, Jul 22, 1967
Time 90:75, Jul 14, 1967
Vogue 150:225, Sep 1, 1967

Who's Who in Hell?
    Productions:
    Opened December 9, 1974 for 8 performances.
    Reviews:
        New York Times Critics' Reviews 1974:156
        New York Times p. 56, Dec 10, 1974
        New Yorker 50:53, Dec 23, 1974
        The Progressive 39:39, Apr 1975

VAJDA, ERNST

The Crown Prince
    Productions:
        Adapted by Zoë Akins. Opened March 23, 1927 for 45
            performances.
    Reviews:
        Bookman 65:448, Jun 1927
        Life (NY) 89:18, Apr 14, 1927
        New York Times p. 23, Mar 24, 1927

Fata Morgana (Mirage)
    Productions:
        Translated by James T. A. Burrell and Philip Moeller.
        Opened March 3, 1924 for 120 performances.
        Opened December 25, 1931 for 27 performances.
    Reviews:
        American Mercury 2:116, May 1924
        Bookman 59:331, May 1924
        Independent 112:231-2, Apr 26, 1924
        Life (NY) 83:18, Mar 27, 1924
        Nation 118:321, Mar 19, 1924
        New Republic 38:128, Mar 26, 1924
        New York Times p. 16, Mar 4, 1924
                       VIII, p. 1, Mar 9, 1924
                       p. 15, Dec 26, 1931
        Theatre Magazine 39:15, May 1924

Grounds for Divorce
    Productions:
        Adapted by Guy Bolton. Opened September 23, 1924 for
            127 performances.
    Reviews:
        Nation 119:394-5, Oct 8, 1924

New York Times p. 20, Sep 24, 1924

The Harem
  Productions:
    Adapted by Avery Hopwood. Opened December 2, 1924 for
      183 performances.
  Reviews:
    American Mercury 4:245-6, Feb 1925
    Bookman 60:742, Feb 1925
    Dramatist 16:1255, Jan 1925
    Life (NY) 84:18, Dec 25, 1924
    New York Times p. 24, Dec 3, 1924
    Theatre Magazine 40:16, Feb 1925

The Little Angel
  Productions:
    Adapted by J. Jacobus. Opened September 27, 1924 for
      49 performances.
  Reviews:
    American Mercury 3:374-5, Nov 1924
    Life (NY) 84:18, Oct 16, 1924
    New York Times p. 10, Sep 29, 1924
               VIII, p. 1, Oct 5, 1924

Mirage (see Fata Morgana)

VANE, SUTTON

Outward Bound
  Productions:
    Opened January 7, 1924 for 144 performances.
    Opened December 22, 1938 for 255 performances.
  Reviews:
    American Mercury 1:372-3, Mar 1924
    Catholic World 148:599, Feb 1939
    Classic 19:46+, May 1924
    Commonweal 29:302, Jan 6, 1939
    Current Opinion 76:443-50, Apr 1924
    Dial 76:293-4, Mar 1924
    Freeman 8:473, Jan 23, 1924
    Independent 112:231-2, Apr 26, 1924
    Life (NY) 83:18, Jan 31, 1924
    Nation 148:44, Jan 7, 1939
    New York Times p. 26, Jan 8, 1924
               p. 16, Dec 23, 1938
               XI, p. 1, Jan 1, 1939
    Stage 16:12-13, Feb 1939
    Theatre Arts 23:97+, Feb 1939
    Theatre Magazine 39:26+, May 1924
    Time 33:25, Jan 2, 1939
    Woman Citizen ns8:23, Mar 8, 1924

VERNEUIL, LOUIS

Affairs of State
   Productions:
      Opened September 25, 1950 for 610 performances.
   Reviews:
      Catholic World 172:149, Nov 1950
      Christian Science Monitor Magazine p. 6, Sep 30, 1950
      Commonweal 53:15, Oct 13, 1950
      Nation 171:321, Oct 7, 1950
      New Republic 123:21, Oct 16, 1950
      New York Theatre Critics' Reviews 1950:267
      New York Times p. 37, Sep 26, 1950
                  II, p. 1, Oct 1, 1950
                  II, p. 3, Feb 4, 1951
                  p. 12, Aug 22, 1952
      New Yorker 26:52, Oct 7, 1950
      Newsweek 36:84, Oct 9, 1950
      Saturday Review 33:24, Nov 4, 1950
      Theatre Arts 34:12, Nov 1950
      Time 56:85, Oct 9, 1950

Cousin Sonia
   Productions:
      Translated by Herbert Williams. Opened December 7, 1925
         for 30 performances.
   No Reviews.

First Love
   Productions:
      Adapted by Zoe Akins from Pile ou Face. Opened
         November 8, 1926 for 50 performances.
   Reviews:
      Life (NY) 88:23, Nov 25, 1926
      New York Times p. 31, Nov 9, 1926
      Theatre Magazine 45:16+, Feb 1927

Jealousy (see also Obsession)
   Productions:
      Adapted by Eugene Walter. Opened October 22, 1928 for
         136 performances.
   Reviews:
      New York Times p. 32, Oct 23, 1928
      Theatre Magazine 49:45-6, Jan 1929
                  49:30-1+, Feb 1929

Love and Let Love
   Productions:
      Opened October 19, 1951 for 51 performances.
   Reviews:
      Catholic World 174:229, Dec 1951
      Commonweal 55:117, Nov 9, 1951
      New York Theatre Critics' Reviews 1951:198

New York Times p. 11, Oct 20, 1951
New Yorker 27:68, Oct 27, 1951
Newsweek 38:84, Oct 29, 1951
Theatre Arts 35:21+, Nov 1951
                35:3, Dec 1951
Time 58:38, Oct 29, 1951

The Love Habit
Productions:
Adapted by Gladys Unger. Opened March 14, 1923 for
    69 performances.
Reviews:
New York Clipper 71:14, Mar 21, 1923
New York Times p. 17, Mar 15, 1923
Theatre Magazine 37:15, May 1923

Matrimony PFD
Productions:
Adapted by Grace George and James Forbes. Opened
    November 12, 1936 for 61 performances.
Reviews:
Catholic World 144:473, Jan 1937
Nation 143:642, Nov 28, 1936
New York Times p. 28, Nov 6, 1936
                p. 26, Nov 13, 1936
Theatre Arts 21:20+, Jan 1937
Time 28:36, Nov 23, 1936

Obsession (see also Jealousy)
Productions:
Adapted by Jane Hinton from Jealousy. Opened October 1,
    1946 for 31 performances.
Reviews:
New York Times p. 39, Oct 2, 1946
New Yorker 22:49, Oct 12, 1946
Newsweek 28:104, Oct 14, 1946
Time 48:100, Oct 14, 1946

Oh Mama
Productions:
Adapted by Wilton Lackaye and Harry Wagstaff Gribble.
    Opened August 19, 1925 for 70 performances.
Reviews:
Dramatist 16:1287-8, Oct 1925
New York Times p. 22, Aug 20, 1925
Theatre Magazine 42:14-15, Oct 1925

Pile ou Face (see First Love)

VILDRAC, CHARLES

Michel Auclair

Productions:
Opened March 4, 1925 for 19 performances.
Reviews:
Nation 120:334-5, Mar 25, 1925
New York Times p. 23, Mar 5, 1925
Theatre Arts 8:13-18, Jan 1942

The Pilgrim
Productions:
(Off Broadway) Translated by Ruth Collins Allen.   Opened
February 11, 1938 for one matinee.
Reviews:
No Reviews.

S. S. Tenacity
Productions:
Opened January 2, 1922 for 67 performances.
Reviews:
Bookman 55:61, Mar 1922
Dramatic Mirror 95:17, Jan 7, 1922
Independent 108:92, Jan 28, 1922
Nation 114:103, Jan 25, 1922
New Republic 29:251, Jan 25, 1922
New York Clipper 69:20, Jan 18, 1922
New York Times p. 20, Jan 3, 1922
                      VI, p. 1, Jan 15, 1922
                      VI, p. 1, Feb 5, 1922
Theatre Magazine 35:166-7, Mar 1922

VON HOFMANNSTHAL, HUGO

Elektra
Productions:
Adapted from Sophocles. Opened December 26, 1930 for
8 performances.
(Off Off Broadway) Translated by Cari Richard Mueller.
Opened February 3, 1974.
Reviews:
New York Times p. 16, Dec 27, 1930
                 VIII, p. 3, May 24, 1931
                 p. 22, May 24, 1974
                 II, p. 1, Jun 9, 1974

Everyman (see also Jedermann)
Productions:
(Off Broadway) Translated by George Sterling.   Opened
May 8, 1941 in repertory.
Reviews:
New York Times p. 19, May 9, 1941

Jedermann (see also Everyman)
Productions:

Based on the English morality play.   Music by Einar Nilson.
Opened December 7, 1927 for 14 performances.
Reviews:
New Republic 53:164-5, Dec 28, 1927
New York Times p. 4, Aug 1, 1927
                    IV, p. 16, Sep 11, 1927
                    p. 30, Sep 19, 1927
                    p. 33, Dec 8, 1927
                    IX, p. 6, Dec 18, 1927
                    VIII, p. 4, Dec 25, 1927
Theatre Arts 12:90-91, Feb 1928
Theatre Magazine 47:58, Feb 1928
Vogue 71:100, Feb 1, 1928

VON KLEIST, HEINRICH

Amphitryon
    Productions:
        (Off Broadway) Adapted from Molière.   Opened November 17,
            1970 for 8 performances.
    Reviews:
        New York Times p. 40, Nov 18, 1970
        New Yorker 45:57-8+, Feb 14, 1970

The Broken Jug
    Productions:
        Adapted by David Harron.   Opened April 1, 1958 for 12
            performances.
    Reviews:
        New York Times p. 36, Apr 2, 1958

The Prince of Homburg
    Productions:
        (Off Broadway) English version by James Kirkup; adapted by
            Robert Kalfin.   Opened November 3, 1976 for 40 per-
            formances.
    Reviews:
        Nation 223:538-9, Nov 20, 1976
        New Republic 175:18, Nov 20, 1976
        New York Times Critics' Reviews 1976:90
        New York Times p. 57, Nov 1, 1976
                        II, p. 3, Nov 7, 1976
        New Yorker 52:109-10, Nov 22, 1976
        Newsweek 88:105, Nov 22, 1976

WEDEKIND, FRANK

The Awakening of Spring   (see also Birabeau's Dame Nature)
    Productions:
        (Off Broadway) Translated by Mascha Beyo.   Adapted by
            Arthur A. Seidelman and Donald Levin.   Opened

May 12, 1964 for eight performances.
(Off Off Broadway) Opened June 11, 1975 (Roundabout).
(Off Off Broadway) Opened June 12, 1975 (Circle Repertory).
(Off Off Broadway) Translated by Mary Eileen O'Donnell.
Adapted by Carol Corwen. Opened April 16, 1977.
Reviews:
New York Times p. 30, Oct 10, 1955
        p. 50, May 13, 1964
        p. 42, Sep 9, 1974

Death and the Devil
    Productions:
        (Off Off Broadway) Opened October 21, 1976.
    No Reviews.

Earth Spirit
    Productions:
        (Off Broadway) Opened June 1950 in repertory.
    Reviews:
        New York Times p. 33, Jun 7, 1950

Franziska
    Productions:
        (Off Off Broadway) Opened April 6, 1977.
    No Reviews.

*King Nicolo
    Reviews:
        New York Times p. 16, Jun 24, 1955

The Loves of Lulu   (see also Lulu)
    Productions:
        Translated by Samuel A. Eliot, Jr.   Opened May 11, 1925
            for 15 performances.
    Reviews:
        New Republic 43:20-21, May 27, 1925
        New York Times p. 26, May 12, 1925
        New Yorker 34:89-90, Oct 11, 1958

Lulu   (see also The Loves of Lulu)
    Productions:
        (Off Broadway) Translated by Mari Saville and Morton Siegel.
            Opened March 27, 1970 for one performance.
        (Off Off Broadway) Adapted by Ron Cowan.   Opened May 1,
            1974.
    Reviews:
        New York Times p. 24, Sep 30, 1958
            p. 32, Mar 28, 1970

Spring's Awakening   (see The Awakening of Spring)

The Tenor
    Productions:

Adapted by Andre Tridon. Opened October 4, 1915 in
repertory (Washington Square Players).
Reviews:
Dramatic Mirror 75:8, Jan 22, 1916
New York Times p. 11, Jan 11, 1916

WEISS, PETER

The Bogeyman of Lusitania (see Song of the Lusitanian Bogey)

*Discourse on Vietnam
Reviews:
New York Times p. 55, Mar 21, 1968
                II, p. 22, Mar 31, 1968

*Hölderlin
Reviews:
Newsweek 78:92, Oct 11, 1972

How Mr. Mockinpott Was Cured of His Suffering
Productions:
(Off Off Broadway) Opened May 25, 1973 in repertory.
No Reviews.

The Investigation
Productions:
English version by Jon Swan and Ulu Grosbard. Opened
October 4, 1966 for 103 performances.
Reviews:
America 115:525, Oct 29, 1966
Christian Century 83:1540-1, Dec 14, 1966
Commentary 42:75-6, Dec 1966
Commonweal 85:139-41, Nov 4, 1966
Life 61:8+, Oct 28, 1966
Nation 203:395-6, Oct 17, 1966
New Republic 155:42-4, Nov 26, 1966
New York Theatre Critics' Reviews 1966:281
New York Times p. 30, Apr 22, 1966
                p. 40, Oct 5, 1966
                II, p. 1, Oct 16, 1966
                II, p. 1, Nov 13, 1966
New Yorker 42:118, Oct 15, 1966
Newsweek 68:98, Oct 17, 1966
Saturday Review 49:72, Oct 22, 1966
Time 88:93, Oct 14, 1966
Vogue 148:99, Nov 15, 1966

Marat/Sade (The Persecution and Assassination of Marat as Per-
formed by the Inmates of the Asylum of Charenton Under
the Direction of the Marquis de Sade)
Productions:
Opened December 27, 1965 for 144 performances.

Opened January 3, 1967 for 55 performances.
(Off Off Broadway) Season of 1971-1972.
Reviews:
America 114:181-2, Jan 29, 1966
Catholic World 203:63-4, Apr 1966
Commentary 41:75-6, Mar 1966
Commonweal 83:476-7, Jan 21, 1966
          83:636-8, Mar 4, 1966
Harper's 232:124, Apr 1966
Life 60:26-27, Mar 11, 1966
Look 30:106-10, Feb 22, 1966
Nation 202:82-4, Jan 17, 1966
New Republic 154:23-4+, Jan 22, 1966
New York Theatre Critics' Reviews 1965:212
                                   1967:398
New York Times p. 42, May 1, 1964
             p. 14, Aug 21, 1964
             p. 29, Aug 25, 1964
             II, X, p. 3, Dec 26, 1965
             p. 35, Dec 28, 1965
             II, p. 1, Jan 9, 1966
             p. 34, Jan 4, 1967
             II, p. 1, Jan 15, 1967
             p. 53, Oct 4, 1971
New Yorker 40:204-6, Sep 19, 1964
Newsweek 67:63, Jan 10, 1966
        69:93, Jan 16, 1966
Reporter 34:48-9, Jan 27, 1966
Saturday Review 49:45+, Jan 15, 1966
Time 87:51, Jan 7, 1966
Vogue 144:94, Oct 15, 1964
     147:102-5, Jan 1, 1966
     147:56, Feb 15, 1966

The Persecution and Assassination of Marat ... (see Marat/Sade)

Sangen om Skrapuken (see Song of the Lusitanian Bogey)

The Song of the Horrible Demon (see Song of the Lusitanian
     Bogey)

Song of the Lusitanian Bogey
  Productions:
    (Off Broadway) Translated by Lee Baxandall. Opened
       January 2, 1968 for 40 performances.
    (Off Broadway) Opened July 23, 1968 for 24 performances
       in repertory.
  Reviews:
    America 118:132, Jan 27, 1968
    Nation 206:125, Jan 22, 1968
    New York Theatre Critics' Reviews 1968:265
    New York Times p. 76, Feb 19, 1967
                II, p. 1, Apr 9, 1967

New York Times p. 52, Jan 3, 1968
New Yorker 43:57-8, Jan 13, 1968
Newsweek 71:79, Jan 15, 1968
Reporter 38:40, Feb 8, 1968
Saturday Review 51:18+, Jan 20, 1968
Time 91:40, Jan 12, 1968

The Tower
    Productions:
        (Off Off Broadway) Opened April 24, 1974.
    No Reviews.

*Trotsky in Exile
    Reviews:
        New York Times II, p. 5, Feb 1, 1970

WERFEL, FRANZ

The Eternal Road
    Productions:
        Adapted by William A. Drake. Translated by Ludwig
            Lewisohn. Opened January 7, 1937 for 153 performances.
    Reviews:
        Nation 144:109, Jan 23, 1937
        New Republic 90:19-20, Feb 10, 1937
        New York Times p. 29, Dec 14, 1936
                        X, p. 7, Dec 27, 1936
                        X, p. 1, Jan 3, 1937
                        X, p. 8, Jan 17, 1937
                        p. 30, May 13, 1937
                        p. 23, May 15, 1937
        Saturday Review 15:17+, Feb 27, 1937
        Stage 13:62-4, Dec 1935
        Theatre Arts 21:180+, Mar 1937
        Time 29:47-8, Jan 18, 1937

The Goat Song
    Productions:
        Translated by Ruth Langner. Opened January 25, 1926
            for 58 performances.
        (Off Broadway) Season of 1953-1954.
    Reviews:
        Bookman 63:213, Apr 1926
        Dramatist 17:1289, Jan 1926
        Independent 116:275, Mar 6, 1926
        Literary Digest 88:25, Feb 13, 1926
        Nation 122:187, Feb 17, 1926
        New Republic 46:17, Feb 24, 1926
        New York Times p. 18, Jan 26, 1926
                        VII, p. 1, Feb 7, 1926
        Theatre Magazine 43:16, Apr 1926
        Vogue 67:134, Mar 15, 1926

Jacobowsky and the Colonel

Productions:

Adapted by S. N. Behrman. Opened March 14, 1944 for 417 performances.

(Off Broadway) Season of 1953-1954.

Reviews:

Catholic World 159:169-70, May 1944
    159:457-8, Aug 1944
Commonweal 39:589-90, Mar 31, 1944
Life 16:49-50+, Apr 10, 1944
Nation 158:373, Mar 25, 1944
    158:429-30, Apr 8, 1944
New Republic 110:307, Mar 27, 1944
New York Theatre Critics' Reviews 1944:243
New York Times VI, p. 24, Mar 5, 1944
    II, p. 1, Mar 12, 1944
    p. 17, Mar 15, 1944
    II, p. 1, Mar 19, 1944
New York Times Magazine pp. 24-5, Mar 5, 1944
    p. 16+, Apr 9, 1944
New Yorker 20:52, Mar 25, 1944
Newsweek 23:105-6, Mar 27, 1944
Theatre Arts 28:143-5, Mar 1944
    28:204, Apr 1944
    28:261-2+, May 1944
Time 43:60+, Mar 27, 1944

Juarez and Maximillian

Productions:

Opened October 11, 1926 for 48 performances.

Reviews:

Dial 81:522, Dec 1926
Independent 117:621, Nov 1927
Life (NY) 88:21, Nov 4, 1926
Literary Digest 91:26-7, Oct 30, 1926
Nation 122:587, May 26, 1926
    123:435, Oct 27, 1926
New Republic 48:271-2, Oct 27, 1926
New York Times p. 31, Oct 12, 1926
    VIII, p. 1, Oct 17, 1926
Theatre Arts 10:813-14+, Dec 1926
Theatre Magazine 44:15, Dec 1926
    44:26-8+, Dec 1926
Vanity Fair 27:63+, Nov 1926
Vogue 68:83, Dec 1, 1926

Schweiger

Productions:

Translated by Jack Charash and William A. Drake. Opened March 23, 1926 for 30 performances.

Reviews:

Bookman 63:467-8, Jun 1926
Life (NY) 87:23, Apr 15, 1926

368 / WERFEL

New York Times p. 20, Mar 24, 1926
Theatre Magazine 43:16, Jun 1926

WESKER, ARNOLD

Chips with Everything
Productions:
Opened October 1, 1963 for 149 performances.
Reviews:
America 109:496, Oct 26, 1963
Commonweal 79:139-41, Oct 25, 1963
79:570-1, Feb 7, 1964
84:473, Jul 22, 1966
Nation 197:267-8, Oct 19, 1963
New Republic 149:30-1, Oct 19, 1963
New York Theatre Critics' Reviews 1963:236
New York Times p. 33, Sep 23, 1963
p. 49, Oct 2, 1963
New Yorker 38:160, May 12, 1962
Newsweek 62:72, Oct 14, 1963
Reporter 27:48+, Sep 13, 1962
Saturday Review 46:30, Oct 19, 1963
Theatre Arts 48:10-11, Jan 1964
Time 82:72+, Oct 11, 1963
Vogue 143:62, Feb 1, 1964

The Four Seasons
Productions:
Opened March 14, 1968 for 6 performances.
Reviews:
New York Times p. 32, Mar 15, 1968
New Yorker 44:102, Mar 23, 1968
Time 91:64, Mar 22, 1968

*The Friends
Reviews:
New York Times p. 41, May 22, 1970
p. 17, Jul 24, 1970
II, p. 1, Aug 30, 1970

The Kitchen
Productions:
(Off Broadway) Opened May 9, 1966 for three performances
(New Theatre Workshop).
(Off Broadway) Opened June 13, 1966 for 137 performances.
Reviews:
Life 61:17, Aug 12, 1966
New York Times p. 50, Jun 14, 1966
Newsweek 67:89, Jun 27, 1966
Saturday Review 49:36, Jul 2, 1966

The Old Ones
    Productions:
        (Off Off Broadway) Opened December 7, 1974.
    Reviews:
        New York Times p. 16, Aug 26, 1972
                     p. 69, Dec 15, 1974

Roots
    Productions:
        (Off Broadway) Opened March 6, 1961 for 72 performances.
        (Off Broadway) Opened January 8, 1965 for nine perform-
            ances.
    Reviews:
        Horizon 3:117-18, Jul 1961
        Nation 192:272, Mar 25, 1961
        New Republic 144:30, Mar 27, 1961
        New York Times p. 40, Mar 7, 1961
                     II, p. 1, Mar 19, 1961
        New Yorker 37:126+, Mar 18, 1961
        Theatre Arts 45:56, May 1961
        Time 77:42+, Mar 17, 1961

WHEELER, HUGH

Big Fish, Little Fish
    Productions:
        Opened March 15, 1961 for 101 performances.
        (Off Off Broadway) Opened September 11, 1974.
    Reviews:
        Commonweal 74:255-6, Jun 2, 1961
        Nation 192:292, Apr 1, 1961
        New Republic 144:22, Apr 1, 1961
        New York Theatre Critics' Review 1961:323
        New York Times p. 42, Mar 16, 1961
                     II, p. 1, Mar 26, 1961
                     p. 32, Sep 18, 1974
        New Yorker 37:113, Mar 25, 1961
        Newsweek 57:82, Mar 27, 1961
        Reporter 24:46, Apr 13, 1961
        Saturday Review 44:32, Apr 1, 1961
        Theatre Arts 45:56-7, May 1961
        Time 77:52, Mar 24, 1961

Look: We've Come Through!
    Productions:
        Opened October 25, 1961 for five performances.
        (Off Off Broadway) January 10, 1974.
        (Off Off Broadway) March 4, 1976.
    Reviews:
        Commonweal 72:210-11, Nov 17, 1961
        New York Theatre Critics' Reviews 1961:198
        New York Times p. 40, Oct 26, 1961

New York Times p. 31, Jan 15, 1974
New Yorker 37:128, Nov 4, 1961
Newsweek 58:69, Nov 6, 1961
Reporter 25:46, Nov 23, 1961
Saturday Review 44:39, Nov 18, 1961
Theatre Arts 46:14-15, Jan 1962

We Have Always Lived in the Castle
  Based on Shirley Jackson's novel.
  Productions:
    Opened October 19, 1966 for 9 performances.
  Reviews:
    Commonweal 85:167, Nov 11, 1966
    New York Theatre Critics' Reviews 1966:266
    New York Times p. 53, Oct 20, 1966
                  p. 48, Oct 24, 1966

WHITING, JOHN

Conditions of Agreement
  Productions:
    (Off Broadway) Opened May 29, 1972 for one performance.
  Reviews:
    New York Times p. 43, May 30, 1972
    Newsweek 79:109, Jun 12, 1972

The Devils
  Productions:
    Based on Aldous Huxley's The Devils of Loudun.   Opened
      November 16, 1965 for 63 performances.
    (Off Off Broadway) Opened January 28, 1973 in repertory.
    (Off Off Broadway) Opened January 10, 1975.
  Reviews:
    Catholic World 202:255-6, Jan 1966
    Commonweal 79:371, Dec 20, 1963
              83:348-9, Dec 17, 1965
    Nation 201:483-4, Dec 13, 1965
    National Review 18:38-9, Jan 11, 1966
    New Republic 153:28, Dec 18, 1965
    New York Theatre Critics' Reviews 1965:255
    New York Times p. 41, Feb 21, 1961
                  p. 25, Nov 5, 1963
                  II, p. 1, Nov 17, 1963
                  p. 51, Nov 17, 1965
                  II, p. 1, Nov 28, 1965
                  p. 21, Jan 4, 1966
                  p. 20, Jan 6, 1966
    New Yorker 37:168-9, Apr 22, 1961
              41:170+, Nov 27, 1965
    Newsweek 66:91, Nov 29, 1965
            62:77, Nov 11, 1963
    Reporter 33:46+, Dec 16, 1965

Saturday Review 46:35, Nov 23, 1963
                48:76, Dec 4, 1965
                50:50, Apr 15, 1967
Time 86:67, Nov 26, 1965
Vogue 147:72, Jan 1, 1966

*The Gates of Summer
   Reviews:
      New York Times p. 53, Jun 16, 1970

Marching Song
   Productions:
      (Off Broadway) Season of 1959-1960.
   Reviews:
      America 102:483, Jan 16, 1960
      New York Times p. 20, Dec 29, 1959

WILDE, OSCAR

*The Florentine Tragedy
   Reviews:
      New York Times p. 24, Feb 14, 1956

An Ideal Husband
   Productions:
      Opened September 16, 1918 for 80 performances.
   Reviews:
      Dramatic Mirror 75:8, Mar 18, 1916
                      79:471, Sep 28, 1918
      Independent 96:37, Oct 12, 1918
      Green Book 20:952-4, Dec 1918
      Life (NY) 77:572-3, Apr 21, 1921
      New York Clipper 69:19, Apr 6, 1921
      New York Times p. 11, Sep 17, 1918
                    IV, p. 2, Sep 22, 1918
                    p. 20, Feb 28, 1946
                    II, p. 2, Apr 14, 1946
      Theatre Magazine 28:278+, Nov 1918
      Weekly Review 4:378-80, Apr 20, 1921

The Importance of Being Earnest
   Productions:
      Opened November 14, 1910 for 48 performances.
      Opened January 20, 1921 for 44 performances.
      Opened May 3, 1926 for 50 performances.
      Opened January 12, 1939 for 61 performances.
      Opened March 3, 1947 for 81 performances.
      (Off Broadway) Opened February 25, 1963 for 164
         performances.
      (Off Off Broadway) Season of 1974-1975.
      (Off Off Broadway) Opened November 22, 1975.
      (Off Off Broadway) Opened July 1976. Reopened January 1977.

Reviews:
Blue Book 12:892-3, Mar 1911
Catholic World 148:730, Mar 1939
              165:70-1, Apr 1947
Commonweal 29:413, Feb 3, 1939
              45:565-6, Mar 21, 1947
Life 22:123-4+, Mar 31, 1947
Life (NY) 56:911, Nov 24, 1910
Munsey 44:564, Jan 1911
Nation 148:128, Jan 28, 1939
      164:338-9, Mar 22, 1947
New Republic 116:41, Mar 17, 1947
New York Theatre Critics' Reviews 1947:439
New York Times p. 30, May 4, 1926
              p. 16, Jan 13, 1939
              p. 18, Jan 24, 1947
              II, p. 3, Mar 2, 1947
              p. 30, Mar 4, 1947
              II, p. 1, Mar 9, 1947
              p. 18, Jan 20, 1961
              p. 5, Feb 27, 1963
              p. 9, Jul 6, 1968
              p. 33, May 30, 1974
              p. 12, Jun 12, 1976
              II, p. 3, Jun 12, 1977
              III, p. 5, Jun 17, 1977
              p. 18, Aug 8, 1977
New Yorker 23:53, Mar 15, 1947
        39:132+, Mar 9, 1963
        53:54, Jun 27, 1977
Newsweek 29:97, Mar 17, 1947
        61:86, Mar 11, 1963
Pearson 25:121, Jan 1911
Saturday Review 108:125, Dec 4, 1909
             150:79, Jul 19, 1930
             30:22-4, Mar 29, 1947
Theatre Arts 23:174, Mar 1939
          23:253, Apr 1939
          31:16-17+, Apr 1947
Theatre Magazine 44:14-15, Jul 1926
Time 33:21, Jan 23, 1939
     49:39, Mar 17, 1947
     109:61, Jun 27, 1977
Weekly Review 4:184-5, Feb 23, 1921

Lady Windermere's Fan
  Productions:
    Opened March 14, 1914 for 72 performances.
    Opened January 26, 1932 for four performances.
    Opened October 14, 1946 for 228 performances.
  Reviews:
    Catholic World 164:262, Dec 1946
    Commonweal 44:551-2, Sep 20, 1946

Dramatic Mirror 71:13, Apr 1, 1914
Green Book 11:1913-14, Jun 1914
Life 20:119-20+, Apr 15, 1946
Nation 98:372, Apr 2, 1914
        163:510, Nov 2, 1946
New Republic 115:556, Oct 28, 1946
New York Theatre Critics' Reviews 1946:307
New York Times p. 11, Mar 31, 1914
                p. 19, Jan 27, 1932
                II, p. 1, Oct 13, 1946
                p. 29, Oct 15, 1946
                II, p. 3, Nov 17, 1946
                VI, p. 23, Dec 8, 1946
New Yorker 22:51, Oct 26, 1946
Newsweek 28:86, Oct 28, 1946
Saturday Review 29:34-6, Nov 9, 1946
School and Society 65:182-3, Mar 8, 1947
Theatre Arts 30:691+, Dec 1946
Theatre Magazine 19:259-60, May 1914
Time 38:63, Oct 28, 1946

Mr. and Mrs. Daventry
    Productions:
        Opened February 23, 1910 for four performances.
    Reviews:
        Dramatic Mirror 63:6, Mar 5, 1910

Nihilists (see Vera, or the Nihilists)

Salome
    Productions:
        Opened October 31, 1917 in repertory (Washington Square
            Players).
        Opened May 22, 1922 for eight performances.
        Opened May 7, 1923 for eight performances.
        (Off Off Broadway) Season of 1967-1968.
        (Off Broadway) Adapted by Lindsay Kemp.   Opened January
            8, 1975 for 30 performances.
        (Off Off Broadway) Opened April 15, 1977.
    Reviews:
        Drama 12:335-7, Sep 1922
        Dramatic Mirror 78:620, May 4, 1918
        Green Book 20:4-5+, Jul 1918
        Life (NY) 71:722, May 2, 1918
        Life 21:87, Aug 5, 1946
        New York Clipper 70:20, May 31, 1922
        New York Times p. 12, May 23, 1922
                        p. 22, May 8, 1923
                        VII, p. 1, May 20, 1923
                        p. 24, Feb 14, 1956
                        p. 33, May 30, 1974
                        p. 26, Jan 14, 1975

Poet Lore 30:433-5, Autumn 1919
Theatre Magazine 27:355+, Jun 1918

Vera, or the Nihilists
Productions:
(Off Off Broadway) Opened April 15, 1976.
No Reviews.

A Woman of No Importance
Productions:
Opened April 14, 1916 for 56 performances.
Reviews:
Book News 34:431-2, Jun 1916
Dramatic Mirror 75:8, Apr 29, 1916
Green Book 16:71, 80-1, Jul 1916
Nation 102:525, May 11, 1916
New York Times p. 9, Apr 25, 1916
　　　　　　　　VII, p. 7, Apr 30, 1916
　　　　　　　　II, p. 6, May 14, 1916
Saturday Review 36:24, Aug 1, 1953
Theatre Magazine 23:334, Jun 1916

WILLIAMS, EMLYN

*Accolade
Reviews:
Christian Science Monitor Magazine p. 7, Sep 30, 1950

A Boy Growing Up   (see also Dylan Thomas Growing Up)
Productions:
Based on the stories of Dylan Thomas.   Opened October 7,
1957 for 17 performances.
Reviews:
New York Times p. 41, Oct 8, 1957

The Corn Is Green
Productions:
Opened November 26, 1940 for 477 performances.
Opened May 3, 1943 for 56 performances.
Opened January 11, 1950 for 16 performances.
(Off Broadway) Season of 1953-1954.
(Off Broadway) Opened September 30, 1961 for 10
performances.
Reviews:
Catholic World 152:469-70, Jan 1941
　　　　　　　　155:299, Jun 1943
Commonweal 33:209, Dec 13, 1940
Independent Woman 20:24, Jan 1941
Life 9:25-8, Dec 23, 1940
Nation 151:585, Dec 7, 1940
New Republic 103:789, Dec 9, 1940

New York Theatre Critics' Reviews 1940:209+
1941:454+
Nation 151:585, Dec 7, 1940
New Republic 103:789, Dec 9, 1940
New York Theatre Critics' Reviews 1940:209+
1941:454+
New York Times p. 27, Nov 27, 1940
X, p. 1, Dec 1, 1940
IX, p. 1, Feb 16, 1941
IV, p. 2, Apr 27, 1941
p. 24, Apr 6, 1943
II, p. 1, May 2, 1943
p. 18, May 4, 1943
II, p. 1, May 9, 1943
p. 33, Jan 12, 1950
II, p. 1, Jan 22, 1950
p. 10, Feb 27, 1954
Stage 1:31, Dec 1940
1:19+, Jan 1941
Theatre Arts 25:91-3, Feb 1941
34:15, Mar 1950
Time 36:69, Dec 9, 1940

*Druid's Rest
Reviews:
Theatre Arts 28:342, Jun 1944

Dylan Thomas Growing Up (see also A Boy Growing Up)
Productions:
(Off Broadway) Based on the stories of Dylan Thomas. Opened October 12, 1976. Reopened November 26, 1976 for a total of 36 performances.
Reviews:
New York Theatre Critics' Reviews 1976:124
New York Times p. 34, Oct 13, 1976
III, p. 4, Nov 26, 1976

The Light of Heart (see Yesterday's Magic)

A Month in the Country (see entry under Turgenev, Ivan)

The Morning Star
Productions:
Opened September 14, 1942 for 24 performances.
Reviews:
Commonweal 36:565, Oct 2, 1942
Nation 155:278, Sep 26, 1942
New Republic 107:381-2, Sep 28, 1942
New Yorker 18:34, Sep 26, 1942
New York Theatre Critics' Reviews 1942:239
New York Times IX, p. 2, Dec 28, 1941
VIII, p. 3, Feb 15, 1942
p. 18, Sep 15, 1942
VIII, p. 1, Sep 20, 1942
Newsweek 20:62, Sep 20, 1942

Theatre Arts 26:677-9, Nov 1942
Time 40:47, Sep 28, 1942

A Murder Has Been Arranged
Productions:
(Off Broadway) Opened November 1949 in repertory.
No Reviews.

Night Must Fall
Productions:
Opened September 28, 1936 for 64 performances.
(Off Broadway) Opened July 3, 1939 for two weeks.
(Off Off Broadway) Opened March 28, 1969 for 9
performances.
(Off Off Broadway) Opened June 27, 1974.
(Off Off Broadway) Opened April 1975.
(Off Off Broadway) Opened August 8, 1975.
Reviews:
Catholic World 144:213, Nov 1936
Commonweal 24:532, Oct 2, 1936
Literary Digest 122:28, Oct 10, 1936
Nation 143:426-7, Oct 10, 1936
New Republic 88:284, Oct 14, 1936
New York Times p. 34, Sep 29, 1936
          p. 41, Sep 29, 1975
Newsweek 8:29, Oct 10, 1936
Stage 14:44-5, Oct 1936
Theatre Arts 20:847-8, Nov 1936
Time 28:52, Oct 12, 1936

Someone Waiting
Productions:
Opened February 14, 1956 for 15 performances.
Reviews:
America 94:646, Mar 10, 1956
New York Theatre Critics' Reviews 1956:365
New York Times p. 51, Nov 26, 1953
          II, p. 1, Feb 12, 1956
          p. 26, Feb 15, 1956
New Yorker 32:93-4, Feb 25, 1956
Theatre Arts 40:21, Apr 1956
Time 67:61, Feb 27, 1956

*Trespass
Reviews:
Theatre Arts 31:36, Oct 1947

*Wind of Heaven
Reviews:
New York Times II, p. 2, Apr 22, 1945

Yesterday's Magic (The Light of Heart)
Productions:

Opened April 14, 1942 for 55 performances.
Reviews:
    Catholic World 155:340, Jun 1942
    Commonweal 36:38, May 1, 1942
    New York Theatre Critics' Reviews 1942:312+
    New York Times X, p. 3, Mar 3, 1940
                  IX, p. 2, Jun 15, 1941
                   p. 27, Apr 15, 1942
                VIII, p. 2, May 17, 1942
    New Yorker 8:30, Apr 25, 1942
    Theatre Arts 26:357, 360, Jun 1942
    Time 39:61, Apr 27, 1942

WILSON, JOHN

Hamp
    Productions:
      (Off Broadway) Based on the novel by J. L. Hodson.
        Opened March 9, 1967 for 101 performances.
    Reviews:
      America 116:508+, Apr 1, 1967
      New York Times p. 25, Aug 18, 1964
                  p. 32, Mar 10, 1967
      New Yorker 43:123, Mar 18, 1967
      Time 89:62, Mar 17, 1967

WINTER, KEITH

The Rats of Norway
    Productions:
      Opened April 15, 1948 for 4 performances.
    Reviews:
      New York Theatre Critics' Reviews 1948:292
      New York Times p. 27, Apr 16, 1948
      New Yorker 24:50, Apr 24, 1948

The Shining Hour
    Productions:
      Opened February 13, 1934 for 121 performances.
    Reviews:
      Catholic World 139:88-9, Apr 1934
      Nation 138:258, Feb 28, 1934
      New Outlook 163:32-3, Mar 1934
      New Republic 78:78, Feb 28, 1934
      New York Times p. 22, Feb 14, 1934
      Newsweek 3:34, Feb 24, 1934
      Review of Reviews 89:57, Apr 1934
      Stage 11:18-19, Mar 1934
           11:18-21, Apr 1934
      Theatre Arts 18:245+, Apr 1934

Worse Things Happen at Sea
Productions:
(Off Broadway) Opened April 24, 1938 in repertory.
Reviews:
New York Times p. 8, Apr 25, 1938

WOLF, FRIEDRICH

Professor Mamlock
Productions:
Translated by Anne Bromberger. Opened April 13, 1937
for 74 performances (Federal Theatre Project).
Reviews:
New York Times p. 30, Apr 14, 1937
X, p. 1, Apr 25, 1937

Sailors of Cattaro
Productions:
Translated by Keene Wallis. Adapted by Michael Blankfort.
Opened December 10, 1934 for 96 performances.
Reviews:
Catholic World 140:600, Feb 1935
Commonweal 21:236, Dec 21, 1934
Golden Book 21:30a, Feb 1935
Nation 139:749, Dec 26, 1934
New Republic 81:223, Jan 2, 1935
New York Times p. 28, Dec 11, 1934
Theatre Arts 19:100+, Feb 1935
Time 24:13, Dec 24, 1934

WOOD, MRS. HENRY

East Lynne
Productions:
Opened March 10, 1926 for 35 performances.
Reviews:
Bookman 63:344, May 1926
New Republic 46:173-4, Mar 31, 1926
New York Times p. 18, Mar 11, 1926
Vogue 67:88-9, May 1, 1926

YEATS, WILLIAM BUTLER

*Calvary
Reviews:
New York Times p. 13, Jul 22, 1960

The Countess Cathleen
Productions:
Opened February 4, 1913 in repertory.

(Off Off Broadway) Adapted by Donna Carlson as <u>Pinion.</u>
Opened Season of 1969-1970.
Reviews:
Christian Science Monitor Magazine p. 5, Mar 18, 1950
Dramatic Mirror 69:7, Feb 26, 1913
Everybody's Magazine 28:680, May 1913

The Death of Cuchulain
Productions:
(Off Broadway) Opened season of 1958-1959.
Reviews:
New York Times p. 34, Apr 13, 1959

*A Full Moon in March
Reviews:
New York Times p. 48, Sep 20, 1960

*Herne's Egg
Reviews:
New York Times p. 48, Sep 20, 1960

*The Hour Glass
Reviews:
New York Times p. 33, Oct 17, 1955

Kathleen ni Houlihan
Productions:
Opened November 20, 1911 in repertory.
Opened February 4, 1913 in repertory (The Irish Players).
Opened in the Fall of 1934 in repertory for one perform-
ance (Abbey Theatre Players).
Reviews:
Dramatic Mirror 66:6, Dec 6, 1911
Weekly Review 3:76, Jul 21, 1960

Masks of Love and Death
Productions:
(Off Off Broadway) Opened February 1976.
No Reviews.

The Moon Mysteries
Productions:
(Off Off Broadway) Opened November 17, 1972.
(Off Off Broadway) Opened December 19, 1973.
(Off Off Broadway) Opened April 1976.
Reviews:
New York Times p. 47, Jan 18, 1973
p. 30, Dec 30, 1973

*On Baile's Strand
Reviews:
New York Times p. 21, Dec 27, 1954
p. 34, Apr 13, 1959

The Only Jealousy of Emer
  Productions:
    (Off Off Broadway) Opened season of 1969-1970.
    (Off Off Broadway) Opened January 23, 1972.
  Reviews:
    New York Times p. 36, Mar 25, 1970
                  p. 26, Jan 25, 1972

Pinion   (see The Countess Cathleen)

The Player Queen
  Productions:
    Opened October 16, 1923 for 49 performances.
  Reviews:
    Nation 117:496, Oct 31, 1923
    New Republic 36:257, Oct 3, 1923
    New York Times p. 14, Oct 17, 1923

*Purgatory
  Reviews:
    New York Times p. 48, Sep 20, 1960

The Resurrection
  Productions:
    Opened November 19, 1934 for one performance.
  Reviews:
    New York Times p. 24, Nov 20, 1934

The Unicorn from the Stars
  Productions:
    (Off Off Broadway) Opened season of 1969-1970.
  No Reviews.

ZUCKMAYER, CARL

The Captain of Koepenick
  Productions:
    Opened December 1, 1964 for 8 performances in repertory.
  Reviews:
    New York Times p. 60, Dec 2, 1964

*Devil's General
  Reviews:
    New York Times II, p. 3, Oct 11, 1953
    Theatre Arts 33:29-30, Jun 1949

*Somewhere in France (with F. Kortner)
  Reviews:
    New York Times p. 16, Apr 29, 1941

ZWEIG, STEFAN

Jeremiah
Productions:
Translated by Eden Paul and Cedar Paul. English Version
by John Gassner and Washington Miner. Opened
February 3, 1939 for 35 performances.
Reviews:
Catholic World 148:731, Mar 1939
Commonweal 29:469, Feb 17, 1939
Nation 148:212, Feb 18, 1939
New York Times p. 11, Feb 4, 1939
One Act Play Magazine 2:747-8, Feb 1939
Theatre Magazine 23:248, Apr 1939
Time 33:24, Feb 13, 1939

Sword by His Side
Productions:
(Off Broadway) Opened season of 1947-1948 in repertory.
No Reviews.

Volpone (with Jules Romains)
Productions:
Translated by Ruth Langner. Based on Ben Jonson's play.
Opened April 9, 1928 for 46 performances.
Opened March 10, 1930 for 8 performances.
Opened January 30, 1957 in repertory.
Reviews:
America 96:566, Feb 16, 1957
Catholic World 127:340-3, Jun 1928
Dial 84:528-30, Jun 1928
Dramatist 19:1365-6, Apr 1928
Life 92:12, Jul 12, 1928
Nation 126:495, Apr 25, 1928
184:174, Feb 23, 1957
New Republic 54:295-6, Apr 25, 1928
New York Times Critics' Reviews 1957:361
New York Times p. 32, Apr 10, 1928
IX, p. 1, Apr 22, 1928
p. 24, Mar 11, 1938
p. 27, Jan 8, 1957
II, p. 10, Jan 13, 1957
p. 27, Feb 5, 1957
Outlook 148:665, Apr 25, 1928
Saturday Review 40:26, Mar 2, 1957
Theatre Arts 12:387-90, Jun 1928
41:21, Apr 1957
Theatre Magazine 47:37-9, Jun 1928
Vogue 71:78, Jun 1, 1928

ABOUT THE DRAMATISTS

Dramatist	Nationality	Dates
Abelman, Paul	English	born 1927
Andreyev, Leonid Nikolayevitch	Russian	1871-1919
Anouilh, Jean	French	born 1910
Ansky, S.	Russian (Jewish)	1863-1920
Archer, William	English	1856-1924
Auden, W. H.	English	born 1907
Ayckbourn, Alan	English	born 1939
Aymé, Marcel	French	1902-1967
Bagnold, Enid	English	born 1889
Bahr, Hermann	Austrian	1863-1934
Barrie, James M.	English	1860-1937
Baum, Vicki	German	1888-1960
Beckett, Samuel	Irish (writes in French)	born 1906
Becque, Henry	French	1837-1899
Behan, Brendan	Irish	1925-1964
Benavente, Jacinto	Spanish	1866-1954
Benelli, Sem	Italian	1877-1949
Bergstrom, Hjalmer	Danish	1868-1914
Bernard, Jean-Jacques	French	born 1888
Besier, Rudolph	English	1878-1942
Betti, Ugo	Italian	1892-1953
Birabeau, André	French	born 1890
Bjornson, Bjornestjerne	Norwegian	1832-1910
Bolitho, William	English	1890-1930
Bolt, Robert	English	born 1924
Bolton, Guy	English	born 1884
Borchert, Wolfgang	German	1921-1947
Bourdet, Edouard	French	1887-1945
Bowen, John	English	born 1924
Brecht, Bertolt	German	1898-1956
Bridie, James	Scottish	1888-1951
Brieux, Eugène	French	1858-1932
Bruckner, Ferdinand	Austrian	1891-1958
Büchner, Georg	German	1813-1837
Camus, Albert	French	1913-1960
Capek, Karel	Czech	1890-1938
Carroll, Paul Vincent	Irish	1900-1968
Casella, Alberto	Italian	born 1891
Chambers, C. Haddon	English	1861-1921
Chekhov, Anton	Russian	1860-1904

Dramatist	Nationality	Dates
Chiarelli, Luigi	Italian	1886-1947
Christie, Agatha	English	1890-1976
Claudel, Paul	French	1868-1955
Cocteau, Jean	French	1889-1963
Colton, John	English	1886-1946
Copeau, Jacques	French	1878-1949
Coward, Noel	English	1899-1973
Dane, Clemence	English	1888-1965
D'Annunzio, Gabriele	Italian	1863-1938
de Ghelderode, Michel	Belgian	1898-1962
de Hartog, Jan	Dutch	born 1914
Delaney, Shelagh	English	born 1940
de Montherlant, Henri	French	1896-1972
de Musset, Alfred	French	1810-1857
dePorto-Riche, Georges	French	1849-1930
Deval, Jacques	French	1893-1972
Drinkwater, John	English	1882-1937
Dumas, Alexandre, fils	French	1824-1895
Dunsany, Lord	English-Irish	1878-1957
Dürrenmatt, Friedrich	Swiss	born 1921
Dyer, Charles	English	born 1928
Echegaray, Jose	Spanish	1832-1916
Eliot, T. S.	American-English	1888-1965
England, Barry	English	born 1934
Ervine, St. John	Irish	1883-1971
Fabbri, Diego	Italian	born 1911
Feydeau, Georges	French	1862-1921
Frank, Bruno	German	1887-1945
Freeman, David E.	Canadian	born 1945
Friel, Brian	Irish	born 1930
Frisch, Max	Swiss	born 1911
Fry, Christopher	English	born 1907
Fugard, Athol	South African	born 1932
Galsworthy, John	English	1867-1933
García-Lorca, Federico	Spanish	1899-1936
Genêt, Jean	French	born 1910
Geraldy, Paul	French	born 1885
Gide, André	French	1869-1951
Giraudoux, Jean	French	1882-1944
Gorki, Maxim	Russian	1868-1936
Granville-Barker, Harley	English	1877-1946
Gray, Simon	English	born 1936
Greene, Graham	English	born 1904
Gregory, Lady	English-Irish	1859-1932
Griffiths, Trevor	English	born 1935
Guitry, Sacha	French	1885-1957
Hamilton, Patrick	English	born 1904
Hampton, Christopher	English	born 1946
Harwood, H. M.	English	1874-1959
Hauptmann, Gerhart	German	1862-1946
Hebbel, Friedrich	German	1813-1863

Dramatist	Nationality	Dates
Heijermans, Herman	Dutch	1864-1924
Hochhuth, Rolf	German	born 1931
Hochwalder, Fritz	Austrian	born 1911
Hopkins, John	English	born 1931
Houghton, Stanley	English	1881-1913
Housman, Laurence	English	1865-1959
Hugo, Victor	French	1802-1885
Huxley, Aldous	English	1894-1963
Ibsen, Henrik	Norwegian	1828-1906
Ionesco, Eugene	French	born 1912
Jerome, Helen	Australian	born 1883
Job, Thomas	Welsh	1900-1947
Johnston, Denis	Irish	born 1901
Jones, Henry Arthur	English	1851-1929
Joyce, James	Irish	1882-1941
Kaiser, Georg	German	1878-1945
Katayev, Valentin	Russian	born 1897
Kipphardt, Heinar	German	born 1922
Knott, Frederick	English	born 1919
Kops, Bernard	English	born 1926
Labiche, Eugene	French	1815-1888
Lawler, Ray	Australian	born 1922
Lenormand, Henri René	French	1882-1951
Levy, Benn W.	English	1900-1973
Lonsdale, Frederick	English	1881-1954
Luke, Peter	English	born 1919
McCarthy, Justin Huntley	Irish	1830-1912
Maeterlinck, Maurice	Belgian	1862-1949
Marceau, Felicien	Belgian	born 1913
Marcel, Gabriel	French	1890-1973
Marcus, Frank	English	born 1928
Martínez-Sierra, Gregorio	Spanish	1881-1947
Masefield, John	English	1878-1967
Maugham, W. Somerset	English	1874-1965
Mauriac, Francois	French	1885-1970
Milne, A. A.	English	1882-1956
Molnar, Ferenc	Hungarian	1878-1952
Morley, Robert	English	born 1908
Munro, C. K.	English	born 1889
Murray, T. C.	Irish	1873-1959
Nestroy, Johann	Austrian	1801-1862
Nichols, Peter	English	born 1927
Nichols, Robert	English	1893-1944
Obey, Andre	French	born 1892
O'Casey, Sean	Irish	1884-1964
Orton, Joe	English	1933-1967
Osborne, John	English	born 1929
Pagnol, Marcel	French	1895-1974
Parker, Louis N.	English	1852-1944
Phillips, Stephan	English	1868-1915
Pinero, Arthur Wing	English	1855-1934

Dramatist	Nationality	Dates
Pinero, Miguel	Puerto Rican	born 1946
Pinter, Harold	English	born 1932
Pirandello, Luigi	Italian	1867-1936
Priestley, J. B.	English	born 1894
Quintero, Joaquin Alvarez	Spanish	1873-1944
Quintero, Serafin	Spanish	1871-1938
Rattigan, Terence	English	born 1911
Robertson, Thomas William	English	1829-1871
Robinson, Lennox	Irish	1886-1958
Romains, Jules	French	1886-1972
Rostand, Edmond	French	1869-1918
Rudkin, David	English	born 1936
Salacrou, Armand	French	born 1899
Sardou, Victorien	French	1831-1908
Sartre, Jean-Paul	French	born 1905
Saunders, James	English	born 1925
Savoir, Alfred	French	1883-1934
Schnitzler, Arthur	Austrian	1862-1931
Shaffer, Anthony	English	born 1926
Shaffer, Peter	English	born 1926
Shairp, Mordaunt	English	1887-1939
Shaw, George Bernard	English-Irish	1856-1950
Shaw, Robert	English	born 1927
Sherriff, R. C.	English	1896-1975
Shiels, George	Irish	born 1886
Sigurjonsson, Johann	Icelandic	1880-1919
Simonov, Konstantin	Russian	born 1915
Simpson, N. F.	English	born 1919
Slade, Bernard	Canadian	born 1930
Smith, Dodie	English	born 1896
Sternheim, Carl	German	1878-1942
Stoppard, Tom	English	born 1937
Storey, David	English	born 1934
Strindberg, August	Swedish	1849-1912
Sudermann, Hermann	German	1857-1928
Synge, John Millington	Irish	1871-1909
Tabori, George	Hungarian-English	born 1914
Taylor, Tom	English	1817-1880
Thomas, Brandon	English	1857-1914
Thomas, Dylan	Welsh	1914-1953
Toller, Ernst	German	1893-1939
Tolstoy, Leo Nikolayevitch	Russian	1828-1910
Turgenev, Ivan	Russian	1818-1883
Ustinov, Peter	English	born 1921
Vajda, Ernst	Hungarian-American	1887-1954
Vane, Sutton	English	1891-1963
Verneuil, Louis	French	1893-1952
Vildrac, Charles	French	born 1882
Von Hofmannsthal, Hugo	German	1874-1929
Von Kleist, Heinrich	German	1777-1811
Wedekind, Frank	German	1864-1918

Dramatist	Nationality	Dates
Weiss, Peter	German	born 1916
Werfel, Franz	Austrian	1890-1945
Wesker, Arnold	English	born 1932
Wheeler, Hugh	English	born 1916
Whiting, John	English	1917-1963
Wilde, Oscar	English-Irish	1854-1900
Williams, Emlyn	English	born 1905
Wilson, John	Scottish	born 1921
Winter, Keith	English	born 1906
Wolf, Frederich	German	1888-1953
Wood, Mrs. Henry	English	1814-1887
Yeats, William Butler	Irish	1865-1939
Zuckmayer, Carl	German	1897-1977
Zweig, Stefan	Austrian	1881-1942

PROLIFIC FOREIGN DRAMATISTS

Dramatist	Plays Reviewed
Shaw, G. B.	50
Coward	34
Brecht	30
Anouilh	29
Ionesco	26
Chekhov	25
Priestley	24
Barrie	23
Maugham	23
Molnar	20
Strindberg	19
O'Casey	18
Pirandello	18
Bolton	17
Ibsen	17
Pinter	17
Rattigan	17
Beckett	16
Giraudoux	15
Yeats	15
Feydeau	14
Galsworthy	14
Lonsdale	13
Ustinov	13
Deval	12
Osborne	12
Sartre	12
Williams	12
Duerrenmatt	11
Gorki	11
Gregory	11
Levy	11
Pinero, A. W.	11
Carroll	10
Christie	10
Cocteau	10
Fry	10
Harwood	10
Maeterlinck	10
Schnitzler	10

FREQUENTLY PRODUCED FOREIGN DRAMATISTS

Dramatist	Productions	Productions over 100 performances
Shaw, G. B.	190	25
Ibsen	112	8
Chekhov	110	4
Coward	58	12
Strindberg	55	0
Beckett	53	4
Brecht	52	4
Pinter	51	10
Anouilh	51	5
O'Casey	47	3
Ionesco	45	1
Barrie	40	4
Pirandello	39	3
Synge	38	0
Maugham	31	8
Molnar	29	7
Priestley	27	3
Giraudoux	26	4
Sartre	24	1
Williams	23	2
Gorki	21	0
Gregory	21	0
Rattigan	21	7
Wilson	21	1
Yeats	21	0
Robinson	20	0
García-Lorca	19	0
Milne	19	6
Pinero, A. W.	19	0
Rostand	18	2
Bolton	17	6
Feydeau	17	1
Christie	16	2
Cocteau	16	0
Durrenmatt	15	1
Eliot	15	2
Galsworthy	15	5
Genêt	15	2
Lonsdale	15	3
Maeterlinck	15	1
Osborne	15	3

SUCCESSFUL FOREIGN PRODUCTIONS

Off Broadway productions indicated by *. Performances in paren-
theses indicate play still running as of June 1, 1977.

Performances	Play and Year of Production	Author
*1,408	The Blacks (1961)	Genêt
1,295	Angel Street (1941)	Hamilton
1,222	Sleuth (1970)	A. Shaffer
(1,068)	Equus (1974)	P. Shaffer
(927)	Same Time, Next Year (1975)	Slade
*672	The Balcony (1960)	Genêt
657	Blithe Spirit (1942)	Coward
648 (see 104)	Rain (1922)	Colton
645	Witness for the Prosecution (1954)	Christie
637	A Man for All Seasons (1961)	Bolt
632	The Fourposter (1951)	deHartog
610	Affairs of State (1950)	Verneuil
592	Absurd Person Singular (1974)	Ayckbourn
*582	Krapp's Last Tape (1960)	Beckett
*578	The Collection (1962)	Pinter
*578	The Dumbwaiter (1962)	Pinter
*545 (see 127)	The Hostage (1961)	Behan
*529 (see 136)	Six Characters in Search of an Author (1963)	Pirandello
522	Dial "M" for Murder (1952)	Knott
517	Victoria Regina (1935)	Housman
500	Bird in Hand (1929)	Drinkwater
485	Journey's End (1929)	Sherriff
477	The Corn Is Green (1940)	Williams
*465	After Magritte (1972)	Stoppard
*465	The Real Inspector Hound (1972)	Stoppard
459	Grand Hotel (1930)	Baum
452	O Mistress Mine (1946)	Rattigan
430	Uncle Harry (1942)	Job
426	Ten Little Indians (1944)	Christie
*424	Brecht on Brecht (1962)	Tabori
420	Rosencrantz and Guildenstern Are Dead (1967)	Stoppard
417	Jacobowsky and the Colonel (1944)	Werfel

390

Performances	Play and Year of Production	Author
409	The Cocktail Party (1950)	Eliot
407	Look Back in Anger (1957)	Osborne
389	Romanoff and Juliet (1957)	Ustinov
385	The Last of Mrs. Cheyney (1925)	Lonsdale
376	A Taste of Honey (1960)	Delaney
373	Wait until Dark (1966)	Knott
370	The Barretts of Wimpole Street (1931)	Besier
368	The Madwoman of Chaillot (1948)	Giraudoux
356	Tovarich (1936)	Deval
359	Hadrian VII (1969)	Luke
352	The First Mrs. Fraser (1929)	Ervine
348	The Respectful Prostitute (1948)	Sartre
*343	The Room (1964)	Pinter
*343	A Slight Ache (1964)	Pinter
*340	Hedda Gabler (1960)	Ibsen
337	Black Comedy (1967)	P. Shaffer
337	Five Finger Exercise (1959)	P. Shaffer
337	White Lies (1967)	P. Shaffer
332	Separate Tables (1956)	Rattigan
326	Philadelphia, Here I Come! (1966)	Friel
324	The Homecoming (1967)	Pinter
321	Mrs. Moonlight (1930)	Levy
321	Peter Pan (1950)	Barrie
316	The Deputy (1964)	Hochhuth
315	Polly with a Past (1917)	Bolton
312	Adam and Eva (1919)	Bolton
310	The Ivory Door (1927)	Milne
295 (see 100)	Man and Superman (1947)	Shaw
280	Disraeli (1911)	Parker
*277	Waiting for Godot (1971)	Beckett
274	Shadow and Substance (1936)	Carroll
272	Anastasia (1954)	Bolton
268	The Man in the Glass Booth (1968)	R. Shaw
264	The Concert (1910)	Bahr
261	Royal Hunt of the Sun (1965)	Shaffer
260	Edward, My Son (1948)	Morley
260 (see 244)	The Play's the Thing (1926)	Molnar
256	Fanny's First Play (1912)	Shaw
256 (see 248 and 204)	Private Lives (1931)	Coward
255	Outward Bound (1938)	Vane
255	The Perfect Alibi (1928)	Milne
255	The Swan (1923)	Molnar
251	Spring Cleaning (1923)	Lonsdale
248	The Guardsman (1924)	Molnar
248 (see 256 and 204)	Private Lives (1948)	Coward

Performances	Play and Year of Production	Author
248	Time Remembered (1957)	Anouilh
246	Michael and Mary (1929)	Milne
244 (see 260)	The Play's the Thing (1948)	Molnar
*240	The Blood Knot (1964)	Fugard
240	Rhinoceros (1961)	Ionesco
239	Fallen Angels (1956)	Coward
233	Charley's Aunt (1940)	B. Thomas
233 (see 138)	The Constant Wife (1926)	Maugham
232 (see 193)	Cyrano de Bergerac (1923)	Rostand
232	Major Barbara (1956)	Shaw
229	The Lark (1955)	Anouilh
228	Lady Windermere's Fan (1946)	Wilde
228	The Norman Conquests (1975)	Ayckbourn
*224	What the Butler Saw (1970)	Orton
220	Loyalties (1922)	Galsworthy
219	Pride and Prejudice (1935)	Jerome
218	Clutterbuck (1949)	Levy
217	Tiger at the Gates (1955)	Giraudoux
*216	Ghosts (1961)	Ibsen
215	The Winslow Boy (1947)	Rattigan
211	Luther (1963)	Osborne
210	Autumn Crocus (1932)	Smith
210	Cynara (1931)	Harwood
206	Dangerous Corner (1932)	Priestley
206	Shanghai Gesture (1926)	Colton
*205	Boesman and Lena (1970)	Fugard
205	The Killing of Sister George (1966)	Marcus
204	The Dover Road (1921)	Milne
204 (see 256 and 248)		
	Private Lives (1969)	Coward
204	Redemption (1918)	Tolstoy
*203	A Country Scandal (1960)	Chekhov
*202	Under Milk Wood (1961)	D. Thomas
199	In Praise of Love (1974)	Rattigan
199	Springtime for Henry (1931)	Levy
196	Write Me a Murder (1961)	Knott
195 (see 142)	Saint Joan (1923)	Shaw
194	Call It a Day (1936)	Smith
193	Abraham Lincoln (1919)	Drinkwater
193	Becket (1960)	Anouilh
193 (see 232)	Cyrano de Bergerac (1946)	Rostand
192	The Changing Room (1973)	Storey
191	Song of Songs (1914)	Sudermann
*189 (see 180 and 110)		
	Arms and the Man (1967)	Shaw
189	Deburau (1920)	Guitry
189	The Visit (1958)	Duerrenmatt
184	Dear Brutus (1918)	Barrie
184	Polly Preferred (1923)	Bolton
184	R. U. R. (1923)	Capek

Performances	Play and Year of Production	Author
183	The Harem (1924)	Vajda
183	Old English (1924)	Galsworthy
182	The Chalk Garden (1955)	Bagnold
182	He Who Gets Slapped (1922)	Andreyev
180 (see 189 and 110)		
	Arms and the Man (1925)	Shaw
180	Death Takes a Holiday (1929)	Casella
180	Mima (1928)	Molnar
179	The Jest (1919)	Benelli
179 (see 143)	Pygmalion (1945)	Shaw
177	John Ferguson (1919)	Ervine
*176	Red Roses for Me (1961)	O'Casey
176	The Skin Game (1920)	Galsworthy
175	The Circle (1921)	Maugham
175	The Green Goddess (1921)	Archer
*175	Man Is Man (1962)	Brecht
*175	A Man's Man (1962)	Brecht
173	A Bill of Divorcement (1921)	Dane
173	Escape (1927)	Galsworthy
172	The Lie (1914)	Jones
168	Lovers and Friends (1943)	Smith
168	Secrets (1922)	Besier
167	Under Orders (1918)	B. Thomas
166	The Green Bay Tree (1933)	Shairp
166	Inadmissible Evidence (1965)	Osborne
165	The Caretaker (1961)	Pinter
*164	The Importance of Being Earnest (1963)	Wilde
163	The Private Ear (1963)	Shaffer
163	The Public Eye (1963)	Shaffer
161	The Nest (1922)	Geraldy
161	Sleeping Partners (1918)	Guitry
160	The Captive (1926)	Bourdet
159	Bitter Sweet (1929)	Coward
159	Dirty Linen and New-Found-Land (1977)	Stoppard
159	Photo Finish (1963)	Ustinov
159	Ross (1961)	Rattigan
159	Sizwe Banzi Is Dead (1974)	Fugard
159	Topaze (1930)	Pagnol
158	Present Laughter (1946)	Coward
157	Ondine (1954)	Giraudoux
157	This Year of Grace (1928)	Coward
157	The Vortex (1925)	Coward
*156 (see 146)	Misalliance (1961)	Shaw
156	When We Are Married (1939)	Priestley
155	Bluebeard's Eighth Wife (1921)	Savoir
155	Travesties (1975)	Stoppard
154	A Day in the Death of Joe Egg (1968)	P. Nichols
153	Amphitryon 38 (1937)	Giraudoux

Performances	Play and Year of Production	Author
153	The Eternal Road (1937)	Werfel
152	A Kiss for Cinderella (1916)	Barrie
151	The Good Fairy (1931)	Molnar
151	The Lady's Not for Burning (1950)	Fry
150	Quadrille (1954)	Coward
149	Caesar and Cleopatra (1949)	Shaw
149	Chips with Everything (1963)	Wesker
148	Lovers (1968)	Friel
148	The Unknown Soldier and His Wife (1967)	Ustinov
*147	The Basement (1968)	Pinter
147	Easy Virtue (1925)	Coward
*147	Green Julia (1972)	Abelman
*147	Tea Party (1968)	Pinter
146 (see 156)	Misalliance (1953)	Shaw
*145	Ashes (1977)	Rudkin
145	Comedians (1976)	Griffiths
144	Chicken Feed (1923)	Bolton
144	Conduct Unbecoming (1970)	England
144 (see 111)	A Doll's House (1937)	Ibsen
144	The High Road (1928)	Lonsdale
144	Marat/Sade (1965)	Weiss
144	Outward Bound (1924)	Vane
144	The Passion Flower (1920)	Benavente
143	Borstal Boy (1970)	Behan
143	Candida (1924)	Shaw
143	Pomander Walk (1910)	Parker
143	The Potting Shed (1957)	Greene
143 (see 179)	Pygmalion (1926)	Shaw
142	As You Desire Me (1931)	Pirandello
142 (see 195)	Saint Joan (1951)	Shaw
*141	The Exception and the Rule (1965)	Brecht
141	The Love of Four Colonels (1953)	Ustinov
141	Within the Gates (1934)	O'Casey
140	Noel Coward in Two Keys (1974)	Coward
138 (see 233)	The Constant Wife (1951)	Maugham
136	Jealousy (1928)	Verneuil
136	The Legend of Leonora (1914)	Barrie
136	The Mind-the-Paint Girl (1912)	Pinero
136 (see 529)	Six Characters in Search of an Author (1922)	Pirandello
136	The White Steed (1939)	Carroll
135	Butley (1972)	Gray
135	Design for Living (1933)	Coward
135	Find Your Way Home (1974)	Hopkins
135	Nobody Home (1915)	Bolton
(135)	Otherwise Engaged (1977)	Gray

Performances		Play and Year of Production	Author
132		The Deep Blue Sea (1952)	Rattigan
132		The Rubicon (1922)	Bourdet
132		The Waltz of the Toreadors (1957)	Anouilh
131		The Grand Duke (1921)	Guitry
131		Laburnum Grove (1935)	Priestley
128	(see 112)	Our Betters (1928)	Maugham
127		The Devil's Disciple (1950)	Shaw
127		An Enemy of the People (1927)	Ibsen
127		Grounds for Divorce (1924)	Vajda
127	(see 545)	The Hostage (1960)	Behan
127		Mary Rose (1920)	Barrie
127		The Phantom Rival (1914)	Molnar
126		The Birthday Party (1967)	Pinter
125	(see 112)	Heartbreak House (1920)	Shaw
124		The Apple Cart (1956)	Shaw
124		Mr. Pim Passes By (1921)	Milne
124		Mixed Marriage (1920)	Ervine
124		Passers-by (1911)	Chambers
123	(see 119)	The Three Sisters (1942)	Chekhov
121	(see 115)	The Doctor's Dilemma (1941)	Shaw
121		Joseph and His Brethren (1913)	Parker
*121		Play (1964)	Beckett
121		The Shining Hour (1934)	Winter
120		The Betrothal (1918)	Maeterlinck
120	(see 111)	The Dybbuk (1925)	Ansky
120		Fata Morgana (1924)	Vajda
120		Peer Gynt (1923)	Ibsen
119		Old Times (1971)	Pinter
*119		Rosmersholm (1962)	Ibsen
119	(see 123)	The Three Sisters (1964)	Chekhov
118		Tonight at Eight-Thirty (1936)	Coward
117		The Confidential Clerk (1954)	Eliot
116		Vivat! Vivat! Regina (1972)	Bolt
115	(see 121)	The Doctor's Dilemma (1927)	Shaw
*113		Camille (1974)	Dumas
113		Red Gloves (1948)	Sartre
112		Getting Married (1919)	Shaw
112	(see 125)	Heartbreak House (1959)	Shaw
112		Jane Clegg (1920)	Ervine
112	(see 128)	Our Betters (1917)	Maugham
112		Smith (1910)	Maugham
111	(see 144)	A Doll's House (1971)	Ibsen
111	(see 120)	The Dybbuk (1926)	Ansky
111		French without Tears (1937)	Rattigan
111		The World We Live In (1922)	Capek
110	(see 189 and 180)	Arms and the Man (1950)	Shaw
110		Home (1970)	Storey
110		The Rehearsal (1963)	Anouilh

Performances	Play and Year of Production	Author
108	The Chinese Prime Minister (1964)	Bagnold
108	Hotel Paradiso (1957)	Feydeau
108	In the Matter of J. Robert Oppenheimer (1969)	Kipphardt
108	Squaring the Circle (1935)	Katayev
108	The Truth about Blayds (1922)	Milne
105	Don Juan in Hell (1952)	Shaw
105	Juno and the Paycock (1940)	O'Casey
105	Once Is Enough (1938)	Lonsdale
*105	The Sea Gull (1973)	Chekhov
104	Androcles and the Lion (1938)	Shaw
104	Another Love Story (1943)	Lonsdale
104	How the Other Half Loves (1971)	Ayckbourn
104	Justice (1916)	Galsworthy
104	The Letter (1927)	Maugham
104	Prunella (1913)	Housman
104 (see 648)	Rain (1924)	Colton
*103	Corruption in the Palace of Justice (1963)	Betti
103	The Investigation (1966)	Weiss
103	Mademoiselle (1932)	Deval
103	The Philanderer (1913)	Shaw
103	The Wild Duck (1925)	Ibsen
*102	Measures Taken (1974)	Brecht
102	Short Eyes (1974)	M. Pinero
102	Too Many Husbands (1919)	Maugham
101	Big Fish, Little Fish (1961)	Wheeler
101	The Complaisant Lover (1961)	Greene
*101	Hamp (1967)	Wilson
100	East of Suez (1922)	Maugham
100	Her Cardboard Lover (1927)	Deval
*100 (see 295)	Man and Superman (1964)	Shaw
100	Rope's End (1929)	Hamilton
100	The Whole World Over (1947)	Simonov

NEW YORK DRAMA CRITICS' AWARDS
(BEST FOREIGN PLAY)

1937-1938	Shadow and Substance (Carroll)
1938-1939	The White Steed (Carroll)
1939-1940	no award
1940-1941	The Corn Is Green (Williams)
1941-1942	Blithe Spirit (Coward)
1942-1943	no award
1943-1944	Jacobowsky and the Colonel (Werfel)
1944-1945	no award
1945-1946	no award
1946-1947	No Exit (Sartre)
1947-1948	The Winslow Boy (Rattigan)
1948-1949	The Madwoman of Chaillot (Giraudoux)
1949-1950	The Cocktail Party (Eliot)
1950-1951	The Lady's Not for Burning (Fry)
1951-1952	Venus Observed (Fry)
1952-1953	The Love of Four Colonels (Ustinov)
1953-1954	Ondine (Giraudoux)
1954-1955	Witness for the Prosecution (Christie)
1955-1956	Tiger at the Gates (Giraudoux)
1956-1957	Waltz of the Toreadors (Anouilh)
1957-1958	Look Back in Anger (Osborne)
1958-1959	The Visit (Duerrenmatt)
1959-1960	Five Finger Exercise (Shaffer)
1960-1961	A Taste of Honey (Delaney)
1961-1962	A Man for All Seasons (Bolt)
1962-1963	no award
1963-1964	Luther (Osborne) Best play of the year regardless of category.
1964-1965	no award
1965-1966	Marat/Sade (The Persecution and Assassination of Marat as Performed by the Inmates of the Asylum of Charenton Under the Direction of the Marquis de Sade) (Weiss) Best play of the year regardless of category.
1966-1967	The Homecoming (Pinter) Best play of the year regardless of category.
1967-1968	Rosencrantz and Guildenstern Are Dead (Stoppard) Best play of the year regardless of category.
1968-1969	no award
1969-1970	Borstal Boy (Behan) Best play of the year regardless of category.

1970-1971	Home (Storey) Best play of the year regardless of category.
1971-1972	The Screens (Genêt)
1972-1973	The Changing Room (Storey) Best play of the year regardless of category.
1973-1974	The Contractor (Storey) Best play of the year regardless of category.
1974-1975	Equus (P. Shaffer) Best play of the year regardless of category.
1975-1976	Travesties (Stoppard) Best play of the year regardless of category.
1976-1977	Otherwise Engaged (Gray) Best play of the year regardless of category.

INDEX OF CO-AUTHORS, ADAPTORS, AND TRANSLATORS

Abdullah, A. 161
Addinsell, Richard 99
Akins, Zoë 357, 359
Allen, Donald M. 187, 190
Allen, Ruth Collins 361
Alsberg, Henry G. 12
Amiel, Denys 235, 236
Andrews, Charlton 293
Andrews, D. H. 87
Antoon, A. J. 339
Archer, Charles 184, 185
Arrieu, Claude 235
Ashmore, B. 74

Baker, Melville 225, 230
Baron, Henry 48
Barrault, Jean-Louis 146
Bartenieff, Irma 197
Bartlett, Sir Basil 221
Baxandall, Lee 55, 365
Behrman, S. N. 146, 367
Belasco, David 160, 227
Belmonte, Nene 214
Bennett, Dorothy Cheston 47
Bennett, Richard 60
Bentley, Eric 50, 51, 52, 54,
  55, 56, 266, 333
Bermel, Albert 86
Bernauer 250
Bernstein, Herman 1, 2, 3,
  198
Beyo, Mascha 362
Bialik, H. N. 12
Bjorkman, Edwin 36, 339,
  342
Black, Kitty 7, 8
Blanchard, Benjamin F. 60
Blankfort, Michael 378
Blau, Herbert 62
Blitzstein, Marc 62
Bolitho, Hector 275
Bolton, Guy 220, 357
Booth, Howard 124

Borden, Ethel 179
Bowles, Paul 289
Bowman, John 339
Boyd, Ernest 36, 108
Boyd, Jullianne 341
Bragg, Bernard 75, 350
Bridie, James 127
Bromberger, Anne 378
Bromfield, Louis 48
Brooks, Jeremy 151, 153
Browne, Maurice 234
Bruce, Renaud C. 105
Brynner, Roc 87
Bulling, Erich 57
Burell, Randal C. 64
Burrell, James T. A. 357

Calderon, George 71
Canfield, Mary Cass 179
Cannan, Denis 7
Capek, Joseph 65
Carlson, Donna 379
Carlson, Jon 126
Carlton, Tom 44
Carr, Philip 150
Carson, Murray 251
Casalis, Jeanne de 328
Caylor, Rose 80
Chappell, Edna and Delos 114
Charash, Jack 367
Clauyel, D. 187
Clift, Montgomery 76
Coghlan, Charles 114
Collinge, Patricia 40
Conlin, Richard 170
Coppel, Alec 174
Corvo, Baron 208
Corwen, Carol 363
Cournos, John 74
Cowan, Ron 363
Crankshaw, Edward 352
Creighton, Anthony 245
Croue, Jean 89

D'Augugan, Jean 202
Davidson, S. E. 343
Davis, J. P. 71
Davis, Owne 65
de Nejac, Emile 287
DeVallieres, Maurice 125
Ditrichstein, Leo 18
Donnelly, Dorothy 294
Dostoevski, F. M. 64
Drake, Alfred 39
Drake, William A. 26, 127, 366, 367
Draper, Samuel 102
Duke, W. A. 26
Dukes, Ashley 32, 161, 197
Duncan, Ronald 86
Dunlop, Geoffrey 62

Eager, Edward 39, 263
Edgington, May 38, 39
Eisler, Hanns 55
Eliot, Samuel A. 363
Erskin, Chester 293
Esslin, Martin 50

Faber, Max 183, 186
Fassett, Jacob J. Jr. 273
Fauritz, Frank 267
Fay, Francis C. 18
Feist, Gene 76, 80, 126, 178, 181, 340
Feydeau, Georges 92
Fjelde, Rolfe 178, 185
Ferris, Walter 68
Fishe, Harrison Grey 177
Forbes, James 360
Forslund, R. V. 182
Forsyth, James 283
Fox, Paul Hervey 203
Frank, Charles 87
Frechtman, Bernard 143, 144
Freund, Mrs. F. E. Washburn 19
Freund, Dr. Washburn 18
Fry, Christopher 9, 147, 150

Galantiere, Lewis 3
Garnett, Constance 71, 76, 80, 353
Gassner, John 381
George, Grace 107, 145, 360
Gielgud, John 74
Gillpatrick, Walter 117

Ginsburg, Norman 184
Giovanni, Paul 148
Glazer, Benjamin 18, 26, 225, 227
Glenville, Peter 125
Goldbaum, Peter 341
Golden, John 26
Gore-Browne, R. F. 164
Gorelik, Mordecai 130, 131
Gorki, Maxim 55
Graham-Lujan, James 142, 143
Granville-Barker, Harley 160, 172, 213, 214, 272, 273, 281, 294
Granville-Barker, Helen 153, 213, 214, 272, 273
Grayson, Helen 36
Green, Paul 184
Gribble, Harry Wagstaff 360
Griffith, Hubert 127
Grosbard, Ulu 364
Grossman, Susan 124, 126
Guerney, Bernard Guilbert 77
Guimera, Angel 117
Guthrie, Judith 2
Guthrie, Tyrone 64, 78, 267

Hahn, Reynaldo 161
Hampton, Christopher 175, 179
Hands, Terry 143
Harris, Neil 256
Harron, Donald 362
Hart, Howard 85
Hauger, George 101, 102
Heijermans-Houwink, Caroline 167, 168
Heinmann, Philip 274
Helburn, Theresa 41
Hellman, Lillian 6
Herbert, Henry 59
Hewlett, Maurice 154
Hill, Lucienne 4, 5, 6, 8, 11
Hingley, Ronald 81
Hinton, Jane 48, 226, 360
Hodson, J. L. 377
Hollo, Anselm 53
Hooker, Brian 161, 283
Hopwood, Avery 358
Hornblow, Arthur Jr. 47, 60, 161, 164

Horst, Louis 236
House, Roy Temple 70
Howard, Sidney 228, 248, 285
Hunter-Blair, Kitty 151, 153

Irving, Laurence 59, 61
Isherwood, Christopher 14
Ivan, Rosalind 89

Jackson, Shirley 370
Jacobs, W. W. 249
Jacobus, J. 358
James, Agnes Hamilton 201
James, Henry 44
Jay, William 45
Jerrell, Randall 77
Jesse, F. Tennyson 164, 165
John, Miriam 10
Johnson, Pamela Hansford 8
Jones, Frank 51
Jones, Robert Edmund 114
Jonson, Ben 381
Joseph, Robert L. 340

Kafka, Franz 146
Kalfin, Robert 362
Kani, John 136
Kanin, Garson 212
Kastner, Rose and Martin 57
Katzin, Winifred 202, 293
Kemp, Lindsay 373
Kipnis, Leonid 78
Kirkup, James 112, 362
Knoblock, Edward 269
Kortner, F. 380
Kronenberger, Louis 7
Kummer, Clare 292

Lackaye, Wilton 360
Landis, Joseph 12
Langley, Noel 231
Langner, Ruth 366, 381
Laughton, Charles 52
Laurence, William L. 2, 151
LeGallienne, Eva 71, 76, 170, 177, 179, 181, 185, 186
LeGallienne, Julie 179
Lessing, Gotthold Ephraim 61
Levin, Donald 362
Levy, Benn W. 127, 248
Lewisohn, Ludwig 366
Leyssac, Paul 179
Littell, Philip 230, 295

Livingston, Arthur 265
Lovell, Roderick 352
Luce, Thomas 36
Ludlam, Charles 114
Lyons, Eugene 198

McCarthy, Kevin 76
McCormick, Elizabeth 74
MacDonald, Ann Sprague 264
MacDonald, Robert D. 169
McHaffie, M. A. 332
Mack, Willard 124
McMahon, Frank 32
Malamuth, Charles 198
Mallen, Miles 65
Mandel, Frank 45, 46
Manheim, Ralph 52, 55
Marburg, Guido 117
Marcin, Max 45
Marquina, Eduardo 214
Martens, G. M. 235
Martin, Christopher 63, 179
Mattos, Alex. T. de 208
Maugham, Somerset 82, 88
Maurette, Marcelle 43
Mayer, Paul Aliva 267, 339
Mayo, Margaret 287
Meader, Clarence A. 3
Meinhard 250
Meltzer, Charles Henry 294
Melville, A. 82
Meriwether, William 40
Merwin, W. S. 143
Metcalf, Henriette 114
Meyer, Adolphe E. 198
Meyer, Michael 175, 179, 181, 183, 184
Middleton, George 43, 44, 45, 46, 47, 59
Miles, Carleton 88
Miles, Dorothy 350
Millay, Edna St. Vincent 226
Miller, Arthur 176
Miller, Gilbert 225
Miner, Washington 381
Moeller, Philip 210, 357
Molière 362
Moorat, J. 172
Moore, Irene 71
Moore, Sonia 71
Morgan, David 353
Morner, Palaemona 338, 341, 343

Morrison, Mary 167
Moss, Arnold 303
Moyes, Patricia 11
Mueller, Cari Richard 361
Murdock, Iris 271
Murray, William 264, 265, 266, 268
Mussman, Linda 338

Nellhaus, Gerhard 53, 54
Nichols, Mike 80
Nicolaeff, Ariadne 74
Nilson, Einar 362
Nivoix, Paul 248
Ntshona, Winston 136

O'Brien, Justin 63, 288
O'Connell, Richard L. 142, 143
Odets, Clifford 329
O'Donnell, Mary Eileen 363
Oland, Edith 342
Oland, Warner 342
Oppenheimer, George 106
Osbourne, Lloyd 154
Ostrow, Dimitri 198, 263

Parker, Louis N. 282, 284
Pauker, John 16
Paul, Cedar 381
Paul, Eden 381
Paulson, Arvid 41
Peters, Paul 55
Picard, Andre 164
Pollock, John 59
Powys, Stephen 160
Prouse, Derth 187, 191

Rafalowicz, Mira 63
Randolph, Clemence 88
Reed, Henry 39, 40
Reel, Arthur 182
Reich, Richard 63
Reznich, E. H. Von 250
Rice, Elmer 18
Rich, Stephen 264
Richepin, Jean 35
Rizzo, Gino 40
Robson, Cecil 5
Roeder, Ralph 106, 210, 248
Rohe, Alice 267
Rolfe, Fr. 208
Romains, Jules 381

Rosen, Samuel 77
Ross, Carmel 175, 177, 185, 353
Rostova, Mina 76
Rothenberg, Jerome 168
Rubens, Paul 45
Rublee, George 295

San Francisco Mime Troupe 55
Saunders, Lilian 167, 168
Savacool, John K. 148
Saville, Mari 363
Schack, William 351
Schlitt, Robert 211
Schmidt, Henry J. 63
Schnee, Thelma 329
Scholtz, August 353
Scott, Fred Newton 3
Seidelman, Arthur A. 362
Seltzer, Thomas 3
Selver, Paul 65
Semple, Lorenzo Jr. 107
Shantl, Susan 63
Sharpe, R. Farquharson 175, 177
Shaw, Barnett 125
Sherwood, Robert E. 108
Short, Robin 341
Shyer, Paul 338
Siegel, Morton 363
Sill, L. M. 85
Simmon, Louis 63
Skariatina, Irina 71
Sophocles 361
Spacek, R. 338, 341, 343
Spiers, Ruth 199
Spottiswood, Sybil 38
Sprigge, Elizabeth 338, 339
Sterling, George 361
Stern, Ann Ward 124
Stern, Edward 124
Stevenson, Robert Louis 154
Storer, Edward 267
Strange, Michael 173
Strindberg, August 112
Swan, Jon 364
Swartz, Marlene 80, 178
Szogyi, Alex 4, 73, 74, 76, 81, 152

Tabori, George 49, 130, 341, 343

Taylor, Deems 235,
Teradash, Daniel 290,
Teta, John 197,
Thomas, Dylan 374, 375
Todd, Albert 80,
Tophoven, Elmar 31,
Trapani, Lou 131,
Tridon, André 295, 364
Tulane, Paul 201,
Tunney, Kiernan 344,

Underhill, John Garrett 34,
    213,
Unger, Gladys 360
Untermeyer, Louis H. 351,

Valency, Maurice 113, 147,
    148, 149,
Van Itallie, Jean-Claude 72,
Vidal, Gore 112,
Vogel, S. J. 295,
Volanakis, Minos 145,

Wagner, Michael 267,
Wallis, Keene 378
Walpole, Hugh 203,
Walter, Eugene 359,
Watson, Donald 188, 189,

190, 192
Watt, Hannah 352
Wedekind, Frank 40
Weissman, José A. 141
Wells, H. G. 123
Wendel, Beth 174
White, Kenneth S. 102
Whitehead, Paxton 124, 126
Whittier, Robert 340
Wilder, Thornton 175, 233,
    235, 291
Wildman, Carl 87
Williams, Emlyn 353
Williams, Herbert 359
Wilmurt, Arthur 236
Wilson, Forrest 351
Winslow, Charles Edward
    Emory 343
Winston, M. 343
Wodehouse, P. G. 107, 229
Wolas, Eva 290
Wright, Barbara 143
Wyngate, Valerie 107

Young, Stark 76, 78, 80
Yurka, Blanche 214

Zilboorg, Gregory 2

INDEX OF TITLES

Abraham Lincoln 109
Absurd Person Singular 15
Accolade 374
Accused 59
Ace of Clubs 89
Act without Words 26
Adam and Eva 43
Admirable Bashville 300
Admirable Crichton 19
Adored One (see Legend of Lenora)
Adventure Story 273
Affairs of Anatol 294
Affairs of State 359
Affinity 59
Afore Night Come 285
After Liverpool (see Games / After Liverpool)
After Magritte 333
After the Ball 89
After the Rain 48
L'Aiglon 281
Aimer (see To Love)
Air Walker 187
Alice-Sit-by-the-Fire 19
Alien Shadow (see Strange Shadow)
L'alouette (see The Lark)
Amazons 252
Amédée, or How to Disentangle Yourself 187
Americans in France 59
Amoureuse 106
Amphitryon (von Kleist) 362
Amphitryon 38 (Giraudoux) 146
Anastasia 43
Anathema 1
Anatol 294
Anatomist 57
Andorra 130
Androcles and the Lion 300
Angel Comes to Babylon 111
Angel Street 162

Annajanska, the Bolshevik Empress 301
Anniversary 70
Another Evening with Chekhov 70
Another Love 106
Another Love Story 205
Antigone (Anouilh) 3
Antigone (Cocteau) 86
Apollo of Bellac 147
Apple Cart 301
Applicant (see Local Stigmatic)
L'Appolon de Marsac 147
L'archipel Lenoir 286
Ardèle 4
Aren't We All? 205
Ariadne 221
Arms and the Man 302
Art and Mrs. Bottle 202
Arturo Ui 49
As You Desire Me 263
Ascent of F6 14
Ashes 285
Asmodée (see Intruder)
Assumption of Hannele (see Hannele)
Astonished Heart (see Tonight at Eight-Thirty)
At Mrs. Beam's 231
At the Bottom 151
Attendant Godot (see Waiting for Godot)
Augustus 4
Augustus Does His Bit 303
Autumn Crocus 331
Autumn Fire 232
Awakening of Spring 40, 362
Azrael 86

B-Beaver Animations 27
Baal 50
Baby Elephant 50

Bacchus 86
Back to Methuselah 303
Balcony 143
Bald Soprano 187
Banco 292
Barbara's Wedding 20
Barchester Towers 193
Barretts of Wimpole Street 37
Basement 256
Bathsheba 106
Battering Ram 128
Battle of Shrivings 296
Bear 70
Beau-Strings 232
Beautiful Sabine Women (see Sabine Women)
Beauty and the Barge 249
Becket 4
Bedlam Galore (see Plays by Eugene Ionesco)
Bedtime Story 236
Beffa (see Jest)
Before Sundown 166
Before Sunset (see Before Sundown)
Belinda 221
Belissa in the Garden 141
Bequest to the Nation 273
Best Sellers 47
Betrothal 208
Between Two Thieves 124
Biedermann und die Brandstifer (see Firebugs)
Big Fish, Little Fish 369
Big Scene 294
Bill of Divorcement 99
Billeted 164
Bird in Hand 109
Bird in the Hand 124
Birthday Party 257
Birthright 232
Bishop's Bonfire 237
Bit of Love 137
Bitter Oleander (see Blood Wedding)
Bitter Sweet 90
Black Comedy 296
Black Mask 164
Blacks 144
Blind Men (see 3 by Ghelderode)
Blithe Spirit 90
Blood Knot 135

Blood of the Bambergs (see Two Plays for England)
Blood Wedding 141
Bloody Laughter 351
Bloomers 332
Blow Your Own Trumpet 354
Blue Bird 209
Blue Comedy 1
Bluebeard's Eighth Wife 293
Bodas de Sangre (see Blood Wedding)
Boesman and Lena 135
Bogeyman of Lusitania (see Song of the Lusitanian Bogey)
Bolshevik Empress 304
Bond 337
Bond Honored 244
Bonds of Interest 34
Boor 71
Borstal Boy 32
Boubouroche 235
Boudoir 106
Boy David 20
Boy Growing Up 374
Boy with a Cart 131
Boyd's Daughter 121
Brand 175
Breadwinner 215
Break of Noon 84
Breakfast in Bed 124
Brecht on Brecht 347
Bridal Crown 337
Broken Jug 362
Brothers Karamazov 89
Brouhaha 347
Browning Version 273
Bugiarda 124
Buoyant Billions 304
Bürger Schippel 332
Burgomaster of Belgium 209
Burnt Flowerbed 39
Business First (see Ariadne)
Butley 154

Caesar and Cleopatra 304
Caesar's Wife 215
Caligula 63
Call Home the Heart 99
Call It a Day 331
Call It Virtue 263
Call of Life 294
Calvary 378

Camel's Back 215
Camille 113
Canaries Sometimes Sing 205
Candida 305
Cannibals 347
Cantatrice Chauve (see Bald Soprano)
Caprice 105
Captain Brassbound's Conversion 307
Captain of Koepenick 380
Captive 47
Cardinal of Spain 104
Caretaker 257
Carnival 225
Caroline 216
Carving a Statue 156
Cascando 27
Case of J. Robert Oppenheimer (see In the Matter of J. Robert Oppenheimer)
Caste 279
Castle in the Air 82
Cataline 175
Caucasian Chalk Circle 50
Cause of It All 352
Cave Girl 44
Cavern 5
Celebration 71
Censor and the Dramatists 20
Chairs 188
Chaises 188
Chalk Garden 16
Changing Room 335
Chantecler 282
Charley's Aunt 349
Chekhov Portfolio 71
Chemin de Fer 124
Chemmy Circle 125
Cher Antoine (see Dear Antoine)
Cherry Orchard 71
Chicken Feed 44
Child of Fortune 44
Children 44
Children of the Sun 151
Chinese Prime Minister 17
Chinese Wall 130
Chips with Everything 368
Christophe Colomb 84
Christopher Columbus (see 3 by Ghelderode)
Chronicles of Hell 101

Church Street 279
Circle 216
Citta Morta 101
Clair de Lune 173
Clerambard 16
Clutterbuck 203
Coats 157
Cock-a-Doodle Dandy 237
Cock o' the Walk 195
Cocktail Party 117
Coggerers 66
Collection 258
College Sinners (see First Episode)
Colombe (see Mademoiselle Colombe)
Colombyre 212
Come and Go 27
Come into the Garden Maude (see Noel Coward in Two Keys)
Come of Age 99
Comedian 160
Comedians 159
Comment s'en de'Barrasser 188
Complaisant Lover 156
Comrades 338
Concert 17
Condemned of Altona 288
Conditions of Agreement 370
Conduct Unbecoming 121
Confidential Clerk 118
Constant Wife 216
Contractor 336
Conversation Piece 90
Corn Is Green 374
Corruption in the Palace of Justice 39
Coufontaine Trilogy 84
Countess Cathleen 378
Countess Julia 338
Country People 151
Country Scandal 73
Country Woman 353
Courageous One 151
Cousin Muriel 100
Cousin Sonia 359
Crabbed Youth and Age 279
Cradle Song 213
Creditors 338
Creeps 128
Crime and Crime 338

Crime Passionel 288
Crimes of Passion 242
Criminals 61
Cromwell 336
Crown Colony 170
Crown Prince 357
Crusts (see Coufontaine Trilogy)
Cry of the Peacock 5
Crysal and Fox 128
Curtmantle 132
Cynara 164
Cyrano de Bergerac 283

Damaged Goods 59
Dame aux Camélias (see Camille)
Dame Nature 40
Damer's Gold 158
Dance of Death 14, 338
Dandy Dick 252
Dangerous Corner 268
Danton's Death 62
Danton's Tod 62
Daphne Laureola 57
Dark Is Light Enough 132
Dark Lady of the Sonnets 307
David Garrick 279
Day after Tomorrow 205
Day in the Death of Joe Egg 233
Days of the Commune 51
Dead City (see La Citta Morta)
Dear Antoine 5
Dear Brutus 20
Dear Departed Mother-in-Law (see Feu la Mère de Madame)
Dear Miss Phoebe 20
Dear Octopus 20
Death and the Devil 363
Death as a Life Force 264
Death of Cuchulain 379
Death of Tintagiles 210
Death Takes a Holiday 68
Deathwatch 144
Deburau 160
Deep Blue Sea 274
Deferential Prostitute (see Respectful Prostitute)
Deirdre of the Sorrows 344
Delicate Story 225

Demonstration (see Nigger-lovers)
Deputy 168
Desert Highway 268
Design for Living 91
Devil and the Good Lord 288
Devil Came from Dublin 66
Devil in the Mind 2
Devil Passes 203
Devil to Pay 167
Devils 370
Devil's Disciple 308
Devil's General 380
Devils of Loudon (see Devils)
Diable et le Bon Dieu (see The Devil and the Good Lord)
Dial "M" for Murder 199
Dindon 125
Dinner with the Family (see Le Rendevous de Senlis)
Diplomacy 286
Dirty Linen & New-Found-Land 333
Discourse on Vietnam 364
Disraeli 249
Divine Drudge 26
Divorcons 287
Doctor and the Devil 350
Dr. Angelus 58
Dr. Knock 281
Doctor's Dilemma 308
Dog Beneath the Skin 14
Doll's House 175
Don 37
Don Juan in Hell 309
Don Juan in the Russian Manner 74
Doña Rosita La Sotera 142
Donogoo 281
Don't Listen, Ladies 160
Dover Road 221
Dragon 158
Dragon's Mouth 268
Drama at Inish 280
Dream of Peter Mann 201
Dream Play 339
Drifting 87
Druid's Rest 375
Drums in the Night 51
Drums of Father Ned 237
Duel of Angels 147
Duke in Darkness 162

Dumbwaiter 258
Dutch Uncle 155
Dutiful Prostitute (see Respectful Prostitute)
Dwarfs 259
Dybbuk 12
Dylan Thomas Growing Up 375

Each in His Own Way 264
Eagle (see L'Aiglon)
Eagle Has Two Heads 86
Earth Spirit 363
East Lynne 378
East of the Suez 217
Easter One Day More 340
Easy Virtue 91
Economic Necessity 171
Eden End 269
Edward, My Son 231
Edward II 51
Egg 211
Egoists 221
Ehe des Herrn Mississippi 111
Einen Jux Will Er Sich Machen 233
Elder Statesman 119
Elektra 361
Elephant Calf 51
Elizabeth von England (see Gloriana)
Embers 27
Emperor Henry IV (see Henry IV)
Emperor's Clothes 347
Enchanted 147
Enchanted Cottage 252
End of the Beginning 237
Endgame 27
Enemies 151
Enemy of the People 176
Enter a Free Man 333
Entertainer 244
Entertaining Mr. Sloane 243
Epitaph for George Dillon 245
Equus 297
Erpingham Camp (see Crimes of Passion)
Errand for Bernice 106
Escape 137
Escurial 101
Et l''Enfer Isabella 107
Eternal Road 366

Eurydice (see Legend of Lovers)
Evening of Brecht 51
Evening with Shaw 310
Ever Since Paradise 269
Everyman (Beckett) 28
Everyman (von Hofmannsthal) 361
Exception and the Rule 51
Exiles 197
Exit the King 188
Expelled 28
Explorer 217
Eyvind of the Hills 329

Failures 202
Faith Healer 128
Faithful 214
Fake 206
Fall and Redemption of Man 49
Fallen Angels 91
Fallen Idol 44
Family Album (see Tonight at Eight-Thirty)
Family Reunion 119
Fancy Free 171
Fanny Hawthorne (see Hindle Wakes)
Fanny's First Play 310
Far-Fetched Fables 311
Far-Off Hills 280
Farm 336
Fashions for Men 225
Fata Morgana 357
Father 340
Fear 202
Fedora 287
Feu la Mère de Madame 125
Field of Ermine 34
Fighting Cock 6
Figuro in the Night 238
Fil a la Patte 125
Fin de Partie 28
Find Your Way Home 171
Firebugs 130
Fireworks on the James 74
First Episode 274
First Love 359
First Mrs. Fraser 121
Firstborn 132
Five-Finger Exercise 297
Five Million 45

Flare Path 274
Flea in Her Ear 125
Flies 288
Flight into Egypt 348
Florentine Tragedy 371
Floriani's Wife 264
Flowering Cherry 42
Folie de Chaillot 148
Fools Are Passing Through 111
For Lucretia 148
For Services Rendered 217
For the Time Being 14
For Two or More (see Plays by Eugene Ionesco)
Foreigners 206
Forget-Me-Not-Lane 234
Fortunato 272
Four Seasons 368
Fourposter 103
Foursome (see Plays by Eugene Ionesco)
Frank V 111
Franziska 363
Freedom of the City 128
French without Tears 274
Frenzy 354
Friends 368
From Morn to Midnight 197
Fugitive 137
Full Moon in March 379
Fumed Oak (see Tonight at Eight-Thirty)
Funeral Games 243

Galileo 52
Gambler 39
Game Is Up (see Fin de Partie)
Games/After Liverpool 292
Gaol Gate 158
Gas 198
Gas Light (see Angel Street)
Gates of Summer 371
Gay Lord Quex 253
Geneva 311
Genius and the Goddess 174
Gentle Jack 42
Gertie 17
Getting Married 311
Ghost Sonata 341
Ghosts 177
Giaconda Smile 174

Gil Blas 174
Give Me Yesterday 222
Glass Cage 269
Glass Slipper 225
Glimpse of the Domesticity of Franklin Barnabas (see Back to Methuselah)
Gloriana 61
Go Back for Murder 82
Goal 195
Goat Song 366
God and Kate Murphy 344
God and the Devil (see The Devil and the Good Lord)
Gods of the Mountain 115
Golden Cuckoo 194
Golden Doom 115
Golden Wings 45
Goldfish (see Les Poissons Rouges)
Good Companions 269
Good Fairy 226
Good Hope 168
Good Night, Children? 269
Good Soup 212
Good Woman of Setzuan 52
Grand Duchess and the Waiter 293
Grand Duke 161
Grand Hotel 26
Granite 100
Great Broxopp 222
Great Catherine 312
Great Pursuit 69
Great Rage of Philip Hotz (see Die Grosse Wut des Philip Hotz)
Green Bay Tree 299
Green Cockatoo 295
Green Goddess 13
Green Julia 1
Grey Farm 275
Grosse Wut des Philip Hotz 131
Grounds for Divorce 357
Grüne Kakadu 295
Guardsman 226
Guerillas 169
Guerre de Troie n'Aura pas Lieu (see Tiger at the Gates)
Guilty (see Therese)
Guns of Carrar 53

Guntower 256

Hadrian VII 208
Half an Hour 20
Halfway up the Tree 354
Hall of Healing 238
Hamlet at Wittenberg 166
Hamlet of Stepney Green 201
Hamp 377
Hands across the Sea (see
    Tonight at Eight-Thirty)
Hank's Night (see Blue
    Comedy)
Hannele 166
Happy Days 28
Harem 358
Harlequinade 275
Harvest 280
Hay Fever 92
He 293
He Wants to Have a Good
    Time (see Einen Jux Will
    Er Sich Machen)
He Who Gets Slapped 2
Heartbreak House 312
Hedda Gabler 179
Hello and Goodbye 135
Henry IV 264
Her Cardboard Lover 107
Her Country 38
Herne's Egg 379
Herod 252
Hiatus (see Intermezzo)
Hidden Horizon 82
High Road 206
Highway of Life 250
Hindle Wakes 171
His Widow's Husband 34
Hoboes in Heaven 235
Hofmeister 53
Hölderlin 364
Hole 330
Home 337
Home at Seven 327
Home Is Tomorrow 269
Homecoming 259
Hop, Signor 101
Hostage (Behan) 33
Hostage (Claudel) (see Coufon-
    taine Trilogy)
Hotel in Amsterdam 245
Hotel Paradiso 125
Hour Glass 379

House in Berlin 131
House of Bernarda Alba 142
House of Regrets 355
How He Lied to Her Husband
    313
How Mr. Mockinpott Was
    Cured of His Suffering 364
How the Ohter Half Loves 15
How They Are at Home 269
How to Disentangle Yourself
    (see Amédée, or How to
    Disentangle Yourself)
Huis Clos (see No Exit)
Human Voice 86
Humiliated Father (see
    Coufontaine Trilogy)
Humulus the Great 6
Hundred Years Old 272
Hunger and Thirst 189
L'Hurluberlu 6
Hyacinth Halvey 158

I Forgot 74
I Have Been Here Before 269
Ideal Husband 371
Idiot 155
Idlers (see Great Pursuit)
If 115
If Five Years Pass 142
If I Were King 208
If I Were You 203
Image 158
Importance of Being Earnest
    371
L'Impromtu (see Plays by
    Eugene Ionesco)
In Celebration 337
In Good King Charles' Golden
    Days 314
In Praise of Love 275
In Search of Justice (see
    An Evening of Brecht)
In the J. Robert Oppenheimer
    Affair (see In the Matter
    of J. Robert Oppenheimer)
In the Jungle of Cities 53
In the Matter of J. Robert
    Oppenheimer 199
In the Shadow of the Glen 344
Inadmissible Evidence 245
Indifferent Shepherd 355
Infernal Machine 86
Informer 54

Insect Comedy (see World We
    Live In)
Inspector Calls 270
Interior 210
Intermezzo 148
Interview (see Local Stig-
    matic)
Intimate Relations 87
Intruder (Maeterlinck) 210
Intruder (Mauriac) 221
Investigation 364
Invitation to a Voyage 36
Is Life Worth Living? (see
    Drama at Inish)
Island 136
Island Fling 92
Island of Goats 40
Ivan the Terrible 352
Ivanoff 74
Ivory Door 222

Jack 189
Jack MacGowran in the Works
    of Samuel Beckett 29
Jack, or the Submission 189
Jackass 111
Jackdaw 158
Jacob 172
Jacobowsky and the Colonel
    367
Jail Gate (see Gaol Gate)
Jane Clegg 122
Jane Eyre 192
Jar 264
Jealousy 359
Jeanne au Bucher 85
Jeannette (see Romeo and
    Jeannette)
Jedermann 361
Jenny Villiers 270
Jeremiah 381
Jest 35
Jeune Fille a Marier 189
Jewish Wife (see Evening
    of Brecht)
Joe Egg (see A Day in the
    Death of Joe Egg)
Johannes Kreisler 250
John Bull's Other Island 314
John Ferguson 122
John Gabriel Borkman 181
Joseph and His Brethren 250
Josephine 18

Journey's End 327
Juarez and Maximilian 367
Judith (Giraudoux) 148
Judith (Hebbel) 167
Jumpers 333
Juno and the Paycock 238
Justice (Brecht) 54
Justice (Galsworthy) 137

Karen 36
Katerina 2
Kathleen ni Houlihan 379
Kean (Dumas) (see The
    Royal Box)
Kean (Sartre) 289
Keep Your Eyes on Emily
    (see Occupe-toi d'Amélie)
Keyholes 212
Killer 189
Killing Game 189
Killing of Sister George 212
Kindred 66
King Argimenes 115
King Nicolo 363
Kingdom of God 213
Kiss for Cinderella 21
Kiss of Importance 164
Kitchen 368
Klienburgerhochzeit 54
Komedie (see Makropoulos
    Secret)
Konzert (see Concert)
Krapp's Last Tape 29
Kreutzer Sonata 352

Laburnum Grove 270
Lacune 189
Lady Frederick 218
Lady from Alfaqueque 153
Lady from Lobster Square
    126
Lady from Maxim's 126
Lady from the Provinces 353
Lady from the Sea 181
Lady Jane 164
Lady of Coventry 251
Lady of Dreams 284
Lady of the Camellias (see
    Camille)
Lady Patricia 38
Lady Windermere's Fan 372
Lady's Not for Burning 132
L'Alouette (see Lark)

Land of Promise 218
Land's End 193
Landscape 260
Landslide at North Station 40
Lark 6
Last Dance 341
Last Night of Don Juan 285
Last of Mrs. Cheyney 206
Last to Go (see The Local
 Stigmatic)
Laughter of the Gods 115
Launzi 226
Lazurus 265
Leader (see Plays by Eugene
 Ionesco)
Leave It to Jeeves 45
League of Youth 182
Legend of Leonora 21
Legend of Lovers 7
Leonce and Lena 63
Lesson 190
Lesson in Love 38
Letter 218
Letter from Paris 332
Letter of the Law 60
Liar 124
Liars 195
License 265
Lie 195
Life Class 337
Life of Man 3
Light of Heart (see Yester-
 day's Magic)
Light of the World 45
Liliom 227
Limping Devil 161
Linden Tree 270
L'Invitation au Chateau (see
 Ring Around the Moon)
Lion in Love 104
Lion Tamer 293
Literature 295
Little Angel 358
Little Boxes 49
Little Dark Horse 41
Little Eyolf 182
Little Man 138
Little Minister 22
Living Corpse (see Redemption)
Living Mask (see Henry IV)
Living Room 156
Living Together (see Norman
 Conquests)

Lizzie McKay (see Respect-
 ful Prostitute)
Local Stigmatic 260
Look after Lulu 92
Look Back in Anger 246
Look: We've Come Through!
 369
Loot 243
Lorelei 107
Lorenzaccio 105
Losers (see Lovers)
Lost Leader 280
Lost Ones 30
Louisiana 16
Love and Let Love 359
Love from a Stranger 83
Love Habit 360
Love in Idleness (see O Mis-
 tress Mine)
Love of Don Perlimplin 142
Love of Four Colonels 355
Love of One's Neighbor 3
Lover 260
Lovers 129
Lovers and Friends 332
Lover's Luck 106
Loves of Cass McGuire 129
Loves of Lulu 363
Lower Depths 152
Loyalties 138
Lucky One 222
Lucrèce 235
Lulu 363
Luther 246
Lydia Gilmore 196

Macbett 190
Machine Infernale (see In-
 fernal Machine)
Madame Pierre 60
Madame Sans-Gêne 287
Mademoiselle 107
Mademoiselle Colombe 7
Madly in Love (see Blue
 Comedy)
Madras House 153
Madwoman of Chaillot 148
Magda 343
Magistrate 253
Magnanimous Lover 122
Maids 144
Main Passe (see Chemmy
 Circle)

Mains Sales (see Soiled Hands)
Major Barbara 314
Makropoulos Secret 64
Malvaloca 272
Man and Boy 275
Man and Dog (see Niggerlovers)
Man and His Phantoms 202
Man and Superman 315
Man and the Masses 351
Man for All Seasons 42
Man in Possession 165
Man in the Glass Booth 326
Man in the Raincoat 355
Man Is Man 54
Man of Destiny 316
Man Who Laughed (see Clair de Lune)
Man with Red Hair 203
Man with the Flower in His Mouth 265
Man's a Man 54
Man's House 110
Marat/Sade 364
Marching Song 371
Margot 47
Maria Rosa 117
Mariana Pineda 142
Marie Tudor 174
Mariners 100
Marius 248
Marquise 92
Marriage 75
Marriage of Mr. Mississippi 111
Marriage Proposal 75
Marseilles 248
Martine 36
Mary Goes First 196
Mary Magdalene 210
Mary, Mary, Quite Contrary 123
Mary Rose 22
Mary Stuart 110
Mary Stuart in Scotland 41
Maschera e il Volto (see Mask and the Face)
Mask and the Face 82
Masks of Love and Death 379
Master 18
Master Builder 183
Master of Santiago 104
Master Puntila and His Valet,

Matti (see Squire Puntila and His Servant)
Maternity 60
Matrimony PFD 360
Matter of Gravity 17
Maurice Harte 232
Measures Taken 55
Medea 8
Meet the Prince 223
Merchants of Glory 248
Merchants of Yonkers 233
Michael and Mary 223
Michel Auclair 360
Mid-Channel 253
Midwife 169
Million Torments 198
Millionairess 316
Mima 227
Mind-the-Paint Girl 253
Miracle in the Mountains 228
Miracle of St. Anthony 210
Mirage (see Fata Morgana)
Misalliance 317
Miss Julia (see Miss Julie)
Miss Julie 341
Miss Mabel 328
Miss Marlowe at Play 223
Miss Thompson (see Rain)
Mr. and Mrs. Daventry 373
Mr. Bolfry 58
Mr. Fox of Venice 200
Mr. Gillie 58
Mr. Pim Passes By 223
Mrs. Dane's Defense 196
Mrs. Dot 218
Mrs. Moonlight 204
Mrs. Mouse, Are You Within? 213
Mrs. Warren's Profession 318
Misunderstanding 64
Mixed Marriage 123
Mob 139
Moment of Truth 355
Mongrel 18
Month in the Country 353
Moon in the Yellow River 194
Moon Mysteries 379
Moon Shines on Kylenamoe 239
Moonbirds 16
Morning Star 375
Morning to Midnight (see From Morn to Midnight)

Morris Dance 154
Morts sans Sepulture (see Un-
 buried Dead)
Mother (Brecht) 55
Mother (Capek) 65
Mother Courage and Her
 Children 55
Motherlove 342
Mountain Giants 265
Mousetrap 83
Mozart 161
Mundy Scheme 129
Murder Has Been Arranged
 376
Murder in the Cathedral 120
Music by Night 271
Music Cure 318
Mystery at Greenfingers 271

Naked 265
Nan (see Tragedy of Nan)
Nathan the Wise 61
National Health 234
Ne Reveillez pas Madame 8
Neighbors 292
Nekrassov 289
Nest 145
New-Found-Land (see Dirty
 Linen & New-Found-Land)
New Gossoon 328
New Tenant 190
New Word 23
Next Time I'll Sing to You
 292
Niggerlovers 348
Night 261
Night at an Inn 116
Night Lodging 152
Night Must Fall 376
Nightcap 45
Nights of Fury (see Nuits de
 la Colère)
Nights of Wrath (see Nuits
 de la Colère)
Nihilists (see Vera, or the
 Nihilists)
Nina 127
Nine Pine Street 88
No Exit 289
No Man's Land 261
No More Peace 351
No Sign of the Dove 355
No Trifling with Love 105

Noah 236
Noble Spaniard 219
Nobody Home 45
Nobody's Business 46
Noces d'Argent (see Nest)
Noel Coward in Two Keys 93
Noontide 85
Norman Conquests 15
Not I 30
Notes on a Love Affair 213
Nouveau Locataire (see New
 Tenant)
Nude with Violin 93
Nuits de la Colère 286

O Mistress Mine 276
Obsession 360
Occupe-toi d'Amélie 126
Offense 300
O'Flaherty, V. C. 319
Oh, Brother! 107
Oh! Les Beaux Jours (see
 Happy Days)
Oh Mama 360
Oktobertag (see Phantom
 Lover)
Old English 139
Old Folks at Home (see
 Lady Jane)
Old Foolishness 66
Old Friends 23
Old Lady Says "No" 194
Old Lady Shows Her Medals
 23
Old Ones 369
Old Times 261
Olive Latimer's Husband 38
Olympia 228
On Approval 206
On Baile's Strand 379
On My Coral Islands 219
On Ne Badine Pas Avec
 L'Amour (see No Trifling
 with Love)
On the Harmfulness of To-
 bacco 75
On the Hazards of Smoking
 Tobacco (see On the Harm-
 fulness of Tobacco)
On the High Road 75
On the Highway (see On the
 High Road)
On the Rocks 319

Once Is Enough 207
Ondine 149
One, Two, Three 228
One-Way Pendulum 330
Only Jealousy of Emer 380
Only Sense Is Nonsense 330
Opium 87
Orphée 87
Other Rose 47
Otherwise Engaged 155
Our American Cousin 349
Our Betters 219
Outside the Door 47
Outward Bound 358
Overruled 319
Overture 41

Pacifica 1860 93
Pain Dur 85
Pan and the Young Shepherd
    154
Pantagleize 102
Paolo and Francesco 252
Paper Chase 251
Paravents 145
Parents Terribles (see Inti-
    mate Relations)
Pariah 342
Parisienne 32
Partage de Midi (see Noon-
    tide)
Passers-By 69
Passion Flower 34
Passion, Poison, and Putre-
    faction 319
Pasteur 161
Patient 83
Patriot for Me 247
Patriotic War of 1812 352
Patriots 280
Pauvre Bitos (see Poor
    Bitos)
Peace in Our Time 93
Pedestrian in the Air 190
Peer Gynt 184
Pelican 165
Pelleas and Melisande 211
Penelope 219
People Are Living There 136
Perfect Alibi 223
Perfect Gentleman 219
Persecution and Assassination of
    Marat as Performed by the In-
mates of the Asylum of
    Charenton Under the Direc-
    tion of the Marquis de Sade
    (see Marat/Sade)
Peter Pan 23
Phantom Lover 198
Phantom Rival 228
Philadelphia, Here I Come!
    129
Philanderer 319
Philanthropist 163
Philip Hotz (see Die Grosse
    Wut des Philip Hotz)
Phipps 172
Phoenix Too Frequent 133
Photo Finish 355
Physicists 112
Pieton de l'Air (see Pedes-
    trian in the Air)
Pigeon 139
Pile ou Face (see First
    Love)
Pilgrim 361
Pillars of Society 185
Pin to See the Peepshow 165
Pinch Hitter 165
Pinion (see Countess Cath-
    leen)
Pinkville 348
Platonov 75
Play 30
Play Strindberg 112
Playboy of the Western
    World 344
Player Queen 380
Playing with Fire 342
Plays by Eugène Ionesco 191
Play's the Thing 229
Please Help Emily 166
Plough and the Stars 239
Point of Departure 8
Point Valaine 94
Poissons Rouges 8
Polly Preferred 46
Polly with a Past 46
Pomander Walk 251
Poor Bitos 8
Poor Fool 19
Port-Royal 104
Portrait of a Planet 112
Possessed 64
Posterity Be Damned 33
Potting Shed 157

Pound on Demand 240
Pour Lucrèce (see For Lucretia)
Power of Darkness 352
Present Laughter 94
Preserving Mr. Panmure 254
Press Cuttings 320
Pride and Prejudice 192
Prince of Homburg 362
Princess Lointaine (see Lady of Dreams)
Prisonnière (see Captive)
Private Ear 298
Private Enterprise 123
Private Life of the Master Race 56
Private Lives 94
Proces (see Trial)
Professor Bernhardi 295
Professor Mamlock 378
Professor's Love Story 24
Proposal 75
Prunella 172
Public Eye 298
Public Prosecutor Is Sick of It All 131
Puntila (see Squire Puntila and His Servant)
Puntila and the Hired Man (see Squire Puntila and His Servant)
Purgatory 380
Purple Dust 240
Putain Respectueuse (see Respectful Prostitute)
Pygmalion 320

Quadrille 95
Quare Fellow 33
Queen after Death 105
Queen and the Rebels 40
Queen's Comedy 58
Queen's Enemies 116

R. A. F. (see Golden Wings)
R. U. R. 65
Raft of the Medusa 198
Rain 88
Rape of the Belt 204
Rats 83
Rats of Norway 377
Ratten 166
Rattle of a Simple Man 116

Real Inspector Hound 334
Red Devil 152
Red Gloves 290
Red Mill (see Mima)
Red Peppers 96
Red Robe (see Letter of the Law)
Red Roses for Me 240
Redemption 352
Rehearsal 8
Reigen 295
Reine Morte 105
Relative Values 96
Rendevous de Senlis 9
Repetition 9
Repetition ou L'Amour Puni 9
Representative (see Deputy)
Request Stop (see Local Stigmatic)
Resistible Rise of Arturo Ui (see Arturo Ui)
Resounding Tinkle 330
Respectful Prostitute 290
Restless Heart 9
Resurrection 380
Return to Tyassi 204
Rhinoceros 191
Riders to the Sea 346
Rifles of Mother Carrar 56
Right You Are If You Think You Are 266
Ring Round the Moon 9
Rise and Fall of the City of Mahagonny 56
Rising of the Moon 158
Road to Happiness 214
Robert E. Lee 110
Roi Se Meurt (see Exit the King)
Romanoff and Juliet 356
Romantic Age 224
Romantic Young Lady 214
Romeo and Jeannette 10
Romulus 112
Ronde 295
Roof 140
Room 262
Roots 369
Rope (see Rope's End)
Rope's End 162
Rosalind 24
Rose Bernd 166
Rosemary 251

Rosencrantz and Guildenstern
  Are Dead 334
Rosmersholm 185
Ross 276
Rossom's Universal Robots
  (see R. U. R.)
Round and Round the Garden
  (see Norman Conquests)
Royal Box 114
Royal Hunt of the Sun 298
Rubicon 48
Ruffian on the Stair 244
Rule of Three 46
Rules of the Game 266
Ruling the Roost 126
Russian People 329
Russian Question 329
Russians (see Russian
  People)
Ruy Blas (see Gil Blas)

S. S. Tenacity 361
Sabine Women 3
Sacred Flame 219
Sailors of Cattaro 378
St. Helena 328
Saint Joan 321
St. Joan of the Stockyards 56
Saint Wench 89
Salome 373
Samaritaine 285
Same Time, Next Year 331
Sangen om Skrapuken (see
  Song of the Lusitanian
  Bogey)
Sarah Simple 224
Satin Slipper 85
Saturday Night 35
Savages 163
Saving Grace 69
Say It with Flowers 267
Scent of Flowers 292
School 279
School for Buffoons 102
Schweiger 367
Schweik in the Second World
  War 57
Scrap of Paper 287
Screens 145
Sea Gull 75
Second Mrs. Tanqueray 254
Secrets 39
Sense of Detachment 247

Separate Tables 276
Sequestres d'Altona (see
  Condemned of Altona)
Severed Head 271
Sex Fable 48
Sexe Faible (see Sex Fable)
Shadow and Substance 66
Shadow of a Gunman 241
Shadow Play (see Tonight at
  Eight-Thirty)
Shall We Join the Ladies? 24
Shanghai Gesture 89
She Had to Know 145
Shepherd's Chameleon 191
Sheppy 220
Shewing-up of Blanco Posnet
  324
Shining Hour 377
Shoemaker's Prodigious Wife
  143
Short Eyes 256
Short Story 231
Siegfried 150
Sigh No More 96
Silence 262
Silver Box 140
Silver Tassie 241
Simpleton of the Unexpected
  Isles 324
Sister Beatrice 211
Six Characters in Search of
  an Author 267
Six of Calais 324
Sizwe Banzi Is Dead 136
Skin Game 140
Skipper Next to God 103
Sleep of Prisoners 133
Sleeping Clergyman 58
Sleeping Partners 161
Sleeping Prince 277
Sleuth 296
Slice of Life 24
Slight Ache 262
Smith 220
Snob 332
Soif de la Faim 191
Soiled Hands 291
Soldat Tanaka 198
Soldiers 169
Someone Waiting 376
Somewhere in France 380
Song at Twilight 96
Song of Songs (Giraudoux) 150

Song of Songs (Sudermann) 343
Song of the Horrible Demon
    (see Song of the Lusitanian
    Bogey)
Song of the Lusitanian Bogey
    365
Songs from Milk Wood 350
Sorceress 287
South Sea Bubble 96
Spider's Web 83
Spook Sonata 342
Spreading the News 159
Spring 233
Spring Cleaning 207
Spring in Autumn 214
Spring's Awakening (see A-
    wakening of Spring)
Springtime for Henry 204
Springtime of Others 36
Squaring the Circle 198
Squire Puntila and His Ser-
    vant 57
Staircase 117
Star Turns Red 242
Stellvertreter (see Deputy)
Still Life (Coward) 96
Still Life (Molnar) 230
Storm over Patsy 127
Straight from the Ghetto 256
Strange Rider (see 3 by
    Ghelderode)
Strange Shadow 329
Straw Hat 201
Strife 140
Strings, My Lord, Are False
    67
Strong Are Lonely 170
Stronger 342
Submission (see Jack, or
    the Submission)
Success (see Give Me Yes-
    terday)
Suite in Three Keys 96
Summer Day's Dream 271
Summer in the Country (see
    A Chekhov Portfolio; and
    Another Evening with Chekhov
Summer Night 26
Summer of the 17th Doll 201
Summerfolk 153
Summertime 40
Sun Always Shines for the Cool
    256

Sunny Morning 273
Sur la Terre Comme au Ciel
    170
Susannah and the Elders 58
Swan 230
Swan Song 77
Sweeney Agonistes 120
Sword by his Side 381

Table by the Window (see
    Separate Tables)
Table Manners (see Norman
    Conquests)
Table Number Seven (see
    Separate Tables)
Tableau 192
Tale of the Wolf 230
Tante 69
Taste of Honey 104
Tea Party 263
Temps Difficiles (see Times
    Have Changed)
Ten Little Indians 83
Tenor 363
Tents of the Arabs 116
Tête d'Or 85
That Worthless Fellow Plato-
    nov (see Fireworks on
    the James)
That's All (see Local Stig-
    matic)
That's Your Trouble (see
    Local Stigmatic)
Theatre 220
There Is a Play Tonight 230
There's One in Every Mar-
    riage 126
Therese 193
They Came to a City 271
They Don't Mean Any Harm 224
Thief 70
Thieves' Carnival 10
Things That Are Caesar's 67
This Happy Breed 97
This Sporting Life 337
This Story of Yours 171
This Time Tomorrow 103
This Was a Man 97
This Woman Business 205
This Year of Grace 97
Thor, with Angels 134
Three Actors and Their
    Drama 102

3 by Ghelderode 102
Three Daughters of Monsieur
    Dupont 61
Three Guardsmen 115
Three Sisters 77
Thunderbolt 254
Ticket of Leave Man, or
    Hawkshaw the Detective 349
Tidings Brought to Mary 85
Tiger and the Horse 42
Tiger at the Gates 150
Time and the Conways 271
Time Is a Dream 202
Time of Vengeance 40
Time Present 248
Time Remembered 11
Time to Go 242
Times Have Changed 48
Tinker's Wedding 346
To Clothe the Naked 268
To Damascus 343
To Have the Honor (see
    Meet the Prince)
To Love 145
Tobias and the Angel 58
Tombless Dead (see Un-
    buried Dead)
Tonight at Eight-Thirty 97
Tonight in Samarkand 107
Tonight We Improvise 268
Too Many Husbands 220
Too True to Be Good 324
Topaze 248
Total Eclipse 163
Tovarich 108
Tower 366
Tragedian in Spite of Himself
    80
Tragedy of Nan 215
Travails of Sancho Panza 292
Traveller without Luggage 11
Travelling Man 159
Travesties 335
Treasure on Pelican 272
Trelawney of the Wells 255
Trespass 376
Trevor 49
Trial 146
Triumph of Death 192
Trotsky in Exile 366
Trouble in the Works (see
    Local Stigmatic)
Troubled Waters 40

Trumpets and Drums 57
Truth about Blayds 224
Tsar Fyodor Ivanovitch 353
Tumbler 205
Tutor (see Der Hofmeister)
Twelve-Pound Look 25
Twelve Thousand 127
Two by Ibsen (see Doll's
    House and Hedda Gabler)
Two Plays for England 248
Typewriter 87
Tyranny of Tears 70

Ugly Duckling 225
Unburied Dead 291
Uncle Harry 194
Uncle Vanya 80
Under Milk Wood 350
Under Orders 350
Under Plain Cover (see Two
    Plays for England
Underpants 333
Unicorn from the Stars 380
Unknown Soldier and His Wife
    356
Unquiet Spirit 36
Unshaven Cheek 202

Variations on a Theme 278
Venus Observed 134
Vera, or the Nihilists 374
Vicar (see Deputy)
Vicar of Christ (see Deputy)
Vicious Circle (see No Exit)
Victims of Duty 192
Victoria Regina 173
Victors 291
Vient de Paraître (see Best
    Sellers)
Vikings of Helgeland 186
Village Wooing 325
Violet 230
Virtuous Island 151
Visit 113
Vivat! Vivat! Regina! 42
Volpone 381
Vortex 98

Wages for Wives (see Chick-
    en Feed)
Wait until Dark 200
Waiting for Godot 31
Waiting in the Wings 98

Waltz of the Dogs 3
Waltz of the Toreadors 11
Was He Anyone? 330
Waste 154
Watched Pot 232
Way Things Go 207
Way Things Happen 100
Ways and Means (see To-
  night at Eight-Thirty)
Wayward Saint 67
We Can't Be as Bad as All
  That 196
We Have Always Lived in
  the Castle 370
We Were Dancing (see To-
  night at Eight-Thirty)
Weak Woman 108
Weaker Sex (see The Sex
  Fable)
Weavers 167
Wedding 81
Wedding Feast (see Die
  Kleinbürgerhochzeit)
Well of the Saints 346
What Every Woman Knows 25
What the Butler Saw 244
What's in It for Me? 325
When Did You Last See My
  Mother 163
When the Young Vine Blooms
  41
When We Are Married 272
When We Dead Awaken 186
Where Ignorance Is Bliss 230
While the Sun Shines 278
Whims 105
White Countess 272
White-Headed Boy 281
White Liars 299
White Lies 299
White Steed 68
Who Is Sylvia? 278
Whole World Over 329
Who's Who in Hell 357
Why She Would Not 325

Widower's Houses 325
Wife with the Smile 236
Wild Duck 186
Will 25
Will Shakespeare 100
Wind of Heaven 376
Windows 141
Wings of the Dove 44
Wings over Europe 234
Winners 130
Winslow Boy 278
Wipe-Out Games 192
Wise Child 155
Wise Have Not Spoken 68
Within the Gates 242
Witness for the Prosecution
  84
Woman of It 207
Woman of No Importance 374
Women at the Tomb 102
Women Have Their Way 273
Wonderful Visit 123
Wood Demon 81
Workhouse Ward 159
World of Paul Slickey 248
World We Live In 65
Worse Things Happen at Sea
  378
Woyzeck 63
Write Me a Murder 200

Yard of Sun 135
Yegor Bulichov 153
Yekaterina Ivanovna (see
  Katerina)
Yerma 143
Yesterday's Magic 376
You Never Can Tell 326
Young Idea 99
Young Madame Conti 127
Younger Generation 172
You're Gonna Be Alright,
  Jamie Boy 128

Zykovs 153